The Cambridge Guide to Teaching English to Speakers of Other Languages

The Cambridge Guide to Teaching English to Speakers of Other Languages

edited by

Ronald Carter and David Nunan

CAMBRIDGE
UNIVERSITY PRESS

PUBLISHED BY THE PRESS SYNDICATE OF THE UNIVERSITY OF CAMBRIDGE
The Pitt Building, Trumpington Street, Cambridge, United Kingdom

CAMBRIDGE UNIVERSITY PRESS
The Edinburgh Building, Cambridge CB2 2RU, UK
40 West 20th Street, New York, NY 10011–4211, USA
10 Stamford Road, Oakleigh, Melbourne 3166, Australia
Ruiz de Alarcón 13, 28014 Madrid, Spain

http://www.cambridge.org

First published 2001

Printed in the United Kingdom at the University Press, Cambridge

Typeset in Times 9/13 pt   System 3b2   [CE]

A catalogue record for this book is available from the British Library

ISBN 0 521 80127 3 hardback
ISBN 0 521 80516 3 paperback

CONTENTS

FIGURES

ABBREVIATIONS

AAVE   African American Vernacular English
CALL   computer-assisted language learning
CDA   critical discourse analysis
CLT   communicative language teaching
EAL   English as an additional language
EAP   English for academic purposes
EFL   English as a foreign language
ELT   English language teaching
EMT   English as a mother tongue
EOP   English for occupational purposes
ESL   English as a second language
ESOL   English for speakers of other languages
ESP   English for specific purposes
EST   English for science and technology
EWL   English as a world language
IELTS   International English Language Testing Service
IPA   International Phonetic Alphabet
IRF   initiation, response, follow-up (see Glossary)
L1   first language
L2   second language
NES   native English speaker
SLA   second language acquisition
TBL   task-based learning
TEFL   Teaching of English as a foreign language
TESL   Teaching of English as a second language
TESOL   Teaching of English to speakers of other languages
TOEFL   Test of English as a foreign language

ACKNOWLEDGEMENTS

The authors wish to thank Mickey Bonin, our commissioning editor at CUP, and Martin Mellor, our copy-editor, for their seminal help, advice and expertise in the writing and editing of this book. Mickey has been a constant source of informed and insightful comment on all the chapters. His input has gone far beyond the realms of duty, exceeding publishing responsibilities and providing academic and professional guidance and advice, which we have always greatly appreciated and learned from. In Martin we have also been fortunate to have a colleague whose informed advice and sharp editorial eye have done much to improve both the editorial design and the academic organisation of the manuscript. We remain greatly indebted to them both. We also thank Sanny Kwok for her unfailing efficiency and continuing support from the very earliest stages of the book. Last but not least, we thank our contributors for demonstrating the very highest standards of professionalism from the earliest stages of gestation – as we worked out a format – to the final stages of refinement. They have all been willing to devote large amounts of time to the project in the midst of very busy professional lives. We thank them for their patience, generosity and cooperation throughout.

The editors also wish to place on record their sincerest thanks and appreciation to four anonymous readers who worked very hard, with great perception and with much critical understanding of the field to assist us in the shaping of the book. We thank all of them, in particular for their attention to detail. Needless to say, however, any errors remain our responsibility.

Ronald Carter and David Nunan

CONTRIBUTORS

Kathleen M. Bailey, Professor of Applied Linguistics, Graduate School of Languages and Educational Linguistics, Monterey Institute of International Studies, Monterey, California, USA

Michael P. Breen, Professor of Language Education, Centre for English Language Teaching, University of Stirling, UK

Geoff Brindley, Senior Lecturer in Linguistics, Department of Linguistics, and Research Co-ordinator, National Centre for English Language Teaching and Research, Macquarie University, Sydney, Australia

Martin Bygate, Senior Lecturer in TESOL, School of Education, University of Leeds, UK

Ronald Carter, Professor of Modern English Language, School of English Studies, University of Nottingham, UK

Beverly Derewianka, Associate Professor, Faculty of Education, University of Wollongong, Australia

Tony Dudley-Evans, Reader in English for Specific Purposes, English for International Students Unit, University of Birmingham, UK

Donald Freeman, Professor of Second Language Education and Director of Center for Teacher Education, Training and Research, Department of Language Teacher Education, School for International Training, Brattleboro, Vermont, USA

Fred Genesee, Professor, Psychology Department, McGill University, Montreal, Canada

Jennifer Hammond, Senior lecturer, Faculty of Education, University of Technology, Sydney, Australia

Liz Hamp-Lyons, Chair Professor of English, Hong Kong Polytechnic University, Hong Kong SAR, China

Elizabeth Hanson-Smith, Educational Computing Consultant, and Professor Emeritus, TESOL Program, California State University, Sacramento, California, USA

Claire Kramsch, Professor of German and Foreign Language Education, German Department, University of California at Berkeley, USA

Agnes Lam, Associate Professor, English Centre, University of Hong Kong, Hong Kong SAR, China

Diane Larsen-Freeman, Professor of Applied Linguistics, Department of Language Teacher Education, School for International Training, Brattleboro, Vermont, USA

Alan Maley, Dean, Institute for English Language Education, Assumption University, Bangkok, Thailand

Michael McCarthy, Professor of Applied Linguistics, School of English Studies, University of Nottingham, UK

David Nunan, Professor of Applied Linguistics, English Centre, University of Hong Kong, Hong Kong SAR, China

Rebecca Oxford, Director of Second Language Education, University of Maryland, College Park, USA

Joy Reid, Professor of English, Department of English, University of Wyoming, USA

Jack Richards, Adjunct Professor, South East Asian Ministers of Education Organization, Regional Language Centre (RELC), Singapore

Michael Rost, University of California at Berkeley, USA

Thomas Scovel, Professor of Applied Linguistics, College of Humanities, San Francisco State University, San Francisco, California, USA

Barbara Seidlhofer, Associate Professor of Applied Linguistics, Department of English, University of Vienna, Austria

Sandra Silberstein, Professor of English, Department of English, University of Washington, Seattle, USA

Brian Tomlinson, Reader in Language Learning and Teaching, Centre for Language Study, Leeds Metropolitan University, UK

Amy B.M. Tsui, Professor, Department of Curriculum Studies, University of Hong Kong, Hong Kong SAR, China

Leo van Lier, Professor of Educational Linguistics, Graduate School of Language and Educational Linguistics, Monterey Institute of International Studies, Monterey, California, USA

Catherine Wallace, Senior Lecturer in Education, Languages in Education, Institute of Education, University of London, UK

Mark Warschauer, Director of Educational Technology, Integral English Language Program/ AMIDEAST, Cairo, Egypt

Ron White, former Director, Centre for Applied Language Studies, University of Reading, UK

Dave Willis, Senior Lecturer, Centre for English Language Studies, Birmingham University, UK

Jane Willis, Teaching Fellow, Language Studies Unit, Aston University, Birmingham, UK

Introduction

The aim of this introductory chapter is to lay the ground for the book as a whole. It does this by looking at what we mean when we refer to the teaching of English to speakers of other languages (**TESOL**). In the course of the discussion, we offer definitions of terms and concepts that are subsumed within the concept of **TESOL**. The chapter includes a discussion of what we mean by the terms 'applied linguistics' as well as differences and distinctions between widely used acronyms in the field such as **ESOL, ELT, ESL, EFL, EAL, EWL, ESP, EAP** and **ESL** (for details of these terms, see below). As we provide definitions, we look at ways in which second language (L2) teaching is differentiated from foreign language teaching.

In addition to providing definition, description and exemplification of key terms, we look at the impact of economic and technological globalisation on English language teaching, as well as the standardisation of English in relation to different sociocultural contexts. In the final part of the chapter, we provide a rationale for the book and an outline of the organisation and sequencing of the chapters.

What is TESOL?

TESOL is an acronym which stands for **Teaching English to speakers of other languages** and is a 'blanket' term covering situations in which English is taught as an L2, as well as those in which it is taught as a foreign language. **ESOL (English for speakers of other languages)** is a term widely used throughout the world, especially in the United States. The field is also sometimes referred to as **English language teaching (ELT)**, although this wrongly suggests that only teachers of English as a second or foreign language and not teachers of **English as a mother tongue (EMT)** have an interest in developing the language of their students.

Some definitions

We begin this section with the term **applied linguistics**, because it is the most general of all the terms to be discussed here. Applied linguistics is a general term covering many aspects of language acquisition and use. It is an amorphous and heterogeneous field drawing on and interfacing with a range of other academic disciplines including linguistics, psychology, sociology, anthropology, cognitive science and information technology. Along with specialists from other disciplines, applied linguists generally aim to provide practical applications of theory and research to solving problems in sub-disciplines. Applied linguists participate to a greater or lesser degree within the following sub-disciplines: second and foreign language learning, literacy, speech pathology, deafness education, interpreting and translating, communication practices, lexicography and first language (L1) acquisition. In this book, the focus is restricted to the teaching and learning of second and foreign languages.

In our introductory statement, we suggested a distinction between **ESL (English as a second language)** and **EFL (English as a foreign language)**. The term **ESL** is used to refer to situations in which English is being taught and learned in countries, contexts and cultures in which English is the predominant language of communication. The teaching of English to immigrants in countries such Australia, Canada, New Zealand, the United Kingdom and the United States typifies ESL. In these countries, individuals from non-English-speaking backgrounds may speak their L1 at home, but will be required to use English for communicating at work, in school and in the community in general. The term is also current in countries where English is widely used as a lingua franca. These include the Special Administrative Region of Hong Kong (where its usage reflects the Region's recent past as a colony of the United Kingdom), Singapore (a multilingual society with English as a lingua franca) and India (where the populations speak a range of other languages, and where English – as well as Hindi – enables communication between these diverse linguistic groups).

EFL is used in contexts where English is neither widely used for communication, nor used as the medium of instruction. Brazil, Japan, Korea, Thailand and Mexico are countries where English is taught as a foreign language, either as part of the elementary and high-school curriculum, or in private schools and other educational settings.

The ESL/EFL distinction has been an important one in language pedagogy for many years because, in each case, the context in which the teaching takes place is very different, requiring different materials, syllabuses and pedagogy. In most EFL settings there is limited exposure to the language outside of the classroom, and often limited opportunity to use it. The syllabus therefore needs to be carefully structured with extensive recycling of key target-language items. In addition, the burden for providing the cultural dimension to the curriculum very much rests with the teacher. Teaching is also complicated by the fact that teachers are usually non-native speakers of English who may lack opportunities to use the language, or lack confidence in using it. In such situations it is important for the materials to provide the sort of rich and diverse linguistic input that ESL learners encounter in the world beyond the classroom.

For many years, the ESL/EFL distinction has been widely used and generally accepted and, as we have indicated above, it has provided a useful conceptual framework. (Note, however, that in some contexts the term **English as an additional language** or **EAL** is preferred.) Nonetheless, we find the distinction increasingly problematic, for a number of reasons. In the first place, the contexts in which L2s are taught and used differ considerably. Teaching English in Japan, for instance, is a very different experience from teaching it in Brazil. Also impinging on the distinction is the growth of **English as a world language (EWL)**. In fact, with globalisation and the rapid expansion of information technologies, there has been an explosion in the demand for English worldwide. This has led to greater diversification in the contexts and situations in which it is learned and used, as well as in the nature of the language itself. English no longer belongs to the United Kingdom, nor to the United States. It is an increasingly diverse and diversified resource for global communication.

In the 1970s, with the development of **communicative language teaching (CLT)**, the focus in syllabus design shifted from a focus on English as a system to be studied to a focus on English as a tool for communication. Syllabus designers, materials writers and teachers began to select content not because it was 'there' in the linguistic systems of the language, but because it matched learners' communicative needs. This shift of focus led to needs-based syllabus design and to the emergence of differentiated courses to match the differentiated needs of learners. Courses in which the goals, objectives and content are matched to the communicative needs are known as **ESP (English for**

specific purposes) courses. These are further differentiated into courses in **EAP** (**English for academic purposes**), **EST** (**English for science and technology**) and so on.

A global language or languages

The rapid expansion in the use of English has also led to the questioning of the distinction between English as a first language (L1) and as a second language (L2). In his opening plenary at the 1999 TESOL Convention in New York, David Crystal gave an illustration of the growing uncertainty surrounding the terms 'first language' and 'second language'. Imagine a couple who meet and marry in Singapore, the male from a German first-language background and the woman from a Malaysian first-language background. The couple subsequently move to France for employment purposes. They have children and raise them through the medium of English. In which contexts and for whom is English a first, a second or a foreign language? What or who is a native speaker, and whose English do they use?

This situation is neither fanciful nor unusual. In becoming the medium for global communication, English is beginning to detach itself from its historical roots. In the course of doing so, it is also becoming increasingly diversified to the point where it is possible to question the term 'English'. The term 'world Englishes' has been used for quite a few years now, and it is conceivable that the plural form 'Englishes' will soon replace the singular 'English'.

ENGLISHES AND STANDARDS

The above descriptions and definitions of key terms and situations suggests that the uses of English in different contexts and for different purposes are neutral. However, the reality of day-to-day teaching and learning of English brings with it a series of interrelated social and political questions.

As is the case with other ex-imperial languages, such as Spanish and Arabic, native speakers of English throughout the world acquire and develop regional varieties of the language. These varieties are not especially marked in the written language but are often marked in speech. Thus, just as there are native speaker varieties of Mexican Spanish or Egyptian Arabic, so we speak of Australian English, South African English and Canadian English. Speakers of such varieties identify with their language and normally have no need to learn other Englishes. For purposes of international communication through English, their spoken variety does not normally lead to significant difficulties, and international varieties of the written language manifest in any case only minimal variations.

Non-native speaker varieties of English have also developed around the world, particularly in former colonial territories. Such varieties normally exist along a continuum which includes *standard* versions of the language which are taught and learned in school and which are recognised internationally to be of economic and political significance. Individual learners are also conscious that their own social mobility and economic power can be enhanced by access to a standard international variety of English. However, some of these varieties of the language may be deliberately spoken in ways which are markedly different from the standard native speaker versions. Speakers using such varieties may do so in order to identify themselves with a variety of the language which is perceived as theirs and not the property of others.

It may seem too that definitions of the terms **native speaker variety** and **non-native speaker varieties** of a language are also neutral and unproblematic. In some countries – e.g. the Republic of Singapore, a former British colony – English plays a major role as an L2 for the majority of the population. A continuum of varieties exists for communication through English as a lingua franca and through standard versions of English for international communication. In Singapore, however, English has furthermore been selected by the government as a medium of instruction in schools. It may even be chosen by some families as a main language spoken at home, although the mother tongue of these speakers may be a Malay or Tamil or Chinese language. The choices may reflect recognition of the socio-economic power of the language, but such contexts and practices also raise questions about the status of a native speaker of a language. Learners of English as a foreign language often need English as a tool of communication; however, in some ESL territories differences and distinctions between standard and non-standard varieties and native and non-native speakers of a language become blurred.

Issues of personal identity come to the fore too where, for economic reasons, learners need an international standard version of English but, for more personal and social reasons, they need a variety through which they are more able to find an expression of their own identity, or even their national identity. In contexts of teaching and learning, their needs may not be entirely met either by a particular national variety because different national varieties carry with them political and ideological baggage. Some countries may, therefore, elect to teach American English because a British English variety was the language of a coloniser. Other countries may elect to teach British or Australian English for reasons ranging from geographical proximity to ideological opposition to aspects of the foreign policies of the United States. And individuals may make other decisions for purely personal reasons. There are, thus, immovable issues of cultural politics in all parts of the world from which discussions of the teaching and learning of English cannot be easily uncoupled.

MODELS OF ENGLISH AND PEDAGOGY

The teaching of standard varieties of a language cannot be divorced either from the role of the teacher or from the relationship between the teacher and the learner in this process. For example, is the language best taught by native speakers of one of the standard national varieties? Is their knowledge of their native language superior to that of non-native speaker teachers? Will they also necessarily possess an insider's understanding of the culture of the target language which renders them superior to non-native speaker teachers in helping learners towards such understanding? Alternatively, is the non-native speaker better positioned because of his or her insider's knowledge of the language of the learners and because – given the monolingual background of many native speakers of English – they (the non-native speakers) have understood first-hand the processes involved in the acquisition and uses of English? Additionally, does the native speaker bring to the classroom cultural assumptions about pedagogy which do not fit locally and which the non-native teacher may again be better positioned to mediate? And, as far as language is concerned, is an authentic native speaker version of the language preferable to one which is less 'real' but judged pedagogically to be more in the interests of learners (many of whom are likely in any case only to interact with other non-native speakers).

Again, these issues are political and impinge culturally and socially on the teaching and learning process because a government may decide to employ native speaker teachers in preference to or alongside non-native speakers; or it may have a narrow definition of what a native speaker is. Such decisions can materially affect the position of the non-native speaker economically, culturally and in the eyes of their students. This analysis suggests that there is no such thing as a neutral description of the teaching and learning of Englishes in the world.

The rationale for and organisation of this book

When we planned this book, we wanted to provide an introduction to the field of foreign and L2 teaching and learning written by top scholars in the field. We wanted to provide more background to key topics than is typically contained in dictionaries and encyclopedias yet, at the same time, to keep entries shorter than the typical book chapter. Although we wanted entries to be accessible to the non-specialist, we also wanted the topics to be dealt with in some depth. At the end of each chapter, we wanted the reader to know the history and evolution of the topic discussed, be familiar with key issues and questions, be conversant with the research that has been carried out, and have some idea of future trends and directions. We hope these objectives have been met in each case.

The book is aimed at teachers, teachers in preparation, and undergraduate and graduate students of language education and applied linguistics. It is intended to provide a general background as well as to provide pointers for those who want a more detailed knowledge of any of the topics introduced here. The latter is given in references to the literature throughout each chapter and also in the list of **key readings** at the end of each chapter. Each list of key readings provides abbreviated details, with full publication details in the list of **references** at the end of the book. We are conscious that some will feel that topics have been left out and, of course, omissions and absences can be identified in any book due, in part at least, to the predilections and preferences of the authors and editors. For example, we are conscious that chapters could have been provided in the rapidly developing areas of **pragmatics** and **corpus linguistics**. We could have provided a chapter on **communicative language teaching** as the most well established of methodologies of the late twentieth century. We hope that these and related topics are treated and developed in other chapters in the book and that the **index** provided will help readers to navigate topics and themes which are not necessarily signalled in individual chapter headings. We also provide a glossary at the end of the book; this is not a comprehensive **glossary** of the terms used in TESOL but refers to the terms most frequently used in the chapters in this book. Key terms in the text are highlighted in bold, and many of these appear in the glossary.

There is no immutable logic to the order in which the chapters in the book have been arranged. We have placed chapters concerned with language organisation and basic skills at the beginning since, in part at least, many of the other chapters derive progressively from this base. There is, however, no reason why the chapters cannot be read in a different sequence. Similarly, there is the following basic structure to each chapter: **introduction**, **background**, overview of **research**, consideration of the relevance to **classroom practice**, reflection on **current and future trends and directions** and a **conclusion**. Although the structure does not apply equally to all topics, authors of chapters have followed this framework as far as possible.

Conclusion

One of the debates currently taking place within the field concerns the question of whether language teaching constitutes a profession. One of the characteristics of professions such as medicine and law is that they have a body of knowledge upon which there is relative agreement, as well as agreed-upon principles of procedure for generating and applying knowledge (although, of course, such knowledge can be and is disputed within the profession). While language pedagogy is nowhere near developing an agreed-upon set of 'rules of the game', there is a rapidly growing knowledge base. What we have tried to do here is provide a snapshot of that knowledge base. We hope that, in some small way, the volume contributes towards a more developed sense of professionalism.

Key readings

There are no obvious follow-ups to the issues covered in this short introduction. However, the following titles, all published in the 1990s, discuss further points on applied linguistics, the place of English in the world, the position of the native speaker and the sociocultural nature of the teaching and learning process. Many of the same titles also provide further definitions of terms in use in the field.

Canagarajah (1999) *Resisting Linguistic Imperialism in English Teaching*
Crystal (1997) *English as a Global Language*

Holliday (1994) *Appropriate Methodology*
Kachru (1990) *The Alchemy of English*
Kramsch (1993) *Context and Culture in Language Teaching*
Medgyes (1994) *The Non-Native Teacher*
Pennycook (1994) *The Cultural Politics of English as an International Language*
Phillipson (1992) *Linguistic Imperialism*
Richards *et al.* (1992) *A Dictionary of Applied Linguistics*
Tollefson (1995) *Power and Inequality in Language Education*
Widdowson (1990) *Aspects of Language Teaching*

Ronald Carter, University of Nottingham
and David Nunan, University of Hong Kong
March 2000

CHAPTER 1

Listening

Michael Rost

Introduction

The term **listening** is used in language teaching to refer to a complex process that allows us to understand spoken language. Listening, the most widely used language skill, is often used in conjunction with the other skills of speaking, reading and writing. Listening is not only a skill area in language performance, but is also a critical means of acquiring a second language (L2). Listening is the channel in which we process language in real time – employing pacing, units of encoding and pausing that are unique to spoken language.

As a goal-oriented activity, listening involves 'bottom-up' processing (in which listeners attend to data in the incoming speech signals) and 'top-down' processing (in which listeners utilise prior knowledge and expectations to create meaning). Both bottom-up and top-down processing are assumed to take place at various levels of cognitive organisation: phonological, grammatical, lexical and propositional. This complex process is often described as a 'parallel processing model' of language understanding: representations at these various levels create activation at other levels. The entire network of interactions serves to produce a 'best match' that fits all of the levels (McClelland 1987; Cowan 1995).

Background

Listening in language teaching has undergone several important influences, as the result of developments in anthropology, education, linguistics, sociology, and even global politics. From the time foreign languages were formally taught until the late nineteenth century, language learning was presented primarily in a written mode, with the role of descriptive grammars, bilingual dictionaries and 'problem sentences' for correct translation occupying the central role. Listening began to assume an important role in language teaching during the late-nineteenth-century Reform Movement, when linguists sought to elaborate a psychological theory of child language acquisition and apply it to the teaching of foreign languages. Resulting from this movement, the spoken language became the definitive source for and means of foreign language learning. Accuracy of perception and clarity of auditory memory became focal language learning skills.

This focus on speech was given a boost in the 1930s and 1940s when anthropologists began to study and describe the world's spoken languages. Influenced by this anthropological movement, Bloomfield declared that 'one learns to understand and speak a language primarily by hearing and imitating native speakers' (Bloomfield 1942). In the 1940s American applied linguists formalised this 'oral approach' into the audiolingual method with an emphasis on intensive oral–aural drills and extensive use of the language laboratory. The underlying assumption of the method was that learners could be 'trained' through intensive, structured and graded input to change their hearing 'habits'.

In contrast to this behaviourist approach, there was a growing interest in the United Kingdom in situational approaches. Firth and his contemporaries (see, e.g., Firth 1957; Chomsky 1957) believed that 'the context of situation' – rather than linguistic units themselves – determined the meaning of utterances. This implied that meaning is a function of the situational and cultural context in which it occurs, and that language understanding involved an integration of linguistic comprehension and non-linguistic interpretation.

Other key background influences are associated with the work of Chomsky and Hymes. A gradual acceptance of Chomsky's innatist views (see Chomsky 1965) led to the notion of the meaning-seeking mind and the concept of a 'natural approach' to language learning. In a natural approach, the learner works from an internal syllabus and requires input data (not necessarily in a graded order) to construct the target language system. In response to Chomsky's notion of language competence, Hymes (1971 [1972, 1979]) proposed the notion of 'communicative competence', stating that what is crucial is not so much a better understanding of how language is structured internally, but a better understanding of how language is used.

This sociological approach – eventually formalised as the discipline of 'conversation analysis' (CA) – had an eventual influence on language teaching syllabus design. The Council of Europe proposed defining a 'common core' of communicative language which all learners would be expected to acquire at the early stages of language learning (Council of Europe 1971). The communicative language teaching (CLT) movement, which had its roots in the 'threshold syllabus' of van Ek (1973), began to view listening as an integral part of communicative competence. Listening for meaning became the primary focus and finding relevant input for the learner assumed greater importance.

In the late 1960s and early 1970s, applied linguists recognised that listening was the primary channel by which the learner gains access to L2 'data', and that it therefore serves as the trigger for acquisition. Subsequent work in applied linguistics (see especially Long 1985b; Chaudron 1988; Pica 1994) has helped to define the role of listening input and interaction in second language acquisition. Since 1980, listening has been viewed as a primary vehicle for language learning (Richards 1985; Richards and Rodgers 1986; Rost 1990).

Research

Four areas affecting how listening is integrated into L2 pedagogy are reviewed here; these are: listening in SLA, speech processing, listening in interactive settings and strategy use.

LISTENING IN SLA

In second language acquisition (SLA) research, it is the 'linguistic environment' that serves as the stage for SLA. This environment – the speakers of the target language and their speech to the L2 learners – provides linguistic input in the form of listening opportunities embedded in social and academic situations. In order to acquire the language, learners must come to understand the language in these situations. This accessibility is made possible in part through accommodations made by native speakers to make language comprehension possible and in part through strategies the learner enacts to make the speech comprehensible.

Building on the research that showed a relationship between input adjustments and message comprehension, Krashen (1982) claimed that 'comprehensible input' was a necessary condition for language learning. In his 'input hypothesis', Krashen says further development from the learner's current stage of language knowledge can only be achieved by the learner 'comprehending' language that contains linguistic items (lexis, syntax, morphology) at a level slightly above the learner's current knowledge ($i+1$). Krashen claimed that comprehension is necessary in order for input to become 'intake', i.e. language data that is assimilated and used to promote further development. The ability to understand new language, Krashen maintained, is made possible by speech adjustments made to learners, in addition to the learner's use of shared knowledge of the context (Larsen-Freeman and Long 1991).

Although Krashen does not refer to strategic adjustments made by the learner to understand new language, the work of Pica *et al.* (1996) examines the role of adjustments in great detail. Their research has helped delineate how different task types (e.g. one-way vs. two-way information gap exchanges), interaction demands of tasks and interaction adjustments made by speaker and listener address the L2 learner's needs and boost subsequent development. This research outlines the dimensions of activity and strategy use required for successful listening development.

SPEECH PROCESSING

Speech-processing research provides important insights into L2 learning. Several factors are activated in speech perception (phonetic quality, prosodic patterns, pausing and speed of input), all of which influence the comprehensibility of input. While it is generally accepted that there is a common store of semantic information (single coding) in memory that is used in both first language (L1) and L2 speech comprehension, research shows that there are separate stores of phonological information (dual coding) for speech (Soares and Grosjean 1984; Sharwood Smith 1994). Semantic knowledge required for language understanding (scripts and schemata related to real world people, places and actions) is accessed through phonological tagging of the language that is heard. As such, facility with the phonological code of the L2 – and with the parallel cognitive processes of grammatical parsing and word recognition – is proposed as the basis for keeping up with the speed of spoken language (Magiste 1985).

Research in spoken-language recognition shows that each language has its own 'preferred strategies' for aural decoding, which are readily acquired by the L1 child, but often only partially acquired by the L2 learner. Preferred strategies involve four fundamental properties of spoken language:

1. the phonological system: the phonemes used in a particular language, typically only 30 or 40 out of hundreds of possible phonemes;

2. phonotactic rules: the sound sequences that a language allows to make up syllables; i.e. variations of what sounds can start or end syllables, whether the 'peak' of the syllable can be a simple or complex or lengthened vowel and whether the ending of the syllable can be a vowel or a consonant;

3. tone melodies: the characteristic variations in high, low, rising and falling tones to indicate lexical or discourse meanings;

4. the stress system: the way in which lexical stress is fixed within an utterance.

In 'bounded' (or 'syllable-timed') languages – such as Spanish and Japanese – stress is located at fixed distances from the boundaries of words. In 'unbounded' (or 'stress-timed') languages – such as English and Arabic – the main stress is pulled towards an utterance's focal syllable. Bounded languages consist of binary rhythmic units (or feet) and listeners tend to hear the language in a binary fashion, as pairs of equally strong syllables. Unbounded languages have no limit on the size of a foot, and listeners tend to hear the language in clusters of syllables organised by either trochaic (strong–weak) rhythm or iambic (weak–strong) rhythm. Stress-timing produces numerous linked or assimilated consonants and reduced (or weakened) vowels so that the pronunciation of words often seems slurred.

Differences in a learner's L1 and L2 with respect to any of these possible distinctions – phonology system, phonotactic rules, use of tone and use of stress – are likely to cause difficulties in spoken-word recognition, at least initially and until ample attention is devoted to learning new strategies. Similarities in a learner's L1 and L2 with respect to one or more of these distinctions are likely to allow the learner greater ease and success with listening, and with word recognition in particular. For example, Japanese learners often have difficulty identifying key words in spoken English, due in part to the different stress systems; on the other hand, Danish learners of English typically have little difficulty learning to follow colloquial conversation, due in part to the similarities of stress, tone, phonology and phonotactic rules in English and Danish.

Of these four components in word recognition, stress is often reported to be the most problematic in L2 listening. In English, L2 listeners must come to use a metrical segmentation strategy that allows them to assume that a strong syllable is the onset of a new content word and that each 'pause unit' of speech contains one prominent content word (Cutler 1997).

Another research area related to speech perception is the effect of variable speech rate on comprehension. Findings clearly show that there is not an isomorphic relationship between speed of speech and comprehension (for a summary, see Flowerdew 1994b). One consistent finding is that the best aid to comprehension is to use normal speaking speed with extra pauses inserted.

LISTENING IN INTERACTIVE SETTINGS

Studies of L2 listening in conversational settings help explain the dynamics of interactive listening and the ways in which L2 speakers participate (or, conversely, are denied participation) in conversations. Such issues have been researched at the discourse analysis level, looking at how control and distribution of power is routinely employed through the structure (i.e. implicit rules) of interactions.

Research in cross-cultural pragmatics is relevant in understanding the dynamics of L2 listening in conversation. In general, cultures differ in their use of key conversation features, such as when to talk, how much to say, pacing and pausing in and between speaking turns, intonational emphasis, use of formulaic expressions, and indirectness (Tannen 1984b). The Cross-Cultural Speech Act Realization Project (CCSARP; Blum-Kulka *et al.* 1989) documents examples of cultural differences in directness–indirectness in several languages and for a number of speech acts (notably apologies, requests and promises). Clearly, knowledge of speakers' cultural norms influences listening success.

Conversational analysis is used to explore problems that L2 listeners experience. Comprehension difficulties in conversation arise not only at the levels of phonological processing, grammatical parsing and word recognition, but also at the levels of informational packaging and conceptual representation of the content. Other comprehension problems include those triggered by elliptical utterances (in which an item is omitted because it is assumed to be understood) and difficulty in assessing the point of an utterance (speaker's intent). In any interaction such problems can be cumulative, leading to misunderstandings and breakdowns in communication.

Bremer *et al.* (1996) document many of the social procedures that L2 listeners must come to use as they become more successful listeners and participants in conversations. These procedures include identification of topic shifts, providing backchannelling or listenership cues, participating in conversational routines (providing obligatory responses), shifting to topic initiator role, and initiating queries and repair of communication problems. Much research on L2 listening in conversation clearly concludes that, in order to become successful participants in target-language conversation, listeners need to employ a great deal of 'interactional work' (including using clarification strategies) in addition to linguistic processing.

STRATEGY USE

Listening strategies are conscious plans to deal with incoming speech, particularly when the listener knows that he or she must compensate for incomplete input or partial understanding. For representative studies in this area, see Rost and Ross 1991; Kasper 1984; Vandergrift 1996.

Rost and Ross's (1991) study of paused texts found that more proficient listeners tend to use more 'hypothesis testing' (asking about specific information in the story) rather than 'lexical push-downs' (asking about word meanings) and 'global reprises' (asking for general repetition). They also report that, following training sessions, listeners at all levels could ask more hypothesis testing questions. Their comprehension, measured by written summaries, also improved as a result.

Kasper's (1984) study using 'think aloud' protocols found that L2 listeners tend to form an initial interpretation of a topic (a 'frame') and then stick to it, trying to fit incoming words and propositions into that frame. L1 listeners were better at recognising when they had made a mistake about the topic and were prepared to initiate a new frame.

Vandergrift's (1996) study involving retrospective self-report validated O'Malley and Chamot's (1990) strategy classifications. He found explicit examples of learner use of both meta-cognitive strategies (such as planning and monitoring), cognitive strategies (such as linguistic inferencing and elaborating) and socio-affective strategies (such as questioning and self-encouragement). He also found a greater (reported) use of metacognitive strategies at higher proficiency levels. Based on his findings, Vandergrift proposes a pedagogic plan for encouraging the use of metacognitive strategies at all proficiency levels.

Practice

The teaching of listening involves the selection of input sources (which may be live, or be recorded on audio or video), the chunking of input into segments for presentation, and an activity cycle for learners to engage in. Effective teaching involves:

- careful selection of input sources (appropriately authentic, interesting, varied and challenging);
- creative design of tasks (well-structured, with opportunities for learners to activate their own knowledge and experience and to monitor what they are doing);
- assistance to help learners enact effective listening strategies (metacognitive, cognitive, and social); and
- integration of listening with other learning purposes (with appropriate links to speaking, reading and writing).

This section reviews some of the key recommendations that have been made by language educators concerning the teaching of listening. The notion of listening for meaning, in contrast to listening for language practice, became a standard in teaching by the mid-1980s. Since then, many practitioners have proposed systems for teaching listening that have influenced the language teaching profession. These can be summarised as follows:

- Morley (1984) offers an array of examples of selective listening materials, using authentic information and information-focused activities (e.g. notional–informational listening practice, situation–functional listening practice, discrimination-oriented practice, sound–spelling listening practice).
- Ur (1984) emphasises the importance of having listening instruction resemble 'real-life listening' in which the listener has built a sense of purpose and expectation for listening and in which there is a necessity for a listener response.
- Anderson and Lynch (1988) provide helpful means for grading input types and organising tasks to maximise learner interaction.
- Underwood (1989) describes listening activities in terms of three phases: pre-, while- and post-listening activities. She demonstrates the utility of using 'authentic' conversations (many of which were surreptitiously recorded).
- Richards (1990) provides an accessible guide for teachers in constructing exercises promoting

'top-down' or 'bottom-up' processing and focusing on transactional or interactional layers of discourse.

- Rost (1991) formalises elements of listening pedagogy into four classes of 'active listening': global listening to focus on meaning, intensive listening to focus on form, selective listening to focus on specific outcomes and interactive listening to focus on strategy development.

- Nunan (1995c) provides a compendium of recipes for exercises for listening classes, organised in four parts: developing cognitive strategies (listening for the main idea, listening for details, predicting), developing listening with other skills, listening to authentic material and using technology.

- Lynch (1996) outlines the types of negotiation tasks that can be used with recorded and 'live' inputs in order to require learners to focus on clarification processes. Lynch also elaborates upon Brown's (1994) guidelines for grading listening materials.

- White (1998) presents a series of principles for activities in which learners progress through repeated listenings of texts. She indicates the need to focus listening instruction on 'what went wrong' when learners do not understand and the value of having instructional links between listening and speaking.

Another area of focus in the practice of teaching listening is learner training. Rubin (1994) and Mendelsohn and Rubin (1995) discuss the importance of strategy training in classroom teaching. Mendelsohn (1998) notes that commercially available materials increasingly include strategy training, particularly 'activation of schemata' prior to listening. Rost (1994) presents a framework for incorporating five types of listening strategies into classroom instruction: predicting, monitoring, inferencing, clarifying and responding.

Numerous published materials incorporate principles that have been gleaned from research and practice. Many coursebooks treat development of listening in interesting and innovative ways. Among them are *Headway* (Soars and Soars 1993), *New Interchange* (Richards *et al.* 1998) and *English Firsthand* (Helgesen *et al.* 1999).

Another aspect of listening pedagogy is the use of the target language for instruction. From simpler notions like 'teaching English through English' (J. Willis 1981), through teaching 'sheltered content' courses in the target language (Brinton *et al.* 1989) to full-scale immersion programmes (Genesee 1984), the benefits for learning content through listening are far-reaching. Not only do the learners have an ongoing demonstration of the importance of listening, but they also have continuous opportunities for integrating listening with other language and academic learning skills, and for using listening for authentic purposes. For a review of issues in assessment, see Brindley (1998b) and Chapter 20 of this volume.

Current and future trends and directions

LISTENING PEDAGOGY

One important trend is the study of individual learners' listening processes, both in specific tasks and longitudinally. Lynch (1996) provides insightful studies of individual listeners, particularly ones experiencing difficulties in making progress. He documents learner changes in product (how much the learner understands), process (the strategies the learner uses to gain understanding) and perception (how the learner views or experiences his or her own difficulties and progress). Similarly, Robbins (1997) tracks several ESL learners, observing how their listening strategies with native-speaker conversation partners develop over time.

The role of phonology in L2 listening is beginning to receive attention. Studies such as Kim (1995), Ross (1997) and Quinn (1998) examine spoken word and phrase recognition by L2 learners, in native speaker–non-native speaker interactions and in fixed-input tasks. Such studies help show the kind of specific phonological strategies needed to adjust to an L2, and the kind of compensatory strategies needed when listeners experience gaps in input.

A promising area of SLA work that affects listening pedagogy is 'input enhancement' (R. Ellis 1994); this is the notion of marking or flooding listening input with the same set of grammatical, lexical or pragmatic features in order to facilitate students' noticing of those features. As the notion of 'awareness-triggering learning' takes hold, the role of listening instruction in this regard will become even more important.

Another trend is renewed interest in 'academic listening', or extended listening for specific purposes. An edited volume by Flowerdew (1994b) reviews several lines of research on lecturing styles, speech perception, text-structure analysis, note-taking and aural memory. As the information revolution progresses, the need for the 'traditional' skills of selective and evaluative listening will become more important.

LISTENING TECHNOLOGY

The widespread availability of audiotape, videotape, CD-ROMs, DVDs and internet downloads of sound and video files has vastly increased potential input material for language learning. Consequently, selection of the most appropriate input, chunking the input into manageable and useful segments, developing support material (particularly for self-access learning) and training of learners in the best uses of this input is ever more important (Benson and Voller 1997).

The development of computerised speech synthesis, speech enhancement and speech-recognition technology has also enabled learners to 'interact' with computers in ways that simulate human interaction. Here also, the use of intelligent methodology that helps students focus on key listening skills and strategies is vital so that 'use of the technology' is not falsely equated with instruction.

Conclusion

Listening has rightly assumed a central role in language learning. The skills underlying listening have become more clearly defined. Strategies contributing to effective listening are now better understood. Teaching methodology in the mainstream has not yet caught up with theory. In many language curriculums, listening is still often considered a mysterious 'black box', for which the best approach seems to be simply 'more practice'. Specific skill instruction as well as strategy development still need greater attention in order to demystify the listening process. Similarly, materials design lags behind current theory, particularly in the areas of input selection and strategy development. Also, the assessment of listening, especially, remains far behind current views of listening. Although there have been marked advances, still in many areas (e.g. curriculum design, teaching methodology, materials design, learner training and testing) much work remains to be done to modernise the teaching of listening.

Key readings

Bremer et al. (1996) *Discourse in Intercultural Encounters*
Brindley (1998b) Assessing listening abilities
Flowerdew (1994b) Research related to second language lecture comprehension
Mendelsohn and Rubin (1995) *A Guide for the Teaching of Second Language Listening*
Nunan (1995c) *New Ways in Teaching Listening*
Rost (1990) *Listening in Language Learning*
White (1998) *Listening*

CHAPTER 2

Speaking

Martin Bygate

New dofer test for this?

Introduction

Speaking in a second language (L2) involves the development of a particular type of communication skill. Oral language, because of its circumstances of production, tends to differ from written language in its typical grammatical, lexical and discourse patterns. In addition, some of the processing skills needed in speaking differ from those involved in reading and writing. This chapter outlines the place of speaking in oral methodology, the conceptual issues involved in oral language pedagogy, and it reviews relevant research and pedagogical implications.

Background

Speaking in an L2 has occupied a peculiar position throughout much of the history of language teaching, and only in the last two decades has it begun to emerge as a branch of teaching, learning and testing in its own right, rarely focusing on the production of spoken discourse. There are three main reasons for this. The first is tradition: grammar–translation approaches to language teaching still have a huge influence in language teaching, marginalising the teaching of communication skills. The second is technology: only since the mid-1970s has tape-recording been sufficiently cheap and practical to enable the widespread study of talk – whether native speaker talk (Carter and McCarthy 1997: 7) or learner talk – and use of tape recorders in the language classroom. Due to the difficulty of studying talk, it was easier for teachers, methodologists, applied linguists and linguists to focus on written language than spoken language (for nearly 20 years the TESOL convention has run annual colloquia on the teaching of reading and writing, but not on speaking or listening).

The third reason for its peculiar development might be termed 'exploitation': most approaches to language teaching other than grammar–translation (the direct method, the audiolingual approach) as well as more marginal approaches (such as the Silent Way, Community Language Learning and Suggestopedia) exploited oral communication centrally as part of their methodology: not as a discourse skill in its own right, but rather as a special medium for providing language input, memorisation practice and habit-formation (see, e.g., Howatt 1984: 192–208). Most of the focus in teaching oral skills was limited to pronunciation. As Howatt comments of the late-nineteenth-century Reform Movement, 'it was essential that the learner's pronunciation should be correct before moving on to texts' (Howatt 1984: 172). Even for those such as Sweet, for whom pronunciation was crucial at the beginning, 'spoken interaction, or conversation, was the end-point of classroom instruction, not its point of departure' (1984: 187). Hence, speaking was mainly associated with pronunciation, and with getting new language noticed and integrated into the learner's competence. Oral discourse was only possible at the end. This confusion of speaking as a skill in its own right with speaking as a central medium for learning continues in current developments. Recently, however, speaking has increasingly emerged as a special area in language pedagogy.

Within existing approaches to the teaching of language, one of the first to offer a clear perspective on the teaching of oral skills was audiolingualism. Audiolingualism appreciated the importance of input before output. And with oral skills preceding written, the four phase cycle of listening–speaking–reading–writing was applied in sequence for each structure (rather than as an argument for providing extensive listening input as in other approaches). More centrally, audiolingualism was based on behaviourist theories of learning and assumed that language was little more than overt, observable behaviour. Its proponents believed that repetition was central to learning, since this has been shown to help memorisation, automaticity and the formation of associations between different elements of language, and between language and contexts of use. Hence, teaching oral language was thought to require no more than engineering the repeated oral production of structures in the target language, concentrating on the development of grammatical and phonological accuracy, combined with fluency; representative examples of materials include Fries 1952; English Language Services 1964; Alexander 1967; O'Neill *et al.* 1971. When tape recorders and language laboratories gradually came into existence in the 1950s, they were mainly used for pronunciation, grammar and translation practice, often in the context of courses named as such.

In the 1970s, language teaching became increasingly influenced by cognitive and socio-linguistic theories of language and learning. Specialists realised that audiolingual approaches omitted to take account of two aspects of language in communication: first, it neglected the relationship between language and meaning; and, second, it failed to provide a social context within which the formal features of language could be associated with functional aspects, such as politeness. A communicative approach developed in two ways. First, a notional–functional approach attempted to extend the teaching of grammar to include the teaching of interactional notions (paying attention to factors of formality and functions, such as making requests, apologies, invitations and introductions). Second, a learner-centred approach emerged which emphasised the importance for learning of starting from the meanings learners wanted to communicate, and working out how to express them.

Nonetheless, at best these approaches were based on the identification of speech acts; in contrast with the teaching of reading and writing, none were anchored in the study of naturally occurring oral interactive discourse, or in the study of the development of oral L2 skills. More recently, skills-based models have been used to study oral L2 use, within the context of a task-based approach.

To some extent this has been influenced by developments in the study of oral discourse in a first language (L1). Conversation analysts (see Yule 1996) and discourse analysts (see Cook 1989; Hoey 1991; Carter and McCarthy 1997) have revealed features of oral discourse which differ from written discourse and across languages; they illustrate the kinds of features learners need to learn. Studies of L2 use have shown the kinds of problems L2 learners face – and the skills they need to overcome them – to communicate in an L2 (e.g. Bialystok 1990). Finally, studies of oral L2 performance within task-based contexts have identified the problems of using more accurate, fluent and complex language, and have started to explore the ways in which learners' communicative performance can be influenced through communication practice.

Research

CHARACTERISTICS OF SPEECH

To understand what is involved in developing oral L2 skills, it is useful to consider the nature and conditions of speech. Most current approaches draw on a psycholinguistic skills- (or 'information-')processing model. Levelt (1989) proposed that speech production involves four major processes: **conceptualisation, formulation, articulation** and **self-monitoring** (for an accessible account, see Scovel 1998). **Conceptualisation** is concerned with planning the message content. It draws on background knowledge, knowledge about the topic, about the speech situation and on knowledge of patterns of discourse. The conceptualiser includes a 'monitor', which checks everything that occurs in the interaction to ensure that the communication goes to plan. This enables speakers to self-correct for expression, grammar and pronunciation. After conceptualisation, the **formulator** finds the words and phrases to express the meanings, sequencing them and putting in appropriate grammatical markers (such as inflections, auxiliaries, articles). It also prepares the sound patterns of the words to be used: L1 errors of pronunciation very commonly involve switching sounds between words that are separated from each other; such switches suggest that the pronunciation of words must be prepared in batches prior to pronunciation. The third process is **articulation**. This involves the motor control of the articulatory organs; in English: the lips, tongue, teeth, alveolar palate, velum, glottis, mouth cavity and breath. **Self-monitoring** is concerned with language users being able to identify and self-correct mistakes.

All this happens very fast and, to be successful, depends on automation: to some degree in conceptualisation, to a considerable extent in formulation and almost entirely in articulation. Automation is necessary since humans do not have enough attention capacity consciously to control the three types of process. Hence, for an elementary L2 speaker it will be difficult to manage this speech fluently and accurately, since they lack automation and/or accuracy, and it is difficult for them to pay attention to all these processes simultaneously under pressure of time.

The skills are also affected by the context. Speaking is typically **reciprocal**: any interlocutors are normally all able to contribute simultaneously to the discourse, and to respond immediately to each other's contributions. Further, in oral communication many people can participate in the same interaction, making it somewhat less predictable than written interaction. Oral interaction varies widely in terms of whether participants have equal speaking rights, or whether one of the speakers adopts or is accorded special rights, such as in doctor–patient, teacher–pupil, professor–student, examiner–examinee, parent–offspring, adult–child interactions. Symmetry affects the freedom of speakers to develop or initiate topics, ask for clarification or close the interaction. Further, speaking is **physically situated face-to-face** interaction: usually speakers can see each other and so can refer to the physical context and use a number of physical signals to indicate, for instance, attention to the interaction, their intention to contribute and their attitude towards what is being said. Hence, speech can tolerate more implicit reference.

Finally, in most speech situations speech is produced 'on line'. Speakers have to decide on their message and communicate it without taking time to check it over and correct it: any interlocutors cannot be expected to wait long for the opportunity to speak themselves. Hence, time pressure means that the process of conceptualisation, formulation and articulation may not be well planned or implemented, and may need pauses and corrections.

These conditions and processes affect the language that is typically produced. For instance, speech more often than writing refers to the interlocutors and the physical time and place of the communication. In addition, speech typically expresses politeness so as to protect the **face** of the interlocutors (Scollon and Scollon 1983), and to structure the dialogue in stages (see Widdowson 1983). The discourse typically results in patterns which are distinct from those normally found in writing (such as the beginnings, endings and intervening phases of a doctor–patient or teacher–student interaction). Selinker and Douglas (1985), Zuengler and Bent (1991) and Bardovi-Harlig and Hartford (1993) showed that familiarity with interlocutor, content and type of speech act could impact on non-native speaker talk.

Further, the on-line processing conditions produce language that is grammatically more 'fragmented', uses more formulaic ('pre-fabricated') phrases, and tolerates more easily the repetition of words and phrases within the same extract of discourse. Finally, the inevitable adjustments that occur in speech are overt and public. These include:

- changing the message or its formulation before it is expressed ('communication strategies'), whether or not interactively negotiated (Yule and Tarone 1991);
- self-correction after the message has been expressed; and
- various kinds of hesitation, introduced to slow down output and create planning time.

Hence, oral language differs from written language both in process and product (although of course spoken language can resemble written language, and written language can simulate spoken patterns). The implication for teaching is that oral skills and oral language should be practised and assessed under different conditions from written skills, and that, unlike the various traditional approaches to providing oral practice, a distinct methodology and syllabus may be needed. We return to this issue below.

DEVELOPMENT IN L2 SPEECH

Given that the limit to a speaker's attention capacity requires automation, how can attention be shifted and automation developed? Skehan (1998) suggests that speakers' fluency, accuracy and complexity of speech demand capacity, and that there is likely to be a trade-off between these aspects of the skill. Increasing attention to one would limit one's capacity for the others, with developmental implications (Skehan 1998). Getting learners to focus on accuracy is likely to encourage a less exploratory or fluent use of the language. Pushing them to develop fluency, on the other hand, might encourage greater use of formulaic chunks of language, discouraging attention to accuracy and reducing speakers' capacity for processing complex language. Leading them to experiment with new expressions or new combinations of words and phrases might jeopardise their accuracy or fluency. Hence, the task focus could affect learners' development.

Skehan and Foster (1997) and Foster and Skehan (1996) showed that different task types can differ in their impact: some led to more accurate and fluent but less complex language, others produced more complex and accurate language, while yet others generated more complex but less accurate language. Linguistic complexity seemed affected by the cognitive complexity of the tasks.

It remains to be seen whether the use of such tasks has long term effects on learners' oral language development. However, task repetition has been shown to have effects on subsequent performance. A student repeating a task carried out two days earlier without any warning on the second occasion produced significantly more accurate vocabulary, improved a number of collocations and produced more accurate grammar. Bygate (1999) confirmed this effect for complexity and fluency, although this time not for accuracy. Students who repeated two tasks, having first performed them ten weeks earlier, completed them more fluently and with greater complexity on the second occasion when compared with their performance of a new task of the same kind on the same day.

The implications emerging from these studies are, first, that task selection is likely to affect learners' language and language processing. Second, some form of task repetition can enable learners to shift their attention from the problem of conceptualisation towards that of formulation. Task recycling seems to provide the basis for learners to integrate their fluency, accuracy and complexity of formulation around what becomes a familiar conceptual base. This research is ongoing, but suggests interesting implications for the teaching of oral skills.

Practice

In terms of language teaching methodology, the communicative approach proposes that tasks should provide the opportunity for learners to use language in order to communicate meanings without focusing on accuracy. This would encourage fluency (Brumfit 1984a) and lead learners to explore creatively ways of expressing themselves using their knowledge of the language. This view led to the publication of a range of materials aimed to set learners talking (e.g. Geddes and Sturtridge 1979; Ur 1981, 1988). However, two problems lurked behind this approach: first, how can accuracy and fluency be brought together and, second, what range of discourse skills should be practised within an 'oral language' syllabus. Although offering stimulating substantial interaction, materials were unsystematic, with no clear relationship between one task and another, or between a speaking task and other aspects of the teaching programme.

Major implications of the work reviewed in the early part of this chapter are the following:

- A range of different types of interaction need practising.
- The conditions of oral tasks need to differ from those for written skills.
- Improvised speech needs practice, but around some content familiarity.
- Overt oral editing skills need to be encouraged, including the use of communication strategies.
- Oral language processing requires integration of accuracy, complexity and fluency.
- For learners' oral abilities to develop, courses need to vary the emphasis on fluency, accuracy and complexity.

Integrated coursebooks began to respond to the need to provide different types of interaction. Whereas hitherto such materials had used oral interaction principally to practise grammatical structures, gradually new generations of coursebooks included a distinct oral syllabus, largely organised around functions (e.g. Richards *et al.* 1998; Swan and Walter 1992; Nunan 1995a). However, on the whole such materials did not offer an explicit syllabus of oral discourse types. Of the exceptions, one is Dörnyei and Thurrell (1992), which consists of tasks specifically targeting the development of communication strategies. Lynch and Anderson (1992) is unusual in focusing exclusively on spoken skills.

In terms of integrating fluency and accuracy, Bygate (1987) suggested that learners can usefully practise different patterns of discourse, in terms of 'interaction routines', or 'information routines'. An early example of this approach, although largely structured around topics, was the use by Abbs and Sexton (1978) of thematically linked 'chains' of tasks to structure parts of units. Similarly Geddes (1986) uses the topics of units to generate genuine oral activities. In a related approach, J. Willis (1996) proposed the use of a cycle of activities around a central task, involving an 'input phase', a 'rehearsal phase' and a 'performance phase': learners first hear a recording of native speakers undertaking a similar task to the one they are to do, providing them with a rough model; they then perform the task in small groups, during which students express themselves without worrying about errors; the teacher observes and provides feedback; finally, students perform the task before the class, with the focus on all-round performance. This approach is built into the course materials written by Willis and Willis (1988). Yule and Gregory (1989) provide a worked example of an oral task type which can be exploited in this way.

Repetition is central to this cycle, but with the assumption that fluency, accuracy and complexity will only be integrated towards the end of the cycle. This view is supported by evidence from studies by Bygate (1996, 1999), which demonstrated a potentially valuable effect for repetition. The notions of rehearsal, repetition and recycling pose interesting challenges to materials writers, since they imply organising tasks to give pedagogically useful connections between them. Central is the opportunity for learners to become familiar with the meaning content, and materials increasingly use the notion of content recycling to facilitate the integration of work within a familiar conceptual frame.

Current and future trends and directions

A basic issue concerns whether or not tasks can involve learners in working with particular kinds of language feature, or whether use of tasks is a kind of 'blind' pedagogy, whereby allowing learners to express themselves in whatever way they wish is believed to lead to development. There are conflicting views on this point. Brumfit (1984a) stressed that fluency activities should provide learners with the freedom to improvise their own expression. Duff (1993) reports that the tasks she used to elicit speech from a learner did not consistently elicit the same kinds of speech. J. Willis (1996) and Skehan (1998) share the view that tasks cannot target specific features, but only provide conditions which are capable of influencing the level of complexity, accuracy or fluency that learners will produce. Skehan believes that tasks can only influence attention to accuracy, fluency or complexity.

In contrast, Loschky and Bley-Vroman (1993) argue that tasks can target language features in terms of whether targeted features are likely, useful or necessary to complete a task. Yule (1997) provides a systematic review of tasks from this perspective. Some empirical studies have shown how the language used on tasks can be traced back to features of the input or task design, and occur with statistical significance (Samuda and Rounds 1992; Bygate 1999; Samuda 2001). The implication is that patterning does take place, and that therefore tasks can influence the complexity, accuracy or fluency of particular language features. It is, however, unclear how far or consistently this occurs. Given the widespread belief that discourse patterns are pervasive in L1 talk, it would be a profound inconsistency within the discipline to discover that patterning does not occur within the context of tasks. This is in need of wider study.

Meanwhile, studies into the impact of tasks on students' processing skills are in their infancy, and far more are needed into the longitudinal effects of task type and task conditions. A key issue is how tasks operate within classroom contexts, and how they affect perceptions of learners and teachers. In this area professional understanding will only gradually emerge.

Finally, the oral language syllabus deserves fuller study. Few materials include an oral language syllabus, and this is a major direction for future developments. Study into the discourse patterns generated by different task types (such as convergent and divergent, or collaborative and competitive task types identified by Pica *et al.* 1993) is an area for further study. An encouraging step forwards is provided by Riggenbach (1999). This offers an extensive background to the teaching of oral abilities, offering 14 activities for teachers to use as a basis for generating their own activities to practise macro-skills, such as turn-taking, aspects of exchange structure and oral discourse types; and a further 12 activities as a basis for developing original activities to practise micro-skills (pronunciation, grammar and vocabulary). (For further illustration, see Riggenbach and Samuda 1997; this is, ironically, a textbook concerned with grammar practice.)

A second key direction for development is to explore further how fluency, accuracy and complexity can be integrated, in particular through the use of different combinations and sequences of activity types. One sequence would start with complexity and accuracy activities and move to fluency activities, putting students under increased time pressure to formulate and attempting to force them to 'automatise' (Johnson 1988, 1996b); an alternative would be to engage learners' fluent processing to begin with and only subsequently lead them to integrate accurate language features into that fluent 'base'. A third route might involve encouraging learners to move from fluent and accurate performance to include more complex language. Finally, there is considerable scope for exploring the role of routines in developing discourse skills.

Key readings

Brumfit (1984a) *Communicative Methodology in Language Teaching*
Bygate (1987) *Speaking*
Carter and McCarthy (1997) *Exploring Spoken English*

Cook (1989) *Discourse*
Riggenbach (1999) *Discourse Analysis in the Language Classroom, Vol. 1: The Spoken Language*
Scovel (1998) *Psycholinguistics*
Skehan (1998) *A Cognitive Approach to Language Learning*
Willis and Willis (1996) *Challenge and Change in Language Teaching*
Yule (1996) *Pragmatics*
Yule (1997) *Referential Communication Tasks*

CHAPTER 3

Reading

Catherine Wallace

Introduction

Depending on the perspectives of different fields of study, it is possible, broadly speaking, to see reading as practice, product or process. The first has been the interest of anthropologists and social psychologists whose concern is with reading and writing practices as linked to their uses in everyday life, not merely within schooling. The second orientation focuses on the form and meaning of written texts and their constituent parts. The third perspective pays relatively greater attention to the role of the reader in the ongoing processing of written language and the strategies that she or he draws on in constructing meaning from text.

Background

PRACTICE: FOCUS ON THE USES OF READING

A number of scholars have wished to locate discussion of reading within the wider framework of literacy practices, as specific to particular sociocultural environments. This emphasis is of relevance to teachers whose learners come to English language literacy with diverse experience of literacy in a first or other language. Some will be highly literate in a first literacy; others may be acquiring literacy through the medium of English. In either case it is important to see reading and writing as part of language behaviour beyond the learning of specific skills or strategies. Street (1984) introduces a dichotomy between an autonomous model of literacy which sees reading and writing as the learning of skills which are supposedly universally implicated in literacy instruction, and a view of literacy which is called 'ideological' and by which reading and writing practices have currency and prestige, not because of any inherent value but because of social and historical factors particular to the cultural setting.

PRODUCT: FOCUS ON TEXT

In some accounts of reading, priority is given to the text and parts of texts with varying attention paid to form alone or the relationship between form and meaning. At the same time, particular reader skills may be identified as linked to the focus on specific textual features. One such skill is phonemic awareness, as evidenced by a sensitivity to the sound constituents of words, allowing the learner reader to map the letters in words onto an equivalence of sound. The teaching approach promoting this skill is called **phonics**. Traditionally seen as alternative to phonics approaches in the teaching of initial reading are **look-and-say** or **whole-word** methods where learners are encouraged to acquire a sight vocabulary, largely through memorising. A more analytical approach to word-level study is suggested by Stubbs (1980) who argues that written English has a semantico-grammatical base. This means that it is possible to deduce both the semantic field of words and the grammatical class to which they belong from their systematic visual patterning rather than from symbol to sound relationships; e.g. the word *writer* where *wr* signals a semantic link with cognate words such as *write* and *writing*; similarly, *er* offers one clue to its grammatical class as a noun. Readers are helped by making analogies between new and known words, making wider use of their linguistic knowledge than is involved in grapheme to phoneme decoding alone. The term **bottom-up** has been used for approaches to reading which emphasise text-based features at word and sentence level. A different kind of text-focused approach to reading is exemplified by the genre approach; this approach considers texts as a whole, focusing not on word and sentence level, but emphasising the value for readers of an awareness of the distinctive features of the range of text types characteristic of social settings, particularly related to schooling.

PROCESS: FOCUS ON READER

Process accounts of reading take the reader rather than the text as a point of departure. They are sometimes termed **top-down**, on the grounds that they give greater emphasis to the kinds of background knowledge and values which the reader brings to reading. The nature of this knowledge can be characterised as a 'schema', or mental model, allowing a reader to relate new, text-based knowledge to existing world knowledge. In the 1980s and 1990s the role of the reader shifted. In early accounts of reading the reader was seen as passive: reading, along with listening, was referred to as a 'passive skill'. There was then a shift in emphasis from a passive, acquiescent reader to an active one. Thus, the reader was typically described as 'extracting' meaning from a text. More recently the ground has shifted again to talk of reading as 'interactive' rather than simply 'active'. Readers are seen as negotiating meaning; meaning is partial within the text and writers' intentions may not be privileged over readers' interpretations.

Most accounts of the reading process see it as primarily a cognitive activity (e.g. Weir and Urquhart 1998). Others give greater emphasis to the reader's affective or critical engagement with text. Widdowson (e.g. 1984b) talks of readers taking up an 'assertive' or 'submissive' position. Even novice readers in a first language or second language may be judged, according to their manner of engagement with the text, as more or less critical or reflective. Wells (1991) notes how early as well as proficient readers may draw on what he calls 'epistemic literacy' which involves the ability not merely to understand the events of narratives but to engage with their implications, to move beyond the text to make critical and cognitive links with the readers' own life experience. In a similar vein, Hasan (1996) and Carter (1997: Chapter 5) talk of 'reflection' literacy, to include the ability to reflect on and monitor our own ongoing processing of text.

FIRST AND SECOND LANGUAGE READING

Much of the above background to reading studies deals primarily with first language (L1) reading. How far does reading in a second language (L2) fit these orientations? Alderson (1984) raises a question voiced by others, namely whether reading is a reading problem or a language problem. He concludes, unsurprisingly, that it is both. Much depends on the stage of L2 development. In the early stages L2 knowledge is a stronger factor than L1 reading ability. L2 readers need a minimum threshold level of general L2 language competence before they can generalise their L1 reading abilities into L2. Where proficient L2 learners are good readers in their L1, the consensus view (based on a wide range of research studies and teachers' observation) is that reading abilities can, indeed, be generalised across languages even in the case of differing scripts.

Underpinning the three broad orientations set out above are different views as to what reading itself means. Reading, for some, means reading words, and success is judged by the number of words which can be read out of context; for others, successful reading is judged from the earliest levels, even by beginner readers, in terms of the ability to make sense of continuous text, beyond word level. It is argued that effective reading is judged not by reference to the accurate rendering aloud of a written text, but by strategies which the reader can be observed to draw on which may signal progress, even in the absence of accurate text decoding. For yet others, attention centres on the quality of the engagement with print. It follows that research also takes different perspectives. Below I review different research traditions and particular instances of research relevant for L2 learners at various degrees of proficiency.

Research

READING AS PRACTICE: RESEARCH ON LITERACY PRACTICES

Researchers into literacy as social practice have been mainly interested in investigating literacy practices in their own right, although several also discuss pedagogic implications. Heath (1983), e.g., conducted a longitudinal ethnographic study of the literacy practices of two communities in the United States. She concludes the account of her study with the need for schools to take fuller account of the diverse literacy experiences which children bring to school. Gregory (1996) takes a case-study approach to classroom studies of language minority primary school children in East London. She examines how home literacy practices in a language other than English may impact on how children are socialised into the dominant English-medium ones institutionalised by schooling. Recent publications extend the discussion on literacy to look beyond reading and writing as the reception and production of linear text to new, diverse forms of literacy for a global age, which they term 'multi-literacies' (Cope and Kalantzis 2000).

READING AS PRODUCT: TEXT-FOCUSED RESEARCH

A large body of reading research – especially in the field of cognitive psychology – is concerned with the ability to decode words and with the particular skills judged to be prerequisite to fluent, independent reading. Adams (1990) offers a thorough review of this research, which shows a strong link between phonemic awareness, the ability to process words automatically and rapidly, and reading achievement. Those who have questioned emphasis on skills such as phonemic awareness point out that it is unclear whether they are acquired in advance of or as a consequence of exposure to alphabetic writing systems (Olson 1990). It also remains unproven that learners progress through clear stages, whereby one kind of skill builds on another to produce the mature, skilled reader; e.g. Lunzer and Gardner (1979) failed to find a hierarchy of skills through which readers progress.

A difficulty with attending specifically to sound–symbol relations in texts, as happens with phonic instruction, is that there is often a mismatch between the L2 learner's phonological system of English and Received Pronunciation on which much phonic practice is based. Additionally, people whose L1 is written with great phonic regularity may find it difficult to adjust to the (phonic) irregularity of English (Nuttall 1996). It is consequently helpful to turn to research on textual features, other than grapheme–phoneme correspondences and beyond word-level and sentence-level structure. Chapman (1983), drawing on work on cohesion (Halliday and Hasan 1976), noted the kinds of difficulties which cohesive ties in texts, such as pronouns, cause for L1 learners as old as 14. Such difficulties are likely to be correspondingly greater for L2 learners. Weir and Urquhart (1998: 59–62) discuss the role of grammatical processing by L2 learners, claiming this as a neglected area of research. The genre theorists (e.g. Martin 1989; Cope and Kalantzis 1993) seek to make explicit to learners the salient grammatical and lexical features not just of written texts in general but of different types of texts. They recommend providing students with extensive, specific knowledge about how texts work, particularly important, it is claimed, for many L2 and minority children who may be less familiar than mainstream learners with a wide range of genres.

READING AS PROCESS: READER-FOCUSED RESEARCH

This research approach is concerned with the strategies or resources which readers employ in reading and learning to read. Major figures in this tradition are Goodman (e.g. 1967) and Smith (e.g. 1971). They are known as 'psycholinguists' on the grounds that they view reading as a language activity as well as a psychological process. Goodman and Smith argued that reading is best seen not as the matching up of visual symbol to sound realisation in a linear manner, but as a process heavily mediated by the reader's ability to make informed predictions as he or she progresses through the text. The context facilitates informed guessing, with some options being much more likely than others on syntactic, semantic and phonological grounds; e.g. the opening part of the sentence 'The man opened his . . .' is much more likely to continue 'case' than 'but' or 'plop' or 'cheese'. This view of reading as a partial, highly selective process was subsequently challenged by laboratory-based experiments which showed that, far from processing text selectively, readers in fact read almost every word on the page, albeit rapidly and automatically (Rayner and Pollatsek 1989).

Both Goodman and Smith see the reader as making use of three cue systems represented by three levels of language within the text. Goodman terms these 'graphophonic', 'syntactic' and 'semantic': first, readers make use of their knowledge of the visual and phonetic features of English; second, they draw on knowledge of syntactic constraints (such as possible word order); and, third, they are aware of semantic constraints related to knowledge of word meanings and collocations. In the case of early readers who read aloud, the reading process can be monitored by observing **miscues**, Goodman's term which labels cases in which readers replace, in systematic ways, a word in the text with one comparable graphophonically, semantically or syntactically. Miscues should not be judged negatively: they are part of the reader's 'meaning-making process' in the ongoing sampling of text. They offer insight into strategies which readers use.

The strategies of early L2 learners were considered in a series of studies by Hosenfeld (1977, 1984) who asked successful readers, as judged by conventional test scores, to report their own reading strategies. Readers reported that they skipped inessential words, guessed from context, read in broad phrases and continued reading text when they came across a new word. Drawing on such studies, other researchers (e.g. Block 1986) have investigated the range and nature of strategies used by successful and less successful readers, in particular the role of metacognitive strategies by which readers monitor their own reading process.

READING AS A SOCIAL PROCESS: CRITICAL READING

More recently there has been interest in reading as a social, critical process (Wallace 1992a; Baynham 1995). This strand of enquiry pays greater attention to social and ideological factors which mediate in readers' access to text. Critical reading is concerned less with the individual author's communicative intent than with ideological effect: the claim is that readers need not accept the words on the page as given, but that a range of interpretations are legitimate, providing that textual warrants are offered. L2 readers, in particular, may bring different kinds of cultural and ideological assumptions to bear on L2 texts, thereby offering, it is argued, fruitful challenges to mainstream or conventional readings.

Practice

READING AS PRACTICE: FOCUS ON USE

Relatively little methodology centres around discussion or awareness-raising of literacy as practice, although it is possible to devise simple literacy awareness tasks which involve L2 students observing who reads what kinds of material in different social settings. It also means inviting students to consider their own needs and roles as readers in both a first and foreign language. Some of these awareness tasks are offered in Wallace (1992a) and can be appropriate for both early readers and more proficient ones. They involve, e.g., students devising matrices of the reading activities which they observe in their everyday environments, keeping a diary of their own reading activities and noting the range of textual material which surrounds them, either or both in the L1 or target L2 setting.

READING AS PRODUCT: FOCUS ON TEXT

Early reading

Eskey (1988) and Paran (1996) discuss the need for reading teachers to 'hold in the bottom' on the grounds that 'top-down' orientation leads to neglect of the language data that the reader is necessarily drawing on. Eskey proposes activities which encourage automated processing of words by asking students to discriminate rapidly between graphophonically similar words, such as *see*, *sea*, *sew*, *saw*. Others favour emphasis on syntactic awareness of word and sentence structure (see also Research section above). One teaching resource which is based on this principle is the *Breakthrough to Literacy* approach, first put forward by Mackay *et al.* (1970), where students construct sentences either from words and morphemes provided in a folder or from self-generated words. In doing so they are able to see the systematic nature of English word order and morphology. This kind of work also allows them to develop a metalanguage for talk around texts, including items such as 'word', 'sentence', 'letter' and 'inflectional ending'. Work on both phonic and morphological analysis of words is now included in the National Literacy Strategy introduced in England and Wales in 1999.

Intermediate to advanced reading

For intermediate to advanced students text-focused literacy study involves practical work with more complex sentence structure, the structure of whole texts and cross-text features of texts such as reference and cohesion. Course materials may offer texts where students are asked to identify co-reference (i.e. reference to the same person; e.g. *John, her husband* or *the man next door* all referring to one man). At this level students are helped by seeing how different kinds of textual features characterise different genres. Modality will, thus, be salient in discursive texts, and temporal sentence connectors in narratives. At the same time genres will be identified by distinctive kinds of rhetorical structures. Foll (1990) offers activities calculated to show the stylistic and structural features of different text types. Davies (1995) describes activities called directed activities related to texts (DARTS) which require readers to identify, analyse and manipulate text structure. Nuttall (1996) further exemplifies text-focused activities which involve, e.g., the matching of diagrams to text structure or the reconstruction of rhetorical structure. This interest in text structure has been continued by practitioners following the genre approach, who point to the need for minority and working-class children to be given specific help with unfamiliar text types. In this tradition, Derewianka (1990) notes, in a series of lesson plans, how children can be offered explicit terminology to support understanding of story structure and other text types related to schooling (such as recounts and arguments).

READING AS PROCESS

Early reading

For early readers **miscue analysis** can be used by teachers to assess the quality and quantity of learner errors in their processing of text. First, this is especially useful for L2 learners who – because their interlanguage system may show systematic syntactic and phonological departures from Standard English – may miscue on the basis of their current use of English rather than because of text misunderstanding. Second, 'language experience' approaches can be encouraged whereby early readers first construct their own simple texts, stories, recounts or descriptions with the help of the teacher as scribe. They then have relatively predictable material available to read back. Another source of material is provided by graded or simplified readers where consistent use of tenses, predictable word order and familiar content give readers the opportunity to increase fluency in the processing of L2 texts, particularly in extensive, out-of-class reading.

Intermediate to advanced reading

A reader-centred approach is evidenced in reading instruction which focuses, first, on what the reader brings to reading in schematic world knowledge and language knowledge and, second, on their ability and willingness to draw on productive strategies in the course of reading. More traditional reading pedagogy emphasised comprehension in the form of the presentation of text followed by post-reading questions on the text. Process approaches attend, first, to the need to prime the reader with new knowledge or prompt the reader to recover existing knowledge (in advance of reading the text) and, second, to make maximum use of cognitive and linguistic resources during text processing. This involves providing 'pre-reading' tasks (such as brainstorming, semantic mapping, true–false or agree–disagree tasks), as well as 'while-reading' tasks (such as margin prompts, encouraging the linking or cross-referencing of one part of a text to another, or encouraging first skim readings followed by closer, more focused ones). Many contemporary coursebooks (e.g. Rossner 1988; Murphy and Cooper 1995) offer a range of such tasks.

A key principle in the design of these tasks is the encouragement of flexible and reflective reading. Flexibility might be promoted by devising tasks encouraging readers to read a range of texts in different ways (e.g. a close detailed reading for some genres and a scanned and later more focused reading for others). Reflective reading, where the reader is engaged with the text, might be encouraged by the interspersion of questions or prompts during the text to encourage interrogation of text. More recent studies of reader strategies (e.g. Janzen and Stoller 1998) invite readers to reflect more specifically on their own reading strategies and to judge the effectiveness of those of other readers.

READING AS SOCIAL CRITICAL PROCESS

Pedagogies which attend to reading as a critical process encourage what Cope and Kalantzis (2000) call 'critical framing' of texts: readers are encouraged to consider the underlying cultural contexts and purposes of texts. Wallace (1992a) and Lankshear *et al.* (1997) have developed activities for classroom use based around media or educational texts which use text analytic procedures to scrutinise the ideological effect of a writer's lexical and syntactic choices. Readers are initially asked why, by and for whom, and in whose interests, texts are written. The aim is not so much to comprehend what has been written as to critique the way in which the text has been written, and what has motivated a writer's choices of lexis, syntax and overall style and presentation. Materials, mainly produced for L1 readers which take a critical perspective, include: *Making Stories* and *Changing Stories* (Mellor *et al.* 1984a; 1984b) and, more recently, *Language, Power and Society* (Butler and Keith 1999).

Future trends and directions

Recent research shows the potential for some rapprochement between opposing camps, particularly those who favour a focus on texts and aspects of texts and those who privilege readers' engagement with texts. It seems that, regardless of the use made by readers of text-based features, automatised processing will quickly fail without the kind of active and selective engagement which readers in real-life settings, if not in laboratory ones, make use of. Research (e.g. Oakhill and Bryant 1998) continues to show that a substantial minority of children develop competence in single-word recognition but do not integrate text with their world knowledge in ways which good comprehenders do. The latter make inferences across texts and monitor their own ongoing processing of the text in much the ways process-oriented teaching of reading has encouraged. One can reasonably conclude that learners, both L1 and L2, require not just support with the mechanical aspects of learning to read but also specific help with effective processing of text. Such processing is aided, moreover, by an understanding of the sociocultural origins of texts and literacy practices. At the same time the process-oriented group have neglected useful kinds of analytical text-focused study which directs learners attention to the particular characteristics of the English writing system (both within words and sentences and, more importantly, the distinctive structure of different text types or genres). Moreover, attention to form – both at sentence level and across whole texts – can be harnessed to the relatively new interest in critical reading, where learners are invited to consider the ideological effects created by the exercise of particular kinds of syntactic and lexical choice.

Conclusion

In this chapter I offer an overview of different orientations to reading research and the implications for practice. All of these orientations can be brought into play in a principled way in the teaching of reading to L2 learners. An understanding of ways in which literacy practices in the learners' L1 context may differ from those dominant in the L2 context provide initial grounding for pedagogy; the specific, judicious teaching of formal aspects of written English texts scaffold a broadly process-favoured teaching approach which, in turn, can be broadened out to include attention to ideological as well as cognitive aspects of literacy, as suggested by the recent interest in critical reading approaches.

Key readings

Alderson and Urquhart (1984) *Reading in a Foreign Language*
Carrell *et al.* (1988) *Interactive Approaches to Second Language Reading*
Davies (1995) *Introducing Reading*
Nuttall (1996) *Teaching Reading Skills in a Foreign Language*
Smith (1971) *Understanding Reading: A Psycholinguistic Analysis*
Wallace (1992b) *Reading*

CHAPTER 4

Writing

Joy Reid

Introduction

Teaching English second language (L2) writing differs from teaching other language skills in two ways. First, even as late as the 1970s, L2 writing was not viewed as a language skill to be taught to learners. Instead, it was used as a support skill in language learning to, for example, practise handwriting, write answers to grammar and reading exercises, and write dictation. In fact, while graduate programmes in TESOL regularly offered courses in other skill areas, virtually no coursework was available in teaching L2 writing. Second, as the theory and practice of L2 composition teaching gradually developed, it followed the path of US native English speaker (NES) composition theory. Only recently has English L2 composition theory and pedagogy begun to offer English first language (L1) researchers and teachers insights and pedagogical practices (Silva *et al.* 1997). This chapter focuses mainly on L2 academic writing, although broader issues are also highlighted.

Background

In the 1970s many English L2 language programme writing classes were, in reality, grammar courses. Students copied sentences or short pieces of discourse, making discrete changes in person or tense. The teaching philosophy grew directly out of the audiolingual method: students were taught incrementally, error was prevented and accuracy was expected to arise out of practice with structures. In the early 1980s, as teachers became more aware of current practices in NES composition, there was a shift from strictly controlled writing to guided writing: writing was limited to structuring sentences, often in direct answers to questions, or by combining sentences – the result of which looked like a short piece of discourse.

The slow but significant shift from language-based writing classrooms to the study of composition techniques and strategies began with (1) researchers' recognition of the newly developing field of NES composition and (2) teachers' realisation of the needs of English L2 students in the academic environment, particularly the role of writing in gate-keeping in post-secondary institutions (e.g. entrance and placement examinations). With the gradual acceptance of error as productive and developmental rather than substandard and deviant, grammatical accuracy became secondary to communication. English L2 composition textbooks reflected the theoretical shift by focusing on the teaching of organisation patterns common in English academic prose: topic and thesis sentences, paragraph and essay modes (e.g. process, comparison–contrast, cause–effect), with the focus primarily on the product, i.e. the resulting paper or essay. This 'current traditional approach' is still widely used.

During the 1980s the 'expressive approach' became prominent in NES composition class-rooms: writing was taught as a process of self-discovery; writers expressed their feelings in a climate of encouragement. In English L2 pedagogy, nearly a decade later, this approach entered the classroom as the 'process movement': a concentration on personal writing (narratives, journals), student creativity, and fluency (Zamel 1982). A false dichotomy between 'process' and 'product' classrooms arose in the L2 literature. Process teachers encouraged students to use their internal resources and individuality; they presumably taught 'writer-based' writing (i.e. writing read only by the writer herself or himself) to the exclusion of external audiences. They neglected accuracy in favour of fluency; the processes (generating ideas, expressing feelings) were more important to individual development than the outcome (the product). In contrast, it was suggested that product teachers focused solely on accuracy, appropriate rhetorical discourse and linguistic patterns to the exclusion of writing processes. They focused primarily on 'reader-based' writing for an academic audience with little or no consideration of the student writer's 'voice', forcing student writing into academic conventions that stifled creativity. In reality, most L2 students were being taught process writing strategies to achieve effective written communication (products), with differences occurring in emphasis.

At the start of the twenty-first century, writing classrooms have achieved a more balanced perspective of composition theory; consequently, new pedagogy has begun to develop: tradi-tional teacher-centred approaches are evolving into more learner-centred courses, and academic writing is viewed as a communicative social act. Despite diverse pedagogical perspectives, most English L2 student writers practise individualised processes to achieve products; courses focus more on classroom community and student responsibility through peer response activities, student selection of topics and evaluation criteria, and collaborative project writing. Focus on the highly complex constructs of audience and purpose have concentrated on author–reader interaction.

The development of multiple drafts to achieve meaningful communication – as well as focus on the problem-solving aspects of identifying and practising discourse conventions – also occupy teachers and L2 students in school-based writing classes. Teachers are designing curriculums based on a balance of institutional, programme and student needs rather than around dogmatic theories or approaches (see Chapter 28).

During the last decade, recognition of the importance of L2 writing in school settings internationally has been demonstrated in three ways. First, the inclusion of direct tests of writing have been included on standardised tests of English language proficiency such as the TOEFL Test of Written English, the University of Michigan's MELAB writing sub-test, and the University of Cambridge Local Examinations Syndicate / British Council's IELTS writing sub-test. Second, the necessity for better teacher preparation in L2 composition has resulted in more courses or at least coursework in graduate TESOL programmes and in more developed materials for L2 writing instruction. Further, there has also been a dramatic increase in textbook writing, conference presentations, and published research and commentary about English L2 writing (for a review, see Cumming 1997). Finally, there are a number of specific series (initiated by major international publishers) devoted to writing development for beginning to intermediate L2 learners of English; e.g. the Cambridge Skills for Fluency Series *Writing, 1, 2, 3, 4* (Littlejohn 1998) and the Oxford Basics Series *Simple Writing* (Hadfield and Hadfield 2000).

In the field of creative writing in TESOL classrooms and in the context of literature in language teaching (see Chapter 26), approaches to writing have been taken that involve strategies such as

- re-writing from different viewpoints;
- shifting registers to explore changing communicative effects;

- writing predictions and completions to texts as part of a process of detailed text study; and
- cross-genre writing (e.g. from poetry to prose and vice versa).

These activities may also be integrated with other competencies; e.g. talking about the content and the planning process prior to and during composition, often in an L1, can lead to greater confidence in the writing process. Such activities encourage learners to write their way into more precise, interpretive readings while at the same time fostering greater attention to forms of writing, to reflection on what is involved in the creation of a text and to adapting writing style to the audience and context of writing. This focus on more literary approaches to writing have strong roots in parts of the world such as Western Europe, especially in secondary school contexts, and increasingly in South East Asia. For coverage of both theory and practice, see Littlefair 1991; Carter and McRae 1996; Grellet 1996; Nash and Stacey 1997.

Research

English L2 writing research has been substantially influenced by – and has often paralleled – NES composition research. For example, L2 researchers have investigated students' composing and revision strategies by ethnographic methods such as case-study and speak-aloud protocols. Much of that research has followed a similarity–deficit model, i.e. ESL writing processes and products follow similar patterns but do everything less well than NES writers. Recommendations following these studies include what Raimes (1991) called the need for 'more of everything for L2 writers': strategy training, direct teaching, support systems, teacher response, practice, etc. Recent research focuses instead on salient and substantial differences rather than deficiencies. Silva's review (1993) of L2 writing research points out that L2 writers differ in their sequence of writing behaviours, the constraints they face in their preponderance and types of evidence, and their knowledge of the expectations of the NES audience. For introductory reviews of L1/L2 practices, see also Hedge 1988; Harris 1993.

Underlying many of these differences are studies in contrastive rhetoric that demonstrate ways that writers from different cultures use culturally appropriate writing conventions (Kaplan 1966; Henry 1993; Connor 1996; Ramanathan and Kaplan 1996). Of course, contrastive rhetoricians understand the limitations of their work: while research results should provide insights for both teachers and students, overgeneralisation of results can disserve individual students and their writing styles. In addition, while cultural differences in rhetorical patterns can adversely affect communication in English, they should not be viewed as deficiencies: 'Invention, arrangement, style, memory and delivery can all be defined, practiced, and valued in ways other than our own' (Matalene 1985: 814).

Increasingly, teacher-researchers have begun asking students about their preferences for and evaluations of techniques, approaches and materials in L2 writing classes. Using interviews, case studies and survey data, researchers are learning more about students' preferences concerning teacher and peer commentary on their written drafts (Ferris 1995, 1997; Zhang 1995; Hedgcock and Lefkowitz 1996; Lee 1997; Lipp and Davis-Ockey 1997; Porte 1997; F. Hyland 1998). Other researchers have sought student input about such diverse issues as strategy training in the English L2 writing class, the roles of teacher and student in individual or small-group writing conferences (Goldstein and Conrad 1990; Patthey-Chavez and Ferris 1997; Nelson and Carson 1998) and the writing tasks students are assigned in their academic classes (Leki and Carson 1997; Spack 1997).

The politics and philosophy of error have occupied many investigations of L2 writing. Researchers have studied reasons for error; e.g. transfer/interference of structures from the students' L1, overgeneralisation of English grammatical rules, and level of difficulty of the structure. A weak form of the contrastive analysis theory has re-entered the literature (Katzner 1986; Danesi 1993): by contrasting L1 and L2 structures, investigators can hypothesise which structures are more likely to be difficult and/or error-causing for some students (Swan and Smith

1987). Moreover, researchers have demonstrated that error should not be stigmatising; rather, it is often systematic and reasonable, occurring in a period of 'interlanguage' in which they are literally and positively developmental (Selinker 1992). Others have investigated the 'acceptance' levels of specific L2 language errors; these error-gravity studies rank which errors are more irritating or grievous to NES readers (Santos 1988; Vann *et al.* 1991).

Assessment is an ongoing area of research in English L2 writing (see Chapter 20), perhaps because, as Kroll (1998: 230) states:

> As we move forward in identifying how to fine-tune our assessment procedures, research continues to uncover the difficulties in controlling for all of the contributing factors simultaneously, to say nothing of the difficulty of identifying what precisely needs to be assessed in the first place.

Hamp-Lyons (1991, 1995, 1997) and others (Hill and Parry 1994) have confronted significant controversies surrounding assessment of large-scale writing tests; e.g. ways in which issues of content knowledge and of the consequent task impact on the writer, problems of task comparability across tests, the use of direct tests of writing as gate-keepers, and the politics of accountability and visibility of large-scale examiners. Hamp-Lyons and Kroll (1996) have reviewed correlative context issues such as writing task types and models of academic writers, issues of design (including prompt development and scoring criteria and procedures, usually holistic, speeded, impressionistic scoring), and selection and training of raters.

Teachers and researchers have also investigated assessment at the programme and classroom level. Because academic writing assignments are almost always a form of testing, issues parallel those in large-scale testing; e.g.:

- cultural bias, level of difficulty and clarity in assignments;
- rationalising assignment choices and assessment criteria for both the teacher and the student writers (Reid and Kroll 1995; Grabe and Kaplan 1996);
- the interrelationships between teacher response and teacher assessment; and
- fair and equitable evaluation processes.

Innovations in English L2 writing assessment include portfolio evaluation, in which several representative, drafted samples of student writing are considered in an overall evaluation. Despite the advantages of authenticity and scope, the assessment process is enormously time consuming, the design of evaluation criteria extremely complex, and results do not seem to differ substantially from more traditional writing assessment formats (Hamp-Lyons 1996).

Finally, a recent research area has extended the areas of contrastive rhetoric and the social-cognitive approach to academic writing in which teachers focus on the context – the writing situation – and the audience of the writing product to the rhetoric of specific genres in different disciplinary 'cultures' (see Chapter 27). Researchers have studied the writing conventions and the expectations of academic readers in such genres as written argumentative and persuasive techniques, written narrative strategies, and expository and report writing (Robinson 1991; Flowerdew 1993; Dudley-Evans 1995, 1997; Meyer 1996; K. Hyland 1998, 2000). Fundamental to this research is the concept of **discourse community**. Most simply, **discourse** involves the writing conventions within an academic group (a community). In a discipline such as chemistry or geology – or in a 'social' context such as a term paper in a psychology class or a case study in a management course – there are substantial differences in how knowledge and ideas are communicated. Swales (1990a: 52) describes genre as writing in which there are 'constraints' in writing conventions in 'content, positioning, and form'. Initial work in genre studies, based on Halliday's functional approach to language (Halliday 1978, 1994; Halliday and Hasan 1985) began in Australia (see Derewianka 1990; Christie 1992; Richardson 1994; Christie and Martin 1997; for a review of genre, see Hyon 1996 and also Chapter 27 of this volume). Results of the research are currently used throughout the Australian NES school system. For reference to L1 and L2 writing in English based mainly on settings in the United Kingdom, see also Littlefair 1991; Kress 1994.

Practice

The pedagogical practices necessary for students to increase their writing competence have been hotly debated. Historically, the question of whether or not writing should (or could) be taught has only recently been answered by research in the relatively new field of composition and rhetoric, and by the advanced degrees that legitimised specialisation in that field. Moreover, few L2 teachers felt prepared to teach composition, and most English L2 learners had received little, if any, directed writing instruction in their L1.

Times have now changed: English L2 writing teachers are better prepared, language programmes recognise the value of L2 writing competencies, and students are more aware of the writing required in school settings. Some pedagogical issues are also similar across language programmes, such as how to provide the most appropriate instruction, how to respond to student work in ways that help their language progress, and how to assess students fairly. Several resource books for English L2 writing teachers offer substantial information about theory and practice, methods and materials, as well as varied pedagogical perspectives.

As ESL research and practices have developed, many techniques and methods have proved successful in English L2 writing classrooms; e.g.:

- careful needs analysis to plan curriculums (Reid 2000);
- co-operative and group work (including collaborative writing) that strengthen the community of the class and offer writers authentic audiences;
- integration of language skills in class activities;
- learning style and strategy training to help students learn how to learn (Reid 1998); and
- the use of relevant, authentic materials and tasks.

In addition, teachers have learned that, in the same way that one size does not fit all, so also one technique, approach, method or material is inadequate in the classroom. As a consequence, eclecticism (the use of a variety of approaches that permits teachers to extend their repertoire), once frowned upon, has become essential for effective teaching.

The use of technology in English L2 writing courses may be the foremost curricular change today. Composition students regularly use word processing, which has revolutionised the writing process. Computer-networked classrooms allow students to communicate both locally and globally; in communicating locally, this may involve students commenting on their peers' writing and working co-operatively on writing projects; globally, this may involve students writing to email 'keypals' and working with another composition class on another continent (Hanson-Smith 1997b). Teachers also communicate and conference by email (Warschauer 1995a; Braine 1997). The exponential growth of the internet since 1994 is causing a revolution in learning (Blyth 1999). Students research topics without time or space constraints; they use available graphics from the internet to enhance their writing; they can access on-line writing centres for consultation. Still another dramatic change is the initiation of the 'virtual classroom' for composition classes, in which students may never meet physically but instead read electronic texts, comment on peers' drafts, communicate in writing with the instructor, and perhaps teleconference with class members and the instructor (for more detailed accounts, see Chapters 15 and 30).

Conclusion: the future

Because the specialisation of English L2 writing is a relatively new area of inquiry, many of the concerns now being investigated (and discussed above) will continue to be refined and revisited in order to provide students with high-quality pedagogy; new technology will continue to be used in the L2 writing class. In particular, teachers are increasingly participating in 'action research', in which teachers ask students for their perspectives and perceptions and/or collaborate with students to discover better classroom practices.

Other ongoing research seeks to identify 'the universe of writing skills . . . needed to succeed in an academic context' (Hamp-Lyons and Kroll 1997: 8) by collecting and analysing writing tasks in selected school and career settings (Hale *et al*. 1996; Dudley-Evans 1997), especially those heavy in ESL enrolment, then developing curriculums with appropriate parameters and pragmatics that will enable English L2 writers to fulfil such tasks. Discourse analysts are using computer text-analysis to explore 'grammar clusters' that typically appear in specific genres (Biber 1988; Biber *et al*. 1998). The results of such research could revolutionise the teaching of grammar structures by demonstrating that the 'same features of grammar are used repeatedly and predictably in clusters that are characteristic of particular types of [written] communication' (Byrd 1998: 92).

Grabe and Kaplan (1997) have contributed the initial critical needs analysis for English L2 writing teacher preparation. They propose that students in such a course:

- explore theories of language as well as writing and literacy development;

- study a wide range of curriculum design;

- investigate cognitive and psycholinguistic processes;

- learn about affect and strategy training; and

- experiment with varied instructional practices.

At the same time, researchers must continue to examine how L2 students learn, how to measure L2 writing development, and how to develop coherent curriculums. Finally, English L2 writing teachers must forge a closer working relationship with NES researchers and practitioners to provide 'a larger, more inclusive, more global perspective on writers and writing' (Silva *et al*. 1997: 425).

Key readings

Bates *et al*. (1993) *Writing Clearly: Responding to ESL Compositions*
Belcher and Braine (1995) *Academic Writing in a Second Language*
Boswood (1999) *New Ways of Using Computers in Language Teaching*
Brock and Walters (1993) *Teaching Composition around the Pacific Rim: Politics and Pedagogy*
Ferris and Hedgcock (1998) *Teaching ESL Composition: Purpose, Process, and Practice*
Freeman and Freeman (1993) *Whole Language for Second Language Learners*
Hamp-Lyons (1991) *Assessing Second Language Writing in Academic Contexts*
Journal of Second Language Writing
Reid (1995b) *Teaching ESL Writing*
Suid and Lincoln (1988) *Recipes for Writing: Motivation, Skills, and Activities*
Swales (1990a) *Genre Analysis: English in Academic and Research Settings*
White (1998) *New Ways in Teaching Writing*
White and Arndt (1991) *Process Writing*

CHAPTER 5

Grammar

Diane Larsen-Freeman

Introduction

The term **grammar** has multiple meanings. It is used to refer both to language users' subconscious internal system and to linguists' attempts explicitly to codify – or describe – that system. With regard to the latter, its scope can be broad enough to refer to the abstract system underlying all languages (i.e. a universal grammar) or, more narrowly, to the system underlying a particular language (e.g. a grammar of English). It can also refer to a particular school of linguistic thought (e.g. a stratificational grammar) or to a specific compendium of facts for a general audience (e.g. *A Comprehensive Grammar of the English Language*; Quirk *et al.* 1985) or to a particular audience (e.g. a pedagogical grammar for students or for teachers).

While these uses may differ in purpose and scope, they seek minimally to explain the same phenomena: how words are formed (morphology) and how words are combined (syntax). Additionally, a study of English grammar includes function words, such as frequently occurring articles, whose role is largely syntactic (i.e. not lexical since they may not have an inherent meaning). Some grammars also include phonology and semantics, but the usual interpretation of grammar is limited to the structural organisation of language.

Background

LINGUISTICS

Linguists make a distinction between two types of descriptive grammars. **Formal grammars** take as their starting point the form or structure of language, with little or no attention given to meaning (semantics) or context and language use (pragmatics). **Functional grammars**, conversely, conceive of language as largely social interaction, seeking to explain why one linguistic form is more appropriate than another in satisfying a particular communicative purpose in a particular context.

FORMAL GRAMMARS

The prevailing formal grammar in the US in the mid-twentieth century was descriptivism or structuralism. Structural linguists based their work on the assumption that grammatical categories should not be established in terms of meaning, but rather in terms of the distribution of structures in sentences (Fries 1952). The dominant school of psychology then was behaviourism, which views all learning as a form of conditioning, brought about through repetition, shaping and reinforcement. This characterisation of learning was thought to apply to language acquisition as well, since language was conceived as verbal behaviour (Skinner 1957).

A clear challenge to this conception of language and language acquisition as a form of conditioning was issued by Noam Chomsky (1959, 1965), who pointed out the limitations of a language-as-behaviour view. Chomsky's primary concern was with grammatical competence: the knowledge of a finite system of rules that enables an ideal language user in a homogeneous speech community to generate and understand an infinite variety of sentences. Chomsky sought to describe the underlying grammatical system (i.e. speakers' competence), rather than what speakers say or understand someone else to say (i.e. their performance). Chomsky's transformational-generative grammar posited the existence of a deep structure that determined the semantic interpretation of a sentence and a surface structure that realised the phonetic form of sentences. The two were linked by a set of transformational rules. The learners' task was – through utilisation of processes such as hypothesis formation and testing – to abstract the rules from the language input to which they were exposed.

According to Chomsky, the input data were degenerate (ill-formed, replete with false starts, fragmented, etc.). Since all children with normal faculties successfully acquired their native language despite the impoverished input, Chomsky reasoned that humans were biologically endowed with an innate language faculty which incorporated a set of universal principles, i.e. a universal grammar (UG). Experience of a particular language served as input to the language faculty which, in turn, provided children with an algorithm for developing a grammar of their native language. The search initially for transformations that connected deep and surface structure and, later, for abstract 'principles' (which must be general enough to account for what all languages have in common) has occupied generative grammarians for decades. A central aim of formal grammars is to explain syntactic facts without recourse to pragmatics, i.e. strictly on the basis of formal grammatical properties of sentences. Formal grammars seek to utilise the least elaborate theory possible, in order to maximize their learnability, a major goal of Chomsky's recent Minimalist Program for linguistic theory (Chomsky 1995).

FUNCTIONAL GRAMMARS

Functional grammarians start from a very different position. Although there are different models of functional grammar (see, e.g., Tomlin 1994), theorists share the conviction that:

> The language system . . . is not considered as an autonomous set of rules and principles, the uses of which can only be considered in a secondary phase; rather it is assumed that the rules and principles composing the language system can only be adequately understood when they are analyzed in terms of the conditions of use. In this sense the study of language use (pragmatics) precedes the study of formal and semantic properties of linguistic expressions.
>
> (Dik 1991: 247)

Thus, where a formal grammarian might accept the challenge to explain how sentence (1) is derived from (2) (by interchanging the subject with the object, inserting *be* and the past participle and the preposition *by* before the displaced subject), a functional grammarian is more interested in explaining the difference in use between these two according to the notion 'perspective'.

1. Mark McGuire and Sammy Sosa broke the home run record.
2. The home run record was broken by Mark McGuire and Sammy Sosa.

A functional grammarian assumes that both sentences describe the same event, but that this event is presented from the participant's viewpoint in (1) and from the viewpoint of the result in (2). He or she is then interested in determining what contextual features influenced the speaker's choosing one version over the other.

Givón (1993) captures the difference between formal grammars and functional grammars succinctly: although grammar consists of a set of rules, what is of interest to the functional grammarian is not that the rules generate grammatical sentences, but rather that the production of rule-governed sentences is the means to coherent communication. Given this communicative orientation, functional grammar's unit of analysis extends beyond the sentence (see Chafe 1980; Longacre 1983) and the explanation for various grammatical structures is sought at the level of discourse. Analysis of spoken and written texts reveals that factors such as information structure and interpersonal patterns of interacting influence grammatical structure. For example, Hopper and Thompson (1980) demonstrated that transitivity is not an *a priori* category, but is rather motivated from its use in discourse. Sequences of verb tense and aspect can similarly only be explained at the discourse level.

Functional grammarians see meaning as central, i.e. grammar is a resource for making and exchanging meaning (Halliday 1978, 1994). In Halliday's systemic-functional theory, three types of meaning in grammatical structure can be identified: experiential meaning (how our experience and inner thoughts are represented), interpersonal meaning (how we interact with others through language) and textual meaning (how coherence is created in spoken and written texts).

GRAMMAR IN LANGUAGE EDUCATION

The simple binary distinction between formal and functional approaches is reflected in language education. The former is the 'structural approach' (Widdowson 1990), and its adherents assume that communicative ends are best served through a bottom-up process: through practising grammatical structures and lexical patterns until they are internalised. Means of inculcating a language's grammar include pattern practice and structural drills, through, for example, the audiolingual method, widely practised in the 1950s and 1960s. Partly due to the influence of transformational grammar, materials in the 1970s featured sentence-based linguistic rules with exercises asking students to transform one sentence pattern into another (Rutherford 1977). Although these teaching practices are still widely used and very visible in current language teaching materials, a major shift occurred during the 1970s.

Factors contributing to the shift include: observations of learners' difficulties in transferring the grammatical structures learned in class to communicative contexts outside, calls to broaden linguistic study from grammatical competence to 'communicative competence' (Hymes 1971 [1972, 1979]), the influence of functional grammar, a research project commissioned by the Council of Europe (1971) and the encouragement of applied linguists (Widdowson 1978; Brumfit and Johnson 1979). A confluence of these factors led language-teaching theorists and practitioners to embrace a new approach to language instruction, i.e. to focus initially on language use rather than formal aspects of language. Initially this translated as advocacy for notional–functional syllabuses rather than ones based on linguistic units, such as had been used up to that point (Wilkins 1976; see also Chapter 22 of this volume). When notional-functional syllabuses themselves were challenged in the 1980s, the commitment to teaching language use remained and was manifest in the 'communicative approach' (Widdowson 1990), which was characterised by, for example, role-playing, jigsaw tasks and information-gap activities. There was, however, often little attempt to control the structural complexity to which learners were exposed. Over time, learners were increasingly expected to approximate target language forms as they used them for communicative purposes.

This major shift in language pedagogy received additional impetus from second language acquisition (SLA) researchers who sought to account for grammatical development by examining how meaning was negotiated in learner interactions (for a review of the literature, see Pica 1994; Gass 1997). SLA researcher Hatch (1978: 409) commented: 'One learns how to do conversation, one learns how to interact verbally and, out of this interaction, syntactic structures are developed'. To this day, communicative language teaching (CLT) prevails, although concern has been expressed that newer approaches are practised at the expense of language form (Widdowson 1990; Bygate *et al.* 1994).

Research

FOCUS ON FORM

To this point, although there is not unanimity (see Krashen 1992; Truscott 1998), many SLA researchers follow Long (1991) in proposing a focus on form (for reviews, see Harley 1988; Long 1988). They work within a meaning-based or communicative approach, setting research agendas which aim to discover what form-focused practices are most effective, when they are best used and with which forms (see Doughty and Williams 1998a). For example, it has also been proposed that, since there is a limit to what humans can pay attention to at any one time and since attending to features of English may be necessary for learning them, grammar instruction may enhance learners' ability to notice aspects of English that might otherwise escape their attention while engaged in communication (Schmidt 1990). There is research (N. Ellis 1993; De Keyser 1995; Robinson 1996) on whether to do so implicitly (by input enhancement; Sharwood Smith 1993) or explicitly (by the teacher's presenting a rule).

Further benefits of focusing on form have been proposed (R. Ellis 1993, 1998b). One is to help students 'notice the gap' between new features in a target language's structure and how they differ from the learners' interlanguage (Schmidt and Frota 1986). Negative evidence that what students have produced does not conform to the target language enhances this focus. A benefit of grammar instruction may therefore be the corrective feedback that students receive on their performance. Grammar instruction can also help students generalise their knowledge to new structures (Gass 1982). Another role of focus on form may be to fill in the gaps in the input (Spada and Lightbown 1993), since classroom language will not necessarily be representative of all grammatical structures that students need to acquire. Finally, a focus on form should also include output practice (Swain 1985), in order to ensure that students are engaged not only in semantic processing but also in syntactic processing.

A contentious, but potentially far-reaching, question is whether learners must be developmentally ready in order for grammar structures to be learnable and, therefore, teachable (Pienemann 1984, 1998). While there may be this need, it may also be the case that grammar instruction in advance of learner readiness (by, e.g., priming subsequent noticing: Lightbown 1998) is positive.

UG-INSPIRED SLA RESEARCH

Theoretical positions taken by Chomsky have been very attractive to certain SLA researchers who have set research agendas to determine the question of UG accessibility by adult second language (L2) learners (e.g. Bley-Vroman *et al.* 1988; Eubank 1991) and the transferability of native-language parametric values to the L2 (e.g. Flynn 1989; White 1989). Schwarz and Sprouse (1994) hypothesise that the whole of the first language (L1) grammar (including its parameter settings) transfer, thus constituting the L2 initial state. In this case, it could be argued that where L1 acquisition may only require positive evidence to introduce a particular structure into the learner's grammar, L2 acquisition may require negative evidence and/or specific structural teaching since learners would need to 'reset' their L1 parameters (White 1987). Along these lines, V. Cook (1994) suggests that one application of a UG perspective for teaching grammar is for the teacher to focus student attention on concentrated sentence examples showing the effects of particular parameters that may need resetting in the target language.

SOCIOCULTURAL THEORY

Research on the learning of grammar has also been conducted using Vygotsky's sociocultural theory as a frame of reference. Donato (1994) studied what he termed 'collective scaffolding' to see how language development was brought about through social interaction. Donato found evidence that participating in collaborative dialogue, through which learners could provide support for each other, spurred development of learners' interlanguage. Goss *et al.* (1994) further concluded that dialogue arising during collaborative problem-solving is an enactment of cognitive activity. Other research (e.g. Swain and Lapkin 1998) corroborates the value of a theoretical orientation towards dialogue as both a cognitive tool and a means of communication which can promote grammatical development.

DISCOURSE GRAMMAR

As mentioned above, one of the functionalists' contributions has been to elevate the focus of linguistic analysis to the discourse level. In investigations of grammar at this level, L2 researchers have discovered interesting patterns (Celce-Murcia 1991a; McCarthy and Carter 1994; Hughes and McCarthy 1998). For example, the present perfect operates at this level to frame a habitual present-tense narrative (Celce-Murcia and Larsen-Freeman 1999). Other work shows how the choice of grammatical form often signals such things as the speaker's attitude, power and identity (Batstone 1995; Larsen-Freeman 2001) and the place of grammar in social interaction (Ochs *et al.* 1996). Other research delves more deeply into the grammar of speech (Biber 1988; Yule *et al.* 1992; Brazil 1995; Carter and McCarthy 1995; McCarthy and Carter 1995) and consequently many grammar teaching materials reflect modality differences (see, e.g., Biber *et al.* 1999).

CORPUS LINGUISTICS

Corpus linguistics is another area with important implications for understanding and teaching grammar (McEnery and Wilson 1996; Biber *et al.* 1998). With technological changes, concordance programs can search massive databases of spoken and written language to identify examples of particular grammatical patterns (Sinclair 1990). For example, using the 320-million-word COBUILD corpus of British, American and Australian English, researchers have found that *insist* typically occurs in the following combinations:

> *insist* (*that*)
> He insisted that he hadn't done it.
> *insist on*
> He insisted on his innocence.
> *insist on* verb + *ing*
> He insisted on testifying.
> *insist* + quote
> He insisted, 'I haven't done it.'

First, what is noteworthy is that not every possible combination of words and grammatical structures occur: there is a finite number of regularly-occurring patterns. Second, it seems that words are not freely substituted into grammatical patterns: once one word is selected, the likelihood of a particular word or phrase following is increased (e.g. when *insist* is selected, either *on* or *that* is very likely to follow). An implication of corpus-based research is that teachers of grammar should pay more attention to conventionalised lexicogrammatical units – i.e. semi-fixed units comprised of words and grammar structures, such as 'the sooner, the better' – since these units contribute extensively to native speaker fluency (Pawley and Syder 1983; Nattinger and DeCarrico 1992; Lewis 1997).

CONNECTIONISM

Connectionists maintain that although language can be described by rules, it does not necessarily follow that language use is a product of rule application (Gasser 1990). Interest in the architecture of the human brain motivates connectionists to seek answers by modelling neural networks rather than following innatist claims. They show how parallel systems of artificial neurons can extract regularities from masses of input data which, in turn, produce output that appears to be rule-governed. Such a simulation by Rumelhart and McClelland (1986) shows that a simple connectionist network can learn to generate both regular and irregular English past tense forms from verb stems without explicit rules, and to roughly follow the same kinds of stages as humans appear to as they learn the same forms. Although early connectionist work was criticised for various reasons (Pinker and Prince 1988), more recent models successfully demonstrate that morphology acquisition (Ellis and Schmidt 1997) and syntax (MacWhinney 1997) may be accounted for by simple associative learning principles (N. Ellis 1996, 1998).

Practice

Binary distinctions – such as those between formal and functional linguistics or structural and communicative approaches – are convenient for classification; however, they can be simplistic. Many teachers clearly attempt to combine the teaching of communication with the teaching of structure. Importantly, structural and communicative approaches have a common overarching goal: to teach students to communicate. The debate continues on the best means to this end.

The structural approach calls for the teacher to present students with an explicit description of grammatical structures or rules which are subsequently practised, first in a mechanical or controlled manner and later in a freer, communicative way. This is often called the present, practice, produce (PPP) approach to grammar teaching. Although this remains a common sequence and many teachers have used it successfully, some question its value; e.g. presentation of abstract rules can be inappropriate for younger learners. Further, if learners learn grammatical structures only when they are ready to do so, they wonder if gains from practice will have an enduring effect. In support of this concern it is not uncommon for students to be able to supply the correct form in a practice exercise, but then be unable to transfer that ability to immediate communicative use outside class.

A traditional response to this issue is to spiral the syllabus, i.e. to keep returning to and expanding upon the same grammatical structures over time. In any case, it is clear that acquisition of grammatical structures is not linear, i.e. one structure is not completely mastered before another is attempted. Rutherford (1987) suggests that an optimal approach to dealing with the non-linearity of grammatical acquisition is when teachers help students understand the general principles of grammar (e.g. how to modify basic word order) rather than concentrating on teaching structure-specific rules.

Implementing a communicative approach requires a different starting point. Instead of starting with a grammar point, a lesson might revolve around students' understanding content or completing a task. When a grammatical problem is encountered, a focus on form takes place immediately by drawing students' attention to it, i.e. promoting their noticing. At a later point, activities may be introduced which highlight that point in the target language (Loschky and Bley-Vroman 1993).

Stemming from a similar approach is the use of input-processing (Lee and van Patten 1995) and consciousness-raising tasks (Rutherford and Sharwood Smith 1988) which also do not require students to produce the target structure. Instead, the teacher makes students aware of specific grammatical features using tasks (Dickens and Woods 1988); e.g. students are given a set of examples and asked to figure out for themselves the rule regarding the correct order of direct and indirect objects in English:

I bought many presents for my family.
I bought my family many presents.
She cooked a delicious dinner for us.
She cooked us a delicious dinner. [etc.] (after Fotos and Ellis 1991)

Students work in small groups so that they simultaneously use the target language communicatively as they induce the grammatical rule.

Others have not abandoned productive practice in learning grammar. Indeed, Gatbonton and Segalowitz (1988) argue that practice can lead to automatisation of certain aspects of performance, which in turn frees up students' attentional resources to be allocated elsewhere. Larsen-Freeman (1991b; 2001) has coined the term 'grammaring' in proposing that the ability to use grammatical structures accurately is a skill requiring productive practice (Anderson 1982). Note that, following the need to focus on form within CLT, such practice is meaningful, not decontextualised and mechanical.

Moreover, since it is important that students not only learn to produce grammatical structures accurately but also learn to use them meaningfully and appropriately, Larsen-Freeman (1997a) asserts that grammar is best conceived as encompassing three dimensions: form, meaning and use. For instance, it is not sufficient for students to practise the singular and plural forms of demonstrative adjectives and pronouns (*this*, *that*, *these*, *those*), or to distinguish the distal and proximal meaning difference among them. It is also necessary for students to learn when to use them (e.g. *this*/*that* versus the personal pronoun *it* in discourse) and when not to use them (e.g. in answer to a question such as *What's this?*). While productive practice may be useful for working on form, associative learning may account more for meaning, and awareness of and sensitivity to context may be required for appropriate use. Since grammar is complex, and students' learning styles vary, learning grammar is not likely to be accomplished through a single means (Larsen-Freeman 1992).

While most teachers value using feedback to help students bring their interlanguage into alignment with the target language, questions of how much and what sort of feedback to give students on their grammatical production are unresolved. Various proposals are, e.g., for teachers to:

- lead students 'down the garden path', i.e. deliberately encourage learners to make over-generalisation errors which are then corrected (Tomasello and Herron 1988);

- provide explicit linguistic rules when errors are made (Carroll and Swain 1993);

- provide negative feedback by recasting (reformulating correctly a learner's incorrect utterance) or leading students to self-repair by elicitation (e.g. 'How do we say that in English?'), clarification (e.g. 'I don't understand'), metalinguistic clues (e.g. 'No, we don't say it that way') or repetition (e.g. 'A books?') (Lyster and Ranta 1997).

Clearly choices among these and other techniques depend upon the nature of the current activity, the teacher, the students, the trust that has been established and the social dynamics of the classroom.

Current and future trends and directions

Corpus-based research is likely to lead to developments in this field since more data will be available for theory-building. Another important development is research on grammars for spoken as well as written language, stimulating the search for more dynamic models of grammar than currently exist (Halliday 1994; Larsen-Freeman 1997b). Connectionism is likely to be influential in this regard (Elman *et al*. 1996; N. Ellis 1998). Another area of interest is the formal study of teachers' conceptions of grammar, and how these concepts inform their practice (see Eisenstein Ebsworth and Schweers 1997; Borg 1998; Johnston and Goettsch 1999). Borg (1999) researches teachers' use of metalanguage to teach grammar, the effectiveness of which, as Sharwood Smith (1993) has noted, is still an open question.

Conclusion

There is little disagreement that L2 learners need to learn to communicate grammatically. How to characterise the grammar and help L2 learners acquire it is more controversial. It is doubtful that a single method of dealing with grammar in class would work equally well for all learners. It should be noted that, as a consequence of the renewed attention grammar has recently received, the complexity of the challenge faced by teachers and researchers is more fully appreciated.

Key readings

Bygate *et al.* (1994) *Grammar and the Language Teacher*
Celce-Murcia and Larsen-Freeman (1999) *An ESL/EFL Teacher's Course* (teachers' grammar)
Davis and Rinvolucri (1995) *More Grammar Games* (teaching suggestions)
Doughty and Williams (1998a) *Focus on Form in Classroom Second Language Acquisition*
Larsen-Freeman (2001) *Teaching Language: From Grammar to Grammaring*
Lock (1996) *Functional English Grammar* (teachers' grammar)
Odlin (1994) *Perspectives on Pedagogical Grammar*
Rutherford (1987) *Second Language Grammar: Learning and Teaching*
Rutherford and Sharwood Smith (1988) *Grammar and Second Language Teaching*
Ur (1988) *Grammar Practice Activities* (teaching suggestions)

CHAPTER 6

Vocabulary

Ronald Carter

Introduction

Vocabulary and its related research paradigms have many inflections in relation to English language teaching. There is a long tradition of research into vocabulary acquisition in a second and foreign language. These include: classroom-based studies exploring different methodologies for vocabulary teaching; a long history of lexicographic research with reference to English dictionaries for language learners, research which has recently accelerated under the impetus of corpus-based, computer-driven lexical analysis; and new computer-driven descriptions of vocabulary which re-evaluate the place of words as individual units in relation to both grammar and the larger patterns of text organisation.

The main focus in the background section of this chapter is ELT lexicography which provides a relevant basis for several new developments in theory and practice. The focus in the 'research' section is on vocabulary acquisition and description, although this should not imply that there has been no lexicographic research. In the 'practice' section we turn to pedagogic treatments of vocabulary.

Background

VOCABULARY ACQUISITION

Central to research into vocabulary learning are key questions concerning *how* words are learned. Teachers help learners with vocabulary directly or 'explicitly' by means of word lists, paired translation equivalents and in variously related semantic sets. They also help learners by more indirect or 'implicit' means, such as exposure to words in the context of reading real texts. Over many years a key question asked by teachers and researchers is 'What does it mean to learn a word?' A definition of learning a word depends crucially on what we mean by a word, but it also depends crucially on how a word is remembered, over what period of time and in what circumstances it can be recalled and whether learning a word also means that it is always retained.

Much work has therefore involved issues of memorisation, and important questions have been raised concerning whether the storage of second language (L2) words involves different kinds of processing from the storage of first language (L1) words (Aitchison 1994; Singleton 1999). Craik and Lockhart (1972) have been particularly influential in showing how processing of words at different levels is crucial to learning. By different 'levels' is meant an integration in the learning process of sound levels, visual shape and form, grammatical structure and semantic patterns so that processing occurs in 'depth' and not just superficially as may be the case, for example, if a word is learned only in relation to its translation equivalent.

There is now a general measure of agreement that 'knowing' a word involves knowing: its spoken and written contexts of use; its patterns with words of related meaning as well as with its collocational partners; its syntactic, pragmatic and discoursal patterns. It means knowing it actively and productively as well as receptively. Such understandings have clear implications for vocabulary teaching.

LEXICOGRAPHY AND LEXICAL CORPORA

There is a long tradition of ELT lexicography, especially the development of word lists for language teachers and learners, dating from Harold Palmer and Michael West's work in the 1930s and culminating in West's *General Service List* (1953). The most significant developments in lexicography in the past two decades have involved more extensive corpora of spoken and written language and the creation of sophisticated computer-based access tools for such corpora. Innovations have been stimulated by the Collins Birmingham University International Language Database (COBUILD) project at the University of Birmingham, UK. The influence of this work is reflected in the fact that by the late 1990s all major English language learner dictionary projects incorporate reference to extensive language corpora and develop computational techniques for extracting lexicographically significant information from language corpora. COBUILD publications (e.g. CCELD 1987; CCED 1995) rely on the use of authentic, naturally-occurring examples in support of English language teaching and learning (see Sinclair 1991).

Other influential contributions to EFL lexicography have continued with the *Cambridge International Dictionary of English* (CIDE 1995), the *Longman Dictionary of Contemporary English* (LDOCE; 3rd edn 1995) and the *Oxford Advanced Learners Dictionary* (OALD; 5th edn 1995). Although influenced by COBUILD, computational methodology and in particular by the now established pre-requisite of a corpus of linguistic evidence, innovations and developments in these dictionaries evolve according to different presentational principles. The *Longman Language Activator* (LLA 1994) is an innovative, corpus-informed dictionary organised to help learners to *produce* the right word.

In terms of corpora, both LDOCE (1995) and OALD (1995) have benefited from the British National Corpus (BNC), a corpus of 100 million words of written and 10 million words of spoken English; both publishers (Longman and Oxford University Press) were among the development partners. Additionally, Longman has further extensive corpora:

- the Longman Lancaster Corpus (LLC), comprising 30 million words of written English;

- one of American English, which informs all dictionaries including the *Longman Dictionary of American English* (LDAE 1997); and

- a 10-million-word learner corpus which includes written texts from students at all levels from over 70 different language backgrounds, designed to provide evidence of the kinds of lexical mistakes learners most frequently make as well as guidance concerning the kinds of words most likely to be understood by learners of English in dictionary definitions and explanations.

Evidence from spoken corpora, in particular, has also informed LDOCE (1995) in that the top 3000 most frequent words in writing and in speech are marked out for special attention. LDOCE and related materials are corpus based but not corpus bound; i.e. examples are given in an order most likely to help learners rather than solely by frequency. Authentic citations from the corpus are judged not to be always helpful to the learner, and in LDOCE an important principle is that pedagogic mediation should precede the reality of the example (see Owen 1996).

CIDE (1995) and OALD (1995) similarly contain numerous innovations. CIDE draws on the

100-million-word Cambridge International Corpus (formerly the Cambridge Language Survey). It emphasises different national variations in English use, contains practical features such as lists of false friends in English in comparison with 14 other international languages, and contains guide words which, in the case of polysemous words, orient the reader to the main or core meaning of the words listed in a single entry. OALD represents a marked extension of a number of key features and some innovations in other areas, with the 1995 edition offering a treatment of 2800 new words and meanings when compared with earlier editions. Additional features include: 90,000 corpus-based examples (drawn from the BNC and the 40-million-word Oxford American English Corpus); notes and illustrated pages on cultural differences between British and American English; extensive usage notes covering areas of awkward grammar and meaning; and an expanded defining vocabulary (now 3500 words). Bogaards (1996), Herbst (1996) and Scholfield (1997) offer further analysis of recent EFL dictionaries.

Research

VOCABULARY ACQUISITION

We have not been taught the majority of words which we know. Beyond a certain level of proficiency in learning a language – and a second or foreign language in particular – vocabulary development is more likely to be mainly implicit or incidental. In vocabulary acquisition studies one key research direction is, therefore, to explore the points at which explicit vocabulary learning is more efficient than implicit vocabulary learning, to ask what are the most effective strategies of implicit learning, and to consider the implications of research results for classroom vocabulary teaching.

In the late 1980s and 1990s research in these areas developed rapidly. Researchers continue to question what exactly is meant by terms such as 'efficient' and 'effective' in short-term and long-term vocabulary learning. Also, recognition of the importance of implicit vocabulary learning does not preclude continuing exploration of how explicit vocabulary learning can be enhanced. N. Ellis (1995b) identifies four main points on an explicit–implicit vocabulary-learning continuum:

1. A strong implicit-learning hypothesis holds that words are acquired largely by unconscious means.

2. A weak implicit-learning hypothesis holds that words cannot be learned without at least some noticing or consciousness that it is a new word which is being learned.

3. A weak explicit-learning hypothesis holds that learners are active processors of information and that a range of strategies are used to infer the meaning of a word, usually with reference to its context.

4. A strong explicit-learning hypothesis holds that a range of metacognitive strategies such as planning and monitoring are necessary for vocabulary learning; in particular, the greater the depth of processing involved in the learning, the more secure and long term the learning is likely to be.

Hypothesis 1 has been most strongly advanced by Krashen (1988, 1989). Hypothesis 2 draws on observations found in several sources, reporting language-awareness and consciousness-raising research (e.g. Schmidt 1990). Hypothesis 3 draws, in particular, on Sternberg (1987), who reports that most vocabulary is learned from context by inference strategies, and on Hulstijn (1992) who also reports research in which learners retain better words learned in context than in marginal glosses or explanations on the page. Hypothesis 4 draws most strongly on Craik and Lockhart's (1972) work on levels of processing and 'cognitive depth' (see above).

Of these hypotheses Hypothesis 4 has been most actively pursued recently, with conclusions reached in a number of studies (see, in particular, articles in N. Ellis 1994; Coady and Huckin

1997). Craik and Lockhart's conclusion – that the more processes involved in the learning of a word the superior the retention and recall – has been particularly influential; e.g. their experiments asked learners of a word to consider its formal shape, its rhyming words, its synonyms, the semantic field in which it belongs, and the kinds of sentence patterns into which it fits.

Related and subsequent research (e.g. Crow and Quigley 1985; Brown and Perry 1991) involving keyword techniques, mediation between L1 and L2, semantic fields, and inference from context has further underlined what N. Ellis (1995b: 16) effectively summarises:

> Metacognitively sophisticated language learners excel because they have cognitive strategies for inferring the meanings of words, for enmeshing them in the meaning networks of other words and concepts and imagery representations, and mapping the surface forms to these rich meaning representations. To the extent that vocabulary acquisition is about meaning, it is an explicit learning process.

The importance of developing metacognitive strategies should not, however, suggest to teachers and learners that explicit vocabulary learning is to be discouraged. Given the complexities of word knowledge and the range of factors involved in knowing a word, most researchers accept that different types of word knowledge are learned in different ways, i.e. that different strategies entail different purposes for vocabulary use and different kinds of storage of the word in the mind (for discussion on explicit versus incidental learning, see Coady and Huckin 1997). For example, Stanovich and Cunningham (1992) assert that people who read more know more words, not least because reading affords the time to work out meanings from context in ways which are less likely to occur in speech. Note, however, that their findings have not been unequivocally accepted or agreed with. On this and related issues, see Huckin *et al.* (1993).

At advanced levels reading by means of inferential strategies may therefore be central to vocabulary development. At beginning levels, strategies of rote memorisation, bilingual translation and glossing can be valuable in learning, e.g., phonetic and graphological shapes and patterns of words. In learning the surface forms of basic concrete words, explicit learning may be the best route. However, for semantic, discoursal and structural properties of less frequent, more abstract words, implicit learning may be better. Recent vocabulary acquisition research suggests strongly that the explicit–implicit vocabulary-learning continuum is a good basis for research (see Meara 1996, 1997; Coady and Huckin 1997; Schmitt and McCarthy 1997). For general reading on this topic, see Carter and McCarthy 1988; McCarthy 1990; Nation 1990, 2001; Schmitt and McCarthy 1997; Carter 1998.

LANGUAGE DESCRIPTION

Even though words enter into strings which show basic grammatical relations between them, some partnerships between words are primarily semantic or occur because they simply belong together. There has been an unchallenged acceptance of the individual, independent word as a primary repository of meaning. Sinclair has identified a key theoretical issue:

> Words enter into meaningful relations with other words around them, and yet all our current descriptions marginalise this massive contribution to meaning. The main reason for this marginalisation is that grammars are always given priority and grammars barricade them-selves against individual patterns of words.   (Sinclair 1996: 76–77)

Studies of such patterns have lacked a sufficiently systematic description both of the patterns and of the meanings created by the choice of one pattern rather than another. In recent years computational analyses of language corpora have begun to point to new methods and techniques of description. Corpus data can identify the co-occurrence of particular words with particular grammatical patterns; e.g. Francis (1993) points out that two verbs, *find* and *make*, occur in 98 per cent of cases in the extraposed structure with *it* in clauses such as:

> I find *it* amusing that he never replies to my faxes.
> Can you make *it* more exciting?

Until recently, grammars have not made extensive reference to corpus data or had access to the kind of distributional analysis afforded by computer-assisted techniques, and they have consequently tended not to give such information. Conversely, dictionaries – which have tended to concentrate on the unit of the single word – have ignored the kinds of patterns resulting when a word forms different syntactic partnerships. For example Sinclair (1991: 67ff) notes – with reference to the COBUILD corpus – that the verb *set* occurs much more commonly in the form *set* than in other morphologies such as *sets* or *setting*, and that in phrasal verb form *set in* has a negative 'semantic prosody' (i.e. the meaning created by the phrasal verb is almost exclusively negative) and that the accompanying noun is frequently an abstract noun:

> Disillusionment with the government's policies has *set in*.
> Now the rot's *set in*.
> A state of moral decay *set in* without anyone really noticing it.

Hunston *et al.* (1997: 209) comment on this kind of lexico-grammatical insight: 'There are two main points about patterns to be made: firstly, that all words can be described in terms of patterns; secondly, that words which share patterns, share meanings.' However, reservations have been expressed about overreliance on corpus data. Widdowson (1998) points out that much depends on the representativeness of the corpus, and that frequency of occurrence of words and word patterns in a corpus does not guarantee the utility of such items for the learner.

Practice

The rapid growth of computerised corpora of English in the late twentieth century, especially in the 1990s, has provided language teachers and syllabus designers with hitherto unavailable information about word frequency and patterns, and about how words are deployed in a diverse range of spoken and written contexts. These tendencies have led to an increased specification of the type of lexis on which teachers and learners should focus.

Sinclair and Renouf (1988) and D. Willis (1990) argue for what they call a 'lexical syllabus', a syllabus which should take pedagogic precedence over grammar or communicative notions and functions. The lexical syllabus ensures that essential grammatical and other structures and functions will be learned automatically by choosing the most frequent words and word combinations for teaching. Core grammatical words such as *the*, *of*, *I*, *that*, *was*, *a* and *and* make up nearly 20 per cent of a typical English text and in a frequency-based lexical syllabus the main grammatical forms should automatically occur in the correct proportions:

> Almost paradoxically, the lexical syllabus does not encourage the piecemeal acquisition of a large vocabulary, especially initially. Instead it concentrates on making full use of the words the learner already has, at any particular stage. It teaches that there is far more general utility in the recombination of known elements than in the addition of less easily usable items.
>
> (Sinclair and Renouf 1988: 142–143)

Lewis (1993) concentrates for a teaching foundation on what he terms 'lexical chunks'. Lewis stresses the importance of learning chunks of language made up of lexico-grammatical patterns (a large number of which are pre-patterned and may therefore be used in a formulaic rehearsed way) while increasing learning of key structures. This can reduce communicative stress on the part of the user. Developing work by Nattinger and DeCarrico (1992), Lewis argues *inter alia* for the following main characteristics of a 'lexical approach':

1. More time should be spent teaching base verbs than tense formations.

2. Content nouns should be taught in chunks which include frequent adjectival and verbal collocations.

3. Sentence heads such as *Do you mind if . . .* and *Would you like to . . .* should be focused on.

4. Suprasentential linking should be explicitly taught.

5. Prepositions, modal verbs and delexical verbs (such as *take a swim*, *have a rest*) should be treated as if they were lexical items.

6. Metaphors and metaphor sets should be taught on account of their centrality to a language.

Lewis stresses the importance of word and lexico-grammatical frequency but places greater emphasis on usefulness to the learner so that frequency does not become an overriding criterion. In *Implementing the Lexical Approach* (1997) Lewis goes several steps further in elucidating the approach, offering a range of classroom-based studies and a variety of suggested teaching procedures.

Nattinger and DeCarrico (1992) take a particular descriptive interest in institutionalised expressions which may be regularly used to perform social or 'pragmatic' functions and thus provide an easily retrievable frame for written or spoken communication. They point, e.g., to the significance of macro- and micro-organisers in the interactional management of language, underlining how these 'lexical phrases' can be learned and then used and re-used. The increased effort involved in producing new words can be to some extent mitigated by the reduced processing effort of recycled lexical phrases.

Current and future trends and directions

Language description will continue to involve computational processing of millions of words, providing hitherto unseen pictures of languages. In particular, more information will be available concerning patterns of fixed expressions, leading to more dictionaries which assist learners with the collocational and idiomatic character of English. Increasing numbers of corpora of spoken Englishes will allow comparisons between spoken and written forms and be of use to learners in the development of formal and informal lexico-grammatical usage. Indeed, dictionaries will probably include ever more grammatical information, just as grammars will include ever more lexical information. In parallel with these developments vocabulary acquisition research is likely to include greater reference to issues of learning word units as well as individual words, i.e. describing and accounting for the incremental stages of words, word families, lexicogrammatical phrases and word networking which learners pass through as they gain greater L2 lexical competence.

Conclusion

Vocabulary teaching and learning is central to the theory and practice of ELT. Words have a central place in culture, and learning words is seen by many as the main task (and obstacle) in learning another language. Interest in vocabulary – from researchers, teachers and teacher-researchers – is likely to continue to grow apace.

Key readings

Carter and McCarthy (1988) *Vocabulary and Language Teaching*
Carter (1998) *Vocabulary: Applied Linguistic Perspectives*
Coady and Huckin (1997) *Second Language Vocabulary Acquisition*
Lewis (1993) *The Lexical Approach*
McCarthy (1990) *Vocabulary*
Nattinger and DeCarrico (1992) *Lexical Phrases and Language Teaching*
Nation (1990) *Teaching and Learning Vocabulary*
Nation (2001) *Learning Vocabulary in Another Language*
Schmitt and McCarthy (1997) *Vocabulary: Description, Acquisition and Pedagogy*
Sinclair (1991) *Corpus, Concordance, Collocation*
Singleton (1999) *Exploring the Second Language Mental Lexicon*
D. Willis (1990) *The Lexical Syllabus*

CHAPTER 7

Discourse

Michael McCarthy

Introduction

The study of **discourse** is the study of language independently of the notion of the sentence. This usually involves studying longer (spoken and written) texts but, above all, it involves examining the relationship between a text and the situation in which it occurs. So, even a short notice saying *No Bicycles* can be studied as discourse. A discourse analyst would be interested in the following questions about the notice:

- Who wrote the notice and to whom is it addressed (e.g. a person in authority, addressing it to a general public? This might explain what appears to be a rather abrupt, ellipted imperative: 'Don't ride/park your bicycle here!').

- How do we know what it means? In fact, in the situation it was taken from (the window of a bicycle-hire shop), it meant 'We have no more bicycles left to hire out'. The notice was displayed at the high season for bicycle hire, and the most plausible interpretation was that the shop was informing potential customers that it had run out of bicycles. So the grammar was not an imperative, but a statement. What factors enable us to interpret this? They are clearly not 'in' the text, but are an interpretation based on the text in its context.

Grammatical (syntactic) analysis of sentences has no such constraints on it. Sentences can be studied in isolation, as blocks of language, illustrating well- or ill-formed grammar. Sentence-grammarians consider questions about the circumstances of production and reception in contexts as something of a distraction. For them, all that is necessary to know about *No Bicycles* is that it is a noun phrase, one which is licensed to act as a subject (*No bicycles could be seen*) or as an object/complement (*They sold no bicycles*); what is missing from the usual sentence structure are abstract elements such as a verb phrase and (if *no bicycles* is the complement) a noun phrase to act as subject. Who or what the subject is can be specified by the kinds of subject permitted by the chosen verb (e.g. *clouds* are inanimate, therefore cannot sell bicycles; *manufacturers* are animate and human, therefore can sell things, etc.). This is what grammarians mean by well-formedness.

Discourse analysts are also interested in things being 'well formed', but by quite different criteria. For a discourse analyst, the questions of who uttered the words *No bicycles*, where, when and for whom, and with what goal, are all relevant to an interpretation as to whether the act of utterance is well formed. For this reason, discourse analysts work with **utterances** (i.e. sequences of words written or spoken in specific contexts) rather than with **sentences** (sequences of words conforming, or not, to the rules of grammar for the construction of phrases, clauses, etc.).

Background

Discourse analysts study both spoken and written texts (although sometimes a rather artificial distinction is made between those who analyse speech ('discourse analysts' proper) and those who work with written texts ('text analysts'). Generally, different models have grown up for analysing spoken and written language. It is widely agreed that there is no simple, single difference between speech and writing (Chafe 1982). The most useful way to conceive of the differences is to see them as scales along which individual texts can be plotted. For example, casual conversations tend to be highly involved interpersonally (detachment or distancing oneself by one speaker or another is often seen as socially problematic); public notices, on the other hand, tend to be detached (e.g. stating regulations or giving warnings). But note we have to say *tend*; we cannot speak in absolutes, only about what is most typical. Speech is most typically created 'on line' or spontaneously and received in real time. Writing is most typically created 'off line' (i.e. composed at one time and read at another), usually with time for reflection and revision (an exception would be real-time emailing by two computers simultaneously on line to each other, one of the reasons why email is often felt to be more like talk than writing).

The terms **text** and **discourse** are often used interchangeably to refer to language 'beyond the sentence', i.e. the study of any utterance or set of utterances as part of a context. But equally a distinction is sometimes made between texts as products of language use (e.g. a public notice saying *Cycling forbidden*, or a novel, or an academic article, or a transcript of a conversation), and discourse as the process of meaning-creation and interaction, whether in writing or in speech. A further complication is that the terms **text linguistics** and **discourse analysis** have, respectively, become strongly associated with the study of either written texts or spoken recordings or transcripts. Both approaches have made significant contributions to applied linguistics and language teaching, and both go beyond the notion of language as an abstract system to examine language in social contexts, i.e. they focus on the producers and receivers of language as much as on the language forms themselves.

Research

Discourse analysis as a general approach to language and as an influential force first emerged in the early 1970s, and since then has been predominantly associated with studies of the spoken language. In the 1960s, considerable interest built in the sociologically oriented study of language, with Hymes' work (1964) – springing from ethnography and anthropology as much as from linguistics – providing a grounding for a socially oriented model of spoken language. Also, in the 1950s, Mitchell had published a seminal article on the relationship between speech and the situation of utterance, including factors such as participant relationships and roles, and the physical settings in which talk occurred (Mitchell 1957). Discourse analysis emerged in this climate of growing interest in the process of meaning creation in real situations, where texts alone were insufficient evidence for the linguist, and settings, participants and goals of interaction came to the fore. It is this broader emphasis on settings and other non-linguistic features of interaction that sets spoken discourse analysts apart from text linguists, although in recent years, with the emergence of genre analysis (see Swales 1990a; see also Chapter 27 of this volume) and critical discourse analysis (see Current and future trends and directions below), distinctions between (predominantly written) text analysis and (predominantly spoken) discourse analysis have blurred somewhat.

An important and influential study of spoken discourse was carried out by Sinclair and Coulthard (1975), who tape-recorded mother-tongue school classrooms and found repeated patterns of interaction between teachers and pupils. Teacher and pupil behaviour were both constituted and reinforced by many factors, including:

- the setting: typically large, teacher-fronted classes;
- the institutional roles: teacher as knower and source of input, as evaluator of pupil response and as controller of topics; pupils as receptors and respondents, communicating with the teacher, not their peers;
- the goals: transmission of knowledge through question and answer sessions or through controlled discussion; display of key knowledge and testing of its reception.

These contextual features were reflected in structural features (i.e. regular configurations recurred in predictable contexts and sequences, while other, possible sequences, did not). For example, the sequence *teacher–question → pupil–answer → teacher–feedback* was normal, while other possible sequences were proscribed (e.g. an evaluating utterance by a pupil aimed at a teacher's utterance). A typical sequence might be:

Initiation (I)	Teacher:	What does 'slippery' mean?
Response (R)	Pupil:	That you can fall, because the floor is polished.
Follow-up (F)	Teacher:	Yes, you can fall, you can slip, good.

Sinclair and Coulthard's work struck direct chords with those active in language teaching in the late 1970s and early 1980s, and their work played an important role in underwriting the communicative revolution at this time. Their model for teacher–pupil interaction, as stated above, was a structural one built upon a hierarchy with smaller units of interaction such as **moves** (e.g. a teacher question or a pupil answer) combining to form **exchanges**, typically completed sets of question (initiation), answer (response) and follow-up moves, i.e. a structure of IRF, by which name the model is often referred to. This in turn combined to form larger units within the lesson, called **transactions**, to reflect their goal of transmitting key chunks of knowledge to the pupils.

Soon, the Sinclair–Coulthard model was extended outside the classroom (e.g. Hoey 1991), and since its early days it has enjoyed continuous attention by those interested in analysing L2 classrooms. Studies in classrooms have further extended the model, including an attempt to interpret teacher–pupil interaction patterns within a Vygotskian perspective of supportive learning (Jarvis and Robinson 1997), applicability of the model to student interaction in group work (Hancock 1997) and the use of the model to analyse student–computer interaction in computer-assisted language learning (CALL) sessions (Chapelle 1990). In direct applications in language teaching materials, one can often see the Sinclair–Coulthard basic notion of the exchange (with IRF reflected in very practical illustrations for learners) of real day-to-day conversational contexts in which such exchanges might occur.

However, shortly after publication of Sinclair and Coulthard's influential model, Politzer (1980) suggests that its 'objectivity' (in the sense of sequential, structural analysis) was inadequate to the task of properly describing classroom interaction, and that a more sociolinguistics-inspired approach was required. In its institutionalised and rather ritualised context of the classroom, the talk that Sinclair and Coulthard examined appeared to progress steadily and smoothly. Casual and spontaneous talk between equals, on the other hand, does not seem to occur in the same way. Ostensibly it appears to be a precarious, haphazard exercise, with interruptions, diversions, competition for the floor or control of topics, indeterminate in its duration, unpredictable in its outcomes. Talk, therefore, is an achievement rather than a pre-ordained text simply played out like a drama on stage; it is the sense of work towards an achievement that conversation analysts try to capture.

Conversation analysis (CA) is mainly (but certainly not exclusively) associated with socio-linguists and sociologists of language. For good illustrations of the approach, see Schegloff and Sacks (1973) on how participants close down conversations; Sacks *et al.* (1974) on turn-taking in talk; Pomerantz (1984) on how participants agree and disagree. See also the many studies of oral narratives (Labov 1972a; Jefferson 1978; Polanyi 1981) and more general works and collections

```
<Liz>    I've been dreaming about it all night
<Jim>    Well ↑I had a dream about it as well
<Liz>         ⌊So-
<Liz>    I've got to get i- because it's on my mind so much I-
<Jim>    ⌊It's funny              ⌊a really guilty conscience about it=
<Liz>    =Yes, I am, so I must . . . get on and do it. So yes, Thursday at eleven →
<Jim>                                         ⌊Heheheh
<Liz>    will be fine
<Jim>    Ok, we'll just review where we are: an'. what's . . . urgent and what's um . . .→
<Liz>                                         ⌊yeah  ⌊↑um
<Jim>    perhaps not↓ so urgent to do
<Liz>                        ⌊Ok. ↑Rose Downey↓ has just phoned
<Jim>    Yeah
```

Figure 7.1 An extract of conversation recorded and transcribed by Almut Koester (© Almut Koester 1999)

(Atkinson and Heritage 1984; Boden and Zimmerman 1991; Pomerantz and Fehr 1997) within sociolinguistic and CA perspectives. Conversation analysts study **local events** in detail, e.g.:

- how pairs of adjacent utterances constrain each other (adjacency pairs such as *Congratulations → Thanks*);

- how speakers use discourse markers (such as *well* and *you know*) to signal interactive features (Schiffrin 1987);

- how they sum up the gist of the conversation at regular intervals using 'formulations' (Heritage and Watson 1979), etc.

Transcription is very narrow, indicating as many aspects as possible of the way talk occurs, including speaker-overlaps, re-cast words, changes in loudness, drawled syllables, laughter, non-verbal vocalisations, etc. An example of an extract of conversation recorded and transcribed by Almut Koester (a researcher working within the CA tradition at the University of Nottingham) illustrates the level of detail CA analysts attend to.

Overlaps are marked (overlapping turns begin with ⌊ at the point where the overlap occurs), steps up and down in intonation are indicated by vertical arrows (↑, ↓), 'latching' (i.e. no perceptible pause between turns at speaking) is shown by 'equals' signs; also, laughter and false-starts are indicated, because they may be relevant to the analysis. This is quite different from the structure-oriented IRF transcriptions of the Sinclair–Coulthard model. What is central here is not the global, but the local, i.e. what speakers do step by step to build relationships and achieve goals.

In the study of written discourse, a long tradition of text linguistics has persisted in Northern Europe, beginning with attempts to account for how sentences are linked together using linguistic resources. Werlich's (1976) description of how linguistic features characterise different text types (narrative, descriptive, expository and argumentative) was enormously influential among German teachers of English in the 1980s, and is a classic 'text grammar'. Likewise, the Prague school and its followers, among whom was Halliday, focused on how the construction of individual sentences in terms of their theme (their starting point or topic) and rheme (what was being said about that topic) contributed to the larger patterns of information in extended texts (Daneš 1974; Fries 1983; Eiler 1986). Thus, in the sentence *Werlich was enormously influential among German EFL teachers*, the theme (or starting point – usually the grammatical subject) is *Werlich*, and the rheme is what is said about him (that he was influential). Among the interests of the Prague school linguists are the different ways in which themes can be repeated and create patterns over a number of sentences, and the ways in which the rheme of one sentence can become the theme of the next.

The school of text linguistics associated with Northern European scholars such as van Dijk (1972) and de Beaugrande and Dressler (1981) addresses questions concerning cognitive processing of extended written texts. This has influenced views of reading, along with schema theory (a theory accounting for how we relate new information to already existing information we possess about the world and about texts; see Rumelhart 1977). Applied linguists and language teachers have not been slow to see the relevance of such studies for more effective fostering of reading skills (Carrell 1983). Cognitive approaches to text analysis emphasise what readers bring to the text: the text is not a file full of meaning which the reader simply 'downloads'. How sentences relate to one another and how the units of meaning combine to create a coherent extended text is the result of interaction between the reader's world and the text, with the reader making plausible interpretations.

Similar approaches to text analysis may be found in the school of rhetorical structure analysis, where the emphasis is on how units of meaning (which are not necessarily sentences) relate to one another in a hierarchy, and how such devices as exemplification, summary, expansion, etc. build on core propositions to construct the finished text (Mann and Thompson 1988), an approach which in turn owes much to the text linguistics of Grimes (1975) and Longacre (1983). Applications in reading pedagogy and in the study of writing have been explored for these approaches (for an example of a study of student mother-tongue writing using rhetorical structure analysis, see O'Brien 1995). Also influential amongst British applied linguists and language teachers has been the practically orientated types of text analysis, originating in the work of Winter (1977, 1982), usually referred to as clause-relational analysis. Working with everyday written texts, followers of Winter such as Hoey (1983) have demonstrated how culturally common patterns such as the 'situation → problem → response → evaluation → solution' sequence in texts (often referred to as the problem–solution pattern) is constructed by the reader in interaction with the logical relations between clauses within the text and by processing lexical and grammatical signals of the pattern employed by the author.

In attempting to re-construct the mental processes readers go through, cognitive approaches to discourse are seen as offering practical pointers for classroom methods, such as pre-text activities in the reading class designed to activate **background knowledge** (or schemata), or student analyses of their own texts as a step in process approaches to writing skills (for an extended survey of such applications of text linguistic methods, see Connor 1987).

Also influential in shifting attention away from sentence-based study of language is the model of textual cohesion associated with Halliday and Hasan (Halliday and Hasan 1976; Hasan 1984, 1985). The study of cohesion is concerned with surface linguistic ties in the text, rather than cognitive processes of interpretation; thus, its categories are grammatical and lexical ones, and include:

- reference: e.g. how pronouns refer back and forth to people and things in different sentences;
- substitution and ellipsis: how reduced grammatical forms such as co-ordinated clauses without subject-repetition can be interpreted coherently;
- conjunction: how the finite set of conjunctions (*and*, *but*, *so*, etc.) create relations between sentences;
- lexical links across sentences: e.g. repetition, use of synonyms, collocations.

Hasan's work on cohesion, in particular, has an applied educational emphasis, using the framework of analysis to evaluate children's writing and reflect on the relationship between linguistic links across sentences and textual coherence.

Thus, the various schools of text linguistics have taken the study of language beyond the sentence and have brought readers and writers to the fore, laying emphasis on the text as an intermediary between sender and receiver, rather than as a detached object in which meaning is somehow 'stored'. Above all, these approaches see sentences as interacting, emphasising the need to study text rather than individual sentences in isolation.

Practice

The emergence of discourse analysis and CA has shown that social dimensions can be brought into language study and that the creation of meaning can be explained without reference to syntactic rules or sentences. In tandem, applied linguists have published books and articles exploring the possibilities of translating discourse analysis and CA into pedagogical guidelines, teaching materials and practical classroom tasks (e.g. Bygate 1987; Cook 1989; McCarthy 1991; Hatch 1992). Richards (1980: 431), in an early example of accommodating CA insights, stresses the importance of 'strategies of conversational interaction' in the development of conversational competence, referring to CA studies to reinforce his arguments. More specific areas of language teaching activity then came under scrutiny using CA for evaluation; e.g. van Lier (1989) evaluates the oral proficiency interview, drawing on CA insights to answer questions of whether or not conversation should serve as an appropriate model for oral assessment. More recently, some scholars have detected a major shift in approaches to communicative teaching, and a growing orientation towards the bottom-up content of communicative competence, with discourse analysis and CA playing a central role in the re-thinking of what teaching input should be (Celce-Murcia *et al.* 1997).

Discourse analysis has become prominent in language teaching in recent years because teachers feel the need to address certain preoccupations in their professional practice. These include:

- If teaching is to be 'communicative', how does communication actually take place? Knowledge of sentences may not be enough to cover the wide range of resources speakers and writers make use of in creating and receiving real messages.

- If teaching is to be 'skills-based', how does knowledge based on sentence-grammar square with skills such as holding conversations, reading texts for key information, being an active listener, adjusting one's writing for audience and purpose, etc.?

- If skills separate written and spoken aspects of language, how reliable are our conventional resources, which are mainly based on written evidence (e.g. grammar books, dictionaries, usage manuals, etc.)?

- How much of what counts as 'discourse' will be automatically transferred from the first language, and how much needs specifically to be taught or focused on in the syllabus, materials or classroom activities?

As noted above, one of the contributions of discourse analysis is the separation of spoken and written texts for different kinds of scrutiny. The practical importance of examining both written language and spoken language is threefold:

- It has implications for 'skills' approaches to language teaching, in which the four primary skills (reading, speaking, writing and listening) are constructed around a written–spoken dichotomy.

- The description of the target language, in terms of vocabulary and grammar, changes considerably depending on the source of one's data, whether written or spoken.

- The units of acquisition (such as clauses and sentences), the 'rules' underlying them (e.g. word-order and complementation patterns) and the metalanguage used to talk about them are also brought into question.

The intermingling of styles, in which writing borrows from features associated with speech (e.g. email discourse, 'user-friendly' information brochures, advertising copy, etc.), and in which the wider spread of literacy and job opportunity gives greater access to features associated with written styles (e.g. professional presentations, 'eloquent' speech, etc.) has led some to abandon a straight-down-the-middle view of speech versus writing as a model for pedagogy. McCarthy and Carter (1994: Chapter 1) prefer to talk of **modes** of communication (which might be more or less speakerly or writerly), as distinguished from the **medium** of communication (which is either spoken or written). This view suggests a greater integration of the traditional four skills in language teaching, where writing tasks might be 'spoken' in their mode and, vice versa, where spoken tasks may explore different levels of detachment, planning, integration, etc. These acts of integrating the separate skills have direct implications for language teaching methodology, suggesting a recategorisation of tasks detailed in syllabuses and timetables (see also Chapter 22).

Current and future trends and directions

The move away from the sentence as the unit of linguistic investigation by text, discourse and conversation analysts has had profound effects on the description and teaching of grammar. Some linguists have begun questioning the validity of many rules proposed by sentence grammarians and the very meanings of grammatical forms, so long taken for granted but now ripe for re-assessment. Items occurring in texts seem to have meanings in context which extend greatly the 'core semantic' meaning, or which even contradict or downplay such meanings; e.g. in a British service encounter (such as leaving clothes to be cleaned or films to be processed) a customer might be asked *What was the name?*, where any meaning of 'pastness' is largely irrelevant to an account of *was*, and the only sensible statement of 'meaning' is one which foregrounds institutional politeness and the indirectness of the past tense form. Discourse grammars address this type of concern by building descriptions which attempt to explain usage by incorporating language users, textual cohesion and coherence, and relevant features of context.

Beyond-the-sentence investigations of grammatical choices suggest that discourse grammars will do more than just add 'bolt-on' extras to existing sentence grammars, but may precipitate a complete re-assessment of how grammars are written, especially spoken ones. In the pedagogical domain, observations of real spoken data also underscore the need to re-evaluate many of the taken-for-granted rules presented in coursebooks and reference books (e.g. Kesner Bland 1988). Celce-Murcia (1991b) sees value in a discourse-based approach to grammar as stemming from a study of learners' communicative needs and the assembly of a corpus of material relevant to those needs; after these stages, and only then, should decisions be taken as to the most useful grammar to be taught. The teaching of the grammar therefore proceeds on the basis of the relevant discourse contexts and the texts that belong to them (Larsen-Freeman 1991b; see also Chapter 5 of this volume).

Recently there has also been considerable debate over the role of ideology in discourse analysis. A simplified characterisation might be the stance that, at one end of the spectrum, it is the business of linguists and applied linguists simply to describe language and the processes of learning and teaching languages; at the other end is the view that language is never neutral but is always bound up with particular ways of seeing the world, and that applied linguists and teachers are always engaged in a politically and ideologically embedded activity. There are also, of course, many positions in between.

Critical discourse analysis (CDA) – see Fairclough (1989, 1995); Kress (1990) – sees the task of the (applied) linguist as taking a critical stance towards language use, and as analysing texts so as to illuminate and highlight the ideology of their producers. CDA adherents are interested in exposing acts of linguistic manipulation, oppression and discrimination through language and the use of language in the unjust exercise of power. Critical text analyses might, for instance, reveal how language choices – such as transitive versus intransitive verb, or active versus passive voice, or particular choices of modal verbs or pronouns – enable writers to manipulate the realisations (or concealment) of agency and power in the representation of action (for a brief exemplification, see Fairclough 1997).

CDA is not without its critics, sternest among whom recently have been Widdowson (1995a, 1995b) and Stubbs (1997), both of whom have taken it to task for its lack of rigour, its sometimes cavalier attitude to form–functional relations and (particularly from Stubbs) its faith in the usefulness of very small amounts of data. Stubbs (1997), occupying a less opposed position than Widdowson, sees possibilities for CDA to speak with a more persuasive voice by adopting a more corpus-based approach, a comparative methodology (across texts and across cultures) and giving more attention to the reception of texts (readers, intended audiences, etc.), rather than to the agenda of the analyst.

Conclusion

This chapter focuses on language as discourse rather than language as sentences. It takes the line that speech and writing need to be considered in their separate manifestations, and that separating them raises important questions for issues of description. But what unites written and spoken language is that both media of communication can be studied in social contexts, and through real texts. This means, in terms of a theory of language, that the evidence is essentially external, existing in the social world, and not inside the linguist's head (or intuition). This last point has profound resonances in the practical ways in which applied linguists and language teachers conduct their own professional discourse and shape themselves as a professional community, as well as in our attitudes to syllabuses, assessment, input, performance, and all the other key features of the language teaching matrix. In some senses, seeing language as discourse lies at the heart of the whole enterprise.

Key readings

Coulthard (1985) *An Introduction to Discourse Analysis*
Cook (1989) *Discourse*
Hatch (1992) *Discourse and Language Education*
McCarthy (1991) *Discourse Analysis for Language Teachers*
McCarthy and Carter (1994) *Language as Discourse: Perspectives for Language Teaching*
Nunan (1993) *Introducing Discourse Analysis*
Richards (1980) *Conversation*
Sinclair and Coulthard (1975) *Towards an Analysis of Discourse*

CHAPTER 8

Pronunciation

Barbara Seidlhofer

Introduction

When talking about pronunciation in language learning we mean the production and perception of the significant sounds of a particular language in order to achieve meaning in contexts of language use. This comprises the production and perception of **segmental sounds**, of **stressed and unstressed syllables**, and of the 'speech melody', or **intonation**. Also, the way we sound is influenced greatly by factors such as voice quality, speech rate and overall loudness. Whenever we say something, all these aspects are present simultaneously from the very start, even in a two-syllable utterance such as *Hello!*

Pronunciation plays a central role in both our personal and our social lives: as individuals, we project our identity through the way we speak, and also indicate our membership of particular communities. At the same time, and sometimes also in conflict with this identity function, our pronunciation is responsible for intelligibility: whether or not we can convey our meaning. The significance of success in L2 (second language) pronunciation learning is therefore far-reaching, complicated by the fact that many aspects of pronunciation happen subconsciously and so are not readily accessible to conscious analysis and intervention.

All this may explain why teachers frequently regard pronunciation as overly difficult, technical or plain mysterious, while at the same time recognising its importance. The consequent feeling of unease can, however, be dispelled relatively easily once a basic understanding has been achieved.

Background

HISTORY AND DEVELOPMENT

Although sometimes referred to as the 'Cinderella' of foreign language teaching, pronunciation actually stood at the very beginning of language teaching methodology as a principled, theoretically-founded discipline, originating with the late-nineteenth-century Reform Movement. Closely connected with this movement was the founding of the **International Phonetic Association (IPA)** and the development of the International Phonetic Alphabet, which is still the universally agreed transcription system for the accurate representation of the sounds of any language. It is widely used in dictionaries and textbooks (see the IPA website at www.arts.gla.ac.uk/IPA/ipa.html). In the IPA's declaration of principles of L2 teaching, which can be seen as marking the beginning of the modern era, the spoken language is held to be primary, and training in **phonetics** is important for both teachers and learners (see Stern 1983: Chapters 5 and 6).

The legacy of the Reform Movement can be discerned in approaches that developed in the more recent past: between roughly the 1930s and 1960s pronunciation had high priority in both audiolingualism in the United States and the oral approach and situational language teaching in the United Kingdom, which introduced the spoken before the written language and aimed at the formation of 'good pronunciation habits' through drills and dialogues.

However, when in the 1960s both structuralist language description and behaviourist views of language learning came under heavy attack in mainstream language teaching, pronunciation lost its unquestioned role as a pivotal component in the curriculum, and class time spent on pronunciation was greatly reduced or even dispensed with altogether. On the other hand, this time saw a marked increase in the recognition of and demand for 'humanistic' approaches to language teaching; for two of these approaches pronunciation is very important: the Silent Way pays particular attention to the accurate production of sounds, stress and intonation from the very beginning, and Community Language Learning typically allows for a lot of pronunciation practice (compare Richards and Rodgers 1986). What seems of particular interest here is that these two alternative approaches share a principle that is increasingly being recognised in contemporary teaching: it is the belief that success is crucially dependent on learners developing a sense of responsibility for their own learning.

The advent of **communicative language teaching (CLT)** has created a dilemma for methodology. The view that 'intelligible pronunciation is an essential component of communicative competence' (Morley 1991) is generally accepted, and with it the necessity of teaching pronunciation on the segmental and suprasegmental levels. At the same time, the emphasis has shifted from drills and exercises to communicative activities based on meaningful interaction which, if successful, direct learners' attention *away* from language form and towards the messages they want to communicate. However, for language items to be learnt, they must be noticed and therefore highlighted, which, in turn, is difficult to do if the language used should be as communicatively 'authentic' as possible. This fundamental problem seems to underlie all decisions that communicative language teachers have to grapple with, and results in Celce-Murcia *et al.*'s (1996: 8) verdict that 'proponents of this approach have not dealt adequately with the role of pronunciation in language teaching, nor have they developed an agreed-upon set of strategies for teaching pronunciation communicatively'.

However, the absence of one particular methodological orthodoxy can also be seen as an opportunity for teachers to make choices which are most appropriate for the specific learners they are working with. And it is probably not just accidental that this diversification of methodological options has coincided with a diversification of learning goals: recent years have seen a reconceptualisation of the role of English in the world and thus of the purposes of learning it; this has been accompanied by a broadening of attitudes towards different native and non-native varieties, including accents. These developments have increased the complexity of pronunciation teaching enormously, and with it the demands made on teachers' awareness and knowledge in this area.

THE KNOWLEDGE BASE

As we have seen, phonetics provides the technical underpinning of pronunciation teaching, and this is what is traditionally given prominence in introductory books and teacher education courses. However, it is probably more helpful to start with considerations of the role of pronunciation in a broader perspective: the 'macro-conditions' which in combination eventually lead to specific 'micro-decisions' for particular classroom settings. We present this in Figure 8.1.

Starting with *pronunciation in individual and social life*, it is easy to see why the notion of 'correct pronunciation' is questionable as a learning target as soon as we realise how inextricably

BACKGROUND KNOWLEDGE:

PRONUNCIATION IN INDIVIDUAL AND SOCIAL LIFE	PRONUNCIATION IN LANGUAGE USE AND LANGUAGE SYSTEM	PRONUNCIATION IN PEDAGOGY
⇓	⇓	⇓

⇓ ⇓ ⇓

Practice:

Methodology

Figure 8.1   The role of pronunciation

bound up it is with social and individual identity. People's accents express their membership of particular communities, and with it conflicting tendencies such as power and solidarity, in-group and out-group, prestige and stigmatisation. The importance of such socio-economic factors becomes particularly apparent when we consider the phenomenon of 'non-reciprocal' intelligibility between social groups of different prestige (Wolff 1964, discussed in Dalton and Seidlhofer 1994: 10f.). This makes plain that intelligibility, rather than being a purely linguistic matter, is often overridden by cultural and economic factors.

In addition to social identity, pronunciation expresses individual identity and reflects ego-boundaries which can be extremely resistant to change. Daniels (1997) reminds us that the mother tongue, for most people, is 'the language of their first tender exchanges' and, hence,

> a sort of umbilical cord which ties us to our mother. Whenever we speak an L2 we cut that cord, perhaps unconsciously afraid of not being able to find it and tie it up again when we revert to first language (L1). A possible way of avoiding the cut is to continue using the sounds, the rhythms and the intonation of our mother tongue while pretending to speak L2.
>
> (Daniels 1997: 82)

Teachers need to be aware, then, that the process of 'modifying one of the basic modes of identification by the self and others, the way we sound' is located 'at the extreme limits of proficiency' (Guiora 1972: 144). This is why the uniquely sensitive nature of pronunciation teaching in comparison with that of other skills, such as mastering grammar and vocabulary, has come to be generally accepted.

Only when these fundamental issues are understood is it time to move on to the second area in Figure 8.1: *pronunciation in language use and language system*. This concerns the role that pronunciation plays in conveying our meaning in discourse, for practical transactions as well as personal interactions. Here, again, it might be best to move from larger to smaller units. To start with, spoken discourse usually takes place within a specific speech event, such as everyday conversations, service encounters, school lessons or job interviews. The participants involved in these have a topic and a purpose, that is to say, they basically wish to 'get their message across'. In order to do this, speakers package their messages into meaning units, or sense groups, which in turn serve listeners as signals of organisation that facilitate the processing of spoken discourse. These chunks are also called tone units, or intonation groups, because they are characterised by pitch change (the speaker's voice going up or down) on the syllables which are perceived as most important. Intonation is therefore an important vehicle for signalling prominence. Other functions of intonation include conveying social meanings and speaker involvement as well as the management of conversation in terms of turn-taking and signalling the informational value of tone units (Dalton and Seidlhofer 1994: Chapters 5 and 7).

A closely related aspect of **suprasegmental** organisation is stress and unstress, i.e. the stress patterns of words, with strong syllables standing out as more noticeable than weak ones; compare *perMIT* (verb) and *PERmit* (noun). Stressed syllables are pronounced with greater energy, which, in English, manifests itself mainly through extra vowel length. Being able to put the stress on the appropriate syllables is something which is essential for learners of any level or setting: it is crucial for intelligibility and also closely connected with the articulation of individual sound segments.

At the segmental level, it is crucial to understand which sounds in a language are the distinctive ones (i.e. which are **phonemes)**, because they express differences in meaning; compare the vowel sounds of 'feel' and 'fill'. In the Spanish sound system, for example, there is no opposition between /b/ and /v/, which makes it difficult for Spanish learners of English to perceive and to pronounce the difference between /b/ and /v/, as in 'berry' and 'very'. Informed teachers can thus help their students greatly by drawing on their knowledge of the sound systems of both L1 and L2. When certain sounds are experienced as particularly difficult by learners, it is also important for teachers to decide how much effort to put into teaching these sounds in comparison with others. Here it is worth knowing how much 'work' individual sounds, or sound contrasts, actually do in a particular language, that is, whether they have high or low functional load. For English, this is described by Catford (1987) and Brown (1991a).

In addition to oppositions among distinctive sounds, there are also different phonetic realisations of phonemes, called **allophones**, which are non-distinctive and often depend on the sound environment; in English, for example, aspirated and non-aspirated /p/, /t/ and /k/ are non-distinctive. To help their learners effectively, teachers need some knowledge of **articulatory phonetics**, an understanding of how the sounds of the target language are produced (see, e.g., Dalton and Seidlhofer 1994; Celce-Murcia *et al.* 1996).

Moving on to *pronunciation in pedagogy* (see Figure 8.1), and following on from the above, we can derive a few general principles which should be established before considering suggestions and materials for classroom practice. Precisely because of the complex nature of pronunciation, the primary consideration must always be the learners and what they may bring to the classroom in terms of their own identity and their purposes for language learning. Studies such as Yule and Macdonald (1994) suggest that the individual learner may be the most important variable in pronunciation teaching and its success or failure. The wide variety of learner factors emphasises the necessity for teachers to have at their disposal an equally wide range of theoretical knowledge and methodological options.

Celce-Murcia *et al.* (1996: Chapter 2) summarise the most important learner variables and offer suggestions for needs analysis by means of student profile questionnaires. The factors they highlight are age, exposure to the target language, amount and type of prior pronunciation instruction, aptitude, attitude and motivation, and the role of the learner's first language (L1). It should be noted that many of these are dependent on the learning purpose and setting in which instruction takes place. Although seldom explicitly addressed in coursebooks, a crucial factor for any specific pronunciation syllabus is whether it is designed for an EFL or ESL setting. Apart from the obvious influence that the surrounding linguistic environment has on teaching procedures, the complex question of **target norms** and '**intelligibility**' as an objective hinges upon the student's setting and learning purpose. Thus, ESL learners will strive to become comfortably intelligible for the native speakers around them, and ultimately may want to approximate to a native target norm in order to integrate with the native speaker community. In contrast, EFL learners may primarily be aiming for an ability to use English as a lingua franca for communication in international settings, often with a variety of other non-native speakers; in this case sounding like a native speaker may be far less irrelevant. It is therefore essential for teachers to be familiar with the increasingly lively discussion about the range of different models for L2 pronunciation learning, and the socio-economic and social and psychological factors which make intelligibility an inevitably relative notion (see Levis 1999; Jenkins 2000). A distinction must be made here between norms and models: regarding a particular native speaker variety as a norm which has to be imitated independently of any considerations of language use strongly connects it with ideas of correctness. Taken as a model, on the other hand, such a variety can be used as a point of reference, to which learners can approximate more or less closely, depending on the needs of the specific situation. The notion of models privileges the criterion of **appropriacy** over that of **correctness**.

There are therefore some major issues that need to be clear in teachers' minds prior to specific methodological decisions, of which the questions of learning purpose and setting are likely to be the most important ones. Other macro-considerations include insights from general learning theory which have particular significance for pronunciation teaching: that ample opportunity and time needs to be provided for exposure to and *perception* of foreign language sounds before learners are asked to produce them; and, closely connected with this, that *achievability*, i.e. success in little steps, is particularly important as a criterion for grading activities, precisely because many learners feel especially vulnerable and insecure in this area.

Another important consideration to bear in mind is the relationship and mutual dependency of pronunciation and other areas of language use and language learning, in particular listening, speaking, grammar and spelling. The focus on meaningful practice advocated by CLT has encouraged a view of pronunciation that recognises its embeddedness in discourse and so invites the use of materials and techniques that involve learners in contextualised and motivating activities which are suited to integrated pronunciation work. To mention a few examples, Bygate (1987), Anderson and Lynch (1988), Bailey and Savage (1994) and Nunan and Miller (1995) offer an overview of theoretical background and teaching techniques for the areas of listening and speaking respectively, and make it easy to see how these abilities are inextricably bound up with pronunciation. Rost (1990) discusses how listeners depend on stress and intonation as primary clues for processing incoming speech, and Wong (1987) and Gilbert (1994, 1995) make suggestions for the pedagogical exploitation of these interrelationships. Seidlhofer and Dalton-Puffer (1995) argue for linking the teaching of pronunciation with that of lexico-grammar, and Morley (1994) effectively integrates pronunciation with other skills in her 'multidimensional curriculum design for speech–pronunciation instruction' for English for academic purposes.

The explanatory potential of sound–spelling relationships is something teachers should be aware of, since correspondences between orthography and phonology enable students to predict the pronunciation of words from their spelling, and vice versa (see Dickerson 1991, 1994). Guidelines for sound–spelling correspondences can also be found in pronunciation dictionaries such as Wells (1990). Kenworthy (1987) includes a chapter on orthography and grammar, demonstrating how exploiting the morphological regularity of English spelling can facilitate pronunciation teaching. A case in point is the indication of parts of speech (such as verb–noun) by presence or absence of voicing (as in *advise – advice, believe – belief*), or the intelligible rendering of the past tense ending -*ed*, which, depending on the sound preceding it, is pronounced as /t/ (as in *laughed*), /d/ (as in *loved*) or /əd, ɪd/ (as in *needed, knitted*).

Research

LINGUISTIC DESCRIPTION

Considering that the study of sounds dates back to antiquity, it would be practically impossible to summarise the research base of this field in this chapter. Fortunately, there are a number of accessible introductory texts to help teachers with an understanding of **phonetics** and **phonology**, such as Clark and Yallop (1990), Ladefoged (1993) and Roach (2000). Recent introductions written specifically for teachers include Dalton and Seidlhofer (1994), Celce-Murcia *et al.* (1996) and Pennington (1996). For a detailed description of the accents with which English is spoken around the world, readers could consult Wells (1982, 3 volumes) or the more concise Trudgill and Hannah (1995).

Recent advances in linguistic description of particular relevance to pronunciation teaching mainly concern the larger-scale aspects of pronunciation: descriptions not of individual sound segments, but of the **suprasegmental** features of speech stretching over whole utterances (also called **prosody**). In particular, two time-honoured assumptions and pedagogical conveniences have become untenable in the light of empirical research findings, namely the close correspondence of certain intonation contours with attitudes and emotions (O'Connor and Arnold 1973) and the assumption of strict stress-timing in English. Regarding the first of these, Brazil's elegant theory of discourse intonation (1994, 1997), which was already the basis for an innovative book on language teaching in 1980 (Brazil *et al.* 1980) formulates more powerful generalisations about the use of tones in English than overly intricate, context-dependent descriptions and may thus prove more helpful for learning. As for English rhythm, the received wisdom has been that English is a stress-timed language, that is to say stressed syllables occur at regular intervals of time however many unstressed syllables intervene. In contrast, so-called syllable-timed languages allot an equal amount of time to each syllable. This appealingly neat categorisation became very popular in pronunciation teaching, but has been shown to be an over-simplification by careful empirical studies (Dauer 1983; Couper-Kuhlen 1993; Cauldwell 1996).

Another research strand that goes beyond the narrow segmental dimension is the study of so-called articulatory settings, that is to say long-term articulatory postures that make up the global properties of **accents**. English in this respect is characterised by greater laxity and less movement of the articulator than most other languages. Good descriptions of such aspects as the distribution of muscular tension and movements of the speech organs typical of the target language can be exploited to help learners recognise and abandon those 'entrenched' settings of their L1 that are found to interfere with intelligibility. Although not a new idea (see Laver 1980; Honikman 1991) the continuing interest in this area (Esling and Wong 1991; Esling 1994) fits well with the recognition that bottom-up and top-down approaches work best interactively: working on articulatory settings may enable learners to acquire new sounds more easily and to put them together and make smooth transitions and links, thus allowing suprasegmental and segmental aspects to work in unison.

An important development and lively research area is the co-operation between computer technology and phonetics for computer-assisted pronunciation teaching and for compiling and analysing spoken corpora so that pedagogical prescription can build on better linguistic description (e.g. Leech *et al.* 1995).

SECOND LANGUAGE ACQUISITION (SLA) AND PEDAGOGY

A great deal of pronunciation-related research which studies not the language but conditions of learning is carried out in the field of SLA (see Chapter 12) and interlanguage phonology in particular (e.g. collections such as Ioup and Weinberger 1987; Leather and James 1997). Allowing for considerable simplification, it would probably be fair to say that the upshot of the research carried out in this field is, again, that achievement in the area of pronunciation is highly context dependent, and that learning goals may have to be readjusted in many cases, in the sense that the objective of 'native' or 'near-native' pronunciation may have to yield to adequate intelligibility appropriate to context. Research findings pointing in this direction are, for example, the strong evidence for early language learning being an advantage especially in the domain of pronunciation, whether the reasons be physiological/neurological (Scovel 1988; Munro *et al.* 1996) or psycho-sociological (Guiora *et al.* 1972; Schumann 1975). What seems uncontroversial is that the flexibility of our language ego tends to decrease as our investment in the linguistic expression of our identity increases. This means that the demands made upon an individual by language learning in general, and pronunciation in particular, can be considerable. Just how strongly these demands make themselves felt will depend on a combination of motivation, aptitude (Skehan 1989a), social attitudes, and personality factors such as extroversion/introversion, anxiety and empathy. Given this complex situation, it does not seem surprising that a widespread phenomenon is fossilisation, a term coined by Selinker (1972) as a description of a kind of plateau in learners' interlanguage beyond which many people find it extremely difficult or impossible to make any further progress. Another factor being studied as a potential hindrance to pronunciation learning is interference, or negative transfer, in the sense that learners tend to 'filter' their SLA through their L1 and thus transfer features characteristic of their L1 inappropriately to their performance in the L2 (Major 1987; Tarone 1987). Relating this concern to language pedagogy, there are a number of useful sources which list the problems typically experienced by speakers of specific L1s (Nilsen and Nilsen 1971; Kenworthy 1987; Swan and Smith 1987; Avery and Ehrlich 1992; Taylor 1993).

Maybe the biggest overarching question to be asked about all these studies is how their findings can serve the teaching of English not just for communication with native speakers – the predominant explicit or at least implicit goal so far – but also what it can do for formulating criteria for teaching pronunciation for intelligibility of English as an international lingua franca, the majority use of English worldwide (Jenkins 1998, 2000).

Practice

Effective teaching requires at least three kinds of competence of teachers: linguistic proficiency in the target language, knowledge about this language, and the ability to identify and select specific aspects of language and combine them for presentation and practice in ways which are effective for learning. Teachers therefore need to be both good informants (models) and good instructors; what precisely these roles entail varies from one context to another.

Various proposals for classroom procedures are arranged below on a continuum of activity types, ranging between 'skill-getting' and 'skill-using' activities (Rivers and Temperley 1978). We thus move from exercises, which draw attention to specifics of the language code, towards communication tasks, which represent problems of some kind that require the use of language for their solution. For further details see the references given below, especially Dalton and Seidlhofer (1994: 65–150, 'Section 2: Demonstration').

1. Elicited mechanical production: This involves manipulation of sound patterns without apparent communicative reason and without offering learners an opportunity for making motivated choices of sounds, stress patterns, etc. Examples: manipulation of stress for prominence, as in *Would you like to have dinner with us toNIGHT? Would you like to have dinner with US tonight? Would you like to have DINNer with us tonight?*, etc. (compare Ponsonby 1987: 80). For individual sounds, tongue twisters of the *She sells sea shells on the sea shore* kind are useful.

2. Listen and repeat: This is a time-honoured technique involving learners in imitating chunks of language provided by the teacher or a recording; still widely used in coursebooks which are accompanied by CD-ROM or tape and particularly popular in language lab exercises.

3. Discrimination practice: Students listen for sound contrasts to train their ears. Examples: reading contrasting sounds or words to a class and asking them to decide what has been uttered. This can take the form of a bingo-like game (Bowen and Marks 1992: 36f., 'sound discrimination exercise') or 'yes–no game' (Taylor 1993: 87). A variation of this particularly suitable for monolingual classes is 'bilingual minimal pairs' (Bowen and Marks 1992: 21), where learners listen for differences in articulatory settings in lists of L1–L2 word pairs, such as German *Bild* and English *build*.

4. Sounds for meaning contrasts: While 'listen and repeat' is often drill-like, exercises can be modified to make them more meaningful for the learner while retaining a focus on sounds. Most recent textbooks offer such variations, combining an endeavour to relate linguistic form

to pragmatic meaning and action, which involves more active involvement on the part of the learner, a clearer specification of purpose and a stronger element of decision-making. **Minimal pairs** (pairs of words distinguished by one phoneme only) can be embedded in sentences such as Please SIT in this SEAT (Nilsen and Nilsen 1971: 1), which can be used for listening for and learning differences, a technique in which Gilbert (1993) is unsurpassed; e.g.: (a) *He wants to buy my boat.* (b) *He wants to buy my vote.* is to be matched with (a) *Will you sell it?* (b) *That's against the law!*

Bowler and Cunningham (1991: e.g. 24, 91) apply the same principle for teaching how to employ pitch height for contrast: *The HERO of the book is a girl called Alice.* versus *The HEROINE of the book is a girl called Alice.* Similarly, chunking into tone units can be practised with effective information gap activities such as Gilbert's arithmetic pair practice, where the correct answers depend on correct grouping, and students thus get immediate evidence of the importance of chunking, as in: *(2 + 3) × 5 = 25* as *two plus three times five equals twenty-five* versus *2 + (3 × 5) = 17* as *two plus three times five equals seventeen* (Gilbert 1993: 109).

Peer dictation activities also challenge learners as both listeners and speakers. A good source for practising the functions of intonation in context is Bradford (1988).

5. Cognitive analysis: Many learners, particularly more mature ones, welcome some overt explanation and analysis. These notions include a wide range of methodological options, such as:

   • 'talking about it': discussing stereotypic ideas about 'correct' and 'sloppy' speech for introducing assimilation and elision as crucial features of connected speech;

   • phonetic training: explanations of how particular sounds are articulated, and conscious exploration and analysis by learners how they themselves articulate L1 and L2 sounds (see Catford 1988);

   • teaching learners phonemic script: controversial, but appreciated by many students to help them conceptualise the L2 sound system, use pronunciation dictionaries, record pronunciation themselves and draw comparisons with their L1 (see Tench 1992);

   • giving rules, especially when they are simple and comprehensive, e.g. for the pronunciation of the -ed past tense marker and the -s inflectional ending (e.g. Celce-Murcia et al. 1996: Chapter 8); rules for word stress are more complicated but can be usefully summarised (see, e.g., Rogerson and Gilbert 1990: 23);

   • comparison of L1 and L2 sound systems: since learners seem to hear the sounds of a new language through the filter of their L1, it can be very helpful to teach the system of phonemes rather than just the articulation of the new sounds;

   • analysis of sounds in words or texts: Hewings (1993) encourages learners to match up monosyllabic word pairs which contain the same vowel sound; Dalton and Seidlhofer (1994: 58, 91, 128) demonstrate how dialogues not designed for pronunciation work can be used for awareness-raising of the functions of stress and intonation, e.g. pitch height for smooth turn-taking;

   • looking up the pronunciation of new words in a dictionary: excellent for developing learner autonomy.

6. Communication activities and games: While many of the above techniques can contain a game-like element, some activities are primarily focused on a particular communicative purpose or outcome (Hancock 1996); e.g. mini-plays whose interpretation depends entirely on the learners' use of voice quality and intonation (Dalton and Seidlhofer 1994: 162).

7. Whole brain activities: These are intended to activate the right brain hemisphere, often involving music, poetry, guided fantasies and relaxation techniques such as yoga breathing (Graham 1978; Laroy 1995; Vaughan-Rees 1995).

8. Learning strategies: Of key value in learner development is training aiming to foster learner autonomy and enable students to develop strategies for coping on their own and for continuing to learn. Examples: awareness-raising questionnaires (e.g. Kenworthy 1987: 55f.), learner diaries, recording of learners' production, dealing with incomprehensibility and employing correction strategies such as soliciting repetition, paraphrasing and checking feedback (Elson 1992; see also Chapter 24 of this volume).

The teacher's decision on what kind of activities to use in any particular context depends, of course, on a thorough analysis of learner needs and variables such as learning purpose, learners' age and setting. It is worth bearing in mind that, however ambitious the learning objectives may be, it may be realistic to think about the different aspects of pronunciation along a teachability–learnability scale. Distinctions such as those between voiced and voiceless consonants are fairly easy to describe and generalise, and they are teachable. Other aspects – notably the attitudinal function of intonation – are extremely dependent on individual circumstances and are therefore practically impossible to isolate for direct teaching. Some aspects might therefore be better left for learning (or not) without teacher intervention (Dalton and Seidlhofer 1994: 72ff).

Current and future trends and directions

As described above, pronunciation pedagogy is undergoing a move from sound manipulation exercises to communication activities, and from a focus on isolated forms to the functioning of pronunciation in discourse. Task-based instruction (see Chapter 25) offers pronunciation teaching considerable scope for development in this respect; however, its full potential has yet to be explored. As for learning goals, these are not so much formulated in terms of remedial accent reduction, but tend to be seen as 'accent addition' (Olle Kjellin, personal communication) which opens up new communication options for learners. This idea is closely connected with the ELT profession realising that many users of English need the language for lingua franca communication with other 'non-native' speakers as well as with native speakers. The implications of the research in this area will take a while to influence the formulation of learning priorities and targets.

Development of IT offers important opportunities with, e.g., the increase in number and size of spoken corpora of both native and non-native speech, enabling researchers to devise more accurate descriptions of language use. Applied linguists need, in turn, to evaluate these data with a view to improving pedagogy. The rapid development of electronic media has also led to a welcome if somewhat bewildering proliferation of teaching materials. A wide variety of speech samples – such as electronic dictionaries, encyclopedias and sound files on CD-ROM, DVD and the internet – is readily available as teaching input. Also, advances in computerised speech synthesis, speech enhancement and speech recognition have led to the development of sophisticated software for interactive pronunciation learning with visual feedback. See, e.g., Anderson-Hsieh (1992), Brinton and La Belle (1997), the pronunciation interest groups of IATEFL at www.cea.mdx.ac.uk/cea/95–96/iatefl/pronhome.html and of TESOL at www.faceweb.okanagan.bc.ca.spis (and links there).

These developments have increased the potential for learner self-access and autonomy and, concurrently, the need for good support materials. Such rich variety of input therefore affects the teacher's role, with a potential shift from acting as an informant to being instructor or 'speech coach' (Morley 1991). This requires making choices from all options available and employing an appropriate methodology responsive to the needs of specific learners.

Conclusion

The enormous importance of pronunciation for successful communication is now widely accepted. The field has undergone a rapid development in the 1990s, broadening its scope and strengthening its links with other areas of language use and language learning. At the same time, the recognition of the complexity and pervasiveness of pronunciation places responsibility on ELT professionals to ensure that teacher education provides for a thorough understanding of the subject and an awareness of its pedagogic significance.

Key readings

Brown (1991b) *Teaching English Pronunciation*
Celce-Murcia *et al.* (1996) *Teaching Pronunciation*
Dalton and Seidlhofer (1994) *Pronunciation*
Jenkins (2000) *The Phonology of English as an International Language*
Kenworthy (1987) *Teaching English Pronunciation*
Morley (1991) The pronunciation component in teaching English to speakers of other languages
Pennington (1996) *Phonology in English Language Teaching*
Roach (2000) *English Phonetics and Phonology*
Speak Out! The journal of the IATEFL pronunciation special interest group
Wells (1990) *Longman Pronunciation Dictionary*

CHAPTER 9

Materials development

Brian Tomlinson

Introduction

Materials development is both a field of study and a practical undertaking. As a field it studies the principles and procedures of the design, implementation and evaluation of language teaching materials. As an undertaking it involves the production, evaluation and adaptation of language teaching materials, by teachers for their own classrooms and by materials writers for sale or distribution. Ideally these two aspects of materials development are interactive in that the theoretical studies inform and are informed by the development and use of classroom materials (e.g. Tomlinson 1998c).

'Materials' include anything which can be used to facilitate the learning of a language. They can be linguistic, visual, auditory or kinesthetic, and they can be presented in print, through live performance or display, or on cassette, CD-ROM, DVD or the internet. They can be instructional in that they inform learners about the language, they can be experiential in that they provide exposure to the language in use, they can be elicitative in that they stimulate language use, or they can be exploratory in that they seek discoveries about language use.

Background

HISTORICAL DEVELOPMENT

Studies of materials development are a recent phenomenon. Until recently materials development was treated as a sub-section of methodology, in which materials were usually introduced as examples of methods in action rather than as a means to explore the principles and procedures of their development. Books for teachers included examples of materials in each section or separately at the end of a book, usually with pertinent comments (e.g. Dubin and Olshtain 1986; Richards and Rodgers 1986; Stevick 1986, 1989; Nunan 1988a; Richards 1990), but materials development was not their main concern. A few books appeared in the 1980s dealing specifically with aspects of materials development (e.g. Cunningsworth 1984; Sheldon 1987) and some articles drew attention to such aspects of materials development as evaluation and exploitation (e.g. Candlin and Breen 1979; Allwright 1981; O'Neil 1982; Kennedy 1983; Mariani 1983; Williams 1983; Sheldon 1988). However, it was not until the 1990s, when courses started to give more prominence to the study of materials development, that books on the principles and procedures of materials development started to be published (e.g. McDonough and Shaw 1993; Hidalgo *et al.* 1995; Tomlinson 1998a).

An important factor in changing attitudes to materials development has been the realisation that an effective way of helping teachers to understand and apply theories of language learning – and to achieve personal and professional development – is to provide monitored experience of the process of developing materials. Another factor has been the appreciation that no coursebook can be ideal for any particular class and that, therefore, an effective classroom teacher needs to be able to evaluate, adapt and produce materials so as to ensure a match between the learners and the materials they use. 'Every teacher is a materials developer' (English Language Centre 1997). In some ways, this is a formalisation of the implicit understanding that a teacher should provide additional teaching materials over and above coursebook material.

These realisations have led to an increase in in-service materials development courses for teachers in which the participants theorise their practice (Schon 1987) by being given concrete experience of developing materials as a basis for reflective observation and conceptualisation (Tomlinson and Masuhara 2000). It has also led on postgraduate courses to the use of such experiential approaches and to an increase in materials development research. For example, in the USA the Materials Writers Interest Section of TESOL publishes a Newsletter, in Japan the Materials Development Special Interest Group of JALT produced in 2000 a materials development edition of The Language Teacher, and in Eastern Europe there are frequent materials development conferences (e.g. the International Conference on Comparing and Evaluating Locally Produced Textbooks, Sofia, March 2000). Also, in the UK, I founded in 1993 an association called MATSDA (Materials Development Association), which organises materials development conferences and workshops and publishes a journal called FOLIO.

ISSUES IN MATERIALS DEVELOPMENT

The many controversies in the field of materials development include the following questions:

Do learners need a coursebook?

Proponents of the coursebook argue that it is the most convenient form of presenting materials, it helps to achieve consistency and continuation, it gives learners a sense of system, cohesion and progress, and it helps teachers prepare and the learner revise. Opponents counter that a coursebook is inevitably superficial and reductionist in its coverage of language points and in its provision of language experience, it cannot cater for the diverse needs of all its users, it imposes uniformity of syllabus and approach, and it removes initiative and power from teachers (see Allwright 1981; O'Neil 1982; Littlejohn 1992; Hutchinson and Torres 1994).

Should materials be learning or acquisition focused?

Despite the theories of researchers such as Krashen (1982, 1988) who advocate the implicit acquisition of language from comprehensible input, most language textbooks aim at explicit learning of language plus practice. The main exceptions are materials developed in the 1980s which aim at facilitating informal acquisition of communicative competence through communication activities such as discussions, projects, games, simulations and drama (e.g. Maley et al. 1980; Maley and Moulding 1981; Frank et al. 1982; Porter Ladousse 1983; Klippel 1984). These activities were popular but treated as supplementary materials in addition to coursebooks, which still focused on the explicit learning of discrete features of the language.

The debate about the relative merits of conscious learning and subconscious acquisition continues (R. Ellis 1999), with some people advocating a strong focus on language experience through a task-based or text-based approach (e.g. J. Willis 1996) and some advocating experience plus language awareness activities (e.g. Tomlinson 1994); however, most coursebooks still follow an approach which adds communication activities to a base of form-focused instruction (e.g.

Soars and Soars 1996; Hutchinson 1997). The experiential advocates argue that learners need to be exposed to the reality of language use and can be motivated by the sense of achievement and involvement which can be gained from communicating in a language whilst learning it. The counter-argument is that learners can gain confidence and a sense of progress from focusing on a systematic series of discrete features of the language.

Should texts be contrived or authentic?

Materials aiming at explicit learning usually contrive examples of the language which focus on the feature being taught. Usually these examples are presented in short, easy texts or dialogues and it is argued that they help the learner by focusing attention on the target feature. The counter-argument is that contrived examples over-protect learners and do not prepare them for the reality of language use, whereas authentic texts (i.e. ordinary texts not produced specifically for language teaching purposes) can provide meaningful exposure to language as it is typically used. Most researchers argue for authenticity and stress its motivating effect on learners (e.g. Bacon and Finnemann 1990; Kuo 1993; Little *et al.* 1994). However, Widdowson (1984a: 218) says that 'pedagogic presentation of language . . . necessarily involves methodological contrivance which isolates features from their natural surroundings'; Day and Bamford (1998: 54–62) attack the 'cult of authenticity' and advocate simplified reading texts which have 'the natural qualities of authenticity' and R. Ellis (1999: 68) argues for '"enriched input" which provides learners with input which has been flooded with exemplars of the target structure in the context of meaning focused activities'. See also Widdowson (2000).

Should materials be censored?

Most publishers are anxious not to risk giving offence and provide writers of global coursebooks with lists of taboo topics, which usually include sex, drugs, alcohol, religion, violence, politics, history and pork (e.g. *Heinemann International Guide for Writers* 1991). They also provide guidelines to help their writers to avoid sexism and racism (e.g. *On Balance* 1991). Whilst some form of censorship might be pedagogically desirable (distressed or embarrassed learners are unlikely to learn much language) and economically necessary (publishers lose money if their books are banned), many teachers argue that published materials are too bland and often fail to achieve the engagement needed for learning. Wajnryb (1996: 291), for example, complains about the 'safe, clean, harmonious, benevolent, undisturbed' world of the EFL coursebook. Affect is undoubtedly an important factor in learning (Jacobs and Schumann 1992; Arnold 1999) and it is arguable that provocative texts which stimulate an affective response are more likely to facilitate learning than neutral texts which do not. Interestingly, textbook projects supported by a national ministry of education often suffer less censorship and their books are sometimes more interesting to use. For example, the popular Namibian coursebook *On Target* (1996) contains texts inviting learners to respond to issues relating to drugs, pre-marital sex, violence and politics.

Some further unresolved issues in materials development include whether materials should:

- be driven by theory or by practice (Bell and Gower 1998; Prowse 1998);
- be driven by syllabus needs, learner needs or market needs;
- cater for learner expectations or try to change them;
- cater for teacher needs and wants as well as those of learners (Masuhara 1998);
- aim for language development only or should also aim for personal and educational development;
- aim to contribute to teacher development as well as language learning.

Research

There has been little published research in materials development (though in many universities postgraduate students are conducting research in materials development and publishers are commissioning confidential research). The published research has mainly focused on macro-evaluation of materials projects (Rea-Dickins 1994; Alderson 1985), publishers' pilot materials (Donovan 1998) and the evaluation of coursebook materials (Cunningsworth 1984, 1996; Breen and Candlin 1987; Tribble 1996; J.B. Brown 1997; Johnson and Johnson 1998).

One of the problems in **materials evaluation** is the subjective nature of many of the instruments of evaluation with the views of the researcher often determining what is measured and valued; e.g. in J.B. Brown's (1997) evaluation, extra points are awarded for coursebooks which include tests. However, recently there have been attempts to design objective instruments to provide more reliable information about what materials can achieve (R. Ellis 1998a; Littlejohn 1998). No one set of criteria can be used for all materials (Johnson and Johnson 1998), and attention is being given to principles and procedures for developing criteria for specific situations in which 'the framework used must be determined by the reasons, objectives and circumstances of the evaluation' (Tomlinson 1999b). Another problem is that many instruments have been for pre-use evaluation (and are therefore speculative) and they are too demanding of time and expertise for teachers to use. However, recently there have been attempts to help teachers to conduct action research on the materials they use (Edge and Richards 1993; Jolly and Bolitho 1998) and to develop instruments for use in conducting **pre-use**, **whilst-use** and **post-use evaluation** (R. Ellis 1998a, 1998b). Research on the merits of different ways of developing materials – and on the effects of different types of materials with similar goals and target learners – is still needed.

There is little work on theories of materials development, although Hall (1995) describes his theory of learning in relation to materials evaluation, and I have listed theoretical principles for materials development (Tomlinson 1998b) and outlined a principled and flexible framework for teachers to use when developing materials (Tomlinson 1999a). There are also published accounts of how textbooks are produced: Hidalgo *et al.* (1995) include a number of chapters on how textbooks are written, and Prowse (1998) reports how 16 EFL writers develop their materials. These accounts seem to agree with Low (1989: 153) that 'designing appropriate materials is not a science: it is a strange mixture of imagination, insight and analytical reasoning.' Maley (1998b: 220–221), for example, argues that the writer should trust 'intuition and tacit knowledge', and states that he operates with a number of variables which are raised to a conscious level only when he encounters a problem and works 'in a more analytical way'.

Practice

CURRENT TRENDS IN PUBLISHED MATERIALS

There are a number of trends noticeable in commercially produced materials. First, there is a similarity between new coursebooks from different publishers. I compared nine recent lower level coursebooks from different publishers and found that all followed a similar presentation, practice and production (PPP) approach (Tomlinson 1999b). There is a return to a greater emphasis on language form and the centrality of grammar, especially in lower and intermediate level course-books, such as *Lifelines* (Hutchinson 1997) and *New Headway Intermediate* (Soars and Soars 1996). More books are now making use of corpus data reflecting actual language use, rather than using idealised input (for suggestions on using corpus data, see Fox 1998; for an example of a teaching book based on corpus data, see Carter and McCarthy 1997).

There are more activities requiring investment by the learners in order for them to make discoveries (e.g. Bolitho and Tomlinson 1995; Joseph and Travers 1996; Carter and McCarthy 1997). Also, there are more interactive learning packages which make use of different media to provide a richer experience of language learning and to offer the learner choice of approach and route (Parish 1995). There are also more extensive reader series being produced with fewer linguistic constraints and more provocative content (e.g. the *Cambridge English Readers* series launched in 1999). For a detailed evaluation of current EFL coursebooks, see Tomlinson *et al.* (2001).

TRENDS IN PROJECT MATERIALS

In many countries groups of writers produce local materials. From observation of such projects in Bulgaria, China, Indonesia, Ireland, Mauritius, Morocco, Namibia, Norway, Romania, South Korea, Sri Lanka, Singapore and Vietnam, the following trends are noticeable:

- Writing teams often consist of teachers and teacher trainers who are in touch with the needs and wants of the learners.
- Writing teams are often large (e.g. 30 in Namibia; seven in Romania, five in Bulgaria), deliberately pooling the different talents available.
- Materials are content and meaning focused, with English being used to gain new knowledge, experience and skills.

Furthermore, the needs, wants and views of learners and teachers are given consideration (e.g. through questionnaires, meetings and piloting on the Namibian project). Also choices are offered to learners and teachers in the books; e.g. between original or simplified versions of text in *Search 8* (Naustdal Fenner and Nordal-Petersen 1997); of optional activities or 'pathways' in *On Target* (1996) and *A Cow's Head and Other Tales* (1996). The materials are often text driven rather than language driven and the texts are often authentic, lengthy and provocative, e.g. texts on drug dealing and pre-marital sex in *On Target*. Additionally, the focus shifts from local cultures to neighbouring cultures to world cultures, especially in *On Target* and *English for Life* (2000).

Experiments have also been conducted in generating materials for courses rather than relying solely on commercially produced materials; e.g. Hall (1995) reports on a genre-based approach and a student-generated, experiential approach developed at the Asian Institute of Technology in Thailand, and a number of researchers are currently experimenting with experiential approaches to literature on ESP courses in Singapore and Thailand.

Possible future directions

Materials will continue to aim at the development of accuracy, fluency and appropriacy while placing more emphasis on helping learners achieve effect. They will provide less practice of co-operative dialogues and more opportunities to use the language to compete for attention and effect. Materials will stop catering predominantly for the 'good language learner' (who is analytic, pays attention to form and makes use of learning strategies in a conscious way) and will start to cater more for the many learners who are experientially inclined. Materials will move away from spoken practice of written grammar, taking more account of the grammar of speech (McCarthy and Carter 1995; Carter and McCarthy 1995, 1997; Carter *et al.* 1998).

Materials will contain more engaging content, which will be of developmental value to learners as well as offering good intake of language use. Materials will become more international, presenting English as a world language rather than as the language of a particular nation and culture. However, teachers and learners will be helped to localise materials in global coursebooks. Most second language (L2) learners of English are not learning English primarily to communicate with native speakers, either abroad or in English-speaking countries; they are learning it for academic or professional advancement and/or to communicate with other non-native speakers of English at home or overseas. Already major global coursebooks series are moving away from a mono-cultural approach and soon coursebooks focusing on daily life in the USA or the UK will be rare.

More materials will be available on the internet and many will make use of internet texts as sources. For example, in Singapore an English coursebook (*English for Life 2000*) makes extensive use of web search activities and offers accompanying readers on the web. Numerous websites make learning materials available (e.g. Planet English: www.planetenglish.com; www.planetenglish.com) and a joint collaboration by several European universities puts language learners in contact for bilingual email exchanges (www.shef.ac.uk/mirrors/tandem/). Also the US Information Service is active in encouraging the use of American educational websites (e.g. American Studies Electronic Crossroads: http://e.usia.gov/education/engteaching/intl/ieal-ndx.htm) and electronically published materials (e.g. ELLSA American Literary Classics: www.rdlthai.com/ellsa_ellsamap1.html).

Conclusion

The study of the design, development and exploitation of learning materials is an effective way of connecting areas of linguistics such as language acquisition, sociolinguistics, psycholinguistics, language analysis, discourse analysis and pragmatics, of developing teacher awareness of methodological options, and of improving the effectiveness of materials. I believe that it will become increasingly central in teacher training and applied linguistics courses and that the consequent increase in both qualitative and quantitative research will greatly improve our knowledge about factors which facilitate the learning of languages.

Key readings

Balan *et al.* (1998) *English News and Views 11* (textbook)
Byrd (1995) *Material Writers Guide*
A Cow's Head and Other Tales (1996) (textbook)
Cunningsworth (1984) *Evaluating and Selecting EFL Teaching Material*
Cunningsworth (1996) *Choosing Your Coursebook*
Grozdanova *et al.* (1996) *A World of English (textbook)*
Hidalgo *et al.* (1995) *Materials Writers on Materials Writing*
McDonough and Shaw (1993) *Materials and Methods in ELT: A Teachers Guide*
Naustdal Fenner and Nordal-Petersen (1997) *Search 8* (textbook)
On Target (1996) (teachers' book)
Sheldon (1987) *ELT Textbooks and Materials: Problems in Evaluation and Development*
Tomlinson (1998a) *Materials Development for Language Teaching*
Tomlinson *et al.* (2000) *English for Life* (textbook)

CHAPTER 10

Second language teacher education

Donald Freeman

Introduction

SECOND LANGUAGE TEACHER EDUCATION AS SHIFTING CONSTRUCT

Second language (L2) teacher education describes the field of professional activity through which individuals learn to teach L2s. In terms commonly used in the field, these formal activities are generally referred to as **teacher training**, while those that are undertaken by experienced teachers, primarily on a voluntary, individual basis, are referred to as **teacher development**. I return to this issue of nomenclature later on (see 'the role of input'); at this point, however, the reader should understand that the term **teacher education** refers to the sum of experiences and activities through which individuals learn to be language teachers. Those learning to teach – whether they are new to the profession or experienced, whether in pre- or in-service contexts – are referred to as **teacher-learners** (Kennedy 1991).

The shifting ground of terminology has plagued L2 teacher education for at least the past 30 years. The four-word concept has tended to be an awkward integration of subject-matter ('second language') and professional process ('teacher education'). In this hybrid, the person of the teacher and the processes of learning to teach have often been overshadowed. As the relative emphasis has shifted, the focus among these four words has migrated from the *content*, the 'second language', to the *person* of the 'teacher', to the *process of learning* or 'education', thus capturing the evolution in the concept of L2 teacher education in the field. Until the latter half of the 1980s, the emphasis was on L2 teacher education. Primary attention was on the contributions of various academic disciplines – e.g. linguistics, psychology and literature – to what made an individual an 'L2 teacher'.

By 1990, some in the field had begun to argue that it was important to examine *how* people learned to teach languages. Thus, the emphasis began to move to the relationship between L2 as the content or subject matter, and teacher education (Bernhardt and Hammadou 1987) comprising the complementary processes of teacher training and teacher development (Freeman 1982; Larsen-Freeman 1983). The publication of Richards and Nunan's edited volume (1990) helped to mark this change in perspective. In introducing this collection the editors noted:

> The field of teacher education is a relatively underexplored one in both second and foreign language teaching. The literature on teacher education in language teaching is slight compared with the literature on issues such as methods and techniques for classroom teaching.
>
> (Richards and Nunan 1990: xi)

Accompanying professional meetings further served to establish the core interest in teacher education in the field and to articulate central issues (see Flowerdew *et al.* 1992; Li *et al.* 1994). Thus, the emphasis moved to the processes of teacher education inherent in the phrase, L2 *teacher education*, and to examining teacher education in L2s in its own right.

Defining the content and processes of teacher education presents a major set of issues. Understanding how people learn to teach and the multiple influences of teacher-learners' past experiences, the school contexts they must enter and career paths they will follow (e.g. Freeman and Richards 1996) present, among others, an equally critical set of research and implementation concerns. Linking the two, as must be done to achieve fully effective teacher education interventions, is a third critical area of work.

THE GAP BETWEEN TEACHER EDUCATION AND TEACHER LEARNING

It is ironic that L2 teacher education has concerned itself very little with how people actually learn to teach. Rather, the focus has conventionally been on the subject matter – what teachers should know – and to a lesser degree on pedagogy – how they should teach it. The notion that there is a learning process that undergirds, if not directs, teacher education is a very recent one (Freeman and Johnson 1998). There are many reasons for this gap between teacher education and teacher learning. Some have to do with the research paradigms and methods that have been valued and used in producing our current knowledge. In the case of teacher education, these paradigms raise questions about how teaching is defined and studied in education and how teacher education links to the study of teaching (see Freeman 1996a). Other reasons have to do with history. In the case of L2 teacher education, these reasons have raised the issue of how the so-called 'parent' disciplines of applied linguistics – cognitive and experimental psychology – and first language (L1) acquisition have defined what language teachers need to know and be able to do. Still other reasons have had to do with professionalisation and attempts to legitimise teaching through the incorporation of research-driven, as contrasted with practice-derived, knowledge to improve teaching performance.

TEACHER EDUCATION FROM KNOWLEDGE TRANSMISSION TO KNOWLEDGE CONSTRUCTION

In general terms, however, it is fair to say that teacher education has been predicated on the idea that knowledge about teaching and learning can be transmitted through processes of organised professional education to form individuals as teachers. This knowledge has been broadly defined as consisting of subject matter and pedagogy. From this standpoint, pre-service teacher education programmes provide teacher-learners with certain knowledge – usually in the form of general theories about language learning, prescriptive grammatical information about language, and pedagogical methods – that will be applicable to any teaching context. Learning to teach has meant learning *about* teaching, usually in the context of the teacher education programme, and then actually doing it in another context. The bridge to practice has come in observing teachers and in practising classroom teaching (e.g. Johnson 1996c). Teacher-learners then eventually develop their own effective teaching behaviours over time in other classroom contexts during their first years of teaching.

There are many problems with this knowledge-transmission view (see Freeman 1994). Principally, it depends on the transfer of knowledge and skills from the teacher education programme to the classroom in order to improve teaching. Thus, this view overlooks, or discounts, the fact that the teacher learning takes place in on-the-job initiation into the practices of teaching. Further, it does not account for what practising teachers know about teaching and how they learn more through professional teacher education than they receive in-service, during their teaching careers.

Since the 1980s, teacher education has moved from this view of knowledge transmission to one of knowledge construction in which teacher-learners build their own understandings of language teaching through their experience by integrating theory, research and opinion with empirical and reflective study of their own classroom practices (e.g. Tharp and Gallimore 1988: 217–247). To understand this change from knowledge transmission to knowledge construction, I briefly review the research in general education which is relevant to L2 teacher education. This background then frames the discussion of key issues which follows.

Background and research

For many reasons, there has tended to be very little substantial research in teacher education, both in education generally and in the field of language teaching (see Zeichner 1998; in TESOL, see Freeman 1996b). From the 1960s to 1980s, the process–product paradigm which dominated educational research focused researchers on how specific classroom or curricular processes generated particular learning outcomes or products (Dunkin and Biddle 1974). In language teaching throughout the 1970s, process–product research combined behaviourism to emphasise a view of teaching that focused on activity and technique. Effective classrooms were those in which teachers successfully applied learned behaviours to condition their students' mastery of language forms (see Chaudron 1988). Teacher education, if it was thought of at all, was viewed as a technicist undertaking of transmitting knowledge to modify teachers' classroom behaviours and thus improve student learning. Indeed, most teacher preparation in language teaching concentrated on literature; little attention was paid to classroom pedagogy. Thus, L2 teacher education was in many senses an invisible undertaking, unframed by its own theory and undocumented by its own research.

The questions at stake are substantial:

- What is the nature of teaching and of teachers' knowledge?
- How is it most adequately documented and understood?
- How is it created, influenced or changed through the interventions of teacher education?

Thus there have been two ongoing debates in teacher education over the past two decades. First, there has been the issue of how to study the process itself and the content being learned through it, which has raised issues of an appropriate variety in research paradigms, methodologies and what is valued as formal knowledge. Second, there has been the question of participants and settings, and how these influence or even shape what is taught and learned in teacher education. Zeichner (1998: 5) in a review of teacher education research in general education notes:

> Although there were hundreds of studies reported which sought to assess the impact of training teachers to do particular things, very few researchers actually looked at the process of teacher education as it happened over time and at how teachers and student teachers interpreted and gave meaning to the pre-service and professional development program they experienced.

The same can be said, if not more so, for teacher education in L2s.

UNDERSTANDING TEACHING AS THE RESEARCH BASE FOR TEACHER EDUCATION

Research in teacher education has depended, with increasing explicitness, on research on teaching. To put it simply: how you understand teaching will shape how you educate others to do it. Process–product research, which defined teaching as behaviour, clearly played a role in the improvement of teaching. However, many contended that it also overlooked, and even downplayed, the individual experiences and perspectives of teachers (Shulman 1986). Process–product research tended to generate abstract, decontextualised findings which reduced teaching to quantifiable sets of behaviours. Thus, it did not engage with the inherent messiness of classroom teaching and learning. There was also a political problem that, within this research tradition, definitions of teaching and teachers' professional knowledge were determined not by practitioners but by people outside the classroom. For researchers, the aim was to abstract teaching from contextual variables of place and time, and thus to improve its respectability through the use of positivist science. To this end, research focused on teaching as discrete behaviours which could be distanced from the contexts within which they occurred. It thus ignored the perspectives of the teachers who were carrying out the very teaching practices under study. For disciplinary advocates, research issues centred on the fledgling professional knowledge base of L2 teaching and on the role of literature and of language competence for teachers who were not teaching their mother tongue.

The tension between researchers and practitioners, which could be termed 'colonialist', fuelled changes in research paradigms and agendas in education. In the mid-1970s new directions in research started to surface which sought to describe the cognitive processes teachers used in teaching. Variously labelled thoughts, judgements and decisions, these processes were examined for how they shaped teachers' behaviours, interactions and curriculums (see Shavelson and Stern 1981; Clark and Peterson 1986). In this interpretative or hermeneutic research paradigm, teachers were assumed to conduct their work in thoughtful, rational ways, drawing on contextual information about their students, curriculums, school cultures, policies, which was filtered through their own beliefs, judgements and values. Even with this shift in emphasis, however, teachers themselves were minimally included in these research and documentation processes. In fact, the research focused on finding conceptual models of teacher thinking that could be used in educating new teachers 'to perceive, analyse, and transform their perceptions of classroom events in ways similar to those used by effective teachers' (Clark and Peterson 1986: 281).

By the mid-1980s, this field, known as teacher cognition, which sought to examine the thought processes that teachers used in planning and carrying out their lessons, had become more fully established. It is probably not surprising that researchers found classroom teaching to draw on a much wider and richer mental context than the simple, direct links between behaviours and thinking (known as teachers' pre-active and interactive decisions). Qualitative and ethnographic research studies which focused on what teachers did in their classrooms showed them engaging in complex thinking and interpretation as they taught their students in their classrooms (Elbaz 1983; Clandinin 1986). In general, this research presents what teachers know about teaching as largely socially constructed out of their experience as well as the settings in which they work. Teachers are seen to use their knowledge in classrooms in interpretive and socially negotiated ways. This knowledge is not static, but it is continually reshaped by the classrooms and schools in which they are working (Grossman 1990).

Current issues and practices

This brief review of research leads to current issues and practices in L2 teacher education. As stated at the beginning of this chapter, in the following discussion the term **teacher-learner** refers to the person who is learning to teach. There is no implication that this person is a beginning teacher; the term simply focuses on the learning process in which he or she is engaged.

THE ROLE OF INPUT: TEACHER EDUCATION STRATEGIES

As mentioned in the first section, confusing nomenclature has been the Achilles' heel of L2 teacher education. The clearest instance is the co-mingling of the terms **teacher training**, **teacher development** and **teacher education**. Like any form of education, teacher education is based on the notion that some type of input is introduced or created, which then has an impact on the learner. Further, input can be examined for what it is, its **content**, and for how it is introduced or created, the **processes** used, and for the **impacts** or **outcomes** it generates. This tripartite organisation of *what is* taught, *how* and *to what effect* can serve as a basic organising frame to examine educational input. However, it is important to note that some research on classroom teaching has raised complications with casting content and process – or subject-matter and teaching method – as independent of one another, by pointing out that from the students' perspective the content or the lesson and how it is presented are often largely inseparable (see McDiarmid *et al.* 1989; Kennedy 1990). Nevertheless, this tripartite structure of content, process and outcome continues to be a useful way of thinking about input in teacher education.

In the case of L2 teacher education, content and process combine to create two broad strategies for input: **teacher training** and **teacher development** (see Freeman 1989). In **teacher training** the content is generally defined externally and transmitted to the teacher-learner through various processes. Outcomes are assessed on external, often behavioural, evidence that the learner has mastered the content. In a typical postgraduate teacher education programme, for example, the faculty defines the curriculum which teacher-learners must master. Often this content will include course input on language (through the study of phonology and applied linguistics), on learning (through second language acquisition; SLA), on teaching (through methods and testing courses) and so on. The content may be presented through conventional processes – such as lectures, readings and the like – or through more participant-oriented processes – such as project work, case studies and so on. The assessment of impact is usually measured through some form of demonstration – such as exams, academic articles or portfolios. In short-term teacher training courses, the same broad typology holds (for examples, see Woodward 1992; Ur 1996).

In contrast, in **teacher development** the content generally stems from the teacher-learners who generate it from their experience. Thus, the processes engage teacher-learners in some form of sense-making or construction of understandings out of what they already know and can do. Because it depends on teacher-learner generated understandings, the impacts of teacher development are usually self-assessed through reflective practices. Typical teacher development activities can include teacher study groups, practitioner research or self-development activities (for examples, see Nunan and Lamb 1995; Gebhard 1996). In a teacher study group for example, the content can be generated through reflection and discussion, or journal writing, or it may be triggered by a reading or other external input. The emphasis, however, is on how teacher-learners connect the input to their own knowledge, experience and ongoing practice. Assessment focuses on the value to teacher-learners of the development activity. Given the emphasis on teacher-learners' experiences, teacher development is generally viewed as an in-service strategy which can take advantage of the background and practical knowledge of experienced teachers. It is often used in the context of peer-led staff development, peer mentoring or coaching, and other self-organised activities (see Malderez and Bod'Oczky 1999). See Figure 10.1 for an overview of these two strategies.

There are several misconceptions that tend to surround these two strategies. First they are often presented as dichotomous and mutually exclusive, which they are not. Both training and development depend on information which is external to teacher-learners, which they then incorporate through internal processes into their own thinking and practice. The distinction is rather one of emphasis and balance. In training, the information usually originates from sources external to the teacher-learners (e.g. lectures, presentations, readings, demonstrations). In development, the information is often externalised from the teacher-learners' experiences through collaborative work, reflective processes and so on. A second misconception is that training and development are often couched in sequential terms. Although it is true the training tends to be a pre-service strategy, while development is more widely used in in-service contexts, most effective L2 teacher education programmes blend the two. Finally, the nomenclature is not strictly applied, so people may speak of being 'teacher trainers' when in fact as teacher educators they use both strategies. To this end, I think it is useful to preserve **teacher education** as the superordinate term, within which teacher training and teacher development can fit as complementary and integrated strategies (Freeman 1982; Larsen-Freeman 1983; Freeman 1989).

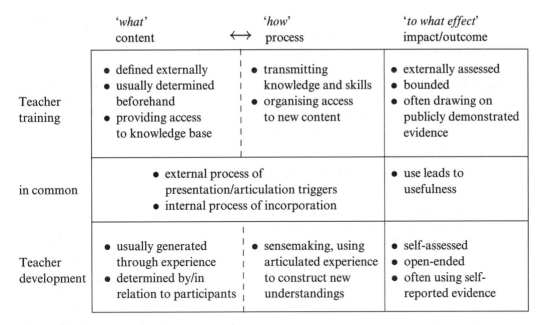

	'what' content	←→	*'how'* process	*'to what effect'* impact/outcome
Teacher training	• defined externally • usually determined beforehand • providing access to knowledge base		• transmitting knowledge and skills • organising access to new content	• externally assessed • bounded • often drawing on publicly demonstrated evidence
in common	• external process of presentation/articulation triggers • internal process of incorporation			• use leads to usefulness
Teacher development	• usually generated through experience • determined by/in relation to participants		• sensemaking, using articulated experience to construct new understandings	• self-assessed • open-ended • often using self-reported evidence

Figure 10.1 Teacher training and teacher development

THE ROLE OF PRIOR KNOWLEDGE: BEFORE FORMAL TEACHER EDUCATION BEGINS

The notion that prior knowledge plays a role in teacher education is a relatively recent one. As discussed in the research section, teacher education has conventionally been framed as a behavioural undertaking in which teacher-learners are to master the new knowledge and skills to which they have been introduced, usually through training strategies. In this view, teacher-learners themselves are seen as blank slates, with no pre-existing ideas about teaching and learning. In 1975, sociologist Dan Lortie exposed this fallacy in one of the first studies of teachers' lives. Coining the phrase 'the apprenticeship of observation' to refer to the time teachers spend as students growing up in classrooms, Lortie made the point that these experiences shape teachers' conceptions of their work in critically important ways. The implications are that as teacher-learners, even beginning teachers bring ideas or beliefs about the nature of the work, about what teaching is or should be, about what students are capable of and so forth (see Pajares 1992). The role of teacher education then becomes one of reshaping existing ideas rather than simply introducing new raw material.

This view of prior knowledge has been slow to influence the practice of teacher education, however, for two reasons. First, there is the complicated task of describing what teacher-learners' prior knowledge is and the forms it may take. Proposals have included such constructs as personal practical knowledge (Elbaz 1983; Clandinin 1986; in TESOL, Golombek 1998), beliefs and values (Pajares 1992; in TESOL, Burns 1996b) and conceptions of teaching (Freeman 1991). Since such knowledge is internal, there can be no definitive way of labelling it, thus competing constructs will continue to exist. Having determined that prior knowledge exists and having tried to label it, however, the second issue then becomes a pedagogical one: how to influence or reshape it (Kennedy 1991). Here teacher education is struggling to reconceive its educational processes so that they encompass and draw on what teacher-learners may already know about teaching (Johnson 1999; Johnson and Johnson 1999).

In L2 teacher education, research by Bailey *et al.* (1996) showed the extent to which teacher-learners' autobiographies can be integrated into course work in order to articulate their prior knowledge as a basis for learning. Similarly L1 strategies of cognitive apprenticeship – of learning to 'think' as practising teachers do – work actively through case studies, problem-solving, portfolios and other techniques to draw on teacher-learners' beliefs and conceptions of teaching (see Johnson 1996a). The challenge lies in helping teacher-learners to articulate their prior knowledge, then in creating substantially meaningful events in their teacher education that can transform that knowledge, and finally in supporting the teacher-learners as they carry these fledgling new ideas into classroom practice. To this end, programmes and courses need to muster both training and development strategies effectively so that teacher-learners can make sense of what they already know and yet not be constrained by their prior values, beliefs and conceptions of the work.

THE ROLE OF INSTITUTIONAL CONTEXT: TEACHER EDUCATION IN PLACE

Acknowledging the existence of prior knowledge in teacher education has led directly to serious reconsideration of the role of institutional contexts in learning to teach. Clearly teacher-learners' ideas about teaching stem from their experiences as students in the context of schools; similarly, their new practices as teachers are also shaped by these institutional environments. The question is, what is the role of schools in learning to teach? In general, little attention has been paid to how the sociocultural forces and values in these institutional environments can shape, impede, encourage or discourage new teachers. Pre-service teacher education has treated schools as places where teacher-learners go to practise teaching in practica or internships, and eventually to work. Classrooms, students and schools have been seen as settings in which teacher-learners can implement what they are learning or have learned in formal teacher education. From a pre-service standpoint, these assumptions and misconceptions have been rarely tested since teacher-learners leave their programmes and go on to teach with relatively little formal feedback on the validity of the connection (Bullough 1989). The dramatic attrition rates among new teachers in the United States in the mid-1980s, with rates that approached 60 per cent or more (Kennedy 1991), focused attention on the complex demands and problems that teachers had 'fitting into' schools as institutions.

In the context of in-service teacher education, however, the role of the institution has been much more central. As researchers have looked at what made certain schools more effective than others, attention shifted to the role of institutional context and its relation to teacher education practices. For example, in the late 1980s, drawing on work in the sociology of education, researchers began to investigate the notion of schools as 'technical cultures' (Rosenholtz 1989). Kleinsasser and Savignon (1992: 293) define these cultures as 'the processes designed to accomplish an organization's goals and determine how work is to be carried out'. This research, as well as other work in teacher cognition (e.g. Clark and Peterson 1986; in TESOL see Tsui 1996a; Ulichny 1996), has helped to establish that learning to teach is not simply a matter of translating ideas encountered in teacher education settings into the classroom. In fact, the conventional notion of turning theory into practice begs the question of how the sociocultural environments of schools can mediate and transform such input as teacher-learners act on it. Unfortunately, the vast majority of in-service teacher education continues to operate within this knowledge-transmission perspective, to be prescriptive and top-down, using highly directive training strategies such as school and district-mandated workshops, relicensure courses and activities, professional upgrading and the like.

There are, however, exemplars of school-based work which counteract this image. Projects which engage an entire school or academic department in rethinking and reworking all aspects of its work (see Hatch 1998) – or ones which link schools and tertiary teacher education institutions in what are known as professional development schools – tend to adopt a systemic approach to educational change (Fullan 1991, 1993). These initiatives are predicated on the notion that teacher education interventions, particularly in-service ones, must be part of a wider strategy of educational change if they are to achieve their goals. This view of systemic change holds that 'no single, discrete entity can be fully understood apart from the complex whole of which it is an integral part. The whole provides the context without which our knowledge of the part is necessarily limited' (Clark 1998: 64). Thus, educating teachers, whether pre- or in-service, must be seen within the context of schools and the social processes of schooling (Freeman and Johnson 1998).

THE ROLE OF TIME: TEACHER EDUCATION OVER TIME

If schools as institutions provide teacher education with a context in space, teacher-learners' personal and professional lives offer a similar context in and through time. Prior to the work of Lortie (1975) and others, the notion of teachers' professional life spans was not a major concern. Major research and conceptualisations by Berliner (1986), Huberman (1993) and others served to establish the concept of professional development throughout a teacher's career. Further, this work pointed to definite stages in the development of knowledge and practice (Genburg 1992; in TESOL see Tsui in press) which could inform teacher education practices. It is clear that at different stages in their careers, teachers have different professional interests and concerns. If, for example, as this research shows, novice teachers (defined as those with less than three years' classroom experience) tend to be concerned with carrying out their images of teaching by managing the classroom and controlling students (Berliner 1986), it would perhaps make sense to focus professional support and in-service education, although not exclusively, on these concerns. Likewise, expert teachers (defined in the research as those with five years or more in the classroom) tend to concern themselves with the purposes and objectives of their teaching and how they may be accomplishing them. Thus, in-service education which draws on development strategies of reflection, self-assessment, inquiry and practitioner research may be more suited for these learners of teaching.

These tensions – in time between specific needs and broad professional development, in place between the school and the teacher education institution, and in knowledge between what teacher-learners believe and what they should know – will always be central in the provision of teacher education. However, the more that providers of teacher education can account for time, place and prior knowledge in their programme designs, the more successful these programmes are likely to be.

Conclusion

There has been an assumption in teacher education that the delivery of programmes and activities is the key to success. In this view, learning to teach is seen as a by-product of capable teacher-learners and teacher educators, and well-structured designs and materials. Thus, in a broad sense, teacher education has depended largely on training strategies to teach people how to do the work of teaching. Underlying these aspects of delivery, however, lies a rich and complex process of learning to teach. Focusing at this level on the learning process, as distinct from the delivery mechanisms, is changing our understanding of teacher education in important ways (Freeman and Johnson 1998). This shift is moving L2 teacher education from its concern over what content and pedagogy teachers should master and how to deliver these in preparation and in-service programmes to the more fundamental and as yet uncharted questions of how language teaching is learned and therefore how it can best be taught. We know that teacher education matters; the question is how, and how to improve it.

Key readings

Chaudron (1988) *Second Language Classrooms*
Freeman and Johnson (1998) Reconceptualizing the knowledge-base of language teacher education
Fullan (1991) *The New Meaning of Educational Change*
Gebhard (1996) *Teaching English as a Second or Foreign Language*
Johnson and Johnson (1999) *Teachers Understanding Teaching*
Richards and Nunan (1990) *Second Language Teacher Education*

CHAPTER 11

Psycholinguistics

Thomas Scovel

Introduction and background

Among the disciplinary hybrids of linguistics which have emerged as new fields of language study over the past decades, few embrace a wider range of inquiry than psycholinguistics. There are several ways this claim can be documented. For one thing, the field itself goes by at least three different names: psycholinguistics (reflecting an emphasis on units of language posited by linguists), the psychology of language (which, as implied, focuses more on using language to validate psychological constructs) and cognitive science (a newer and much broader term, encompassing such disparate fields as artificial intelligence and neurology, which uses language data to help construct a model of human cognition). Cognitive science is also used as a superordinate term to embrace psycholinguistics, psychology of language and other related approaches to linguistics.

Another measure of the diversity of psycholinguistic research is the variety of topics found in most introductory texts: everything from chimps to Chomsky, from brains to baby talk, from meaning to memory, from prototypes to parameters, and from sign language to slips of the tongue. Yet another demonstration of the field's breadth is the way psycholinguists keep appropriating new areas of linguistics for research, thus implicating trends for research in the twenty-first century. For example, one well-known investigator, whose early work was based heavily on psychology (Clark and Clark 1977), has written a recent book which concentrates almost exclusively on how pragmatics and deixis relate to psycholinguistic inquiry (Clark 1996). Finally, psycholinguistics has always been involved with ideas which have traditionally been a part of much older disciplines; for example, philosophy (the relationship between symbol and referent) and anthropology (the Sapir–Whorf theory that languages differ in how they categorise reality).

The heterogeneity of disciplinary traditions and the hodgepodge of topics covered make psycholinguistics exceedingly difficult to define, but for the purpose of this introduction, let us describe it as any inquiry that attempts to use cognitive processing of linguistic data as a window to how the human mind operates. The maze of themes and theories collectively comprising the field can be broken down into five psycholinguistic puzzles:

- How do people comprehend language?
- How do they produce it?
- How do they acquire it?

- How do they lose it?
- How does a particular language affect cognition, if at all?

Research

COMPREHENSION

One common theme that pervades much of psycholinguistic (PL) research is how the linguistic activities most people perceive as simple and commonplace turn out, after scientific scrutiny, to be exceedingly complex processes. Comprehension of speech is a classic example. Someone utters a brief remark and almost always, we 'hear' our interlocutor speak a recognisable string of words. Given the psycholinguistic tasks a listener must accomplish in a brief amount of time, it is quite amazing that we identify individual words in a stream of rapid speech. What makes this exploit more astounding is that psycholinguists are still relatively unclear about how we can instantly recognise individual sounds, let alone the syllables and words composed from these phonemes. The comprehension puzzle has been partially explained by PL research which has demonstrated that we hear speech sounds categorically: the stop phonemes like /b/ and /p/ are not perceived on a range from 'very /b/' to 'very /p/' but are heard as definitely one or the other (Tartter 1986). Psycholinguists have shown that not only do adults perceive these sounds as clearly distinguishable, but the categorical perception of basic speech sounds is found even in tiny babies (Jusczyk 1997), suggesting that at least part of our ability to hear phonemes is 'hard-wired' into our brain at birth. Current PL research suggests that our capacity rapidly to segment the stream of speech into individual phonemes is based partly on categorical perception which is innately programmed, and partly on our prolonged exposure as children to the phonological patterns specific to our mother tongue.

However, psycholinguists would not progress far in understanding comprehension if they limited their investigations to such 'bottom-up' skills as phoneme identification. Another large source of data comes from 'top-down' factors such as the influence of context. Contextual clues can be so strong that they override phonological information, as illustrated, e.g., by experiments in which subjects listen to a set of sentences containing the syllable '-eel', where the initial consonant had been purposely deleted. Subjects claim to hear 'heel' when the sentence contains the phrase '-eel was on the shoe', but 'peel' when the sentence has '-eel was on the orange', etc. So powerful is the constraint of context that it can convince listeners to hear sounds that were never spoken.

Psycholinguists have also studied the effects of syntax on comprehension and discovered, somewhat surprisingly, that the number and type of grammatical transformations used in a sentence do not affect comprehension nearly as much as slight changes in meaning. Early PL work on sentence comprehension was driven by the belief that a 'simple' active sentence would be easier to recall accurately than its more 'complicated' passive counterpart, and some preliminary experiments in the 1970s suggested that subjects tended to have better recall with active sentences like 'The lifeguard rescued the swimmer' than the passive equivalent ('The swimmer was rescued by the lifeguard'). But subsequent studies immediately demonstrated that the effect of syntactic complexity could easily be overridden by semantic factors. Thus, when subjects were given an 'easy' active sentence which was implausible ('The swimmer rescued the lifeguard'), on tests of comprehension and memory, subjects later recalled this sentence in its *passive* form ('The swimmer was rescued by the lifeguard') because it described a much more plausible situation.

The influence of top-down information has also been demonstrated at the discourse level, where experiments on reading short, vaguely written paragraphs have shown that without titles, pictures and other contextual clues, subjects experience great difficulty comprehending and remembering these specially written discourses. However, when provided with contextual information (even just a minimal short title), subjects' ability to comprehend and remember the content of these paragraphs more than doubles (Dooling and Lachman 1971). Of course this does not mean that native speakers constantly and exclusively rely on top-down information to understand spoken or written texts, but it does confirm that heavy reliance on bottom-up details does not significantly facilitate comprehension. This is certainly one PL finding which seems to have great relevance to language teaching.

Which PL models best account for the interaction between fine details of linguistic structure (e.g. phonetic and orthographic information) in comprehension and much broader contexts (e.g. pictures and titles)? Some psycholinguists would agree with Harley (1995) and claim that connectionist models revolutionised the field in the 1990s and provide the most adequate explanation for this interaction. For example, parallel distributed processing (PDP) is a model which allows for the simultaneous processing of bottom-up and top-down linguistic information and also seems to replicate, at least in some ways, how the brain processes information (Seidenberg and McClelland 1989). In sum, although innate factors are of initial assistance in helping infant learners process speech sounds in their mother tongue, all the contextual and semantic information learners acquire over the years from their environment play a vital role in helping them comprehend words and sentences. For mature language users, comprehension is greatly facilitated by the constant interplay between the contextual knowledge the listener or reader brings to the communicative situation and the fine details of the spoken or written code which the linguistic text provides in that situation.

PRODUCTION

Psycholinguists have learned much more about the comprehension of language than its production, largely because it is easier to control for the variables that go into listening and reading than to account for the factors that may shape speaking and writing. Levelt (1989) has posited a model for language production comprising four sequential stages: **conceptualisation**, **formulation**, **articulation** and **self-monitoring**. Except for relying on introspective and anecdotal evidence – two sources of data traditionally avoided by contemporary psychologists of language – we have no way of accessing the initial stage of conceptualisation, although, quite obviously, how people begin to translate thought into speech is a question which lies at the heart of psycholinguistics (for related discussion, see also Chapter 2, p. 16).

A special area of interest in PL research is how the production of a foreign language differs from speaking in one's mother tongue. Key questions addressed include:

- At which production stage is the language of the message decided?
- How are the corresponding first language (L1) and second language (L2) words related and why does code switching (both intentional and unintentional) occur relatively frequently?
- In what ways does our mother tongue interfere with the production of L2 speech?
- Why do we usually speak more slowly and hesitantly in a foreign language than in our mother tongue?
- How do speakers try to compensate for the gaps in their incomplete L2 system?

(For reviews of these issues, see de Bot 1992; Dörnyei and Kormos 1998; Poulisse and Bongaerts 1994; see also Chapter 13 of this volume.)

Slips of the tongue (or the keyboard) provide intriguing glimpses into the second stage of production, **formulation** (Fromkin 1993). Although they often produce nonsense words ('blake fruid' for 'brake fluid') or Spoonerisms ('you noble tons of soil' for 'you noble sons of toil'), slips of the tongue reveal much about how speech is formulated. For one thing, they almost never violate phonotactic rules of a language; i.e. even though 'fruid' is not a word in English, the initial /fr/ consonant cluster is found in many words. Conversely, English speakers never blend words to form /pf/ clusters, which are permissible in languages like German. Similarly, English slips of the tongue also follow English morphological rules; e.g. 'you noble tons of soil', where the /s/ plural suffix is attached to the noun 'ton'. So, it is impossible to find Spoonerisms where this suffix is attached to a preposition, like 'of' here: 'you noble ton ofs soil'. Briefly, slips of the tongue suggest that many structures and rules posited by linguists are 'psychologically real' in that they seem to shape the formulation of speech or writing.

Articulation involves a dramatic shift from the abstract realm of cognition to the physical world of sounds (or letters). Thanks largely to the pioneering work of Lenneberg (1967) – the first psycholinguist to attempt to explore the field from a biological and evolutionary perspective – we now know that the articulation of speech is not just overlaid onto other anatomical structures (i.e. we use our teeth to make an interdental /θ/ sound, although their primary purpose is for mastication), but that articulation also depends on structures that are uniquely designed for speech. The low position of the human larynx in the throat frees the back of the tongue to articulate a wider range of vowel sounds, creates an elongated pharynx and, with it, brings distinct acoustic advantages (Lieberman 1991). Studies of how the various articulators produce speech clearly reveal that co-articulation is the norm, not the exception; i.e. at the same time our tongue positions itself for the initial /s/ of a word like 'sweet', the lips are already puckering up to prepare for the labialised /w/ which follows in the consonant cluster at the start of this word. There is still much to learn about the specifics and the timing of co-articulation in normal speech, let alone about the aetiology of such articulatory pathologies as stuttering.

The final stage, **self-monitoring**, is an area that has been extensively examined by second language acquisition (SLA) researchers (for a recent review, see Kormos 1999). Corder (1967) was one of the first to show that the ability of native speakers (or writers) to self-correct their mistakes demonstrates very clearly that they possess full linguistic competence of their native language. Non-native speakers of a language, on the other hand, frequently commit errors because, even when it is pointed out to them, they are unable to correct the mistake since they lack full competence in the language. For example, because of fatigue, etc. native speakers might say something like 'I should have *went* yesterday', but if the mistake is pointed out to them (and very often the speaker catches the goof automatically) they instantly self-monitor and produce the correct form. Non-native speakers, however, often self-monitor by guessing or creatively forming their own rule; thus, they often 'correct' by substituting one error with another (e.g. 'Oh, I mean I should have *wented* yesterday'). One controversial topic in speech production involving both SLA and PL research is whether or not there is a critical period for acquiring errorless language. Several researchers (e.g. Scovel 1988) promote a strong version of this hypothesis claiming that unless a language is acquired within the first decade of life, errors cannot be self-monitored and will remain in either a speaker's accent or syntax as a permanent feature of production.

ACQUISITION

Most of the PL research reviewed above considers language at a particular moment in time. However, by its very nature, the study of language acquisition is diachronic, covering many years. Until the 1950s linguists devoted little attention to the remarkable fact that virtually every human grows up with complete spoken (i.e. excluding literacy) mastery of one language (their native language) or at least one since a large minority mature into fluent bilinguals or even trilinguals. It had been assumed that children accomplished this feat simply through many hours of daily contact with native speakers (i.e. through nurture); however, psycholinguists have proven that, aside from this simplistic behavioural explanation, infants are born with innate linguistic abilities which help them enormously to make sense out of the linguistic environment (see Jusczyk 1997). Some scholars (Pinker 1994) have further claimed that the most significant features of L1 acquisition are shaped much more by nature than by nurture. However, most contemporary psycholinguists believe that language acquisition is enhanced and shaped by interaction: not just interaction between the linguistic environment and innately specified linguistic abilities (such as universal grammar), but also between children and care-takers. For example, specialists in L1 acquisition have shown that child-directed speech (CDS) used by adult care-takers is profoundly different from normal adult language and, because of features such as exaggerated intonation, it greatly facilitates language learning.

Recently, given the amount of research on child language acquisition, the field has become a separate speciality, although findings continue to influence other areas of psycholinguistics and vice versa. A significant discovery is that although children may differ markedly in their rate of acquisition, especially in the early years, all progress through similar phonological, lexical, syntactic, etc. stages of development. Before twelve months, most infants have picked up basic intonation and/or tonal patterns of their native tongue, along with some consonants; but it takes several years before children have acquired all of the target language's consonants (especially, e.g., certain sounds like /r/ in English). Children also learn words dealing with the here and now long before acquiring the ability to displace time and place. In summary, it appears that because of their innate endowment, prolonged exposure to a native tongue and the constant attention and interaction with their care-takers who use a nurturing CDS, it is almost impossible for human infants not to grow into full-fledged members of a speech community. (For research on bilingualism, see Chapter 13.)

DISSOLUTION

An important arena of PL research is the study of language loss, especially when brought about by brain damage. Nineteenth-century European neurologists such as Broca and Wernicke were the first to localise speech and language to specific areas of the brain, and those early and tentative neuroanatomical associations have spawned the modern fields of **aphasiology** and **neurolinguistics**, two areas of inquiry closely related to psycholinguistics.

Evidence from neurological pathology, such as **aphasia**, reveals several intriguing aspects of how the brain programmes speech. As summarised by Dingwall (1993), neurolinguistic evidence suggests that comprehension and production are relatively independent of each other. Although the central area of the left hemisphere controls most linguistic functions for the majority of people, traumatic injury to this area's more posterior portion creates Wernicke's aphasia, where comprehension tends to be disrupted. A more anterior injury causes Broca's aphasia, where problems in production arise, suggesting that articulation of speech is mediated in this area. Intriguingly, when deaf signers suffer an injury to Broca's area in the left hemisphere, they have as much difficulty producing sign language (e.g. American Sign Language) as hearing people do with the production of speech. Another neurolinguistic finding is that Chinese and Japanese speakers who suffer brain injury in Broca's area experience great difficulty writing the phonological components of their ideographic system, but have no trouble writing or reading the semantic components of the characters. These examples imply that comprehension and production of speech and writing involves co-ordination of several autonomous linguistic sub-systems. With contemporary techniques (e.g. positron emission tomography and regional cerebral blood flow scanning) we continue to learn how language is neurologically produced, processed and remembered in both injured and healthy subjects.

LINGUISTIC RELATIVITY

Finally, a controversial area of psycholinguistics is **linguistic relativity**, or the **Sapir–Whorf hypothesis**, the very popular notion that each language, because of its linguistic uniqueness, creates its own cognitive world. That is, Korean speakers 'think differently' from Spanish speakers because the languages are so different. Despite the pervasiveness and popularity of this belief, most PL evidence fails to support it. Psycholinguists who may differ strongly in other areas are in more agreement in their reluctance to endorse this notion (Steinberg 1993; Pinker 1994). First, many fail to distinguish linguistic relativity from language determinism (Slobin 1971). The former claims that each individual language has a unique relationship to cognition and/or perception; the latter holds that human language, in a very general way, is related to thought. PL research has frequently demonstrated the existence of determinism; e.g. experiments have shown that negatives reduce processing time in any language. However, experimental documentation for relativity is more difficult to obtain. Another major problem with the Sapir–Whorf hypothesis is that it is based on a structural linguistic model observed more than 50 years ago. This has been replaced by generative models, based largely on Chomsky's work, which presuppose one universal grammar (UG) innately shared by all language users (Chomsky 1968). It is therefore difficult to reconcile the psycholinguistic 'uniqueness' of each language with the belief that languages (and presumably the human mind) are more similar than they are disparate. Finally, in its strongest versions, the Sapir–Whorf hypothesis can, albeit unintentionally, foster ethnocentric stereotyping (Tsunoda 1985). However, for a re-thinking of many of these issues, see Gumperz and Levinson (1996).

Practice

One application mentioned above is the realisation that native speakers rely heavily (though not exclusively) on top-down information when listening to speech or reading texts. However, in most foreign language classrooms (especially beginner and intermediate) most of the material deals with the recognition and comprehension of bottom-up details (e.g. the final consonant of a syllable, the gender of a noun, the tense of a verb). PL data from experiments on comprehension suggest that it is profoundly impeded if access to top-down information is ignored. Obviously, current and future SLA research on the relationship between L2 input and learning is closely related to this issue but, in brief, it is clear that learners comprehend content because of context.

Another insight from PL research comes from recent attempts to uncover what linguistic cues native speakers use to help them remember words. Gathercole *et al.* (1999) gave young English-speaking children lists of real and invented words to remember. They found that, although the children not surprisingly remembered the real words better, for the invented words those with more common sounding syllables were recalled best. This study confirms earlier work on PDP, suggesting that people can simultaneously use phonological and lexical information to help them decode and remember language. Experiments like this suggest that language teachers can help students more by using linguistic contexts which provide separate but concurrent cues about the language they introduce (e.g. 'what a beautiful *thing* – a blue sky in *spring* and white clouds on the *wing*').

Finally, a less precise insight comes from PL work on production. Any speaker or writer must progress through various stages of production simultaneously and (at least for speech) in an exceedingly short timespan. A review of research on native-speaking subjects should give language teachers a great sense of empathy for the complexity of the tasks students confront when speaking or writing in another language. PL experiments with highly fluent native speakers show that they often produce slips of the tongue and other errors, especially when pressed for time. An indirect implication of this for language teaching is that more 'wait time' is needed for L2 learners, and teachers should therefore be aware that patience is crucial.

Conclusion

Psycholinguistics is a broad and diverse field, related in many tangential ways to the learning and teaching of an L2. Introductory texts range from detailed texts (Carroll 1994; Harley 1995) to pithy prefaces (Steinberg 1993; Scovel 1998), and any current introduction can demonstrate how complex and stimulating the field can be. Future research will focus on integrating findings from the discipline's various subfields into a more cohesive perspective on cognitive science. Certainly research in neurolinguistics and artificial intelligence will contribute to this integration. Because talk and thought are such vital aspects of all human endeavour, psycholinguistic inquiry will not only indirectly assist us to become more effective language learners and teachers, but may also help us better understand ourselves and each other.

Key readings

Aitchison (1996) *The Seeds of Speech: Language Origin and Evolution*
Altmann (1997) *An Exploration of Language, Mind and Understanding*
Birdsong (1999) *Second Language Acquisition and the Critical Period Hypothesis*
Candland (1993) *Feral Children and Clever Animals*
Carroll (1994) *Psychology of Language*
Obler and Gjerlow (1999) *Language and the Brain*
Pinker (1994) *The Language Instinct*
Scovel (1998) *Psycholinguistics*

CHAPTER 12

Second language acquisition

David Nunan

Introduction

The term **second language acquisition (SLA)** refers to the processes through which someone acquires one or more second or foreign languages. SLA researchers look at acquisition in naturalistic contexts (where learners pick up the language informally through interacting in the language) and in classroom settings. Researchers are interested in both product (the language used by learners at different stages in the acquisition process) and process (the mental process and environmental factors that influence the acquisition process). In this chapter I trace the development of SLA from its origins in contrastive analysis. This is followed by a selective review of research, focusing on product-oriented studies of stages that learners pass through as they acquire another language, as well as investigations into the processes underlying acquisition. The practical implications of research are then discussed, followed by a review of current and future trends and directions.

Background

The discipline now known as SLA emerged from comparative studies of similarities and differences between languages. These studies were conducted in the belief that a learner's first language (L1) has an important influence on the acquisition of a second (L2), resulting in the 'contrastive analysis' (CA) hypothesis. Proponents of contrastive analysis argued that where L1 and L2 rules are in conflict, errors are likely to occur which are the result of 'interference' between L1 and L2. For example, the hypothesis predicted that Spanish L1 learners would tend, when learning English, to place the adjective after the noun as is done in Spanish, rather than before it. Such an error can be explained as 'negative transfer' of the L1 rule to the L2. When the rules are similar for both languages, 'positive transfer' would occur, and language learning would be facilitated. Where a target language feature does not exist in the L1, learning would also be impeded. Thus, English L1 learners will encounter difficulty trying to master the use of nominal classifiers in certain Asian languages such as Cantonese, because these do not exist in English. In terms of pedagogy, contrastivists held that learners' difficulties in learning an L2 could be predicted on the basis of a systematic comparison of the two languages, and that learners from different first language backgrounds would experience different difficulties when attempting to learn a common L2.

The CA hypothesis was in harmony with the prevailing psychological theory of the time:

behaviourism. Behaviourists believed that learning was a process of habit formation. Linguistic habits acquired by individuals as their L1 emerged would have a marked influence on their L2 acquisition. It is no coincidence that research questioning the contrastivist position emerged at about the same time as cognitive psychologists began to challenge behaviourism.

A major shift in perspective occurred in the 1960s, when linguists and language educators turned their attention from the CA of languages and began studying the specific language learners used as they attempted to communicate in the target language. In an important publication, Corder (1967) made a strong case for the investigation of learners' errors as a way of obtaining insights into the processes and strategies underlying SLA. Errors were seen not as evidence of pathology on the part of learners (as suggested by behaviourism), but as a normal and healthy part of the learning process.

The systematic study of learners' errors revealed interesting insights into SLA process. First, learners made errors that were not predicted by the CA hypothesis. Second, the errors that learners made were systematic, rather than random. Third, learners appeared to move through a series of stages as they developed competence in the target language. These successive stages were characterised by particular types of error, and each stage could be seen as a kind of **interlanguage** or 'interim language' in its own right (Selinker 1972).

Not surprisingly, the field of SLA has been strongly influenced by L1 acquisition. SLA researchers have looked to L1 acquisition for insights into ways of investigating the acquisition process as well as the outcomes of the research. Particularly influential was a pioneering study by Brown (1973), who conducted a longitudinal case study of three children acquiring English as an L1. Brown traced the development of 14 grammatical structures, discovering that, contrary to expectations, there was no relationship between the order in which items were acquired and the frequency with which they were used by the parents.

Research

PRODUCT-ORIENTED RESEARCH

During the early 1970s a series of empirical investigations into learner language were carried out which became known as the 'morpheme order' studies. Their principal aim was to determine whether there is a 'natural' sequence in the order in which L2 learners acquire the grammar of the target language. Dulay and Burt (1973, 1974) – the principal architects of the morpheme order studies – found that, like their L1 counterparts, children acquiring an L2 appeared to follow a predetermined order which could not be accounted for in terms of the frequency with which learners heard the language items. Moreover, children from very different L1 backgrounds (Spanish and Chinese) acquired a number of morphemes in virtually the same order. However, the order differed from that of the L1 learners investigated by Brown. A replication of the studies with adult learners produced strikingly similar results to those with children (Bailey *et al.* 1974).

As a result of these and other investigations, it was concluded that in neither child nor adult L2 performance could the majority of errors be attributed to the learners' L1s, and that learners in fact made many errors in areas of grammar that are comparable in both the L1 and L2, errors which the CA hypothesis predicted would not occur. Dulay and Burt (1974) therefore rejected the hypothesis, proposing instead a hypothesis entitled 'L2 acquisition equals L1 acquisition' and indicating that the two hypotheses predict the appearance of different types of errors ('goofs') in L2 learners' speech.

> Briefly the CA hypothesis states that while the child is learning an L2, he [or she] will tend to use his native language structures in his L2 speech, and where structures in his L1 and his L2 differ he will goof. For example, in Spanish, subjects are often dropped, so Spanish children learning English should tend to say *Wants Miss Jones* for *He wants Miss Jones*.

The 'L2 acquisition equals L1 acquisition' hypothesis holds that children actively organize the L2 speech that they hear and make generalizations about its structure as children learning their L1 do. Therefore the goofs expected in any particular L2 production would be similar to those made by children learning the same language as their L1. For example *Jose want Miss Jones* would be expected since L1 acquisition studies have shown that children generally omit functors, in this case the *-s* inflection for third person singular present indicative.

(Dulay and Burt 1974: 96)

The morpheme order studies indicated a predetermined order of acquisition for certain grammatical morphemes. Subsequent research also showed that this order could not be changed by instruction. However, the researchers were unable to explain why certain items were acquired before others. During the 1980s, however, a number of researchers studying the acquisition of German and English proposed an interested explanation for the disparity between instruction and acquisition based on speech-processing constraints (Pienemann 1989). They argued that grammatical items can be sequenced into a series of stages, each more complex than the last. However, this complexity is determined by the demands made on short-term memory, rather than by the conceptual complexity of the items in question. Take, e.g., third person *-s*, which morpheme studies had shown is acquired late. These researchers could explain why this was so. According to pedagogical grammars, the item is relatively straightforward. If the subject of a sentence is singular, add *-s* to the main verb. However, in speech-processing terms it can be quite complex, because the speaker has to hold the information as to whether the noun phrase is singular or plural in working memory. Because many speech-processing operations are very complex, and also because the time available for speaking or comprehending is limited, only part of the whole speech-processing operation can be focused on at one time. These researchers argue that items can only be learned when they are one stage ahead of a learner's present processing capacity. This is called the 'teachability' hypothesis. They further argue that grammatical syllabuses should be structurally graded to reflect these developmental sequences.

In the 1980s Stephen Krashen was the best-known figure in the SLA field. He formulated a controversial hypothesis to explain the disparity between the order in which grammatical items were taught and the order in which they were acquired, arguing that there are two mental processes operating in SLA: conscious learning and subconscious acquisition. Conscious learning focuses on grammatical rules, enabling the learner to memorise rules and to identify instances of rule violation. Subconscious acquisition is a very different process, facilitating the acquisition of rules at a subconscious level. According to Krashen (1982, 1988), when using the language to communicate meaning, the learner must draw on subconscious knowledge. The suggestion of conscious and subconscious processes functioning in language development was not new or radical; however, Krashen's assertion that these processes were totally separate, i.e. that learning could not become acquisition, was. Krashen went on to argue that the basic mechanism underlying language acquisition was comprehension. According to his **comprehensible input** hypothesis, when the student understands a message in the language containing a structure, his or her current level of competence advances by one step, and that structure is acquired. These hypotheses had a marked influence on practice, as outlined below.

PROCESS-ORIENTED RESEARCH

Research reviewed above focused on the products or outcomes of acquisition. A growing body of research considers learning processes, exploring the kinds of classroom tasks that appear to facilitate SLA. The bulk of this research focuses on activities or procedures which learners perform in relation to the input data. Given the extent of research in the field, this review is necessarily selective.

In the first of a series of investigations into learner–learner interaction, Long (1981) found that two-way tasks (in which all students in a group discussion had unique information to contribute) stimulated significantly more modified interactions than one-way tasks (in which one member of the group possessed all the relevant information). Similarly, Doughty and Pica (1986) found that required information-exchange tasks generated significantly more modified interaction than tasks where exchange of information was optional.

The term 'modified interaction' refers to instances during an interaction when the speaker alters the form in which his or her language is encoded to make it more comprehensible. Such modification may be prompted by lack of comprehension on the listener's part. (For further details, see Chapter 25 on task-based learning.) This research into modified interaction was strongly influenced by Krashen's hypothesis that comprehensible input was a necessary and sufficient condition for SLA, i.e. that acquisition would occur when learners understood messages in the target language. Long (1985a: 378) advanced the following arguments (which are paraphrased) in favour of tasks which promote conversational adjustments or interactional modifications on the part of the learner:

> Where (a) is linguistic/conversational adjustment, (b) is comprehensible input and (c) is acquisition: Step 1: show that (a) promotes (b). Step 2: show that (b) promotes (c). Step 3: deduce that (a) promotes (c). Satisfactory evidence of the (a) → (b) → (c) progression would allow the linguistic environment to be posited as an indirect causal variable in SLA. (The relationship would be indirect because of the intervening 'comprehension' variable.)

In a relatively short period of time, SLA researchers have generated an impressive number of empirical studies. For detailed reviews of other studies and issues, see Larsen-Freeman and Long 1991; R. Ellis 1994.

Practice

In this section, practical pedagogical implications of the conceptual and empirical work summarised above are presented and exemplified. I focus particularly on claims made by SLA researchers for product-oriented syllabuses, the implications of the comprehensible input hypothesis, and proposals for task-based language teaching.

Krashen's work on the subconscious acquisition hypothesis and the comprehensible input hypothesis is summarised above. According to these hypotheses, innate processes guide SLA. In practical terms, researchers argued that learners should be provided with much natural input, especially extensive listening opportunities and particularly in the early stages of learning. They also argue that a silent phase at the beginning of language learning (when the student is not required to produce the new language) has proven useful for most students in reducing interlingual errors and enhancing pronunciation. Finally, and most controversially, they argued that formal grammar instruction was of limited utility as it fuelled conscious learning rather than subconscious acquisition (Dulay *et al.* 1982; Krashen and Terrell 1983). While relatively few researchers still subscribe to Krashen's hypotheses, at least in their original form, the value of rich and varied listening input early on has wide support (for more details, see Chapter 1).

Krashen's comprehensible input hypothesis was challenged by Swain (1985), who investigated immersion programmes in Canada in which children receive content instruction in a language other than their L1. Native speakers of English receive instruction in maths, science, etc. in French, and vice versa for French native speakers. These children therefore receive massive amounts of comprehensible input. Despite this, L2 development is not as advanced as it should be according to the comprehensible input hypothesis. Swain found that the basic instructional pattern in class was one in which teachers talked a great deal and students got to say very little. Based on her observations, Swain formulated an alternative hypothesis – the 'comprehensible output' hypothesis – suggesting that opportunities to produce language were important for acquisition.

The idea that grammatically sequenced syllabuses and the conscious learning of grammar were of limited utility in language learning was also vigorously rejected by proponents of the teachability hypothesis. In their view, grammatical structures can be classified according to the demands they make on the learner's working memory. The greater the demands, the more difficult the structure is to learn. An item will only be acquired, and therefore should only be taught, when the learner is developmentally ready to acquire it. The researchers who formulated this hypothesis argued that grammar could and should be taught, but that the timing of instruction should be in accord with the learner's developmental stage.

The process-oriented research work of Long and others provided impetus for the development of task-based language teaching. In task-based language teaching, the start point for designing language courses is not an ordered list of linguistic items, but a collection of tasks. SLA research has informed the work of syllabus designers, methodologists and materials writers by suggesting that tasks encouraging learners to negotiate meaning are healthy for acquisition. The growing importance of 'task' as a fundamental element in curriculums and textbooks of all kinds underlines the growing links between process-oriented research and classroom pedagogy.

Current and future trends and directions

Current SLA research orientations can be captured by a single word: complexity. Researchers have begun to realise that there are social and interpersonal as well as psychological dimensions to acquisition, that input and output are both important, that form and meaning are ultimately inseparable, and that acquisition is an organic rather than linear process.

In a recent study, Martyn (1996) investigated the influence of certain task characteristics on the negotiation of meaning in small group work, looking at the following variables:

- interaction relationship: whether one person holds all of the information required to complete the task, whether each participant holds a portion of the information, or whether the information is shared;

- interaction requirement: whether or not the information must be shared;

- goal orientation: whether the task goal is convergent or divergent;

- outcome options: whether there is only a single correct outcome, or whether more than one outcome is possible.

The results seem to indicate that while task variables appear to have an effect on the amount of negotiation for meaning, there appears to be an interaction between task variables, personality factors and interactional dynamic. This ongoing research underlines the complexity of the learning environment, and the difficulty of isolating psychological and linguistic factors from social and interpersonal ones.

A major challenge for curriculum designers, materials writers and classroom practitioners who subscribe to task-based teaching is how to develop programmes that integrate tasks with form-focused instruction. This is particularly challenging when teaching beginners in foreign language contexts. A number of applied linguists (see, e.g., R. Ellis 1995) are currently exploring the extent to which one can implement task-based teaching with beginner learners, and experiments are under way to establish the appropriate balance and 'mix' between tasks which have non-linguistic outcomes and exercises which have linguistic outcomes.

In searching for metaphors to reflect the complexity of the acquisition process, some researchers have argued that the adoption of an 'organic' perspective can greatly enrich our understanding of language acquisition and use. Without such a perspective, our understanding of other dimensions of language (such as the notion of 'grammaticality') will be piecemeal and incomplete, as will any attempt at understanding and interpreting utterances in isolation from the contexts in which they occur. The organic metaphor sees SLA more like growing a garden than building a wall. From such a perspective, learners do not learn one thing perfectly one item at a time, but learn numerous things simultaneously (and imperfectly). The linguistic flowers do not all appear at the same time, nor do they all grow at the same rate. Some even appear to wilt for a time before renewing their growth. Rate and speed of development are determined by a complex interplay of factors related to pedagogical interventions (Pica 1985); speech-processing constraints (Pienemann and Johnston 1987); acquisitional processes (Pienemann 1989); and the influence of the discoursal environment in which the items occur (Levinson 1983; McCarthy 1991; Nunan 1993, 1999).

Conclusion

In this chapter, I describe the emergence of SLA as a discipline from early work in CA, error analysis and interlanguage development. I examine research into SLA in both naturalistic and instructional settings, considering both process- and product-oriented studies. The chapter also looks at the practical implications of current research for syllabus design and methodology, focusing in particular on the implications of SLA research for syllabus design, the input hypothesis, and task-based language teaching. The final part of the chapter suggests that future work will attempt to capture the complexity of the acquisition process by incorporating a wide range of linguistic, social, interpersonal and psycholinguistic variables into the design of the research process.

Key readings

R. Ellis (1994) *The Study of Second Language Acquisition*
Krashen (1982) *Principles and Practice in Second Language Acquisition*
Larsen-Freeman (1991) Second language acquisition research: Staking out the territory
Larsen-Freeman and Long (1991) *An Introduction to Second Language Acquisition Research*
Lightbrown and Spada (1993) *How Languages are Learned*
Nunan (1999) *Second Language Teaching and Learning*

CHAPTER 13

Bilingualism

Agnes Lam

Introduction

Bilingualism refers to the phenomenon of competence and communication in two languages. A bilingual individual is someone who has the ability to communicate in two languages alternately. Such an ability or psychological state in the individual has been referred to as bilinguality (Hamers and Blanc 2000). A bilingual society is one in which two languages are used for communication. In a bilingual society, it is possible to have a large number of monolinguals (those who speak only one of the two languages used in that society), provided that there are enough bilinguals to perform the functions requiring bilingual competence in that society. There is therefore a distinction between individual bilingualism and societal bilingualism.

The above definitions seem fairly straightforward. What makes it difficult to apply such definitions is the disagreement over what constitutes competencies in two languages. Several questions have been asked:

- Monolingual or communicative norms: Do we measure the competencies of bilingual persons against the respective competencies of monolingual persons? If so, we end up with labelling some bilinguals as perfect bilinguals (a small minority) and others as imperfect bilinguals (the vast majority). Another approach is not to apply monolingual norms in measuring bilingual abilities but just to evaluate the communicative competence of the bilingual as a whole (Grosjean 1992).

- Relative competencies in two languages: Is the bilingual better at one language than the other? If so, the person has dominant bilinguality. If he or she is equally good at both languages, then the term balanced bilingual is used (Hamers and Blanc 2000).

- Domains: Can someone be considered a bilingual if he or she can only function in one language in a few domains (e.g. work), while communicating in another language in other domains (e.g. home)? Essentially, the person only has the registers or varieties of language associated with particular domains for different languages. His or her communicative abilities in one language complement those of the other. I would call this complementary bilinguality.

- Components: Can linguistic competence be subdivided into smaller components? For example, can someone be considered a bilingual if he or she can comprehend two languages but speak and write only one of them? In such circumstances, the person can be described as a receptive bilingual, having the ability to understand both languages. Otherwise, the ability to produce both languages in some manner (speaking and/or writing) is usually assumed when a person is identified as a bilingual.

Apart from bilingual abilities involving two languages, individuals may also have **bidialectal** or **biscriptural** abilities within one language. Bidialectalism refers to the phenomenon whereby someone can communicate in more than two dialects of the same language, e.g. Cantonese and Putonghua for a Chinese speaker. Biscriptural competence is the ability to read more than one script of the same language; e.g. the Chinese language can be written both in the new simplified script and the traditional complex script.

A final definitional issue concerns the relationship between bilingualism and multilingualism. Discussions of bilingualism often include multilingual contexts (Romaine 1996: 572), because in many multilingual societies there are more bilingual than multilingual individuals. There are many patterns of multilingualism based on various combinations of bilingual competencies. For example, individuals in a multilingual society could be bilingual in the dominant language (the language with power or status) and another non-dominant language. The non-dominant language may vary for individuals. Increasingly, however, with the recognition that many societies are multilingual, multilingualism is often discussed as a phenomenon in its own right (Paulston 1994; Cenoz and Genesee 1998).

Background

A multifaceted phenomenon, bilingualism requires multidisciplinary investigations for it to be more completely understood. In their attempts at linguistic representations, linguists differ in the importance they accord to bilingualism. Until recently, linguistic descriptions of languages have often disregarded bilingual considerations, focusing instead on the monolingual speaker–hearer competence in the language. Recently, however, with the emergence of sociolinguistic concerns in the late 1950s and the renewed interest in variation studies as a whole, language change arising from the use of two or more languages in a society is now studied with greater vigour (Thomason 1997). Bilingualism is now directly linked with studies in contact linguistics (Appel and Muysken 1987). The bilingual individual is now recognised as 'the ultimate locus of contact' (Romaine 1996: 572–573, concurring with Weinreich 1968) and accepted as one of the agents of language change arising from contact situations.

Psycholinguistic studies of bilingualism have asked questions such as: how do we become bilingual? How are the two languages represented in the bilingual brain? What happens in real time when a bilingual communicates? To answer the question of how someone becomes bilingual, it is useful to draw a distinction between simultaneous and successive bilingualism: simultaneous bilingualism refers to the acquisition of two languages at the same time while successive bilingualism refers to the acquisition of one language after another. In the latter, the first language (L1) will have been established in some way before the learner is exposed to the second language (L2). To distinguish between the two, McLaughlin (1982: 218) uses the operational definition that if two languages are acquired below three years old, then it is considered simultaneous bilingualism with both languages acquired as L1s; if the learner only starts learning the L2 after three years old, then it is defined as successive bilingualism. The learning of the L2 in successive bilingualism is also referred to as second language acquisition (SLA). (For more discussion of cognitive processing in bilinguals and bilingual memory, see Harris 1992; Paradis 1995; see also Chapter 11 of this volume.)

Sociolinguists ask questions about the relative status and function of the languages in a bilingual community. Governments may decide to help non-dominant or minority groups (e.g. immigrants to America) develop competence in their own L1s while they learn the dominant or official language(s) (e.g. English). If they are successful, then there is language maintenance; if not, there is language shift (the gradual loss of use of the L1 in a particular population). In extreme cases, the result may be language death (the complete loss of speakers of a language). Apart from language planning issues, sociolinguists are also interested in how bilinguals switch between two languages for communicative effect. Related to the study of language switching (Myers-Scotton 1993; Milroy and Muysken 1995) is the research on biculturality, the ability to alternate between two cultures (see also Chapter 14).

To meet the needs of immigrant or non-dominant groups, several governments around the world have attempted to provide bilingual education: education using both languages as media of instruction and/or having bilingualism as a goal of education. Educators are concerned about the types of teaching programmes and classroom techniques that can facilitate the development of bilingual abilities. A whole range of bilingual education models is now available. Some of these models can encourage maintenance of the non-dominant languages while others are likely to lead to language shift. If becoming bilingual helps learners to develop positive attitudes to their native languages and themselves, the phenomenon is called additive bilingualism. If they develop negative attitudes towards their own languages in the process of becoming bilingual, then it is called subtractive bilingualism (Cummins 1984: 57–58). Some researchers have related these positive and negative attitudes to cognitive advantages and disadvantages (Hamers and Blanc 2000).

Research

Although the acquisition of two languages is not a twentieth-century phenomenon, the study of bilingualism, as outlined above, is a relatively modern discipline. In fact, until the middle of the twentieth century most scholarly efforts were not spent on understanding bilingualism as a phenomenon *per se*. The interest in bilingual learners tended to relate to questions on how to enable them to learn languages more efficiently. There was little work on the psycholinguistic processes in a bilingual's brain until the work of Weinreich (1953). The publication of Ferguson's (1959 [1996]) article on **diglossia** – a term used to describe the stable use of two linguistic varieties for different domains of language use in a society – paved the way for the identification of societal bilingualism, but it took a few years before the connection was made by Fishman (1967a). Even then, there was little interest in describing discourse structures of the mixed output of a bilingual communicating with another bilingual as an interesting phenomenon in itself until Gumperz and Hymes' (1972) work. Most linguists in the 1970s were still working within Chomsky's (1965) approach to linguistics which was not designed to handle mixed language output. Much of the early impetus for research into bilingualism came instead from studies in bilingual education, which in turn was the result of a mixture of interacting effects from post-war population movements, post-colonial language policies and the propagation of humanistic and egalitarian ideologies.

With population movements occurring in various parts of the world for two or three decades after the Second World War, laws were passed in some countries to allow members of non-dominant groups to learn in their own languages while at the same time trying to learn the dominant language. In America, the Bilingual Education Act was passed in 1968 (Wagner 1981: 47), while in Canada the Official Languages Act was adopted in 1969 (Shapson 1984: 1). Though not a centre for immigration as America has been in recent decades, the People's Republic of China has 55 minorities or non-dominant groups. Soon after the establishment of the present government in 1949, China passed legislation from the 1950s onwards to provide for education in the non-dominant languages while encouraging, but not requiring, some of these speakers to learn Putonghua, the national mode of communication (Dai *et al.* 1997). Likewise, in multilingual India the Three Language Formula (the regional language and the mother tongue – Hindi or another Indian language – and English or a modern European language) was first devised in 1956 and modified in 1961 (Srivastava 1988: 263). Similar events took place in other countries well into the 1970s.

It is important to note the historical background to studies of bilingual education because it sheds light on their motivation and expected outcomes. Many of the early studies in bilingualism were case studies of particular countries or communities, involving an appreciation of history, politics and demography. *The International Handbook of Bilingualism and Bilingual Education* (Paulston 1988) is one of the most comprehensive research efforts documenting the circumstances in countries such as China (Tai 1988), India (Srivastava 1988), South Africa (Young 1988), the UK (Linguistic Minorities Project 1988) and the US (Ruiz 1988) among others. Other studies appearing from the 1980s include Paulston (1982) on Sweden, Shapson and D'oyley (1984) on Canada, Churchill (1986) on the OECD (Organisation for Economic Co-operation and Development) countries and Baetens Beardsmore (1993) on Europe.

As part of many pilot programmes in bilingual education, models for facilitating bilingual development in schools have been developed. A review of all the models developed (Nunan and Lam 1998) shows that they hinge on two main issues:

- Whether the non-dominant language is used as a medium of instruction.
- Whether the non-dominant language is valued as a cultural asset worth acquiring for itself.

These two parameters can be used to categorise a whole range of bilingual education models. Four examples illustrate this:

1. The *submersion* model of bilingual education: the non-dominant language is neither valued nor used as a medium of instruction.

2. *Transitional bilingualism*: the non-dominant language is used as a medium of instruction for a period but is not eventually valued as a target language.

3. *Heritage language* programmes: the non-dominant language is not used as a medium of instruction but is valued as a target language to be learned

4. The *language exposure* time model: the learner's own language is valued as a target language and also used as a medium of instruction for some subjects.

(For a discussion of other bilingual education models, see Nunan and Lam 1998.)

Since bilingual education involves a large sector of the population and is a social issue often hotly debated upon, the awareness of bilingualism as a phenomenon has grown steadily. So has research in bilingualism. By the 1980s, there are several introductory texts to the field such as Baetens Beardsmore (1982), Alatis and Staczek (1985), Cummins and Swain (1986), Baker (1988) and Hamers and Blanc (2000; 1st edns 1983/1989). Other new books include Hoffman (1991) and Romaine (1995). Apart from general discussions of bilingualism and bilingual education, usually in primary or secondary school settings, there is also a body of research for sub-areas, such as bilingualism and language contact (Appel and Muysken 1987), cognitive processing in bilinguals (Bialystok 1991; Harris 1992), and even what parents can do at home to help children become bilingual (Harding and Riley 1986; Arnberg 1987; Dopke 1992).

In the context of societal bilingualism, language contact effects have often been observed. When two languages are used in the same community, there might be the adoption of vocabulary items or phrases from one language while a person is communicating largely in the other. Observed at any particular point in time, this might only appear as an instance of language switching. If this behaviour spreads to other individuals in that community and the borrowed items become commonly adopted, then there is language change in the form of lexical borrowing. Lexical borrowing may be quite superficial in that the linguistic system is fairly unaffected. The bilingual person's output is still largely recognisable as one language rather than another. When one or more components in two languages become fused into one code for communication, then there is change in the linguistic systems themselves; this phenomenon is called language convergence, i.e. the systematic merging of forms between languages which are in the same geographical speech area or *Sprachbund* (linguistic alliance) (Jakobson 1931). Complete merging of two languages may result in mixed languages such as pidgins (mixed languages with no native speakers) or creoles (pidgins that have acquired native speakers, i.e. children of speakers of a pidgin). It is possible therefore that societal bilingualism over time may give rise to the emergence of a mixed language which in turn may become the common mode of communication.

Another approach to the study of language mixing is to consider what happens in the bilingual's brain. One of the first attempts was Weinreich's (1953) delineation of bilingual memory organisation. In Weinreich's model, there are three types of bilingual memory systems: coexistent bilingualism, merged bilingualism and subordinative bilingualism. In the first type, the two languages are kept separate; in the second, the representations of the two languages are integrated into one system; in the last, L2 is based on the representations of L1. It has been postulated that the way the memory organises the two languages is related to how they are acquired (Ervin and Osgood 1965, cited in Keatley 1992). In the first type, the languages are kept apart in the memory system because they are learned in different environments; in the second type, bilinguals have acquired the languages while using them interchangeably; in the last, L2 is learned on the basis of L1. Ervin and Osgood refer to the first type as co-ordinate bilingualism and the second as compound bilingualism. They consider the third type as a form of the second type since the mental representations of L2 are based on L1 and are therefore not separately stored (on the compound–co-ordinate distinction, see Lambert *et al.* 1958; on neurolinguistic constraints on language learning, see Penfield and Roberts 1959; Scovel 1988).

Since the mid-1950s, much research in the tradition of experimental psycholinguistics has been conducted with the aim of understanding the mental representations of bilingual competencies (for a comprehensive review, see Keatley 1992). There are also studies focused on bidialectal (Lam *et al.* 1991) and biscriptural processing (Lam 1997). While some transfer effects between the two linguistic systems have been observed, the exact nature of bilingual representations or processing is still not entirely clear. Recently, Chomsky's (1965, 1980) ideas on innate mental representations, or universal grammar, have also been revived as a framework for understanding the bilingual's system of communication (Bhatia and Ritchie 1996). It is suggested that the bilingual's system of mixed speech abides by certain grammatical constraints (for other grammatical considerations, see Muysken 1995; Myers-Scotton 1995). Apart from linguistic models, more general problem-solving models from cognitive science and artificial intelligence have also been applied to understand bilingual processing. This is because there is now no general consensus as to where cognition (or thinking) ends and language begins.

Practice

The recognition of bilingualism as a social, individual and linguistic phenomenon has several implications for educational practice. To begin with, teachers have to appreciate the sociolinguistic circumstances surrounding the development of bilingual competencies in their students. If they are in positions of power and influence, they could try to propose to their governments or institutions educational models appropriate for their circumstances. A first task is therefore to understand the sociolinguistic situation in their particular society or community as well as to identify the assumptions behind any bilingual education model.

A survey of the literature also makes apparent that each community is not exactly the same. Although lessons can be learned from understanding another community, a model that may work for one community may not work for another. The earlier the teacher realises this, the more realistic he or she can be. If the teacher is not in a position to influence the model of bilingual education imposed on the classroom, he or she can still try to see what positive attitudes towards bilingualism can be encouraged in the learners. For a start, he or she must realise that demands may be placed on the bilingual ethnic minority child and must be sensitive to cross-cultural identity issues. If the teacher can try to foster cross-cultural openness and learn to become bicultural – if not bilingual – it will provide some motivation to learners. Every effort, no matter how small, to learn the learners' language is usually appreciated. Rather than presenting the learning of two languages as onerous, the teacher can also point out to students the advantages of knowing more than one language and design tasks to enable them to appreciate such enrichment opportunities in their environment. If the teacher is bilingual, it may also be useful to recount to students his or her experience of becoming bilingual. This, in turn, will give rise to opportunities for learners to share their experiences as well. With a positive attitude towards bilingualism, the teacher and learners can then work together to enable the learners to make appropriate language choices for different situations as well as observe the nuances in mixed mode interaction. (For practical guidelines for teacher development, see Nunan and Lam 1998; for cultural identity issues in classroom contexts involving more than one language, see Byram 1998.)

Current and future trends and directions

Although the study of bilingualism was initially motivated by an educational need, and so had a strong pedagogical orientation in the early work, research in the last few decades has brought together the theoretical approaches from several disciplines. This multidisciplinary approach to bilingualism has proved healthy and is likely to continue to be adopted.

At the same time, the recent convergence of theoretical assumptions from various sub-disciplines can enable the researcher in bilingualism to synthesise the findings from various fields more easily than before. For example, the recent emphasis on cross-cultural linguistics or cultural discourse analysis makes it easier for bilingual communication patterns to be described and understood. Sociolinguistic research and linguistic analysis are coming together much more than before. Contact linguistics is now more recognised as a branch of mainstream linguistics. All these advances make it possible for bilingualism to be considered in its own right and for bilingual communities to be recognised and studied on their own terms, rather than according to outdated norms of monolingual homogeneous speech communities.

Technological advances on tracking electrical activity in the brain without surgery or reliance on brain-damaged patients also makes it possible for researchers to undertake non-intrusive studies on brain activation (Caplan 1987), which can offer more empirical evidence for the organisation of bilingual memory. Newer theoretical models of psycholinguistic processing – such as connectionism and spreading activation in neural networks (Dijkstra and de Smelt 1996) – also offer more flexibility in constructs of bilingual mental organisation. With such models, we might be able to account for a greater range of bilingual behaviour using current parameters.

While bilingual education might have been the goal in the 1970s, at the start of the twenty-first century there is the call for multilingualism and multilingual education to be a new target. In multilingual education, the implications for language competencies in the teachers, as well as administrative arrangements for classes streamed according to learners' L1s, are even more enormous and demand even more creative solutions. More than ever, teachers and teacher educators will have to accommodate explicit or covert bilingual or multilingual language-policy considerations as they have direct day-to-day implications on school language policy, curricular organisation, classroom interaction and the development of bilingual or multilingual learners.

Conclusion

The multifaceted nature of the phenomenon of bilingualism needs to be fully appreciated for any pedagogical programme designed to foster bilingual development to succeed. To study bilingualism is to study the interaction between linguistics, psycholinguistics, sociolinguistics, pedagogy and the real world of language politics and policy. To be able to appreciate such interactions in changing times and adjust classroom practice in the light of changes is the hallmark of a professional language teacher.

Key readings

Baetens Beardsmore (1982) *Bilingualism: Basic Principles*
Cenoz and Genesee (1998) *Multilingualism and Multilingual Education*
Cummins and Swain (1986) *Bilingualism in Education*
Fishman (1967a) Bilingualism with and without diglossia; diglossia with and without bilingualism
Grosjean (1992) Another view of bilingualism
Harding and Riley (1986) *The Bilingual Family*
Harris (1992) *Cognitive Processing in Bilinguals*
Paulston (1988) *International Handbook of Bilingualism and Bilingual Education*
Romaine (1996) Bilingualism

CHAPTER 14

Sociolinguistics

Sandra Silberstein

Introduction

Sociolinguistics examines the relationship between language use and the social world, particularly how language operates within and creates social structures. Studies in sociolinguistics explore the commonplace observations that everyone does not speak a language in the same way, that we alter our speech to accommodate our audience, and that we recognise members and non-members of our communities via speech. Sociolinguistic studies have looked at **speech communities** based on social categories such as age, class, ethnicity, gender, geography, profession and sexual identity. To be sure, such categories are fluid: they exist only in context, and rather than standing independent of speech are generally produced through it. In short, these categories exist largely as a matter of social perception.

Background

Sustained interest in sociolinguistics emerged in the 1960s, in part as a reaction to 'autonomous' Chomskian linguistics. In place of the latter's idealised speaker/hearer, for whom social influences are idiosyncratic or irrelevant, the 'hyphenated' field of sociolinguistics sought to explore and theorise the language use of social beings. Capturing the interdisciplinary nature of the enterprise, a distinction is often made between **micro-sociolinguistics** and **macro-sociolinguistics** (Coulmas 1997; Spolsky 1998). Micro-sociolinguistics refers to research with a linguistic slant, often focusing on dialect and stylistic/register variation. Both quantitative and qualitative research methods have been employed to explore such linguistic phenomena as phonological differences between dialects or discourse variation between male and female speakers. Coulmas (1997: v) refers to micro-sociolinguistics as 'social dimensions of language'. In contrast, macro-sociolinguistics (or Coulmas's 'linguistic dimensions of society') looks at the behaviours of entire speech communities, exploring issues such as why immigrant communities retain their native languages in some social contexts but not in others, or how social identity can affect language choice. With the coming-together of (micro-)sociolinguistics in a narrow sense and a macro-sociology of language, we have tools and questions of particular interest to second language (L2) practitioners.

Research

This section explores those aspects of sociolinguistic research that have been particularly productive when viewed through the lens of L2 teaching and learning. For convenience's sake, this work will be discussed within three subcategories: **language variation**, **linguistic relativity** and **languages in contact**.

LANGUAGE VARIATION

One of the earliest studies reported the work of Labov (1972a) and his colleagues among inner-city youth in New York City (for a precursor of this work, see his dialect study of Martha's Vineyard: Labov 1972c [1963]). Far from being 'sloppy or ungrammatical' – as was the prevailing stereotype – the language used by these speakers was shown to be as consistent and rule-governed as any 'standard' or 'prestige' dialect, the result of systematic linguistic and historical processes. The dissemination of Labov's insights within the native-language teaching profession had a profound effect. In 1979, as a result of court testimony by linguists including Labov (1982) and Smitherman (1981), a US federal judge, in what is variously termed the 'Ann Arbor' or 'King' cases, ruled in favour of a group of parents by requiring that the school district first identify children speaking so-called Black English – today more commonly termed African American Vernacular English (AAVE) or Ebonics – and then use linguistic knowledge to teach these students how to read 'standard English' (Labov 1982: 193). A significant outcome was that teachers were schooled in the origin and history of students' native language variety and trained to recognise and address the systematic differences between this variety and the standard or prestige form.

Briefly, **pidginisation** is a process that results from contact of two or more languages in a context where language needs can or must be satisfied through use of a simplified code. Examples include trading contexts or the interactions between colonised people and a conqueror. When social dominance comes into play, the language(s) of the subordinated groups have most of their effect on the grammar, while the socially dominant language contributes more of the vocabulary. Through a **creolisation** process, speakers (generally of succeeding generations) develop an elaborated code that can accommodate the full range of life's functions. A gradual **decreolisation** process can occur as speakers incorporate features from a dominant language. During the 1970s, a number of linguists came to argue that AAVE usage exists on a decreolisation continuum between creoles such as Gullah and a prestige form termed Standard American English (for summaries, see Conklin and Lourie 1983; Labov 1982). More recently, creolisation models in general have been complicated somewhat to acknowledge multidirectional linguistic influences (Myers-Scotton 1993) and the dynamic virtuosity of learners' language use. Pedagogically speaking, variation research has demonstrated the ways in which students' home languages enrich the linguistic landscape, are fundamental to their identities and can be used to aid their learning (see Auerbach 1993; Murray 1998; Smitherman 1998). The examination of languages in contact and, in particular, the pidginisation model was to have an important influence on L2 studies.

For L2 researchers, the notion of a continuum between a first language (L1) and a 'target language' proved productive. A learner's simplified **interlanguage** – a concept developed by Corder (1967) and Selinker (1972) – could be seen to result from a pidginisation process (Schumann 1978). In this model, acquisition takes place through the processes of depidginisation and decreolisation, as learners restructure their interlanguage and move towards an L2 (Anderson 1983). One of several controversial issues is the explanation of sustained pidginisation: Schumann argued that social and psychological distance explain those learners whose speech remains simplified. A re-theorising of social distance appears at the end of this chapter.

Language variation research has focused increasingly on issues of social context, departing from early interpretations which tended to see meaning inhering in linguistic features themselves. For example, the observations of Lakoff (1975) were often interpreted to suggest that women's use of tag questions and hedges *per se* rendered them linguistically less powerful. In the area of social class, debate centred on Bernstein's (1971) suggestion that the less 'elaborated', so-called 'restricted', code he reported for working-class students implied a cognitive deficit. Later thinking suggests a more dynamic process in which context and category reproduce each other through speech. Tag questions of themselves don't create a less powerful speaker, do they? And discourse styles do not necessarily imply cognitive ability. Rather, in a school context where working-class students encounter middle-class teachers, or in contexts where gender relations are unequal, roles are reproduced through contextualised speech activities.

Perhaps one of the most important findings of contemporary sociolinguistic research is the extent to which social categories interact. Examples are studies of the commonly held stereotypes that women speak more grammatically and are more polite than men. This research shows us the extent to which social context is implicated in language use. An early study by Nichols (1976) reports a case where gender and social class interact with respect to grammaticality. Working with a rural Black population in South Carolina, Nichols (1976) found that 'women in the lower socioeconomic group . . . exhibited more conservative linguistic behavior than men in that group; women in the more socially mobile . . . community exhibited more innovative linguistic behavior than . . . men' (p. 110). Building on this observation, Nichols underscores the contextual nature of language use when she speculates that 'perhaps in transitional groups, or in different social situations for the same group, women will exhibit both conservative and innovative behavior' (p. 111).

Freeman and McElhinny (1996: 251) survey the interaction of culture and gender with respect to politeness:

> In societies where politeness is normatively valued or seen as a skill, or where acquisition of politeness is not an automatic part of language learning but requires additional training, men tend to be understood as more polite, and women are understood as impolite (Keenan 1974) or too polite (Smith-Hefner 1988). In societies where directness is valued, and politeness is seen as a form of deference rather than a skill, women tend to be more polite, or at least are perceived as more polite . . .

Freeman and McElhinny note that these commonsense understandings of politeness tell us more about the workings of ideology than the actual use of language. They cite, among others, Keenan (1974) whose work in Malagasy finds men credited as being more skilfully polite because they do *not* use the devalued European politeness system.

A wide variety of ways in which language and society intersect – in which we find social stratification of linguistic variables from phonology and syntax to discourse and narrative conventions – is documented in sociolinguistic research on:

- age (e.g. Schieffelin and Ochs 1986; Silberstein 1988; Scollon and Scollon 1995; Eckert 1997);
- ethnicity (e.g. Scollon and Scollon 1981, 1995; Silberstein 1984; Tannen 1984a; Rampton 1995; Fishman 1997);
- gender (e.g. Graddol and Swann 1989; Coates and Cameron 1988; Coates 1993; Tannen 1993; Bergvall *et al.* 1996; Johnson and Meinhof 1997);
- geography (e.g. Tannen 1984a; Trudgill 1990; Wolfram 1997);
- profession (e.g. DiPietro 1982; Scollon and Scollon 1995);
- sexual identity (e.g. Malinowitz 1995; Livia and Hall 1997; Poynton 1997; Nelson 1999); and
- social class (e.g. Labov 1966, 1972d; Bernstein 1971; Trudgill 1974; for a critique, see Robinson 1979).

LINGUISTIC RELATIVITY

Research on cross-cultural miscommunication explores communicative failures occasioned by the fact that seemingly equivalent language can function quite differently in different cultures (compare this position with that taken within psycholinguistics; see Chapter 11). Thomas (1983) distinguishes between what she calls **pragmalinguistic** and **sociopragmatic failure**. In the former, speakers fail to convey their meaning because the message's pragmatic force is misunderstood. A speaker might translate something from an L1 into a target language without the knowledge that the communicative conventions of the target language are quite different. For example, the formulaic expression 'How are you?' in English generally means little more than 'Hello'. Socio-pragmatic failure occurs when one does not know what to say to whom, a situation that can lead to violating local politeness norms. As examples, which topics are discussed, which questions are appropriately asked of newcomers and which favours one asks differ dramatically across speech communities. For students from many locations outside the US it is odd that American hosts offer food only once and then take it away.

Hymes (1962 [1968]) coined the term **ethnography of speaking** (more recently expanded to **ethnography of communication**) to describe the task of the researcher who is 'concerned with the situations and uses, the patterns and functions, of speaking' (p. 101). As he says, 'it is a question of what a foreigner must learn about a group's verbal behaviour in order to participate appropriately and effectively in its activities' (p. 101). In effect, the task of the researcher becomes the description of what Hymes (1971 [1972, 1979]) termed **communicative competence**. Canale and Swain (1980) and Canale (1983) theorised four components of communicative competence: grammatical competence, discourse competence (coherence and cohesion), strategic competence (skill in coping with communicative breakdowns) and sociolinguistic competence. The last involves appropriate language use based on knowledge of sociocultural conventions and social context. Sociolinguistic knowledge involves sensitivity to issues of context and topic, as well as social parameters such as gender, age and social status.

Scollon and Scollon (1995) present an interactive sociolinguistic framework that addresses communication across social parameters. In their study of intercultural professional communication in English between Westerners and East Asians, they use the term **discourse** more broadly than did Canale and Swain. Scollon and Scollon's **interdiscourse communication** refers to 'the entire range of communications across boundaries of groups [e.g. professional groups] or discourse systems [e.g. a gender system]' (p. xi). They remind us that 'effective communication requires study of cultural and discourse differences on the one hand, but also requires a recognition of one's own limitations' in crossing discourse boundaries (p. 15). (See also Chapter 29 of this volume.)

In sum, research on cross-linguistic communication demonstrates that grammatical knowledge alone does not guarantee communication. With the contemporary emphasis on communicative competence and communicative language teaching (CLT), language teachers have focused increasing attention on sociolinguistic aspects of language use.

LANGUAGES IN CONTACT

When speakers live in a linguistically diverse environment, several alternatives to monolingualism are available to them. In a **diglossic** situation (Ferguson 1959 [1996]; Fishman 1967b; Schiffman 1997) two languages or varieties of a language exist side by side, essentially in complementary distribution. Often one is used for formal situations (e.g. education, religion), the other in informal contexts. Usually one is a high-prestige variety (H), while the other, frequently the vernacular and native language/variety, is considered low (L). This is a complex social context in which language teachers are asked to teach a prestige non-native, perhaps imposed, language variety. Another contact phenomenon is **code-switching**, which occurs when bilingual speakers switch from one language to another in the same discourse, sometimes within the same utterance (Myers-Scotton

1997). Although common throughout the world, one example is the flexible Spanish–English code-switching of Latinos in Anglophone North America. As Myers-Scotton points out, code-switching patterns can announce speakers' relationships to both languages as well as their membership in a particular code-switching community.

Clyne (1997) reminds us that any multilingual situation evidences diverse communication patterns with respect to features such as length of turns, ways of taking and maintaining the floor, and speech acts (such as apologies and complaints); all of these are heavily influenced by cultural values. Teachers of English in multilingual contexts are faced with complex sociolinguistic and cultural phenomena (see also Chapter 29).

Practice

LANGUAGE VARIATION

Students need to develop a critical understanding of the commonplace observation that the same language can be spoken differently by diverse speakers; moreover, the same speakers vary their language (or shift style) depending on which of their sociolinguistic identities is being called upon. This element of communicative competence needs to be explicitly addressed in the language classroom. When encountering an unfamiliar language/culture, students may be sending signals of which they are unaware. For example, it is widely reported anecdotally that female students studying an L2 with a male native speaker or men learning from a female instructor tend to approximate the pitch of their teachers rather than native speakers of their own gender. These language students might want to be aware that their pitch will be a **sociolinguistic marker**, even if they decide that they feel physically or psychologically more comfortable speaking slightly higher or lower than their native-speaking counterparts. Students also typically want to learn when the English they have acquired is overly formal, is slang, or associates them with a particular social class or community. In this context, language teachers are called upon to make conscious decisions concerning which varieties of English and which language strategies they bring into the classroom. It is suggested below that students should hone their observational skills in order to recognise how interactions between language and society affect their communication. One place to begin is with a critical awareness of the social constructions present in their own language textbooks (see Chapters 3 and 9).

LINGUISTIC RELATIVITY

As we have seen, language learners must go beyond grammatical competence if they are to be successful users of a language. One area of sociolinguistic competence is the use of speech acts. As Cohen (1996: 383) points out:

> 'Sorry about that!' may serve as an adequate apology in some [cultural] situations. In others it may be perceived as a rude, even arrogant nonapology. In yet other situations, it may not even be intended as an apology in the first place. Hence, it has become increasingly clear that the teaching of second language words and phrases isolated from their sociocultural context may lead to the production of linguistic curiosities which do not achieve their communicative purposes.

Cohen notes that it may take many years to acquire native-like sociolinguistic competence and recommends classroom activities on speech acts. Adapted from Olstain and Cohen (1991), he recommends five steps: assessment of students' sociolinguistic awareness; presentation and discussion of dialogues focusing on sociocultural factors affecting speech acts; evaluation of situations that might require apologies or complaints; role plays; feedback and discussion. Another centre of cross-cultural difference can be conversation. Phenomena such as turn-taking,

taking and maintaining the floor (Sacks *et al.* 1974) or the uses of silence (Tannen and Saville-Troike 1985) can prove areas of conversational 'failure'. Moreover, text-building itself varies among speech communities. Silberstein (1984) documents cultural differences in story-telling norms within the US. To prepare students to encounter linguistic diversity between and within 'cultures', practitioners (e.g. Silberstein 1984; Kramsch 1993; Canagarajah 1999) have suggested making students critical observers (in effect, ethnographers) of their own and their teachers' instances of cross-cultural confusion.

LANGUAGES IN CONTACT

Heath (1993) has been studying community-based youth groups that develop students' linguistic virtuosity. Through dramas written, cast and directed by young people, inner-city youth retain their L1 or dialect while gaining proficiency in 'standard' US English. Through role-playing, these youths come to take a critical view of language and develop sophisticated abilities to switch languages or dialects depending on the context/role they portray. In later work, Heath (1998) has sought to validate young people's linguistic abilities so they might find employment as translators. Heath's research suggests that teachers can help students exploit their already sophisticated understandings of language use. Rampton (1995) finds another kind of sociolinguistic dexterity in **language crossing** among urban adolescents in Britain who switch to non-hereditary forms: the use of Punjabi by young people of Anglo and Afro-Caribbean descent, the use of Creole by Anglos and Punjabis, and the use of stylised Indian English by all three. These studies underline the complex language identities students can bring to the classroom.

Pratt (1991: 34) uses the term **contact zones** for classrooms and other 'social spaces where cultures meet, clash, and grapple with each other, often in contexts of highly asymmetrical relations of power, such as colonialism, slavery, or their aftermaths'. If the tendency towards domination is resisted, the knowledge born in these tensions can be transformative for all. In contexts where it is important for students to maintain their identification with more than one language – i.e. where code-switching is part of students' linguistic identity – the wisdom of 'English only' classroom policies is certainly brought into question; in fact, a powerful argument against this policy is presented by Auerbach (1993). Where English is used primarily with non-native speakers – or native speakers of local (i.e. postcolonial) varieties of English – teachers need to decide which variety or varieties of English will be taught. Canagarajah (1999) recommends that teachers help students 'appropriate' English on their own terms, according to their own needs, values and aspirations.

Current and future trends and directions

Some of the most exciting new work explores the relationship between identity and language learning. Much of this thinking has been influenced by post-structuralist critiques of traditionally conceived social categories. For example, in place of fixed, *a priori* notions of class and gender, post-structuralists argue that social categories are fluid, that they are created and recreated at the moment of speech through speech, that we all occupy multiple subject positions (a term combining the concept of subjectivity with the subject of traditional grammar) and that individuals can and do resist the hierarchical positions in which they find themselves. Canagarajah's (1999) study of English language teaching in Sri Lanka seeks to be a voice from the 'periphery', documenting how teachers and students in the marginalised postcolonial communities of the developing world subtly negotiate the uses of English and local languages in the English classroom. As Canagarajah (1999: 25) demonstrates, 'it is wrong to assume that the cultures of the subordinate groups are always passive and accommodative'. Canagarajah documents strategies on the parts of teachers and students that negotiate the role of local culture, politics, identity and language in the English class. As examples, teachers or students might code-switch to the local language to build solidarity; and student textbook graffiti can adapt unfamiliar North American figures to a Tamil context. Researchers like Canagarajah help teachers understand the complex strategies of language users in the English class.

Norton Peirce's (1993, 1995) study of immigrant women learning English in Canada challenges second language acquisition theorists to reconceptualise notions of identity and the individual in language learning. (Note that her more recent work is published under Norton.) Working within a post-structuralist tradition, Norton Peirce (1995) conceptualises social identity as 'nonunitary and contradictory . . . changing across time and space'. Documenting the language use of a learner she calls Martina, Norton Peirce reports that 'as a socially constructed immigrant woman . . . [she] never felt comfortable speaking' (pp. 21, 26), but as a mother and primary care-taker 'she refused to be silenced' (p. 21). This kind of social positioning is largely neglected by language acquisition theories that focus on individual motivation while ignoring the impact on learners of 'frequently inequitable social structures' (p. 25). On this basis, Norton Peirce (1993) critiques Schumann's pidginisation hypothesis for overlooking the fact that social and psychological distance between learners and a target language community may be due to power structures that first marginalise learners, then blame them for an inability to acculturate.

Like Canagarajah's work, Norton Peirce's falls within new paradigms that examine the social dimensions of language pedagogy within rubrics that are variously termed critical/postmodern/border pedagogies (Giroux and McLaren 1994), pedagogies of possibility (Simon 1987, 1992) or liberatory pedagogy (Freire 1970 [1996]; Shor 1987). She joins others (e.g. Chick 1996) who call for examining the complex relationship between the language classroom and the larger society. Finally, Norton Peirce (1993: 26) urges language teachers to help 'learners claim the right to speak outside the classroom. To this end, the lived experiences and social identities of language learners need to be incorporated into the L2 curriculum.'

Key readings

Coulmas (1997) *The Handbook of Sociolinguistics*
Coupland and Jaworski (1997) *Sociolinguistics*
Fasold (1984) *The Sociolinguistics of Society*
Fasold (1990) *The Sociolinguistics of Language*
Holmes (1992) *An Introduction to Sociolinguistics*
Hudson (1996) *Sociolinguistics*
McKay and Hornberger (1995) *Sociolinguistics and Language Teaching*
Preston (1989) *Sociolinguistics and Second Language Acquisition*
Romaine (1994) *Language in Society*
Spolsky (1998) *Sociolinguistics*
Trudgill (1995) *Sociolinguistics*
Trudgill and Cheshire (1998) *The Sociolinguistics Reader, Vol. 1:
    Multilingualism and Variation; Vol. 2: Gender and Discourse*
Wardough (1998) *An Introduction to Sociolinguistics*
Wolfson (1989) *Sociolinguistics and TESOL*
Wolfson and Judd (1983) *Sociolinguistics and Language Acquisition*

CHAPTER 15

Computer-assisted language learning

Elizabeth Hanson-Smith

Introduction

In the 1990s the personal computer emerged as a significant tool for language teaching and learning. The widespread use of software, local area networks (LANs) and the internet has created enormous opportunities for learners to enhance their communicative abilities, both by individualising practice and by tapping into a global community of other learners.

Background

Much of the early history of computers in language learning, in the 1980s and 1990s, was concerned with keeping abreast of technological change. Mainframe computers were at first seen as the taskmaster: a number of content courses, particularly in English grammar and computer science were provided by the PLATO system (Bitzer 1960) at many universities. Students 'mastered' each individual topic – which consisted of presentation and 'practice' in the form of tests – in solitary confinement in a language laboratory. However, the continual miniaturisation of electronics has given us increasingly smaller, faster and more powerful desktop computers. At the start of the twenty-first century 'multimedia' has become virtually synonymous with 'computer'. With these changes, issues in computer-assisted language learning (CALL) have also evolved from an early emphasis on how to use the new technology to research on technology's effects on learning. Higgins and Johns (1984) framed the major debate of the 1980s and early 1990s over whether the computer was 'master' of or 'slave' to the learning process: Was the computer to be a replacement for teachers, or merely an obedient servant to students?

Coincidental with the development of the multimedia personal computer were the changes in our understanding of the teaching and learning of languages. Communicative approaches (spawned by Krashen; see in particular Krashen 1982), content-based learning (Cantoni-Harvey 1987) and task-based learning (Nunan 1989a, 1995b) are all enhanced by the use of the computer. CALL has branched out in many ways in communicative pedagogy (see below).

Technology-enhanced language learning was given a huge theoretical boost when Sydney Papert (1993) – creator of the computer language Logo – and others applied the principles of Dewey (1938) and Piaget (1950) to the use of computers. 'Constructivism' involves the use of problem-solving during tasks and projects, rather than or in addition to direct instruction by the teacher. In CALL this theory implies learning by using computer tools to explore simulated worlds, to build presentations and websites that reflect on personally engaging and significant topics, and to undertake authentic communication with other learners around the world.

The constructivist theory of learning dovetails well with the recent recognition in language pedagogy of the need to encompass higher cognitive processes in the learning task. Chamot and O'Malley (1996a), who call this the Cognitive Academic Language Learning Approach (CALLA), are probably the chief proponents of this view. The cognitive approach addresses the need for students to be aware of their own learning processes, and to organise and structure their learning themselves. The plethora of information available electronically makes these cognitive demands on language students, creating a suitably rich setting for the authentic tasks and projects that are seen to promote language acquisition (see activities suggested in Chapter 12). The chaotic information of the internet, with its largely native-speaker-oriented content resources, enhances the necessity for students to deploy schema and strategies for efficient learning. Technology thus becomes an 'environment' for learning, as well as both tutor and tool (Egbert and Hanson-Smith 1999; see also Chapter 30 of this volume).

Research

While the theory of CALL advanced considerably over the days of the mainframe, one difficulty was that until recently most published articles on CALL were concerned with how to implement a system rather than what the best systems for language learning might be. An ancillary effect of rapid change is the difficulty of performing longitudinal studies on computers and their uses.

COMPARATIVE STUDIES

A significant interest of early CALL studies was the comparison of computer-enhanced classes with 'traditional' or conventional classes. However, comparable research variables are difficult to establish since the kinds of activities students carry out in the computer environment may be very different from those in conventional classes. For example, what possible problems are there for a researcher who compares a class contacting 'key pals' (by analogy to 'pen pals') using email (or the real-time system 'MOO'; see below) to a conventional letter-writing class with the longer time scales of conventional post? Warschauer (1996a) attempts to avoid this by comparing informal on-line writing with face-to-face class discussion.

Another area of interest is comparing computer use with other technologies, e.g. computer-based listening activities and audio-taped language materials in a 'traditional' (one student, one machine) language lab (Thornton and Dudley 1997). In the audio lab, students spent 50 per cent more time off task because of the necessity of physically rewinding and locating tape segments. In contrast, computer-assisted students spent less time replaying items because they could guess at answers and receive immediate feedback. They were often satisfied with the feedback, and did not re-listen. Interestingly, both student groups scored about the same on the post-test, with no statistically significant difference (p. 33).

LINGUISTIC ANALYSES AND SKILLS ACQUISITION

Researchers have examined how computers enhance the instructed acquisition, e.g., pronunciation (Eskenazi 1999), grammatical structures (Collentine 2000) and lexical items (Laufer and Hill 2000). Broader skills areas are also receiving attention; e.g. Chun and Plass (1997) examine reading comprehension skills, Negretti (1999) uses conversational analysis in web-based activities, and Sullivan (1998) explores the connections among reading, writing, speaking and critical thinking.

There are positive learning effects of teaching composition with word processing: students write more and can make global revisions. Since the 1980s word processors have been taken for granted in many academic settings with little research undertaken in comparing, e.g., composition revision processes in paper-and-pencil versus computerised classes (for a summary, see Pennington and Brock 1992; Sullivan and Pratt 1996).

Holliday (1993, 1995, 1998, 1999) has examined a large corpus of student email from the *SL-Lists* (international EFL/ESL email student discussion lists; see www.kyoto-su.ac.jp/~trobb/ slinfo.html), comparing it with personal letters and telephone conversations. He has established that electronic communication provides a range and distributive frequency of linguistic features comparable to other genres of writing and speaking. He suggests that the repetitive nature of email, in which writers quote and comment on each other's messages, assists learners in understanding linguistic cues. See also Peyton (2000) who describes a similar experience (called 'language scaffolding') with elementary-school-age deaf children.

THE COMPUTER AS RESEARCH TOOL

Recent studies indicate a growing trend towards using the computer as primary research tool, either to elicit data (e.g. Holliday, above) or to record data indirectly. For example, Liou (1995) reports on using computers to record interactive processes. Wright (1998) is studying the effect that playing simulations has on L2 development. Ehsani and Knodt (1998) explore various speech technologies that might assist in oral language research. Murphy-Judy (1998) includes articles on pronunciation and on-line writing. Hulstijn (2000) provides an excellent summary of computer-elicited data collection techniques and how computerised tools record learner production. With a medium that can record each keystroke, compare huge text corpora and create audio and video files with easy-to-manage technology, researchers should find many new data sources to investigate language acquisition. Chapelle (2001) provides a useful overview of CALL and second language acquisition.

MOTIVATION

From early on, as teachers observed the intensity of student computer use, motivation has been a pervasive theme in CALL, and qualitative studies on attitudes towards computer use quickly emerged (e.g. Phinney 1991), sometimes focusing on 'computer phobia'. However, most reports – based on attitudinal surveys, student portfolios and self-reporting – indicate that students and teachers, with few exceptions, are highly motivated when using computers (Beauvois 1998; Jaeglin 1998).

Many empirical studies also contain qualitative elements. For example, Jakobsdottir and Hooper (1995) found that when computers 'read' a text aloud, learners' listening skills and motivation improve. Soo (1999) links motivation and CALL learning styles: if a teaching style does not match students' learning styles to some degree, instruction may be perceived as boring or incomprehensible, and students are less motivated. Motivation is an area that deserves close study. Cultural and ethnographic issues are aspects which may affect motivation (see Cummins and Sayers 1995; Sullivan 1998; Warschauer 1999). For suggestions of new areas for CALL research, see Chapelle (1997) and Ortega (1997); for a follow-up discussion of Chapelle (1997), see Salaberry (1999).

Practice

DRILL, GRILL AND COMPUTER-ADAPTIVE TESTS

A description of best practices in CALL must include an understanding of how typical classroom activities can be enhanced electronically. Taking the most basic example, as a tool for drill and practice in the four skills (reading, speaking, writing and listening), grammar and vocabulary, the computer has repeatedly demonstrated its usefulness as a patient and obedient taskmaster. Instant feedback to students can be provided for every answer, correct or incorrect. Some instructors teach themselves enough about electronic authoring to create their own tailored interactive drills and tests, either software- or internet-based.

Some sophisticated programs respond to student answers by increasing or decreasing the difficulty of subsequent questions or exercises; this is the basic strategy of computer-adaptive tests (CAT; also called computer-based testing, CBT), such as the computerised TOEFL (Test of English as a Foreign Language; see also Dunkel 1999). Some programs also allow students to proceed as fast as desired through a curriculum roughly tailored to their individual strengths and weaknesses. However, the transfer of knowledge and skills through an instructional delivery system – even with its advantages over a human teacher – does not always match the needs of the language learner, who must ultimately interact, negotiate meaning and communicate with others in various output modes and for various purposes well beyond the acquisition of specific facts.

The four skills, grammar and vocabulary

Besides infinite patience and immediate feedback, tutorial and drill on the computer can provide more than a teacher in the classroom; for example, in the following areas:

Phonetics and phonology

An application such as Pronunciation Power allows the student to see a video of native-speaker facial movements without embarrassing stares, to watch an animated sagittal section demonstrating articulatory organs that are otherwise hidden and to view voice wave forms which plot the student's own recorded speech against a target native model. The activities may be repeated without re-winding a tape or requesting the teacher to reiterate (see the Pronunication Power website at www.pronunciationpower.com/proddemo2.html for a downloadable demonstration of Pronunciation Power 2).

Speaking skills

Speech-recognition technology, although still far from perfect, allows students to control computer actions with speech input. Although accepting such a wide range of accents as to be useless for pronunciation correction, speech-recognition activities allow the shy student to speak up. Many programs, including Dynamic English (1997) and ELLIS (1998), use this technology. Newer technologies allowing, e.g. voice and video email, will no doubt play a role in the design of speaking activities in future.

Listening skills

Students may receive hours of listening input at the computer, with appropriate comprehension questions, easily controlled repetition and immediate playback. The main disadvantage is the lack of verbal interaction and negotiation of meaning, although this may change with newer technologies. On the internet students can self-access much authentic listening content; see, e.g., www.voa.gov (Voice of America) and www.bbc.co.uk/worldservice/ (BBC World Service). Many content CD-ROM and DVDs also provide audio files for the written texts, so that students may listen as they read, often a rare opportunity (particularly for adult learners) to hear the rhythms and accents of the language as written and spoken by native speakers. Real English, a CD-ROM series, incorporates input for beginners from over 850 videotaped interviews of native speakers from three continents (for a full description and ordering information for the program, see the Real English website, www.realenglish.tm.fr).

Reading skills

Although reading long passages on the computer screen is not recommended, reading skills programs can enhance reading speed by paced reading activities, where lines of text are scrolled with pre-determined timing; by automating the creation of cloze passages; by timing students' reading; and by creating jigsaw paragraphs or jumbled texts. Such activities are time consuming for the teacher to prepare manually. A demonstration of a Macintosh software program, NewReader (McVicker 1995), which performs all these tasks, may be obtained from its author.

Writing skill and composition

Perhaps one of the earliest computer technologies readily adapted by language teachers is the word processor. Computers can enhance all aspects of the writing process, allowing easy revision and multiple drafts, spell-checking (which can teach spelling by raising students' awareness levels); also, increasingly sophisticated translation suggestions and grammatical advice are available, which may be used with caution by advanced writers.

Grammar and vocabulary practice

Beyond naked drills and exercises, teachers find that grammar and vocabulary games can be very motivating for learners in twos or threes around one computer screen; e.g. Puzzlemaker (puzzlemaker.school.discovery.com) allows users to construct puzzles on line based on their own word lists.

Concordance programs

These are another means to vocabulary and grammar practice. The programs search a text for a word or phrase, presenting them with about 10 words of surrounding text. Students can view many examples of usage and compare them to their own writing without having to search manually through many pages of text. Concordance software is often published with sets of text specifically designed for classroom use. Mills and Salzmann (1998) have developed what is in effect an on-line concordancer, Grammar Safari (http://deil.lang.uiuc.edu/web.pages/grammarsafar-i.html), which helps students use search engines to find typical collocations and grammatical or rhetorical items on the internet (see also Mills 2000).

AUTHENTICITY, TASKS, CONTENT AND STRATEGIES

Most current practitioners of CALL stress the importance of authentic language and audience; here the computer aids by allowing language learners to communicate with native speakers around the world over the internet. Organised exchanges allow classes to communicate in a safe, guided atmosphere; e.g. Sayer's *Orillas* project for K-12 (Cummins and Sayers 1995; see also http://orillas.upr.clu.edu) and Vilmi's *HUT Internet Writing Project* for university exchanges (www.hut.fi/~rvilmi/Project).

For the more advanced independent learner, many poetry and fiction writers, movie stars and rock bands have websites that encourage fans to post writings and respond to others' work. Because bulletin board software is readily and cheaply available and easy to use, many individual teachers' websites include an opportunity for free-form writing. For teachers wanting to explore ideas for the internet, the collection of lesson plans in Boswood (1999) is a good place to begin learning about how to use email and distance communication effectively (see also Chapter 30).

A more elaborate opportunity for using authentic language is the multi-user object-oriented (MOO) environment, where students enter a virtual reality; see, e.g., schMOOze University

(Falsetti 1998); see also Falsetti and Schweitzer (1995). Students may play language games at the Student Union, and claim and decorate their own dorm room; teachers may schedule a classroom in which to meet and conduct an on-line lesson. Diversity University at Marist College (www.du.org) is one of the first sites designed specifically for classroom distance learning through a MOO environment enhanced by three-dimensional virtual-reality software.

Another highly motivating use of technology are multimedia projects using presentation software such as Microsoft PowerPoint or HyperStudio (for a demonstration of the latter, see wwww.hyperstudio.com). These powerful but simple-to-use programs provide writing and drawing tools, and the means to create animations and insert photos, sound and video files. Projects using such tools form the basis of authentic tasks for ESL students of all ages. They are usually very successful, particularly when assigned as group tasks demanding a variety of skills and intra-group communication (see Hanson-Smith 1997a). Students learn an authentic work skill while exploring topics relevant to themselves. Most authoring software allows projects to be converted into web pages; for examples of web projects, see Gaer (2000) and Robb (2000). For teachers interested in starting student email projects, see Warschauer (1995b).

Rather than studying the language in isolation, an important trend in TESOL is the use of content to build language skills. As content resources, both software and the internet provide much data which students may explore in various modes.

An extremely wide range of content is available on the internet for adaptation to language lessons. Most large organisations now have websites which provide visitors with a wealth of information to exploit: many major museums, for example, even provide ready-made teaching materials and on-line lessons which may be adapted for language learners (see, e.g. The British Museum at www.british-museum.ac.uk and The Smithsonian Institution at www.tsi.org). Ideas can be gleaned from almost any site, e.g. those of TV channels, newspapers, meteorological offices, stock-market traders, fiction writers, medical societies and film makers. Students can be encouraged to post opinions about controversial events, research statistics, participate in live chat or write fan mail. (See also Chapter 30.)

A vast body of knowledge is made available by the enormous storage capacity of CD-ROM, DVD and the internet. While the variety of media (e.g. video, sound, animation, text, graphics) appeals to a wide range of learning and teaching styles, organising the plethora of data is a significant task, especially for students just beginning to learn a language. As internet access expands and learners seek sites that match their personal interests, teachers will need increasingly to help them structure their learning to best take advantage of these language resources. One model program in this area is the Division of English as an International Language (DEIL) LinguaCenter at the University of Illinois (http://deil.lang.uiuc.edu/), which has organised classes around resources on the internet (Mills 2000). Another is the Oregon State University English Language Institute, which uses a self-access lab, individualised learning and teachers trained to give highly personalised guidance to technological resources (Averill *et al.* 2000).

Current and future trends and directions

Until recently technology has driven pedagogy, at first because of its limitations and now because of the increasing availability and speed of computers and the expansion of the internet as a multimedia tool. The cost of computers and connectivity may be the chief limiting factor in what computer-enhanced teaching can achieve. The move from wired to wireless communications and the consolidation of telecommunications into combined telephone–internet–television access will not drive pedagogy in quite the same way as the move to personal computers has done. In some parts of the world it is now theoretically possible to connect every student to on-line education and information through wireless services. Eventually, as miniaturisation progresses, audio and monitor may be embedded in eyeglasses and a voice-controlled computer strapped into a backpack for communication anywhere, anytime. However, advanced technologies increase disparities – at least in the short term – between technology-rich and technology-poor schools, countries and students. Increasingly, a fear that technology may replace teachers is being displaced by the desire to offer all learners access to the information systems that run the world economy. Where technology is deployed to its best advantage, we should see teachers' roles become that of guide and mentor, encouraging students to take charge of their own learning, helping them to learn at their own pace.

Key readings

Boswood (1999) *New Ways of Using Computers in Language Teaching*
Chapelle (2001) *Computer Applications in Second Language Acquisition*
Crookall and Oxford (1990) *Simulation, Gaming, and Language Learning*
Cummins and Sayers (1995) *Challenging Cultural Illiteracy through Global Learning Networks*
Egbert and Hanson-Smith (1999) *CALL Environments*
Hanson-Smith (2000) *Technology-Enhanced Learning Environments*
Language Learning and Technology (On-line journal available at http://llt.msu.edu/)
Pfaff-Harris (2000) *The Linguistic Funland!*
Warschauer (1995b) *On-line Activities and Projects for Networking Language Learners*

CHAPTER 16

Observation

Kathleen M. Bailey

Introduction

Observation, as the term is used here, refers to the purposeful examination of teaching and/or learning events through systematic processes of data collection and analysis. Such events may occur in untutored environments (see Chapter 12) or in formal instructional settings. This chapter focuses on observation in language classroom environments. (See also Nunan 1992: 91–114.)

In language teaching and applied linguistics, classroom observation has historically served four broad functions. First, pre-service teachers are often observed in the practicum context by teacher educators, who typically give them advice on the development of their teaching skills as a regular part of pre-service training programmes (Day 1990). Second, practising teachers are observed either by novice teachers or by colleagues, for the professional development purposes of the observer. Third, practising teachers are observed by supervisors, course co-ordinators, department heads, principals or headteachers, in order to judge the extent to which the teachers adhere to the administration's expectations for teaching methods, curricular coverage, class control, etc. Fourth, observation is widely used as a means of collecting data in classroom research.

In each of the four contexts outlined above, teachers and learners have often been observed by outsiders. Recently, however, teachers themselves have undertaken classroom observation for a variety of reasons. These include peer observation for professional development purposes (Rorschach and Whitney 1986; Richards and Lockhart 1991–92), peer coaching (Joyce and Showers 1982, 1987; Showers 1985; Showers and Joyce 1996) and action research (Kemmis and McTaggart 1988; Mingucci 1999).

Background

Observation in second and foreign language classrooms has been strongly influenced by the traditions of observation in first language (L1) classrooms in general education settings. Concerns that unstructured observation (whether for supervision or teacher education purposes) could be subjective or biased led to the development of 'objective' coding systems, called **observation schedules**, which were used to document observable behaviours in classrooms, either as they occurred ('real-time coding') or with electronically recorded data.

One of the early influential observation systems was Flanders' (1970) 'interaction analysis' instrument. Flanders' system focused primarily on teacher behaviours, and involved tallying instances of 'indirect influence' (accepts feelings, praises or encourages, accepts or uses ideas of students, and asks questions) and 'direct influence' (lecturing, giving directions, and criticising or justifying authority). Student talk was categorised simply as response or initiation. There was also a category for silence or confusion.

Moskowitz (1967, 1971) adapted Flanders' system for use in foreign language education. Her adaptation was called 'FLint' (for 'foreign language interaction') and included categories for using English (assumed to be the learners' L1) as opposed to the target language, as well as for teaching behaviours related to contemporary language pedagogy (such as the teacher directing pattern drills, or the students giving a choral response). Moskowitz used the FLint system to conduct comparative research on the behaviour of outstanding versus typical teachers (1976), in teacher training (1968) and in working with teacher supervisors (1971).

Another influential observation instrument is Fanselow's (1977) 'FOCUS' (foci for observing communications used in settings). Fanselow designed his system by starting with Bellack's four-part structure of classroom talk (see, e.g., Bellack *et al.* 1966). Bellack and his colleagues found that much classroom talk followed a pattern of structure, solicit, respond and react, and that only the third move – respond – was typically carried out by pupils. So, e.g., in traditional teacher-fronted teaching one encounters many examples of interaction such as the following:

T: [structure:] Okay, everyone, today we are going to continue working on negative numbers. Let's just review a bit here. [solicit:] Fred, what happens if you multiply two negative numbers?

S: [respond:] You get a positive.

T: [react:] That's right. Fred's wide awake this morning. You get a positive number.

In addition to these four basic pedagogical moves, Fanselow's observation schedule includes categories for who is communicating, the mediums used, how content areas are communicated and what areas of content are being communicated. Fanselow labels these categories source, pedagogical purpose (i.e. Bellack's four moves), mediums, uses and content.

Observation schedules such as FLint and FOCUS can be used for 'real-time coding' during classroom observations, but some of them can also be used to analyse transcripts, audio recordings or videotapes of lessons. Copies of several such instruments can be found in the original sources cited above and in the appendices to Allwright and Bailey (1991). A very interesting resource is Allwright's (1988) *Observation in the Language Classroom*, which provides a historical overview of the uses of observation in language teaching. It includes both the observation instruments and extensive excerpts of text from the authors' original articles.

The historical development of second language (L2) classroom observation is not limited to the use of observation instruments, and it has not been without problems. Teachers (and perhaps learners) have sometimes felt like objects being observed without input or consultation, whose behaviour and key decisions were reduced to tally marks on a page by observers who might or might not understand the day-to-day workings of the language classroom. As a result, a tension emerged in some areas between the observer and the observed.

Research

As language classroom research developed in the 1970s, many researchers began to feel that the existing instruments were inadequate for evolving research purposes. (For a discussion of problems with such instruments, see Chaudron 1988.) Changes in linguistics and language pedagogy also contributed to new developments in observation practices. Two trends emerged as a result.

The first trend was that new instruments were developed for specific research purposes as a result of developments in linguistics and pedagogy. For instance, Long *et al.* (1976) developed the Embryonic Category System, which was based on speech acts (e.g. student analyses, student classifies, student negates, etc.). Transcribed utterances were categorised under the main headings of pedagogical moves, social skills and rhetorical acts. Long *et al.* used this system to code transcripts of learner speech in two situations: large-group discussions with a teacher and dyadic interactions between two students on the same topic. The authors found that the language learners working in pairs not only talked more in the target language but also performed a wider range of communicative functions than did their classmates interacting with the teacher in the 'lock-step' condition. For a copy of the Embryonic Category System, see Long *et al.* (1976: 144–145) or Allwright and Bailey (1991: 213). Examples of coded data transcribed from recorded lessons is also provided by Long *et al.* (1976: 146–147).

'COLT' ('Communicative Orientation of Language Teaching'; Allen *et al.* 1984) is an example of an observational instrument which was developed as a result of changes in language pedagogy. COLT's categories reflect developments in communicative language teaching (CLT), such as the use of information gap activities. The data yielded by COLT both describe classroom activities and analyse the features of the communication between teachers and students. For a copy of the COLT system, see Allen *et al.* (1984: 251–252) or Allwright and Bailey (1991: 216–219).

A different direction in the emergence of new observation procedures was the development of discourse analysis as a viable subfield in linguistics. Discourse analysis examines both written and spoken texts, so discourse analytic procedures can be brought to bear on classroom speech as a data base. Sinclair and Coulthard (1975), working with transcribed recordings of L1 classrooms in England, developed a system which was subsequently used by language researchers to analyse transcripts from L2 classrooms. The discourse analytic approach to observation spurred by Sinclair and Coulthard typically yielded a finer grained analysis than did the earlier coding systems. For a copy of this system, see Sinclair and Coulthard (1975: 25–27) or Allwright and Bailey (1991: 214–215); Sinclair and Coulthard (1975: 61–111) also provide examples of coded classroom data.

Practice

Freeman (1982) has described three approaches to observing teachers for the purposes of in-service training and professional development. He calls these (1) the 'supervisory approach,' (2) the 'alternatives approach,' and (3) the 'non-directive approach', and relates them to a hierarchy of needs that evolve across a teacher's professional lifetime. These three approaches are distinguished, primarily by the type of feedback the observer gives the teacher rather than how the observations themselves are conducted.

Regardless of the context, one of the problems associated with classroom observations is what Labov (1972b) has called 'the observer's paradox', i.e. by observing people's behaviour we often alter the very behavioural patterns we wish to observe. There are some steps which can be taken to overcome this paradox. For instance, when observing teachers and learners in language class-rooms, it is a good idea to explain the purpose of the observation in general terms. If the learners don't know why an observer is present, they often assume that they and their teacher are being observed for supervisory purposes. This assumption may cause them to either act out or be better behaved than usual!

Also, when using an obtrusive form of data collection, such as a video camera, it can be helpful to familiarise the learners with the equipment. It's also useful to visit the classroom often enough over time that the teacher and the students become desensitised to the presence of the observer and the recording device.

Related to the issue of the observer's paradox is the extent to which the observer participates in the activities being observed. There is a range of possible involvement, from being a non-participant observer to being a full participant observer (see Spradley 1980). In its purest form, participant observation is conducted by someone who is a member of the group under investigation (e.g. the teacher or a student in the classroom). Of course, a visitor observing a lesson can also participate in group work or do the exercises as well.

Another issue is the extent to which observations are conducted overtly or covertly. The assumption underlying covert observations is that if people don't know they are being observed they will behave more naturally. Some schools of education build special observation classrooms with one-way mirrors so that students and teachers can be observed unawares. Some language learners and teachers have kept daily journals as a means of recording their observations, without the other members of the class knowing that data were being collected. Normally, however, in the resulting data, people would be identified only by pseudonyms, and it is generally considered bad form (and is illegal in some places) to tape-record or video-record people's behaviour without asking their permission.

Lately teachers themselves have been utilising classroom observation procedures for their own purposes. These include peer observation for professional development (see, e.g., Rorschach and Whitney 1986) or a more formalised and reciprocal system of peer coaching (Joyce and Showers 1982, 1987; Showers 1985; Showers and Joyce 1996). In peer coaching teachers engage in ongoing reciprocal class observations in which the coaching partners themselves determine the focus for the observation. (For a variety of observation tasks which teachers can utilise, see Wajnryb 1993.)

Teachers also utilise classroom observation procedures to conduct action research (see, e.g., Mingucci 1999). Action research entails an iterative cycle of planning, acting, observing and reflecting (Kemmis and McTaggart 1988). The observation phases can include all the data collection procedures described above, but in this approach they are typically under the teacher's control. Audio- and video-recording and teachers' journals are among the most frequently used forms of data collection in action-research observations.

Current and future trends and directions

As the accessibility of affordable audio and video recorders has increased, the use of transcripts from such recordings has become much more common in classroom research. Very few researchers collect primary data with only 'real-time' coding these days, although many instruments originally designed for real-time coding can be used in the analysis of recordings and the resulting transcripts. Whether transcripts are subjected to coding with an observation schedule or a fine-grained discourse analysis is largely a question of the researcher's purpose.

Producing the original transcript, however, can be a very time-consuming and tedious process. Allwright and Bailey (1991: 62) report that it often takes up to 20 hours of transcription time to produce an accurate and complete transcript of a one-hour language lesson. Depending on what one wishes to observe, transcripts can be simple orthographic renditions of speech or highly detailed linguistic representations which indicate in-breaths, pauses in micro-seconds, hesitations, overlaps, stutter-starts, hesitations and phonetic renderings of utterances. One set of suggested transcription conventions can be found in Allwright and Bailey (1991: 222–223), and van Lier (1988) offers a helpful appendix about transcription in classroom research. For a more detailed treatment of transcription and coding, see the anthology edited by Edwards and Lampert (1993).

In recent years, as introspective and retrospective data have gained wider acceptability (Færch and Kasper 1987), teachers' and language learners' journals documenting classroom events have provided a different sort of observational data for classroom research. (For an analysis of several language teachers' journals, see Bailey 1990.) In some cases, such journal records are used in conjunction with other forms of observational data. For instance, Block (1996) used a combination of students' oral diary entries, the teacher's journal and tape recordings of classes in Spain in his report of teachers' and learners' differing perspectives on classroom events.

The use of multiple data sets (as in Block's study) is an example of what is called **triangulation**, a concept borrowed by anthropologists as a metaphor from land surveying and navigation. The idea is that one can get a better fix on a distant point by measuring it from two different starting points (hence the image of the triangle). In anthropological research, triangulation refers to processes of verification which give us confidence in our observations. Denzin (1970) describes four different types of triangulation (see also van Lier 1988: 13):

- data triangulation, in which different sources of data (teachers, students, parents, etc.) contribute to an investigation;

- theory triangulation, when various theories are brought to bear in a study;

- researcher triangulation, in which more than one researcher contributes to the investigation; and

- methods triangulation, which entails the use of multiple methods (e.g. interviews, questionnaires, observation schedules, test scores, field notes, etc.) to collect data.

Triangulation provides a means for researchers working with non-quantified data to check on their interpretations by providing enhanced credibility through the incorporation of multiple points of view and/or various data sets.

The recent emphasis on transcription is partly due to the fact that, although classroom observation can be guided by the use of an observation schedule, researchers and teacher educators or supervisors often feel that the use of pre-established categories in such instruments – while contributing a clarity of focus – can also produce a sort of 'tunnel vision': the categories determine (and therefore limit or restrict) the kinds of observations one can make while watching a lesson. For this reason, some researchers prefer to take notes during an observation and to create a set of field notes documenting the interactions observed.

Observational field notes can be used either as the sole source of data or in tandem with electronically produced recordings. In classroom observation, the observer's field notes provide a running commentary on the events which occur in a lesson. The field notes must be carefully prepared and detailed enough to be clear and convincing. It is the observer's responsibility to recognise the difference between observations which are data based and his or her inferences (or even opinions). This is not to say that inferences or opinions need to be avoided entirely, but that they must be (1) recognised as inferences or opinions by the observer, (2) supported by verifiable observational data and (3) checked with the observee(s) whenever possible.

Field notes provide a human, interpretive dimension to observational data, which is often absent in videotapes, audiotapes or observation schedules. Well written field notes provide credible documentation of interactions and cases. See, e.g., Carrasco's (1981) description of 'Lupita', a child whom the teacher had viewed as passive or unintelligent until the observer's detailed description documented her interactive skills.

One of the difficulties in analysing field notes and transcripts is that some key issues that emerge may not be easily quantifiable, so a content analysis (or other kinds of qualitative analyses) may be needed to reveal the patterns in the data. Future directions will include the use of computer programs for analysing transcripts and observers' field notes about classroom interaction. Some such programs are already available (see Weitzman and Miles 1995). They work essentially as automatic indexing systems which search for key words and phrases that have been identified by the researcher.

Conclusion

Whether classroom observation is used for teacher education, supervision, teacher development or research, there are now numerous instruments and codified procedures for working with observational data. In addition, in action research, peer observation and peer coaching, teachers themselves use a variety of procedures for observing classroom interaction, and analysing the data collected during observations.

Key readings

Allwright (1988) *Observation in the Language Classroom*
Allwright and Bailey (1991) *Focus on the Language Classroom*
Spradley (1980) *Participant Observation*
van Lier (1988) *The Classroom and the Language Learner*
Wajnryb (1993) *Classroom Observation Tasks*

CHAPTER 17

Classroom interaction

Amy B.M. Tsui

Introduction

The term **classroom interaction** refers to the interaction between the teacher and learners, and amongst the learners, in the classroom. Earlier studies of second language (L2) classroom interaction focused on the language used by the teacher and learners, the interaction generated, and their effect on L2 learning. More recent studies have begun to investigate the underlying factors which shape interaction in the classroom – e.g. teacher and learner beliefs, social and cultural background of the teacher and learners, and the psychological aspects of second and foreign language learning – providing further insights into the complexities of classroom interaction.

Background

L2 classroom interaction research began in the 1960s with the aim of evaluating the effectiveness of different methods in foreign language teaching in the hope that the findings would show the 'best' method and its characteristics. The methodology adopted was strongly influenced by first language (L1) classroom teaching research which was motivated by the need to assess objectively the teaching performance of student-teachers during practical teaching. Various classroom observation instruments have been proposed to capture the language used by the teacher and the interaction generated (see Chapter 16). These interaction analysis studies revealed that classroom processes are extremely complex and that a prescriptive approach to ascertain the 'best' method would be fundamentally flawed if the descriptive techniques are inadequate. Research efforts therefore turned to coping with problems of description (Allwright 1988), and the focus of classroom interaction studies shifted from prescriptive to descriptive and from evaluative to awareness-raising.

Descriptions of classroom interaction focused initially on the language used by the teacher, especially teacher questions and the learner responses elicited, teachers' feedback and turn-allocation behaviour. These features were examined in light of how they affected interaction and the opportunities for learners to engage in language production. Recent studies have paid more attention to learner talk, examining not only the language produced by learners in response to the teacher, but also their communication strategies, and the relation between task types, learner interaction and opportunities for negotiation of meaning.

The study of language and interaction in the classroom is not peculiar to L2 classrooms. In the 1960s, educationists in the UK emphasised the importance of 'language across the curriculum'

(Barnes 1969; Britton 1970). Research was conducted on the questions asked by the teacher and the types of pupil talk generated in various content subjects in L1 classrooms, including mathematics, science and humanities subjects. Comparisons were also made between talk at home and talk at school which showed that the latter was impoverished when compared with the former. Features of talk at home which helped children to learn how to mean were identified, such as care-taker speech, scaffolding, exploratory talk and collaborative construction of meaning. These findings have provided insights for L2 classroom interaction research.

For more than two decades, the focus of classroom interaction research – be it teacher or student talk – had been on what is observable; more recently researchers have begun to question analyses of classroom processes based only on the observable. It was felt that the 'unobservables' in the classroom – such as teachers' and learners' psychological states, including beliefs, attitudes, motivations, self perception and anxiety, learning styles and cultural norms – play an important part in shaping classroom interaction. Approaches to analysing classroom interaction also moved from solely an observer's perspective to include a participant's perspective and using a variety of sources of data apart from classroom discourse data.

Research

Research on the observable aspects of classroom interaction pertain to three main aspects: input, interaction and output. Input refers to the language used by the teacher, output refers to language produced by learners and interaction refers to the interrelationship between input and output with no assumption of a linear cause and effect relationship between the two (see van Lier 1996). Early studies focused on the input provided by the teacher, especially the phonological and syntactic features of teacher speech and teacher questions. These studies show that, in order to make their speech comprehensible to learners, teachers generally speak slower, use simpler syntactic structures, exaggerated pronunciation, clearer articulation, more repetitions and more basic vocabulary than when speaking to native speakers. Such modified speech, which contains features similar to 'care-taker speech', has been referred to as 'foreigner talk'. Investigations have been conducted on whether such modifications do in fact make the input more comprehensible to learners (for a summary of such studies, see Chaudron 1988). The findings were, however, inconclusive, leading researchers to question whether the modification of input by the teacher alone is sufficient to make the input comprehensible, and whether they ought to examine the interaction between the teacher and learners.

Studies of the interaction between the native speaker (NS) and the non-native speakers (NNS) showed that when the input provided by the NS is incomprehensible to the NNS, they enter into a negotiation of meaning in which the NNS asks for clarification, repetition or confirmation, resulting in a modification of the structure of interaction. Drawing on these findings, researchers argue that this kind of negotiation provides optimal comprehensible input to the learner and, hence, facilitates L2 development (see Long 1983b). The following is an example of how a question–answer structure may be modified in the process of negotiation.

1. *T*: . . . what other advantages do you think you may have, if you were the only child in the family? (question)
   S: I'm sorry. I beg your pardon. (request for repetition)
   T: Er, if you were the only child in your family, then what other advantages you may have? What points, what other good points you may have? (modified repetition) (followed by lexical modification)
   S: It's quieter for my study. (answer)
   T: Yes? It's quieter for you to study. Yes? Any other? (confirmation check)
   S: No more. (confirmation)
   T: OK. Fine. (acknowledgement)

   (Tsui 1995: 18)

Studies of interactional modifications have focused largely on the presence of modification devices to determine the amount of comprehensible input made available to learners (see, e.g., Varonis and Gass 1985). There is not, however, much empirical research on the relationship between different kinds of interaction and the rate of L2 development (R. Ellis 1988).

An important dimension of classroom interaction is teacher questions, which has received much attention in both L1 and L2 classroom studies. Barnes' (1969) influential study of L1 classrooms differentiates questions with only one acceptable answer ('closed' questions) and those with more than one answer ('open' questions); a further differentiation is questions to which the teacher has an answer ('display' or 'pseudo' questions) and those to which the teacher does not ('referential' or 'genuine' questions). A similar distinction has been made in L2 classroom studies to examine how these questions affect the types of responses elicited from learners (see Long and Sato 1983; Brock 1986). It was found that 'display' questions were predominant in teachers' interaction with learners, and that 'referential' questions were more conducive to the production of lengthier and more complex responses by learners. For example, in the following two excerpts of data from an L2 primary classroom, both questions asked by the teacher are 'what' questions, but the first one is a 'display' question which has only one correct answer, hence 'closed'. The second is a 'referential' question with no pre-determined answer, hence 'open'.

2. *T*: Last week we were reading 'Kee Knock Stan' [title of a story]. What is 'Kee Knock Stan'? Janice. (display question)
   P: I cannot understand.
   T: Yes. (Tsui 1995: 25: 2c)
3. *T*: What do you think the postman at the post office would do? (referential question)
   P: I think I would divide it if the letters are to Hong Kong or other places.
   T: Yes, I think that's a sensible way, right? Good. (Tsui 1995: 25: 2c)

When teachers fail to elicit any response from the learners, they often need to modify their questions. Long and Sato (1983) identified a number of modification devices used by teachers, including syntactic modifications (such as making the topic salient and decomposing complex structures) and semantic modifications (such as paraphrasing difficult words and disambiguation).

Besides teachers' questions, both turn-allocation by the teacher and turn-taking by learners contribute to learners' opportunities to participate in the interaction. Seliger (1977) investigated learners' turn-taking behaviours and their correlation with second language acquisition (SLA). He found that those who generated high levels of input by initiating and sustaining their turns (called High Input Generators, HIGs) outperformed those who generated low input by being passive and not taking turns unless called upon (called Low Input Generators, LIGs). He concluded that HIGs were better able to turn input into intake because they were testing more hypotheses about the target language and, hence, were more effective language learners (Seliger 1983). Seliger's findings were not, however, confirmed by subsequent studies. For example, Day (1984) and Slimani (1987) failed to find a positive correlation between learners' participation and their L2 achievement. Investigations have also been conducted on factors which could impinge on learners' turn-taking behaviour, such as language proficiency, learning styles and cultural norms (Schumann and Schumann 1977; Allwright 1980; Sato 1982).

The types of task in which learners engage and the number of participants in a task also affect learners' participation. Studies have been conducted on learners' participation in tasks involving pair work, group work and the whole class. It was found that compared to teacher-fronted interaction in whole class work, both pair work and group work provide more opportunities for learners to initiate and control the interaction, to produce a much larger variety of speech acts and to engage in the negotiation of meaning (see Long and Porter 1985; Pica and Doughty 1985, 1988; Doughty and Pica 1986; Johnson 1995). Hence, tasks involving a small number of participants is believed to facilitate better SLA.

Studies of task types and learners' participation investigated how task types affected the quantity and quality of negotiated interaction and learners' language output (see Pica *et al.* 1987). The findings show that two-way tasks which required information exchange in both directions for task completion involved more negotiation than one-way tasks with unidirectional information flow. Similarly, 'closed' tasks led to more negotiation of meaning, more conversational adjustment and more learner speech modifications towards the target language than 'open' tasks in which information exchange was less restrictive (Pica *et al.* 1989; Loschky and Bley-Vroman 1993; Plough and Gass 1993). It has been argued that learners' engagement in the negotiation of meaning facilitates SLA because it provides learners with the opportunity to obtain comprehensible input, to express concepts which are beyond their linguistic capability and to focus on the part of their utterance requiring modification (see Swain 1985; Gass 1988).

Closely related to learners' output is teacher's feedback on the output. Early studies took a simplistic view of teacher feedback as being either negative evaluation or positive reinforcement. More recent studies point out the need to re-consider the notion of 'errors' and to see teacher feedback as providing the scaffolding for learners as they formulate their hypotheses about the language (for a summary of studies conducted on error treatment, see Allwright and Bailey 1991).

The research summarised above focuses primarily on what is observable in the classroom. This focus leads to a partial understanding of classroom processes (see Allwright and Bailey 1991). For example, studies on learner participation focused on observable turns taken by learners as the sole indicator of participation; however, learners could participate by taking private turns or even mental turns which are unobservable (see Allwright 1980).

Current and future trends and directions

Current research on classroom interaction has begun to investigate unobservable aspects of classroom interaction. Observable interaction could be affected by a number of factors, e.g. individual learning styles: while some learn better by actively participating, others learn better by listening and internalising the input. Another factor is learners' psychological state: Horwitz *et al.* (1991) observe that learning a foreign language is a psychologically unsettling process, threatening learners' self-esteem as a competent communicator. To cope with this anxiety, many learners adopt the avoidance strategy of being reticent (see Tsui 1996b). In a study of over 400 secondary school learners in Hong Kong, Walker (1997) found that there is a close relationship between learners' oral participation, their foreign language learning anxiety and their self-esteem as a competent speaker of English.

Yet another factor is cultural norms: Studies of turn-taking behaviour of Asian students showed that their participation is strongly guided by what they believe to be proper classroom behaviour (Sato 1982; Johnson 1995; Tsui 1995). Apart from focusing on observables, most earlier studies were conducted from an observer's ('etic') rather than a participant's ('emic') perspective, and investigations of specific aspects of classroom interaction often failed to take into consideration the entire context of the situation in which the interaction occurred (see Tsui 1997).

Current research adopts an ethnographic approach which investigates classroom events from a participant's perspective, in naturalistic rather than experimental settings and in its entire, 'holistic' context (Hammersley 1990; Nunan 1996). Bailey and Nunan's (1996) collection of classroom studies used data collected from various sources, including teachers' journals, interviews, stimulated recalls and lesson plans, in addition to lesson recordings and transcripts to enable the researcher to analyse classroom events from the participants' perspective. Johnson (1995) includes learners' perception of classroom events as an important part of understanding classroom processes.

Until recently, L2 classroom research was drawing on insights largely from L1 and SLA research because of its focus on linguistic aspects of classroom interaction. However, it is becoming more apparent that dimensions like teacher knowledge, teacher beliefs, teacher thinking and decision-making are very important in understanding teacher behaviour. There is a rich body of research in teacher education which could be drawn upon to illuminate classroom processes. There is also a rich body of research on language and learning in L1 classrooms from which L2 classroom research could benefit (see, e.g., Wells 1986; Norman 1992). Current work on classroom research draws on insights and concepts from various disciplines, including teacher education, learning theory and social interaction theory in order to understand and account for the complex processes involved in classroom interaction (see, e.g., Richards and Lockhart 1994; Johnson 1995; Bailey and Nunan 1996; van Lier 1996).

Practice

A major concern of L2 teachers is how to generate rich and meaningful interaction in the classroom which will facilitate SLA. Many teachers find it difficult to engage students in interaction, especially in teacher-fronted settings. The research findings summarised above have a number of pedagogical implications. First, when students fail to respond to the teacher's question, it may be because the questions were too complex, inappropriately phrased or contained difficult vocabulary items. If the question is too complex, then the modifications should be 'comprehension-oriented', such as paraphrasing difficult words, simplifying syntax and making the main point salient. If it is inappropriately phrased, then the modifications should be 'response-oriented', such as rephrasing into several simple questions to which the students can respond more easily (see Tsui 1995: 56–64). One effective way is to ask teachers to video-tape their own lessons and examine questions which fail to elicit responses. For example, in an L2 lesson the teacher put on the board a newspaper headline 'Police to pursue crooked cabbies' and asked the students 'What *is* it? Never mind what it means but what *is* it?' When no response was forthcoming, he modified it as 'Where would you find this?' However, after 8.5 seconds there was still no response. Finally, he changed the question to 'How can you tell that that belongs in the newspaper?' (Tsui 1995: 60). In the post-observation discussion, the teacher said that he was not sure why his subsequent modification did not work. Upon examining the possible interpretations of the modified question, it became clear to him that the question could mean 'Where would one find police pursuing crooked cabbies?' or 'Where would this line appear?' The discussion helped to raise the teacher's awareness of the importance of introspecting on his own use of language rather than just blaming the students for being passive.

It is also very useful to examine instances of successful modification of questions and discuss why they are successful. For example, in a primary L2 classroom, the teacher read out a sentence describing a dog. She said 'So that's a very good descriptive sentence. It tells you exactly what the dog looks like. Can you picture the dog?' The teacher realised that the use of the word 'picture' might be a bit beyond the pupils' ability level. Therefore, she modified the question to 'If I were to ask you to draw the dog, would you be able to draw the dog?' As a result of her lexical modification, the students immediately responded in chorus by saying 'yes, yes' (see Tsui 1995: 58).

Not giving enough wait-time for learners to process a question and formulate an answer is another reason for the lack of response from students. Many teachers fear that lengthy wait-time slows down the pace of teaching and leads to disruption in the classroom, or that they might appear to be inefficient and incompetent (see Rowe 1969; White and Lightbown 1984; Tsui 1996b). Therefore they often answer their own questions. Holley and King (1974) found that if the teacher allowed longer wait-time after a learner made a mistake or after the teacher posed a question, the learner was much better able to respond correctly. This does not mean that lengthening wait-time necessarily improves students' responsiveness. In a study of teachers' action research, it was found that excessive lengthening of wait-time exacerbated anxiety amongst students. To alleviate L2 learning anxiety, from which many L2 learners suffer, the teacher can provide opportunities for learners to rehearse their responses to a teacher's question by comparing notes with their partners or group members, or writing down their responses before presenting them to the rest of the class (see Tsui 1996b).

The way a teacher allocates turns in the classroom can also affect students' classroom interaction. In classrooms where interaction is highly controlled by the teacher, as in many Asian classrooms, patterns of turn-allocation is an important factor. In a study of his own turn-allocation behaviour by recording the number of turns he allocated to which learner, a teacher found that, contrary to his perception of himself as allocating turns evenly, he frequently allocated turns to the same learners. On reflection, he realised that these learners were those who could usually answer correctly, and that he subconsciously turned to these learners whenever he wanted to progress quickly. To ensure more even turn-allocation, he kept a class list and put a tick against a student whenever he allocated him or her a turn (see Tsui 1993).

The above pedagogical practices to improve classroom interaction must be implemented with the teacher's awareness of L2 learning as a psychologically unsettling and potentially face-threatening experience which can generate debilitating anxiety. The teacher needs to be sensitive to the psychological state of the students and to be supportive and appreciative of any effort made by the students to learn the target language. Only then will the teacher be able to generate the kind of classroom interaction which will facilitate meaningful and enjoyable learning.

Conclusion

Classroom interaction research started off with the aim of investigating the effectiveness of teaching methodologies and the behaviours of effective teachers. Such investigations revealed that classroom processes are extremely complex and the research focus soon shifted from prescription to description, from evaluation to awareness-raising. For a long time, research consisted of largely quantitative studies focusing on observable and linguistic aspects of interaction conducted from an observer's perspective. Recently there has been an increase in classroom interaction research adopting an ethnographic approach. While such studies yielded interesting insights lacking in experimental and quantitative studies, it should be noted that the two approaches are not mutually exclusive paradigms (Tsui 1995). As Hammersley (1986) points out, a good understanding of classroom interaction would require both quantitative and qualitative studies. Classroom interaction studies have benefited and will continue to benefit from an open-minded attitude to an eclectic combination of research methods as well as to insights from a number of disciplines.

Key readings

Allwright and Bailey (1991) *Focus on the Language Classroom*
Bailey and Nunan (1996) *Voices from the Language Classroom*
Chaudron (1988) *Second Language Classrooms*
R. Ellis (1988) *Classroom Second Language Development*
Hammersley (1990) *Classroom Ethnography*
Johnson (1995) *Understanding Communication in Second Language Classrooms*

CHAPTER 18

English for academic purposes

Liz Hamp-Lyons

Introduction

Over the past 25 years TESL/TEFL in universities/colleges and other academic settings – or in programmes designed to prepare non-native users of English for English-medium academic settings – has grown into a multi-million-dollar enterprise around the world. Teaching those who are using English for their studies differs from teaching English to those who are learning for general purposes only, and from teaching those who are learning for occupational purposes.

English for academic purposes (EAP) is not only a teaching approach. It is also a branch of applied linguistics consisting of a significant body of research into effective teaching and assessment approaches, methods of analysis of the academic language needs of students, analysis of the linguistic and discoursal structures of academic texts, and analysis of the textual practices of academics.

Background

The practice of teaching EAP has been with us for a long time – wherever individual teachers of non-native students in academic contexts have taught with a view to the context rather than *only* to the language – but the term 'EAP' first came into general use through the British organisation SELMOUS (Special English Language Materials for Overseas University Students), which was formed in 1972. Although the organisation's first collection of papers from its annual meeting was titled *English for academic purposes* (Cowie and Heaton 1977), it didn't change its name to include the term until 1989, when it became BALEAP (British Association of Lecturers in English for Academic Purposes). The field of EAP was first characterised within a larger perspective by Strevens (1977a). Strevens saw EAP as a branch of the larger field of **English for specific purposes** or **ESP** (which was known in its early days as 'English for special purposes'). He described, first, a move away from an emphasis on the literature and culture of English speakers and towards teaching for practical command of the language; and, second, a move towards a view that the teaching of the language should be matched to the needs and purposes of the language learner.

EAP is an educational approach and a set of beliefs about TESOL that is unlike that taken in general English courses and textbooks. It begins with the learner and the situation, whereas general English begins with the language. Many EAP courses/programmes place more focus on reading and writing, while most general English courses place more focus on speaking and listening. General English courses tend to teach learners conversational and social genres of the language, while EAP courses tend to teach formal, academic genres.

In discussing ESP and EAP, Strevens (1977b) argued that courses can be specific in four ways:

1. by restricting the language taught to only those skills which are required for the learner's immediate purposes;

2. by selecting from the whole language only those items of vocabulary, grammar patterns, linguistic functions, etc., which are required for the learner's immediate purposes;

3. by including only topics, themes and discourse contexts that are directly relevant to the learner's immediate language needs; and

4. by addressing only those communicative needs that relate to the learner's immediate purpose.

It can be seen that when all four kinds of specificity are applied to a course, the result is something quite restricted; this restriction resulted in some dissatisfaction with early approaches to ESP. EAP, on the other hand, has generally managed to escape these problems because the academic context has proved able to provide subject matter that is sufficiently specific and relevant to satisfy learners' needs but also sufficiently general to be applicable across a fairly wide range of contexts. It also offers subject matter that can satisfy some of the broader educational and social aims that learners and teachers bring to the education process. Jordan (1997) offers a useful and comprehensive overview of practice in EAP.

Needs analysis is fundamental to an EAP approach to course design and teaching. If a general approach to an EAP course is taken, the course usually consists primarily of study skills practice (e.g. listening to lectures, seminar skills, academic writing, reading and note-taking, etc.) with an academic register and style in the practice texts and materials. If a needs analysis indicates that the study situation is more specific, many of the same areas of study skills are still taught, but with particular attention to the language used in the specific disciplinary context identified in the needs analysis. The language is attended to at the levels of:

- register: lexical and grammatical/structural features (the best-known work is Ewer and Latorre 1969);

- discourse: the effect of communicative context; the relationship between the text/discourse and its speakers/writers/hearers/readers. See the *Nucleus* series (Bates and Dudley-Evans (eds) 1976–85); see also the *English in Focus* series (Widdowson 1974–(1980)); see also Chapter 7; and

- genre: how language is used in a particular setting, such as research papers, dissertations, formal lectures (the work of Swales has been most influential here; see also Chapter 27).

Needs analysis leads to the specification of objectives for a course or set of courses and to an assessment of the available resources and constraints to be borne in mind, which in turn lead to the syllabus(es) and methodology. The syllabus is implemented through teaching materials, and is then evaluated for effectiveness.

The development of the field of EAP has been rapid in the little more than 20 years since its recognition as a legitimate aspect of ELT. Nowadays it is accepted that TESL/TEFL to learners who are bound for or participating in formal education through the medium of English should include a component of study skills preparation. Even for those who have reached high educational levels in their own language, there are differences in study behaviours in the Anglo tradition, and these differences are becoming increasingly well understood through the research described below.

Research

As is the case in ESP (see Chapter 19), much of the EAP materials development described in the practice section below is underpinned by work in needs analysis. The most thorough EAP needs study was conducted by Weir for the development of the Associated Examining Board's TEAP (Test of English for academic purposes), and is summarised in Weir (1988). A good overview of needs analysis is provided by West (1994), and papers describing needs analyses in particular geographic and educational contexts frequently appear in the journal *English for Specific Purposes*. Jordan (1997: 29) sees four dimensions of needs: those of the target situation, of the employer or sponsor, of the student, and of the course designer and/or teacher. Research into EAP falls within one or more of these areas.

Analyses of the linguistic and discoursal structures of academic texts fall into the 'target situation' category. This work includes macro-level analyses such as studies on: the structure of theses (in particular Dudley-Evans 1991); text features such as hedging (e.g., K. Hyland 1994; Salager-Meyer 1994; Crompton 1997); and analyses of genres which are elements of 'texts', such as paper introductions (e.g. Dudley-Evans and Henderson 1990b) and results sections (e.g., Brett 1994). It also includes micro-level analyses, such as Master's work on the use of active verbs in scientific text (Master 1991).

The term 'texts' is used in the discourse analysis sense here, and EAP research includes studies of spoken texts and genres such as seminars (e.g. Furneaux *et al.* 1991; Prior 1991) and lectures (most notably Flowerdew 1994a). Studies of the textual practices of academics (e.g. Latour and Woolgar 1986; Myers 1990; Dudley-Evans 1993, 1994b) offer another interesting area that feeds into EAP practice and theory: by understanding what 'experts' do, novice academics can shape their own academic language towards those models.

Research into the academic language needs of students is more humanistic than research that looks at texts, genres and academic contexts; it incorporates a wider view of 'needs' and typically includes students 'wants' and preferences as well as more concrete needs. The first major study in this area was Geoghegan (1983), who interviewed non-native students at Cambridge University; this work made clear how students' perspectives can be compared to those of other stakeholders. Research in this area attends to affect, i.e. how students feel about their study experiences (e.g. Casanave 1990; Johns 1992); it also includes studies pointing out differences between students' wants and expectations and staff's expectations (e.g. Channell 1990; Thorp 1991; Grundy 1993). The related field of contrastive rhetoric combines the textual perspective and the student perspective, as it studies how students' academic work (usually written work) in English is affected by what they know about their own language (Kaplan 1966, 1988; Connor and Kaplan 1987; Connor 1996). Some work also queries the consequences for students when they have to accommodate too many of the conventions of English academic discourse practices, perhaps losing to an extent their sense of identity (Spack 1988; Fan Shen 1989). This work is linked to the field of 'critical language awareness' (Fairclough 1992; Ivanič 1998; Tang and John 1999).

Not surprisingly, there is a rich body of research into effective teaching approaches for EAP. EAP practitioners have concentrated on solving the problems closest to home, since EAP is a field firmly grounded in practical needs. The largest and most prolific field is academic writing (e.g. Robinson 1988a; Kroll 1990; Belcher and Braine 1995; Kaplan and Grabe 1996), particularly in the US, but there is also significant work in academic listening (in particular Anderson and Lynch 1988; Flowerdew 1994a), academic reading (principally in the journal *Reading in a Foreign Language*; see also *TESOL Quarterly* and *System*); academic speaking has been mainly ignored (but see McKenna 1987). Swales and Feak (1994) reveal the symbiotic relationship between research and practice in their important research-based textbook, *Academic Writing for Graduate Students*. Other research into advanced research writing includes Sionis (1995) and Bunton (1999). A growing area of research concerns the dissertation student–supervisor relationship and its effectiveness (Belcher 1994; Dong 1998).

There is also significant research into the assessment of EAP. This began at the end of the 1970s with the development of the English Language Testing Service (ELTS) by the British Council under B.J. Carroll, and continued through the 1980s in the work of Weir for the Associated Examining Board on TEAP. As ELTS became the standard measure of English proficiency for non-native speaker applicants to UK and Australian universities, a major validation study (Criper and Davies 1988) was conducted and was followed by a full research and development project (Clapham and Alderson 1996) culminating in the introduction of the IELTS (International English Language Testing Service) in 1989. The major EAP assessment in the US is the Michigan English Language Institute's Academic English Test, which is used almost entirely internally. (For further discussion of assessment and evaluation issues, see Chapters 20 and 21.)

Practice

A main activity of specialists in EAP is materials design and development. In-house materials can be specific to the study context of the students, and can be designed to suit pre-study classes where all the practice materials must be built into the course text, or to concurrent courses where the materials can be closely linked to the teaching going on in a subject class. Published materials, on the other hand, are inevitably fairly general. The fundamental similarities between study demands at the same educational level can be capitalised on in creating materials intended to provide basic preparation for good study habits. Among the earliest books in this area were *Study Skills in English* (Wallace 1980), *Panorama* (Williams 1982) and *Strengthen Your Study Skills* (Salimbene 1985). EAP courses also typically focus attention on the language skills separately: the 'rules' and strategies of academic skills are not like those of the general language skills, and this is acknowledged in books such as *Study Listening* (Lynch 1983), *Study Writing* (Hamp-Lyons and Heasley 1987) and *Study Reading* (Glendinning and Holmstrom 1992). Some of the books in the Cambridge University Press study skills series are a decade old now, but are still popularly used in many countries.

One of the aspects of EAP that attracts the best English language teachers is the potential for developing one's own material based on needs analysis of the immediate situation. In fact, all the textbooks mentioned in this section began as in-house materials and were later polished into textbooks; this is also true of Swales and Feak (1994). In-house materials have the great strength of responding directly to the local needs; however, the more specific materials are to a situation, the less likely it is that they will be published as textbooks for economic reasons.

In the USA a concern with literacy dominates the literature and the terminology of academic skills development (see, e.g., DiPardo 1993; Johns 1997). Readers can usefully refer to the journal *College Composition and Communication*; for attention to the literacy skills of second language (L2) and second dialect users, readers can refer to journals such as *College ESL* and the *Journal of Basic Writing*. The work of John Swales and Ann Johns stands out as exceptions to this generalisation: Swales has been instrumental in developing a more sophisticated understanding of the language needs of postgraduate students in particular (e.g. Swales 1986, 1990a; Swales and Feak 1994).

Current and future trends and directions

We can expect that more attention will be paid to EAP at pre-tertiary (college) levels. It is increasingly understood that children entering schooling can be helped to learn more effectively, as well as to integrate better into the educational structure, if they are taught specifically academic skills and language as well as the language needed for social communication (Heath 1983; Hasan and Martin 1989; Christie 1992).

In counterpoint to the probable increase in attention to EAP in early schooling, thesis writing and dissertation supervision are also receiving more attention at present, as indicated above. The knowledge base which has built around traditional university-based academic needs has led to the understanding that academic language needs neither begin nor end in upper high school/under-graduate education, but span formal schooling at every level. Going still further, a related development is a concern with the English language skills of non-native English speaking academics, especially those teaching and researching in non-English language countries such as Hong Kong and Singapore, and this group's needs are beginning to be addressed (Sengupta *et al.* 1999). We can expect this more all-encompassing view of EAP to develop much further before it is exhausted.

In recent years the term 'academic literacy' has come to be applied to the complex set of skills (not necessarily only those relating to the mastery of reading and writing) which are increasingly argued to be vital underpinnings to the cultural knowledge required for success in academic communities, from elementary school on. The discourse of academic literacy is more usually found outside TESOL: e.g. in the USA in work relating to students from ethnically and dialectally diverse backgrounds (e.g. Berlin 1988; Auerbach 1994; Fox 1994) and in highly politicised terms (e.g., Freire 1970 [1996]; Giroux 1994). In the UK it is associated with the Lancaster critical linguistics group (e.g. Fairclough 1992; Ivanič 1998); and in Australia with the critical genre group (e.g. Cope and Kalantzis 1993; Luke 1996). See also Chapter 27 of this volume. With its basis in educational Marxism and critical linguistics / critical education, 'academic literacy' argues from very different premises than traditional EAP. However, I have argued (Hamp-Lyons 1994) that, despite arising from quite different sociopolitical contexts, the concepts of academic literacy and those of EAP are linguistically and pedagogically quite similar, and certainly the different movements share a common desire to provide appropriate and effective education. The debate over motives and means in this area – in the pages of the *English for Specific Purposes* journal between Pennycook (1997) and Allison (1996, 1998) – provides fascinating insights into these issues. Part of this debate relates to the role of English in the modern and future world, and the evident dominance it now has in scholarly publication in most parts of the world (Swales 1990b; Eichele personal communication 1999; Gu Yue-guo personal communication 1999). We can expect this to be a fruitful and controversial area of research – and polemic – in the first years of the twenty-first century.

Conclusion

EAP is a thriving and important aspect of TESOL that has so far received less attention from researchers than it deserves. It is also more complex and potentially problematic than most English language teachers recognise at the beginning of their EAP teaching. Its greatest strength is its responsiveness to the needs of the learners; but this is its greatest weakness too, making many of its solutions highly contextual and of doubtful transferability. For this reason, it will offer a rich site for study and practice for the foreseeable future.

Key readings

Allison (1996) Pragmatist discourse and English for academic purposes
Connor (1996) *Cross-Cultural Aspects of Second Language Writing*
Hamp-Lyons and Heasley (1987) *Study Writing*
Hutchinson and Waters (1987) *English for Specific Purposes*
Swales (1990a) *Genre Analysis: English in Academic and Research Contexts*

CHAPTER 19

English for specific purposes

Tony Dudley-Evans

Introduction

English for specific purposes (ESP) has for about 30 years been a separate branch of English Language Teaching. It has developed its own approaches, materials and methodology and is generally seen as a very active, even 'feisty' movement that has had considerable influence over the more general activities of TESOL and applied linguistics.

ESP has always seen itself as materials-driven and as a classroom-based activity concerned with practical outcomes. Most writing about ESP is concerned with aspects of teaching, materials production and text analysis rather than with the development of a theory of ESP.

Background

DEFINITION OF ESP

The key defining feature of ESP is that its teaching and materials are founded on the results of **needs analysis**. The first questions when starting preparation for teaching an ESP course is almost always: What do students need to do with English? Which of the skills do they need to master and how well? Which genres do they need to master, either for comprehension or production purposes? Various commentators (notably Brumfit 1984a) have remarked that needs analysis is not exclusive to ESP and that much general TESOL – especially when following the communicative approach – is based on needs analysis. However, in ESP one can be more precise about learners' needs; their needs are defined by a learning or occupational situation in which English plays a key role (see Chapter 18). Specific needs can be identified by examining that situation and the texts (written or spoken) in detail; in contrast, for students not immediately using English, or about to use it, needs are much more general.

Apart from the primacy of needs analysis, defining features of ESP can be difficult to identify. Robinson, in her first overview of ESP (1980), suggested that **limited duration** (i.e. an intensive course of a fixed length) and **adult learners** are defining features of ESP courses. However, in her second survey (1991) she accepts that, although many ESP courses are of limited duration, a significant number are not (e.g. a three- or four-year programme as part of a university degree) and, while it is true that the majority of ESP learners are adults, ESP can be taught at school (even at primary level in English-medium schools where English is not the pupils' first language). Similarly, ESP is generally taught to intermediate or advanced students of English, but can also be taught to beginners.

The above are optional or variable characteristics of ESP. I would add to this list the idea that ESP may be designed for specific disciplines or professions. The ESP teacher needs to bear in mind and exploit if possible this specific subject knowledge, which leads to classroom interaction and teaching methodology that can be quite different from that of general English; however, in some situations – e.g. pre-study or pre-work courses where learners have not started their academic or professional activity and therefore have less subject knowledge – teaching methodology will be similar to that of general English. The use of a distinctive methodology is therefore a variable characteristic of ESP.

We therefore return to the question of the defining features of ESP. Looking closely at 'specific purpose', ESP materials will always draw on the topics and activities of that specific purpose, in many cases exploiting the methodology of the subject area or the profession (Widdowson 1983). For example, an English course for engineers will use engineering situations to present relevant language and discourse; problem-solving activities (calculations, making recommendations) will probably also be used, since they draw on skills and abilities possessed by the students. Similarly, a business English course will use case studies as these are widely used in business training. It must not, however, be forgotten that ESP is concerned with teaching language, discourse and relevant communication skills: it exploits topics and the underlying methodology of the target discipline or profession to present language, discourse and skills.

I thus see the absolute characteristics of ESP as follows:

- ESP is designed to meet the specific needs of the learner.
- ESP makes use of the underlying methodology and activities of the discipline it serves.
- ESP is centred on the language (grammar, lexis, register), skills, discourse and genres appropriate to these activities (Dudley-Evans and St John 1998: 4–5).

The variable characteristics are:

- ESP may be related to or designed for specific disciplines.
- ESP may use, in specific teaching situations, a different methodology from that of general English.
- ESP is likely to be designed for adult learners, either at a tertiary-level institution or in a professional work situation. It could, however, be used for learners at secondary school level.
- ESP is generally designed for intermediate or advanced students. Most ESP courses assume basic knowledge of the language system, but it can be used with beginners (Dudley-Evans and St John 1998: 5).

CLASSIFICATION

As with most branches of TESOL and applied linguistics, ESP is often divided up into various categories with mysterious acronyms. It is usually classified into two main categories: **English for academic purposes (EAP;** see Chapter 18) and **English for occupational purposes (EOP).** EAP largely speaks for itself: it relates to the English needed in an educational context, usually at a university or similar institution, and possibly also at school level. EOP is more complicated: it relates to professional purposes, e.g. those of working doctors, engineers or business people. The biggest branch of EOP is business English, the teaching of which can range from teaching general business-related vocabulary to the teaching of specific skills important in business, e.g. negotiation and meeting skills.

Another key distinction is between more general ESP and more specific ESP. Dudley-Evans and St John (1998) – drawing on an idea from George Blue (Blue 1988) – make a distinction between English for general academic purposes (EGAP) designed for pre-study groups, or groups that are heterogeneous with regard to discipline, and English for specific academic purposes

(ESAP) designed to meet specific needs of a group from the same discipline. A similar distinction can be made between the teaching of general business-related language and skills (English for general business purposes; EGBP) and the teaching of specific business language for skills such as negotiation, or the writing of letters or faxes (English for specific business purposes; ESBP).

It is often convenient to refer to types of ESAP or ESBP by profession, so one commonly hears terms such as medical English, English for engineers or English for administration. These terms may be useful as a quick classification, but may lead to confusion. Medical English may include EAP for students following a degree course in medicine where English is the medium of instruction, or a reading skills course where the subject is taught in a language other than English, but also a type of EOP for practising doctors using English to talk to patients (e.g. Cuban doctors in South Africa) or to write up research in English. Similarly, English for engineers may be for students of engineering, or for practising engineers needing, say, to write reports in English. In the USA, ESAP is often called content-based instruction (CBI), which is seen as separate from ESP (Brinton *et al.* 1989).

Finally, two other commonly used abbreviations are EST (English for science and technology), which was widely used when most EAP teaching was for students of engineering and science. It is thus a branch of EAP. In the USA, EVP (English for vocational purposes) is frequently used for teaching English for specific trades or vocations. This branch of EOP is often sub-divided into vocational English (concerning language and skills needed in a job) and pre-vocational English (concerning skills needed for applying for jobs and being interviewed).

Research

BEYOND NEEDS ANALYSIS

I have emphasised needs analysis as the key defining feature of ESP. The initial needs analysis provides information about the target situation, what learners will have to do in English and the skills and language needed. This is generally called **target situation analysis** (Chambers 1980). While initial needs analysis will always be the first step for ESP, it is usually the next stage that involves the most detailed analysis, and there has been increasing emphasis on investigating these additional factors. Information about the learners – in particular their level in English, weaknesses in language and skills needed (often called lacks), and also their own perceptions of what they need – are increasingly investigated.

Taking an example, the need to understand lectures is an objective need that comes under target situation analysis. Learners' confidence or lack of confidence in their listening abilities, and their perception that they need more vocabulary to understand lectures, is subjective. This investigation of subjectively felt needs, as opposed to the objective needs established by target situation analysis, is called **learning situation analysis**. The investigation of learners' weaknesses or lacks is called **present situation analysis**.

Analysis of the learning situation within the teaching institution or company is also important and is called **means analysis** (Holliday and Cooke 1982). For ESP courses to be successful and to have a lasting effect on learners' ability to study or work using English, the environment in which English is taught versus that in which it is used must be assessed. For example, if learners are used to rote-learning, it may be that a problem-solving approach to learning ESP will be alien to their learning styles and contrary to their expectations. This does not mean that the problem-solving approach cannot be used, but it would be more effective if the factors that militate against its use are known and allowed for.

THE NEED FOR TEXT ANALYSIS

However much priority is given to needs analysis and the various approaches to it outlined above, I believe that the key stage in ESP course design and materials development is the action needed following this needs analysis stage. This next stage is when the ESP teacher considers the (written or spoken) texts that the learner has to produce and/or understand, tries to identify the texts' key features and devises teaching material that will enable learners to use the texts effectively.

ESP work has thus always been interested in the structure of discourse and, indeed, has often been at the forefront of applied linguistic research. For example, early work by Lackstrom *et al.* (1973), Allen and Widdowson (1974), Widdowson (1978) and Trimble (1985) showed ways of analysing scientific and technical text that led to materials production. More recently, work in genre analysis (see Chapter 27) has extended the analyses of the above researchers, relating it more directly to the conventions and expectations of the target discourse communities that ESP learners wish to become members of. The work of Swales (1981, 1990a) on the academic article and Bhatia (1993) on types of business letter are extremely insightful about the ways in which writers manipulate these texts and also very productive in terms of generating appropriate teaching material.

Early work in ESP genre analysis placed the focus on 'moves', i.e. how the writer structures a text or part of a text (such as an article introduction or discussion section) through a series of stratagems. Masuku (1996) argues that moves and genres are elements of discourse and that the difference between them is that moves combine to form genres. At a rank below the move 'we enter the domain of grammar' (Masuku 1996: 117). A move may be defined as 'a meaningful unit represented in linguistic (lexicogrammatical) forms and related to the communicative purpose of the social activity in which members of the discourse community are engaged' (Hozayen 1994: 151). Skelton (1994: 456) takes the definition a stage further by stating:

> Move structure analysis tentatively assigns a function to a stretch of written or spoken text, identifies that function with one, or a set of, exponents which signal its presence, and seeks to establish whether or not the pattern identified is a general one, by reference to ostensibly similar texts. If the pattern can be generalised, its status is confirmed.

Swales (1990a: 141) argues that a writer 'creates a research space' in an article's introduction in order to show the originality of and need for the presented research; the model is thus called the 'creating a research space' (CARS) model (see Figure 27.1, p. 188). Bhatia (1993: 46–47) follows a similar pattern to Swales in establishing the moves for sales promotion letters (letters selling a product to potential customers).

Recently, Swales and others (e.g. Berkenkotter and Huckin 1995; Swales 1998b) have turned away from a reliance on moves to consider in more detail the workings of discourse communities and the role genres play within those communities (see Chapter 27 on three approaches to genre analysis: ESP school, New Rhetoric and systemic linguistics). This greater interest in the workings of discourse communities and the decline in interest in moves have led to an increasing overlap between the ESP and New Rhetoric schools.

While the ESP school is considering higher level issues, research using corpora and concordancing techniques has linked genre analysis with phraseological studies. Gledhill (2000) shows how introductions to medical articles about cancer research use a limited and predictable phraseology. This phraseology can be established by examining the collocations of high-frequency grammatical items (e.g. *of, for, on, but, has, have, were,* etc.). Gledhill can, e.g., show that *has been/have been* are used in cancer research articles to establish a relationship between a drug or biochemical process and a disease (as in *TNF alpha has been shown to deliver the toxicity of ricin A*; Gledhill 2000: 7). This research has great potential, especially the potential of relating the more general findings of genre analysis to specific language use, and thus to materials production.

Concern with the discourse community's work is also characteristic of the teaching of business English, the current growth area in ESP. Needs analysis in business English must establish exactly how the discourse community uses language and text, and the effect of culture (both business or corporate culture and national culture) on the way that discourse is structured. Charles (1994, 1996) shows very effectively how the nature of the business relationship (i.e. whether it is new or old) has a significant effect on the structure of a sales negotiation, and also that there are important differences between British and Finnish styles of negotiation. The same has been shown for Japanese–American negotiations (Neu 1986) and Brazilian–American negotiations (Garcez 1993).

Practice

I have already argued that ESP is a materials-led field. Most materials, however, are prepared by individual teachers for particular situations, and there is not a huge amount of published ESP material. Hamp-Lyons (Chapter 18) discusses a number of coursebooks in EAP. In EOP, especially business English, there is much more material: St John (1996) discusses various types of material, giving brief description of key coursebooks. Research work in genre analysis (see Chapter 27) is beginning to generate textbooks applying its findings to the teaching of academic writing (for examples of textbooks making direct use of genre analysis findings, see Weissberg and Buker 1990; Swales and Feak 1994).

Current and future trends and directions

In discussing needs analysis and genre analysis, I have shown how ESP research and teaching are increasingly focusing on and sensitive to the learners' background and the effects of the environment in which they use English. This leads to an increased awareness of the importance of cross-cultural issues (Connor 1996) and a shift towards further research in this area. The growth of business English will increase the need for such research, particularly as business English is very often used by two or more non-native speakers (St John 1996) using both language and strategies that may be very different from those used by native speakers.

I have also argued for the importance of genre analysis as applied research that leads the course designer from the initial needs analysis to materials production and lesson planning. I would expect future research in genre analysis to go in two directions: first, concern with the broader picture of how discourse communities work and the role text plays within them will continue; second, specific corpora will be used to investigate the phraseology of particular specialist genres in specialist disciplines and professions.

The concern with cultural issues is likely to lead to an increased advocacy role for the ESP teacher. In Johns and Dudley-Evans (1993) I suggested – on the basis of research into the discourse of economics (Dudley-Evans and Henderson 1990a; Henderson *et al.* 1993) – that ESP teachers and researchers can have an increased role as 'genre doctors', advising disciplines and professions on the effectiveness of their communication. I also foresee ESP teachers participating centrally in the debate on the dominance of the Anglo-American rhetorical style in international publication. Many (notably Mauranen 1993; Swales 1998a) argue that journals should be tolerant of different rhetorics when considering manuscripts for publication. This can only happen if journal editors become aware of the issues; the ESP teacher/researcher is clearly well placed to do this. I have the impression that this issue is being increasingly debated, and that attitudes are changing.

A similar type of role for the ESP teacher is envisaged by those who argue that ESP teaching should be concerned with rights analysis as well as needs analysis. Benesch (1999) argues that in collaborative situations where the ESP teacher is working closely with the subject teacher (either together in the classroom or outside in planning classes), the ESP teacher should not act just as interpreter of the way that the subject teacher communicates information in lectures or his/her priorities in marking assignments/examination answers. She suggests that ESP should develop an awareness in ESP students of how they can assert their rights, by, e.g., insisting on asking questions about points the lecturer has not made clear.

It is interesting that the concern with rights analysis has been influenced by the critical discourse analysis movement in applied linguistics (Fairclough 1989; Barton and Ivanič 1991).

However, ESP has its own movements, its own journal and, above all, its own procedures. It is still, however, very much part of applied linguistics and continues to be influenced by developments there; it also plays its own role in the development of applied linguistics.

Key readings

Dudley-Evans and St John (1998) *Developments in English for Specific Purposes*
English for Specific Purposes (in particular the special issue 'Business English' 15(1), 1996)
Hutchinson and Waters (1987) *English for Specific Purposes*
Johns and Dudley-Evans (1993) English for specific purposes
Jordan (1997) *English for Academic Purposes: A Guide and Resource Book for Teachers*
Robinson (1991) *ESP Today: A Practitioner's Guide*
Swales (1990a) *Genre Analysis: English in Academic and Research Settings*

CHAPTER 20

Assessment

Geoff Brindley

Introduction

TERMINOLOGY AND KEY CONCEPTS

The term **assessment** refers to a variety of ways of collecting information on a learner's language ability or achievement. Although **testing** and **assessment** are often used interchangeably, the latter is an umbrella term encompassing measurement instruments administered on a 'one-off' basis such as tests, as well as qualitative methods of monitoring and recording student learning such as observation, simulations or project work. Assessment is also distinguished from **evaluation** which is concerned with the overall language programme and not just with what individual students have learnt (see Chapter 21). **Proficiency assessment** refers to the assessment of general language abilities acquired by the learner independent of a course of study. This kind of assessment is often done through the administration of standardised commercial language-proficiency tests. On the other hand, **assessment of achievement** aims to establish what a student has learned in relation to a particular course or curriculum (thus frequently carried out by the teacher). Achievement assessment may be based either on the specific content of the course or on the course objectives (Hughes 1989).

Assessment carried out by teachers during the learning process with the aim of using the results to improve instruction is known as **formative assessment**. Assessment at the end of a course, term or school year – often for purposes of providing aggregated information on programme outcomes to educational authorities – is referred to as **summative assessment**.

The interpretation of assessment results may be **norm-referenced** or **criterion-referenced**. Norm-referenced assessment ranks learners in relation to each other; e.g. a score or percentage in an examination reports a learner's standing compared to other candidates (such as 'student X came in the top 10 per cent'). Criterion-referencing occurs when learners' performance is described in relation to an explicitly stated standard; e.g. a person's ability may be reported in terms of a 'can-do' statement describing the kinds of tasks he or she can perform using the target language (such as 'can give basic personal information'). The two key requirements for any assessment are that it should be *valid* and *reliable*, i.e. it should assess only the abilities which it claims to assess and do so consistently.

In the field of language assessment, a distinction is made between three types of validity:

1. **Construct validity**: the extent to which the content of the test/assessment reflects current theoretical understandings of the skill(s) being assessed;
2. **Content validity**: whether it represents an adequate sample of ability; and
3. **Criterion-related validity**: the extent to which the results correlate with other independent measures of ability.

Recently, however, largely due to the influence of Samuel Messick, a major figure in educational measurement in the United States, these types of validity have become subsumed into a single *unitary* concept of validity centred around construct validity (Messick 1980, 1989). The unified view of validity also encompasses the notion of **consequential validity**, a term referring to the extent to which a test or assessment serves the purposes for which it is intended. Establishing the validity of a test or assessment may, thus, include an evaluation of the social consequences (both intended and unintended) of a test's interpretation and use (Messick 1989: 84).

Reliability is concerned with ascertaining to what degree scores on tests or assessments are affected by **measurement error**, i.e. by variation in scores caused by factors unrelated to the ability being assessed (e.g. conditions of administration, test instructions, fatigue, guessing, etc.). Such factors may result in inconsistent performance by test takers. To establish the degree to which test results are stable, various approaches can be used. The consistency of test results over time can be estimated in terms of **test–retest reliability**, where the same test is given to a group at two different points in time or by administering two equivalent forms of the same test. To examine whether performance is consistent across different parts of the same test, various kinds of **internal consistency** estimates can be calculated (for more details, see Bachman 1990; J.D. Brown 1996).

PURPOSES

Assessment is carried out to collect information on learners' language proficiency and/or achievement that can be used by the stakeholders in language learning programmes for various purposes. These purposes include:

- selection: e.g. to determine whether learners have sufficient language proficiency to be able to undertake tertiary study;
- certification: e.g. to provide people with a statement of their language ability for employment purposes;
- accountability: e.g. to provide educational funding authorities with evidence that intended learning outcomes have been achieved and to justify expenditure;
- diagnosis: e.g. to identify learners' strengths and weaknesses;
- instructional decision-making: e.g. to decide what material to present next or what to revise;
- motivation: e.g. to encourage learners to study harder.

The relative emphasis given to each of these purposes is influenced to a considerable extent by the social and political context in which assessment takes place. Recently, the accountability function has become paramount in many industrialised countries as educational policy has become increasingly driven by the need to measure outcomes and report against national standards to justify public expenditure (Norton 1997; Brindley 1998a).

Background

Trends in language assessment have tended to reflect prevailing beliefs about the nature of language. In the 1960s and 1970s, under the influence of structural linguistics, language tests were designed to assess learners' mastery of different areas of the linguistic system such as phoneme discrimination, grammatical knowledge and vocabulary. To maximise reliability, tests often used objective testing formats such as multiple choice and included large numbers of items.

However, such **discrete item tests** provided no information on learners' ability to use language for communicative purposes. Language testers therefore began to look for other more global *washback ?* forms of assessment which were able to tap the use of language skills under normal contextual constraints. In the 1970s and early 1980s, this led to an upsurge of interest in **integrative tests**, such as cloze (a technique which consists of deleting every *n*th word in a written or spoken text; the test candidates' task is to supply the missing words in the gapped text) and dictation, which required learners to use linguistic and contextual knowledge to reconstitute the meaning of spoken or written texts. In a series of research studies, John Oller and his colleagues found strong relationships between testees' performance in integrative tests and in the sub-components of various other test batteries testing other language skills, such as writing and speaking. On the basis of these findings, Oller hypothesised that there was a single general proficiency factor which underlay test performance. This became known as the 'unitary competence hypothesis' (Oller 1976; Oller and Hinofotis 1980). However, in the face of critiques of the methodology used in the studies, Oller (1983: 353) subsequently modified the hypothesis, acknowledging that language proficiency was made up of multiple components. It is now generally accepted that a single test of overall ability, such as a cloze passage, does not give an accurate picture of an individual's proficiency and that a range of different assessment procedures are necessary (Cohen 1994: 196).

Another obvious problem with integrative tests is that they are indirect tests, i.e. they do not require the testee to demonstrate the language skills they would need to use in order to communicate in the real world. With the widespread adoption of communicative language teaching (CLT) principles, however, assessment has become increasingly direct. Many language tests and assessments used nowadays often contain tasks which resemble the kinds of language-use situations that test takers would encounter in using the language for communicative purposes in everyday life. The kinds of tasks used in communicative assessments of proficiency and achievement thus typically include activities such as oral interviews, listening to and reading extracts from the media and various kinds of 'authentic' writing tasks which reflect real-life demands (for a range of examples, see Weir 1990, 1993).

Research

There has been an enormous amount of research activity in language assessment in recent years; for a comprehensive overview, see Clapham and Corson (1997). This volume contains state-of-the-art surveys of a wide range of current issues in language assessment. A summary of trends in language testing is also provided by Douglas (1995), while Shohamy (1995) discusses the particular issues and problems involved in the assessment of language performance. Hamayan (1995) describes a variety of assessment procedures not involving the use of formal tests. Kunnan (1997) categorises over a hundred language testing research studies in terms of the framework for language test validation proposed by Messick (1980). Current developments and research in the assessment of the skills of listening, speaking, reading and writing, respectively, are provided by Brindley (1998b), Turner (1998), Perkins (1998) and Kroll (1998).

The brief review of research below focuses on two important issues in language assessment: (1) the key question of how to define language ability and (2) self-assessment of language ability. Among the many important research topics that would merit attention in a longer review include the relationship between test-taker characteristics and test performance (e.g. Kunnan 1997), test-taker strategies (e.g. Storey 1998), test-taker discourse (e.g. O'Loughlin 1997), factors influencing task difficulty (e.g. Fulcher 1996a), rater and interviewer behaviour (e.g. Weigle 1994; McNamara 1996; Morton *et al.* 1997) and applications of measurement theory to test analysis (e.g. Lynch and McNamara 1998). The important question of the impact of assessment and testing on teaching and learning (known as **washback**) is also beginning to receive a good deal of attention in the language assessment literature (Alderson and Wall 1993) as are issues of ethics and fairness (Hamp-Lyons 1998).

RESEARCH INTO THE NATURE OF COMMUNICATIVE LANGUAGE ABILITY

Many assessment specialists would argue that the fundamental issue in language assessment is that of construct validity. In other words, as Spolsky (1985) asks: 'What does it mean to know how to use a language?' To answer this question, it is necessary to describe the nature of the abilities being assessed; this is known as **construct definition**. Thus, if we are developing a test of 'speaking', we need to be able to specify what we mean by 'speaking ability', i.e. what its components are and how these components are drawn on by different kinds of speaking tasks. However, given the multiple, individual and contextual factors involved in language use, this is clearly not an easy task.

In recent years, two approaches to construct definition have been adopted (McNamara 1996). The first approach focuses on compiling detailed specifications of the features of target language performances which learners have to carry out, often on the basis of an analysis of communicative needs (Shohamy 1995). These features form the criteria for assessment and are built into assessment instruments such as proficiency rating scales; e.g. see the well-known scale used by the American Council on the Teaching of Foreign Languages (ACTFL 1986) to assess language ability of foreign language teachers.

The second approach, rather than starting with an analysis of the language that the learner needs to use, employs a theoretical model of language ability as a basis for constructing tests and assessment tools; see Canale and Swain 1980; Bachman 1990 (the latter updated by Bachman and Palmer 1996). Such models provide a detailed and explicit framework for describing the types of abilities involved in communicative language use and have been drawn on in a number of language test construction and validation projects (e.g. Harley *et al.* 1990; Bachman *et al.* 1995; McKay 1995; Milanovic *et al.* 1996; Chalhoub-Deville *et al.* 1997).

Both of these approaches have been criticised. Assessments based on the 'real life' approach which take the context of language use as the point of departure are considered problematic by many measurement specialists since they are not based on an underlying theoretical model of communicative language ability and thus lack generalisability beyond the assessment situation (Bachman 1990; Shohamy 1995; McNamara 1996). On the other hand, although models which have been developed to address this perceived gap provide a useful framework for research and test development, their theoretical status remains to be validated (Skehan 1989b). Additionally, there are doubts about the extent to which such models can represent the multiple factors involved in interactive language use (McNamara 1996). The search for models of language ability which reflect the complexity and multidimensionality of language use is thus ongoing.

RESEARCH INTO SELF-ASSESSMENT

Theoretical developments such as those outlined above have contributed to our understanding of the components of ability underlying performance in language tests and enabled researchers to develop more precise tools for measuring language ability. However, a good deal of assessment taking place in language learning classrooms is aimed not so much at formally measuring outcomes, but rather at improving the quality of learning and instruction. In this context, there has been a considerable growth of interest in the use of **self-assessment** with language learners in various educational settings (Oscarson 1997). Proponents have argued that participating in self-assessment can assist learners to become skilled judges of their own strengths and weaknesses and to set realistic goals for themselves, thus developing their capacity to become self-directed (Dickinson 1987; Oscarson 1997). Research suggests that with training, learners are capable of self-assessing their language ability with reasonable accuracy (Blanche and Merino 1989).

Research into the use of self-assessment has provided a number of insights that can usefully inform language teaching practice. First, evidence suggests that the concept of self-assessment may be quite unfamiliar and threatening to many learners since it alters traditional teacher–learner relationships (Blue 1994; Heron 1988). Guidance in the use of self-assessment techniques is therefore crucial (Cram 1995; Dickinson 1987). Second, the ability of learners to self-assess accurately appears to be related to the transparency of the instruments used. Some research studies suggest that learners find it easier to say what they cannot do, or what they have difficulty doing, than what they can do (Bachman and Palmer 1989; Ready-Morfitt 1991). This finding has implications for the way in which self-assessment scales are worded. Third, learners seem to be able to assess their abilities more accurately when the self-assessment statements are couched in specific terms and are closely related to their personal experience (Oscarson 1997; Ross 1998). Finally, some evidence suggests that cultural factors affect learners' willingness to self-assess as well as the accuracy of these assessments (Blue 1994; von Elek 1985).

Practice

Not only do assessments of language performance need to meet the requirements of validity and reliability, they also need to be practically feasible. Research suggests that the introduction of assessment systems is likely to be affected by a number of pressures and constraints, including the level of available resources (e.g. funding, time and availability of relevant expertise) and demands for external accountability (Wall 1996; Brindley 1998a). These considerations are particularly important when assessment is part of the curriculum and teachers are responsible for the construction and administration of assessments.

Direct assessment of language performance is time consuming and therefore expensive, particularly individualised testing. For example, subjective rating of spoken production through an oral interview entails not only payment of interviewers but also training and periodic retraining of raters. Because of such costs, some large-scale language-proficiency tests do not contain a speaking component. Achievement assessment may also be very resource intensive. For example, in the context of language assessment in British primary schools, Barrs (1992: 55) reports that a common concern regarding the implementation of the Primary Language Record – a detailed observational system for recording students' language use – is the amount of time necessary to document students' performances on an ongoing basis.

Given the potential practical problems arising when new tests or systems are introduced into an existing curriculum, assessment researchers have argued that institutions need to consider carefully resourcing requirements at both the planning and implementation stages. If teachers are required to construct and administer their own assessment tasks, it is crucial to provide adequate support (e.g. professional development, materials development and rater training) and establish systems for ensuring the quality of assessment tools used (Bottomley *et al*. 1994; Brindley 1998a).

Current and future trends and directions

On the theoretical front, one notable recent development is the increasing overlap between second language acquisition (SLA) and language assessment research (Bachman and Cohen 1998). Methods of language analysis developed by SLA researchers are increasingly used to investigate language use in assessment situations (e.g. Ross 1992; Young and Milanovic 1992; Lazaraton 1996) and the results of such research are increasingly employed in constructing tests and assessment procedures (Fulcher 1996b). Also, the notion of 'what it means to know how to use a language' continues to be increasingly refined and elaborated. One important development here is the expansion of recent models of communicative language ability to include what were previously regarded as 'non-language' factors, such as personality and background knowledge. Thus, the framework put forward by Bachman and Palmer (1996) includes the test-takers' **topical knowledge** (knowledge of the world that can be mobilised in tests) and **affective schemata** (emotional memories influencing the way test-takers behave). This is an important development since it recognises the key role that personal characteristics may play in language performance and opens the way for the development of assessment procedures which attempt to build such factors into the assessment situation. However, as McNamara (1996: 88) points out, it also opens a Pandora's box because of the complexity of such variables and the challenges involved in adequately measuring them.

The recent widespread adoption of computer-adaptive assessment enables tasks to be tailored to the test taker's level of ability, and enables test takers to receive immediate feedback on their performance (Gruba and Corbel 1997). Computerised versions of major proficiency tests are increasingly available worldwide (Educational Testing Service 1998). Researchers are also investigating ways in which advances in electronically-mediated communication, computer technology and linguistic analysis can be incorporated into language tests, including automated scoring of open-ended responses, video-mediated testing, and handwriting and speech recognition (Burstein *et al.* 1996; J.D. Brown 1997). The potential of the internet for delivery of language tests is also increasingly being exploited.

A further shift in the assessment landscape is the increasing attention paid to assessment of achievement, an area which was somewhat neglected in the past (Weir 1993; Brindley 1998a). Such developments have resulted in an increase in the use of 'alternative' methods of assessing and recording achievement which can capture the outcomes of learning that occur in the classroom but which do not involve standardised tests (for further discussion of alternative assessment, see Chapter 21). Methods include structured observation, progress grids, learning journals, project work, teacher-developed tasks, peer-assessment and self-assessment (Brindley 1989; Cohen 1994; Hamayan 1995; Genesee and Upshur 1996; Bailey 1998; Shohamy 1998).

Although research has provided some information on how these methods are used in language programmes, the nature and extent of their impact on learning have yet to be fully investigated. One notable gap in the context of language learning concerns the nature and use of teacher-constructed assessment tasks, a question which has been explored in some depth in general education (see, e.g., Linn and Burton 1994).

Conclusion

From this survey, it can be seen that language assessment is a complex and rapidly evolving field which underwent significant change in the 1990s. From a theoretical perspective, considerable progress has been made. Models of ability now underlying language tests are much more sophisticated than the somewhat crude skills-based models characterising earlier periods. At the same time, researchers are beginning to employ insights from linguistic theory and applied linguistic research to enrich the constructs which are the object of assessment. Progress has also been made in test analysis with the advent of measurement techniques which can model the multiple factors involved in test performance (Bachman and Eignor 1997).

Despite the advances in language assessment, a number of important areas are in urgent need of further investigation. More data-based studies of language skills in use are needed to increase our knowledge of the nature of language ability. We need to find cost-effective ways of integrating new technology into the design and delivery of tests, and we also need to study and document the interfaces between teaching and assessment. Finally, in order to formulate ethical standards of practice, we need to find out more about the ways in which tests and other assessments are used. Only through the systematic exploration of such questions will it eventually be possible to improve the quality of information that language assessment provides.

Key readings

Alderson and Wall (1993) Does washback exist?
Bachman (1990) *Fundamental Considerations in Language Testing*

Bachman and Palmer (1996) *Language Testing in Practice*
J.D. Brown (1996) *Testing in Language Programs*
Genesee and Upshur (1996) *Classroom-Based Evaluation in Second Language Education*
Cohen (1994) *Assessing Language Ability in the Classroom*
Hughes (1989) *Testing for Language Teachers*
McNamara (1996) *Measuring Second Language Performance*
Spolsky (1985) An essay on the theoretical basis of language testing
Weir (1993) *Understanding and Developing Language Tests*

CHAPTER 21

Evaluation

Fred Genesee

Introduction

Evaluation in TESOL settings is a process of collecting, analysing and interpreting information about teaching and learning in order to make informed decisions that enhance student achievement and the success of educational programmes (Rea-Dickins and Germaine 1993; Genesee and Upshur 1996; O'Malley and Valdez-Pierce 1996). Three simple examples help explicate the varied forms evaluation can take in TESOL settings:

- Example 1: The English Language Institute at Central University, South Africa offers courses in oral and written English for business purposes to adult non-native speakers of English whose employers want to transfer them to international operations. They have designed an evaluation to determine the effectiveness and usefulness of new textbooks and audiolingual materials to decide whether to continue using them in the coming year. Questionnaires will be used to collect feedback from the students, their teachers and their employers.

- Example 2: Henry Jones is an elementary ESL teacher. He prepares students with little or no proficiency in English for participation in mainstream classrooms where academic instruction is presented only in English. At the end of each year he identifies which of his ESL students can be 'mainstreamed' without special ESL instruction. His decisions are based on specially designed ESL tests administered at the end of each year and on his observation of students' performance in maths and science classes taught in English.

- Example 3: The Republic of Xanadu has implemented a new enriched EFL programme in all of its secondary schools to better prepare its citizens for globalisation. It has planned a longitudinal evaluation of the effectiveness of this programme. The evaluation will compare the performance of students in the new programme to that of students in the 'old' programme using a battery of carefully designed language tests. Also, teachers and school administrators will be interviewed about their impression of the programme. Results from the testing and interviews will be used to decide what aspects of the new programme need revision, and how they should be revised.

These examples illustrate that evaluation can focus on different aspects of teaching and learning: respectively, textbooks and instructional materials, student achievement, and whole programmes of instruction. They also illustrate that evaluation can be undertaken for different reasons, and that the reasons impact in substantial ways. Finally, they illustrate that evaluation is a process that includes four basic components:

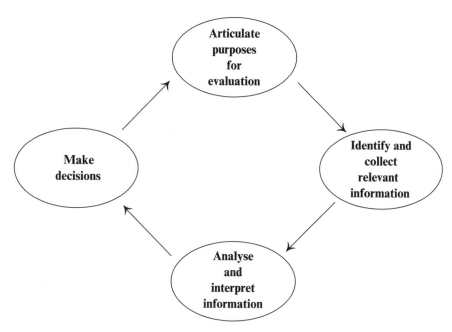

Figure 21.1   Four basic components of evaluation

1. The purpose of the evaluation is first articulated: e.g. to decide whether to continue using new materials (Example 1); to decide which students will be exempt from ESL instruction (Example 2).

2. Information relevant to the purpose of evaluation is identified and collected: e.g. the teacher uses student scores on tests and his observations of performance to make decisions (Example 2); school officials use feedback from teachers and school administrators as well as language test results in the new and regular programmes to decide where and how to revise the new programme (Example 3).

3. Once collected, the information is analysed and interpreted: feedback from students, their employers and teachers is interpreted impressionistically (Example 1); test scores of students in the new programme are compared to those of students in the regular programme and responses to interviews and questionnaires from principals and students are interpreted qualitatively (Example 3).

4. Finally, decisions are taken: the materials are kept, or rejected (Example 1); each student is assigned to an ESL or non-ESL strand (Example 2); decisions are made about how to modify the programme (Example 3).

Figure 21.1 depicts these components of evaluation in a cyclical relationship because they are inter-related and ongoing: each component influences the next in a continuous fashion.

It is important to clarify the distinction between **evaluation** and **assessment**. These terms are often used interchangeably, but they are technically different. Assessment of an individual student's progress or achievement is an important component of evaluation: it is that part of evaluation that includes the collection and analysis of information about student learning. The primary focus of assessment in TESOL has been language assessment and the role of tests in assessing students' language skills (see Chapter 20). Evaluation goes beyond student achievement (and language assessment) to consider all aspects of teaching and learning, and to look at how educational decisions can be informed by the results of alternative forms of assessment.

Background

Evaluation entails consideration of the following issues: purposes of evaluation, participants, kinds of information, information collection, and analysis and interpretation of information.

PURPOSES OF EVALUATION

An important purpose of evaluation is **accountability**: to demonstrate that students are learning to the standards expected of them and/or that a curriculum or programme of instruction is working the way it should. Formal programme evaluation entails the selection of appropriate comparison groups, standardised tests and statistical methods for the interpretation of test results; e.g. French immersion programmes in Canada have been subjected to systematic, formal evaluations to ascertain their effectiveness (for an overview of programme evaluation issues, see Elley 1989). Primary responsibility for formal programme evaluation usually lies with trained researchers or district personnel. Formal programme evaluation is generally **summative**, i.e. it occurs at the end of an extended period of instruction; the resulting decisions tend to have high stakes attached. There is a growing emphasis on ongoing **formative** evaluation for curriculum and programme development (Nunan 1988a; Brown 1995: Chapter 7), i.e. the evaluation serves to individualise the educational treatment of students to optimise their achievement. Ideally, the development of new programmes and curriculums is informed from the beginning by thorough needs analyses and, once implemented, programmes and curriculums are modified continuously in response to ongoing assessments of their effectiveness. In collaborative curriculum/programme evaluation, classroom teachers along with district personnel and/or researchers engage in action research to evaluate and develop ESL/EFL curriculums (for examples, see Brown 1989; Burns 1996a). Teacher engagement in such efforts is predicated on the recognition that the interpretation of 'situated information' collected in context is an important aspect of formative evaluation and, thus, teachers have a valuable contribution to make.

Another important purpose of evaluation is to make placement, advancement/promotion or related decisions about students' status in a programme, course or unit within a course. In these cases, evaluation often relies heavily on language-test results and can involve classroom teachers or other school or district professionals. Evaluation for placement and advancement purposes tends to be summative whereas evaluation to determine the status of students within a programme or course of student is largely formative.

Yet another purpose of evaluation is to guide classroom instruction and enhance student learning on a day-to-day basis. Classroom-based evaluation, while considered informal relative to most programme evaluation, is taking on increased importance as evaluation experts recognise the importance of day-to-day decisions teachers make on student learning and the effectiveness of educational programmes (Richards and Lockhart 1994: Chapter 4). Classroom-based evaluation is concerned, e.g., with questions about:

- suitability of general instructional goals and objectives associated with individual lesson or unit plans;
- effectiveness of instructional methods, materials and activities used to attain instructional objectives;
- adequacy of professional resources required to deliver instruction.

It calls for consideration of numerous classroom-based and other factors that can impinge on the effectiveness of instruction and the success of learning. Classroom-based factors include: students' learning needs and goals; their preferred learning styles; their attitudes toward schooling and second language (L2) learning in particular; and their interests and motivations. Other factors include: community attitudes; availability of resources and time outside school to complete

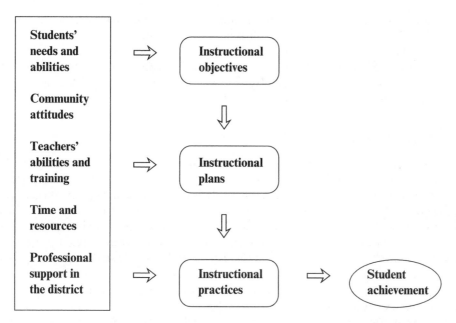

Figure 21.2 Instructional and other factors to consider in classroom-based evaluation

assignments; the level and kind of professional support in the district or community to support teaching and learning. Figure 21.2 presents a schematic representation of these diverse factors and their inter-relationships in classroom-based evaluation.

Classroom-based evaluation under the active management of teachers can also serve important professional development purposes since information resulting from such evaluations provides teachers with valuable feedback about their instructional effectiveness that they can use to hone their professional skills. As part of the reflective teaching movement, teachers are encouraged to conduct research in their own classrooms (Nunan 1989b; Allwright and Bailey 1991; Richards and Lockhart 1994); classroom-based evaluation is an important part of such research.

PARTICIPANTS

As noted earlier, evaluation for purposes of accountability, student placement/advancement and formal programme/curriculum development has relied and continues to rely heavily on the participation of policy-makers and educational leaders at district, state/provincial and national levels. Researchers often play an important role in formal programme evaluation, be it for strictly scholarly purposes or in co-operation with districts as part of their accountability efforts. Classroom-based and collaborative approaches to evaluation call for the involvement of teachers as primary agents in planning, managing and carrying out formative evaluations (Nunan 1988a; Brown 1995; Genesee and Upshur 1996).

In keeping with student-centred approaches to curriculum development and instruction (Nunan 1988a), students are assigned important roles in classroom-based evaluation. This is particularly true of older learners. More specifically, it is argued that including students in the evaluation process as active partners serves to:

- make them aware of learning objectives so they are better able to allocate time and energy to fulfilling designated instructional objectives; and

- instil a sense of ownership and responsibility for learning that can enhance achievement.

While parents of school-aged L2 learners have always had access to their children's test results in report cards and during parent–teacher conferences, they, like students, are increasingly encouraged to become active players in evaluation. For example, educators are encouraged to explain evaluation procedures to parents of young ESL learners and to include parents in reviewing students' achievements. When it comes to decision-making itself, however, it is not clear precisely what role parents will or can play; e.g. there may be cultural and language issues impeding communication between home and school.

KINDS OF INFORMATION

Student achievement has been and continues to be an important focus of evaluation. Teachers, administrators, parents and others need to know what and how much students have learned in order to make appropriate advancement/placement decisions, to develop appropriate curriculum and instruction and to judge the overall success of their education. At the same time, there is growing recognition that effective education calls for the interpretation of student performance in class – be it by tests or during routine instruction – so that teachers can design instruction that corresponds to individual students' needs and characteristics. Formative student evaluation of this sort calls for a great deal of information about the factors influencing the processes of teaching and learning in the classroom; e.g. information about students' interests, language learning needs, prior educational experiences, preferred learning styles and strategies, attitudes toward schooling and themselves as learners, and even medical and family histories. Such information can be particularly important in planning instruction for ESL students since they vary considerably with respect to these factors. Thinking about evaluation has, therefore, evolved significantly to include information that goes beyond student achievement. While some of this information may be quantitative, much of it is qualitative in nature and calls for alternative and diverse methods of information collection.

The specific kinds of information that are collected depend on the purposes for evaluation, i.e. what decisions are to be taken. For example, decisions about student placement in particular programmes call for information about their general language proficiency and prior educational experiences whereas decisions about individualising instruction for students experiencing difficulty with aspects of the language call for information about specific language skills, learning strategies, attitudes toward the instructional materials and so on. Not all information is useful for all evaluation purposes.

INFORMATION COLLECTION

Tests are useful for collecting information about certain aspects of language learning (see Chapter 20). They are not useful for collecting the different kinds of information that educators need to make their day-to-day educational decisions. Alternative methods are available for collecting information about language learning and about student-related factors that influence the processes of language teaching and learning. For example, dialogue journals that are shared with teachers can provide important insights useful for instructional planning and delivery. Portfolio conferences provide a forum for student–teacher discussions where insights can emerge about students' views, etc. which can guide and improve teachers' interpretation of students' classroom performance. Such activities also give students opportunities to use the target language in academic and interpersonal situations that are otherwise difficult to create in classrooms, thus giving teachers evidence of students' communication skills that are difficult to solicit in a whole-class setting; e.g. students' journal writing reveals their use of specific writing strategies; and reading or writing conferences about academic texts give teachers first-hand evidence of individual students' academic language skills.

For tests and alternative forms of language assessment to be useful for classroom-based evaluation, they should be: linked to instructional objectives and activities; designed to optimise student performance; developmentally appropriate, relevant and interesting to students; authentic; fair; and ongoing.

ANALYSIS AND INTERPRETATION OF INFORMATION

In keeping with the expanded view of evaluation that is emerging, multiple frames of reference are called for when analysing and interpreting information for educational decision-making. Clearly, extensive judgement – based on experience, professional training and one's understanding of educational theory – is implicated in the interpretation information collected for classroom evaluation, especially for information emanating from alternative assessment activities (e.g. dialogue journals, portfolio conferences, observation).

ESL/EFL educators increasingly utilise content and, in some cases, performance standards established by educational authorities (Brindley 1998a) and professional associations (ACTFL 1996; TESOL 1997) as benchmarks for evaluating student performance and educational effectiveness. Although content standards seldom provide explicit and discrete criteria for evaluating language learning, they provide a framework for developing instructional curriculums and objectives that provide bases for evaluating student learning. The use of instructional objectives and standards-based curriculums in assessment is part of a shift towards criterion-referenced assessment (for a discussion of criterion- and norm-referenced test interpretation, see Chapter 20).

Practice

The practical implications of classroom-based and collaborative approaches to evaluation for instructional, programme and curriculum planning and development are direct and substantial because these approaches are motivated to provide teachers with the necessary tools for sound educational decision-making and to draw on expertise of classroom teachers for programme-level decision-making. Educational publications increasingly discuss evaluation from the practitioners' viewpoint (see Fradd and McGee 1994; Brown 1995; Genesee and Upshur 1996; O'Malley and Valdez-Pierce 1996), although implementation of such approaches poses challenges. Since the premise of these approaches is that sound evaluation must be tailored to reflect local goals, practices, resources and characteristics, it is not possible to prescribe how they should be conducted. Thus, there can be disagreement about whether such evaluations are adequate for higher-level decision-making. Moreover, although new approaches to evaluation are less technical than traditional approaches, they still require specialised knowledge and skill for appropriate implementation. This poses challenges for pre- and in-service professional development. Practitioner-oriented approaches to evaluation is also time consuming for already busy teachers.

An additional challenge for practitioner-oriented approaches is reconciling individualised teacher-driven evaluations with district- or state-mandated evaluations (Brindley 1998a). At issue is how to incorporate results and implications from highly contextualised classroom-based evaluations with standardised results from more formal evaluations that are often favoured by district and state authorities. Resolution of this issue involves technical (e.g. how to equate evaluation results from different teachers using different procedures) and sociopolitical (e.g. how to convince educational authorities that these innovative approaches are useful) considerations.

Current and future directions

As noted, evaluation in ESL/EFL educational settings has developed significantly in recent years. Programme- and curriculum-evaluation models have expanded to include collaborations between classroom teachers, district personnel and trained researchers (for examples, see Hudelson and Lindfors 1993; Burns 1996a). Another trend is the emphasis on classroom-based evaluation that is linked to classroom teaching. This trend is often identified with the movement towards so-called alternative assessment but, in fact, encompasses issues falling within the evaluation domain. As noted, this approach is characterised by its emphasis on:

1. multiple types of information; e.g. student achievement, attitudes, learning styles, needs and aspirations;

2. alternative and varied methods of information collection to complement tests;

3. concerns for both the processes and the products of teaching and learning;

4. criterion-referenced, standards-based and objectives-based interpretation of student learning; and

5. inclusive participation, including visible and strong roles for teachers, students and (where appropriate) parents.

To date, empirical investigation of these approaches is noticeably lacking, although some largely descriptive reports are in preparation (see Burns 1996a; Brown 1989; Brindley 1998a). Future research is likely to examine how and to what extent these approaches are being adopted, and reflect on their effectiveness.

Conclusion

Evaluation is essential to successful education because it forms the basis for appropriate and effective decision-making. Evaluation in TESOL is the purposeful collection of information to assist decision-making about teaching and learning in ESL/EFL classrooms and programmes. It has evolved in recent years to include informal and formal approaches, bottom-up and top-down perspectives, and alternative forms of information collection and interpretation to complement tests. Classroom-based evaluation is a tool that teachers can use to hone decision-making skills for the benefit of students. Collaborative approaches to evaluation include the teaming up of educational practitioners, trained researchers and district personnel to optimise programme and curriculum development. New evaluation approaches recognise classroom teachers as reflective, self-motivated professionals. Further developments in these approaches are likely, contributing to the array of evaluation perspectives available to educators and researchers interested in improving L2 teaching and learning.

Key readings

Brindley (1998a) Outcomes-based assessment and reporting in language learning programmes
Brown (1995) *The Elements of Language Curriculum*
Genesee and Upshur (1996) *Classroom-Based Evaluation in Second Language Education*
O'Malley and Valdez-Pierce (1996) *Authentic Assessment for English Language Learners*
Rea-Dickins and Germaine (1993) *Evaluation*

CHAPTER 22

Syllabus design

Michael P. Breen

Introduction

Any syllabus is a plan of what is to be achieved through teaching and learning. It is part of an overall language curriculum or course which is made up of four elements: **aims**, **content**, **methodology** and **evaluation**. The syllabus identifies *what* will be worked upon by the teacher and students in terms of content selected to be appropriate to overall aims. Methodology refers to how teachers and learners work upon the content, whilst evaluation is the process of assessing outcomes from the learning and judging the appropriateness of other elements of the curriculum.

A syllabus may be formally documented, as in the aims and content of a national or institutional syllabus for particular groups of learners or (less explicitly perhaps) in the content material of published textbooks. Every teacher follows a syllabus, but it may vary from being a pre-designed document to a day-to-day choice of content which the teacher regards as serving a course's particular aims. In the latter case, the syllabus unfolds as lessons progress.

Any syllabus ideally should provide:

- a clear framework of knowledge and capabilities selected to be appropriate to overall aims;
- continuity and a sense of direction in classroom work for teacher and students;
- a record for other teachers of what has been covered in the course;
- a basis for evaluating students' progress;
- a basis for evaluating the appropriateness of the course in relation to overall aims and student needs identified both before and during the course;
- content appropriate to the broader language curriculum, the particular class of learners, and the educational situation and wider society in which the course is located.

To meet these requirements, syllabus designers – including teachers who develop their own syllabuses – apply principles to the organisation of the content which they intend the syllabus to cover. These principles can be expressed as questions:

1. What knowledge and capabilities should be *focused upon*? A syllabus may give priority to linguistic or broader communicative knowledge and focus upon one or all four skills (reading, speaking, writing and listening) or, more broadly, problem-solving or negotiation capabilities.

2. What should be *selected* as appropriate content? Given a linguistic focus, which particular structures and vocabulary should be covered or, given a communicative focus, which particular uses of language or types of tasks should be selected?

3. How should the content be *subdivided* so that it can be dealt with in manageable units? In other words, what is selected as content may be broken down to contributory or constituent parts for ease of teaching and learning in real time.

4. How should the content be *sequenced* along a path of development? A syllabus may adopt a step-by-step progression from less to more complex knowledge and capabilities, or it may be cyclic where earlier knowledge and capabilities are revisited and refined at later points.

These four principles of organisation define a syllabus. In the history of language teaching, the last 20 years in particular have revealed significant developments in syllabus design that have led to the application of each of these principles in alternative ways.

Background

Generally speaking, there are four types of syllabus currently used in language teaching. Syllabus designers, textbook writers, and teachers have evolved versions of these, but their main characteristics usefully reveal the development of syllabus design over the last 20 years or so. Before describing the types of syllabus, I give a brief history of their emergence to illustrate their differences (for further details of these developments, see Breen 1987; Nunan 1988b; White 1988; Stern 1992).

Before the advent of communicative language teaching (CLT) in the late 1970s, it was widely accepted that the syllabus should focus upon linguistic knowledge and the skills of listening, reading, speaking and writing, usually in that order. In the 1970s, research in the social and conversational use of language, coupled with growing dissatisfaction with learners' apparent failure to use the linguistic knowledge outside the classroom which they had gained within it, initiated a major change in syllabus design. Applied linguists advocated a focus upon *language use* rather than the formal aspects of language (e.g. Council of Europe 1971; Wilkins 1972b; Brumfit and Johnson 1979). The initial phase of this transition was exemplified in the development of functional syllabuses focusing upon particular purposes of language and how these would be expressed linguistically. At the same time – in response to the particular needs of certain groups of learners – special purpose syllabuses and teaching materials were quickly developed focusing upon language knowledge and skills needed for academic study or specific occupations, e.g. engineering or medicine (Mackay and Mountford 1978; Mumby 1978; Trimble *et al.* 1978).

In the early 1980s this functional movement in syllabus design became challenged from two directions. The teaching of a repertoire of functions or special purpose language was considered by some as limiting the learner's potential to certain fixed communicative situations or fixed social and occupational roles. They argued that a focus upon formal aspects of language at least allowed learners to generalise from one situation or communicative demand to another on the basis of the system of rules and the range of vocabulary that they have learned (Brumfit 1981; Wilkins *et al.* 1981).

The second challenge echoed earlier doubts expressed about formal syllabuses. Both types of syllabus could be seen as 'synthetic' in that learners were expected gradually to accumulate separated bits of knowledge, be they forms or functions, largely through de-contextualised *language-focused* activities before applying such knowledge as typically synthesised in real communication. They were also seen as partial because either formal or functional knowledge of linguistic structures or utterances were just two elements within broader communicative competence. Such competence entailed *orchestrating* language forms, the conventions for the social use of language, and the interpretation and expression of meanings as a unified activity (Breen and

Candlin 1980; Canale and Swain 1980). This view was informed by linguistic and sociolinguistic analyses of extended spoken or written discourse and by how it was constructed and participated in by language users (see, e.g., Widdowson 1978, 1989).

During the 1980s, therefore, the wider development of CLT evolved in two new directions subsequent to functionalism. Both reflected a shift in the kind of research on which they were based. As we have seen, formal and functional syllabuses had been based on *how linguists described language*, and the latter were motivated by an extended awareness of the nature of language use in social situations. The two new directions for syllabus design were oriented towards psycholinguistic and educational accounts of *how language learning is actually undertaken* by the learner. Such an orientation led to task-based and process syllabus types.

Task-based syllabuses had their origins in research on second language acquisition (SLA) during the 1980s. Building upon discoveries from first language (L1) acquisition and Krashen's influential view that language was best acquired through the learner's focus upon meaning in the input provided to the learner (summarised in Krashen 1985), researchers began to focus upon how learners interacted in order to negotiate meaning both inside and outside the classroom (Hatch 1978; Long 1981; for a review, see Pica 1994). From this perspective, a learner's use of the formal and social conventions governing language were seen to serve the struggle for meaning during interaction. The goal of the syllabus designer or teacher therefore became the provision of suitable tasks to encourage interaction and, through it, negotiation for meaning. In essence, a learner's expression and interpretation of meaning during appropriate tasks would enable the acquisition and refinement of linguistic knowledge and its social use. Some researchers and practitioners therefore proposed that *task* should be the key unit within the syllabus rather than aspects of language, be these formally or functionally identified (Breen *et al.* 1979; Prabhu 1984; Long 1985b; Candlin and Murphy 1987; Long and Crookes 1992).

Two main task types are identified in task-based syllabus design: a syllabus may be constituted of (1) communicative or target-like tasks or (2) metacommunicative or learning tasks. The former are those involving learners in sharing meaning in the target language about everyday tasks. Any task-based syllabus varies according to the particular curriculum within which it is located. A curriculum serving the needs, for example of school-age learners might include a syllabus of age-appropriate everyday tasks, such as planning a trip or solving a maths/science problem (see Chapters 18, 19 and 27).

The second task type is facilitative of the learner's involvement in communicative or target-like tasks. Metacommunicative or learning tasks (sometimes called pedagogic tasks) involve learners in sharing meaning about how the language works or is used in target situations and/or sharing meaning about students' own learning processes. Typical metacommunicative tasks are deducing verb-form patterns in spoken or written texts, or mapping how, e.g., narratives or scientific reports are structured.

Also focusing upon how language learning is undertaken – specifically in the context of the broader curriculum and the classroom – a second proposal for syllabus design in the 1980s was derived from educational perspectives on curriculum design and the teaching–learning process. A key argument was that *what* learners have to learn and *how* teaching and learning are done are unavoidably interrelated. Content, teaching methodology and learning constantly interact and influence each another during classroom work so that the teaching and learning process is itself a highly significant part of the content of language lessons (Postman and Weingartner 1969; Freire 1970 [1996], 1972; Stenhouse 1975; Breen and Candlin 1980). These ideas coincided with innovations in teaching methodologies which provided alternatives to grammar translation, audiolingual and other teacher modelling and feedback methodologies that had typified the use of formal syllabuses in particular (Stevick 1976, 1980).

This orientation to how language may be learned in ways that could be directly related to how teaching and learning may be done in the classroom had motivated the adoption of tasks as a key component of the syllabus. However, the idea that negotiation for meaning during tasks facilitates language acquisition supported the proposal that learner negotiation could also focus upon the creation of the classroom syllabus itself (Candlin 1984). In essence, collaborative decision-making about different aspects of the teaching–learning process in the classroom could be seen as a *meta-task* which involves learners in authentic opportunities to use and develop their knowledge and capabilities whilst, at the same time, calling upon their responsible engagement in the learning process within the classroom group. A **process syllabus** was therefore proposed as providing a framework for such classroom decision-making (Breen 1984). This type of syllabus identified negotiation about the purposes, contents and ways of working as a meaningful part of the content of lessons or series of lessons. A process syllabus therefore represents an orientation to how learning is done which deliberately locates the selection and organisation of the actual syllabus of the classroom group within the collaborative decision-making process undertaken by teacher and learners in a language class (Breen and Littlejohn 2000).

The distinctive characteristics of the four main types of syllabus described above can be identified with reference to the principles of syllabus organisation identified in the previous section. Figure 22.1 summarises these key characteristics and provides specific information about them. Note that the four syllabus types are prototypical, i.e. actual syllabuses used by teachers in different situations will represent variations on these key characteristics. These four types of syllabus design emerged in the late 1970s and the 1980s; more recent developments within these types are referred to below.

Research

Very little research has been undertaken to evaluate the relative effectiveness of syllabus types. Since a syllabus is implemented in a classroom and operates *within* the wider process of teaching and learning, this would be difficult to do. Just as it has proved virtually impossible to show that one teaching method is more effective than another (Stern 1983; Allwright 1988), variations in teacher interpretations of a syllabus during the course and variations in what students actually learn from the teacher intervene between the syllabus as a plan and the actual outcomes which learners achieve (Allwright 1984; Slimani 1989; Dobinson 1996).

The emergence of task-based syllabuses, however, has coincided with a significant amount of SLA research on the kinds of negotiation that learners undertake during tasks and the kinds of tasks that appear to facilitate best negotiation for meaning (Crookes and Gass 1993a, 1993b; Foster 1998; Skehan 1998; Long in press). Although few studies on task work are classroom based, research continues to inform the selection and sequencing of particular tasks within a syllabus; e.g. the current reassessment of a focus upon formal knowledge of language is of direct relevance for task-based syllabuses. This reassessment has been largely motivated by the discovery that, even after years of rich and meaningful input in content-based or immersion classrooms, learners continue to reveal non-target-like features in their language production. Swain (1995) suggests that the relative lack of opportunity for oral participation by learners in class may explain this. The debate among researchers centres upon whether to focus explicitly on formal features in teaching or more implicitly to enable learners to notice the gap between their own production and correct reformulations provided by a teacher or others as feedback (Spada 1997; Doughty and Williams 1998a). This suggests that follow-up tasks encouraging a focus upon learners' gaps in formal knowledge revealed during earlier more communicative tasks may be a feature of future task-based syllabuses (see also Chapter 25).

Teachers' accounts of negotiation with learners about aspects of the classroom curriculum are becoming increasingly available, and these will inform developments in process syllabuses (Bailey and Nunan 1996; Richards 1998; Breen and Littlejohn 2000). Both kinds of research summarised here – particularly if carried out in real classrooms – can support the efficacy of task-based or process syllabuses, but it remains true that it would be hard to isolate the direct effect upon learning of any syllabus used by a teacher.

Orientation: What is to be learned ⟵ ⟶ *How the learning is done*

	Formal	Functional	Task-based	Process
Knowledge focus	Forms, systems and rules of phonology, morphology, vocabulary, grammar, discourse as text.	Purposes of language use in terms of social functions: e.g. requests, descriptions, explanations, etc.	Meanings derived and created through unified system of linguistic forms and interpersonal conventions.	Overall same as task-based but focus may also narrow at times to Formal/Functional knowledge depending upon identified immediate and long terms needs of learners.
Capabilities focus	Accurate production. 4 skills from receptive to productive.	Social appropriateness based on repertoire of functions. 4 skills related to purposes/needs.	Comprehensible, accurate and appropriate interpretation, expression and negotiation of meanings in tasks. Skills use integrated within tasks.	Same as task-based plus negotiated decision-making within classroom group on aspects of the class curriculum.
Selection and subdivision	Larger units down to smaller units: e.g. sentence types or intonation patterns to modality, inflections, particular vocabulary, single sounds, etc.	Linguistic realisations of superordinate and subordinate functions of language in common use or derived from Needs Analysis for particular Special Purposes; academic or occupational.	*Communicative/target-like tasks:* everyday tasks (e.g. planning a trip) or special purpose tasks (e.g. solving technical problem). *Metacommunicative/learning tasks:* e.g. deducing pattern in verb forms or comparing learning strategies.	*Negotiation cycle:* 1. Decisions made on purposes, content, and ways of working in classroom group; 2. Agreed action – such as tasks/activities; 3. Evaluation of both outcomes and chosen procedures. Cycle applied to all elements in the curriculum so that actual syllabus of the class evolves.
Sequencing	Assumes learner accumulates and synthesises. Simple to complex, or frequent to infrequent, or most useful to less useful.	Assumes learner builds repertoire. Most common linguistic realisations to more subtle or most needed to less needed.	Assumes learner refines knowledge and abilities in cyclic way. Familiar to less familiar or generalisable to less generalisable tasks. Task sequence also shaped by problems in earlier tasks.	Assumes learner refines knowledge and abilities in cyclic way. Sequence of activities and tasks emerges in ongoing way through evaluation stage (3) revealing needs and achievements which inform next decisions (1).

Figure 22.1 Key characteristics of the four main syllabus types

Practice

Currently teachers have a wider choice of alternatives in the focus, selection, subdivision and sequencing of the content of lessons than 20 years ago (see Figure 22.1). The choices depend upon a teacher's answers to two questions:

1. What particular view of language do I hold? Is the view of language expressed in a particular type of syllabus close to the one I seek to convey to students in terms of the knowledge and capabilities on which they should focus and which they should develop?

2. What is my view of language learning? Do the assumptions within a particular type of syllabus concerning how students learn a language provide the scope for the kind of learning process I wish them to experience?

The day-to-day practicalities of teaching a language to particular students in a particular working situation have to be balanced against one's preferred answers to these questions. One of the challenges raised by innovations such as task-based or, particularly, process syllabus types is their feasibility in certain contexts: a challenge always applicable to any innovation in language teaching! The teacher selecting a type of syllabus or its particular characteristics has to take account of:

*   differing student expectations about appropriate content and ways of working in the language classroom;
*   the overall aims and conventions of the immediate working context of the teacher's institution;
*   the possibility that the educational system in which the institution is located may require students to follow an externally designed syllabus or undertake externally designed tests.

These contextual factors lead to a third question which influences the teacher's practical selection of the syllabus and its characteristics:

3. Which type of syllabus is most appropriate to the teaching context in which I am working? Which alternatives in focus, selection, subdivision and sequencing could I implement most easily in the classroom? Which are most feasible, at least initially? Also, if I seek to innovate on the basis of my answers to questions 1 and 2, which particular aspect(s) of the syllabus could I begin with?

Current and future trends and directions

As we have seen, current research on tasks and negotiation for meaning in the classroom continue to inform syllabus design which is more oriented to *how* learning is done (Figure 22.1). However, significant developments in the 1990s particularly influenced syllabuses oriented to *what* is to be learned. Two main trends emerged in which syllabuses have been developed with a focus on lexis or vocabulary, and on outcomes or competencies. Both represent recent extensions of formal and functional types of syllabus.

Lexical syllabuses are motivated by the argument that language learning can be built around a growing repertoire of vocabulary that is relevant and purposeful for the learner (Carter and McCarthy 1988; D. Willis 1990). The proposals for appropriate lexical syllabuses have been significantly mobilised by the coincidental availability of large lexical corpora on computer databases. It is most likely that computer-based corpora of authentic language use will be a major factor in the future organisation of syllabus content.

Outcomes-based education has been a dominant feature of the recent movement towards the assessment of national standards in education in many countries (e.g. Glatthorn 1993; Evans and

---

Language syllabus
Major goal: Proficiency.
Content: the systematic study of the language in terms of its formal and functional characteristics.

Culture syllabus
Major goal: Knowledge.
Content: the systematic study of the people who use the language in terms of their society, history, values, etc.

Communicative activities syllabus
Major goal: Proficiency.
Content: use of language in its socio-cultural context, both inside and outside the classroom.

General language education syllabus
Major goal: Transfer of knowledge and experience.
Content: reflecting on language, cultures, and learning (knowledge about language(s), cross cultural awareness, strategies for learning etc.)

Figure 22.2 Stern's integrated language curriculum

King 1994; McGhan 1994). In this context, curriculum designers have elaborated upon language proficiency in terms of statements describing what a learner may be able to do with the language. The aims of the syllabus may therefore be expressed as target achievements or 'competency statements', and syllabus content would serve to support learners' use of such competencies (Auerbach 1986; Brindley 1995). A major characteristic of current frameworks of competency statements is their distinction between stages or levels of achievement in the four skills of reading, speaking, writing and listening.

Within the current interest in the design of systematic frameworks of stages or levels of achievement in language use is the concept of a syllabus as having several dimensions or strands which would address complementary and interrelated goals. Two examples illustrate a broadening of our view of the kinds of knowledge and capabilities which may be the focus of the syllabus. The first is Stern's proposal for an integrated curriculum: this is a syllabus of syllabuses, each of which entails particular syllabus goals. Figure 22.2 summarises Stern's concept, derived from long research experience of bilingual education in Canada (Stern 1992). Stern's call for focus on the target-language community's culture and the cultural experience and perspectives of learners has been adopted as a significant goal within syllabus development (Byram 1989; Kramsch 1993).

The second example addresses the school-age learner's needs when developing a new language (Scarino et al. 1988). Such needs provide principles on which the goals of a particular language syllabus could be based (Clark 1987). Figure 22.3 illustrates these goals, which echo and extend Stern's.

These brief examples illustrate the recognition that learning a language involves learners in a complex interrelationship of different but complementary areas of knowledge and capabilities. We may regard some of these as part of communicative competence whilst others suggest a broader picture of what it means to be a language learner and user. These developments in *multi-dimensional* syllabuses suggest that syllabus design in the early part of the twenty-first century may reveal a growing synthesis of the two orientations summarised in Figure 22.1.

Conclusion

In general, therefore, there are four main trends in current syllabus design:

Communication
By participating in activities organised around use of the language, learners will acquire communication skills in order that they may widen their networks of relationships, have direct access to information, and use their language skills for study, vocational, and leisure-based purposes.

Sociocultural
Learners will develop an understanding of the culture of the target language community which they can use as a basis for informed comparison with other cultures. Through this, learners will develop an appreciation of the validity of different ways of perceiving and encoding experience and of organising interpersonal relations, and reach a secure acceptance of their own personal identity and value.

Learning-how-to-learn
Learners will be able to take a growing responsibility for the management of their own learning so that they learn how to learn and how to learn a language.

Language and cultural awareness
Learners will reflect upon and develop an awareness of the role and nature of language and of culture in everyday life so that they may understand the diversity of the world around them and act upon it in judicious ways.

General knowledge
Learners will gain knowledge and understanding of a range of subject matter related to their needs, interests and aspirations as well as to other areas of their formal (school) learning.

Figure 22.3   Overall goals of the language syllabus

1. outcomes-based or competency-based planning;
2. the organisation of the syllabus presented through tasks and subdivided and sequenced *as* tasks;
3. shared decision-making through negotiation between teacher and learners;
4. the recent identification of different syllabuses which may serve a range of appropriate language-learning aims; this implies a weakening of the distinctions between the types of syllabus that typified the end of the twentieth century.

These trends suggest that plans for what is to be achieved through teaching and learning which genuinely *integrate* form, function, task and process in different ways will multiply. In addition to ongoing extensions and refinements to these four terms, one feature of this evolution may be the closer integration of syllabus design *within* the whole language curriculum (its aims, content, methodology and evaluation) and within broader educational curriculums (van Lier 1996). This would locate design of the syllabus within language pedagogy rather than it being identified as a separable undertaking.

Key readings

Breen and Littlejohn (2000) *Classroom Decision-Making*
Brumfit (1984b) *General English Syllabus Design*
Clark (1987) *Curriculum Renewal in School Foreign Language Learning*

Crookes and Gass (1993a) *Tasks in a Learning Language Context*
Crookes and Gass (1993b) *Tasks in a Pedagogical Context*
Kramsch (1993) *Context and Culture in Language Teaching*
Long and Crookes (1992) Three approaches to task-based syllabus design
Nunan (1988b) *Syllabus Design*
Prabhu (1984) Procedural syllabuses
van Lier (1996) *Interaction in the Language Curriculum*
D. Willis (1990) *The Lexical Syllabus*

CHAPTER 23

Language awareness

Leo van Lier

Introduction

Language awareness has been conceptualised in several different ways. In a round-table discussion in the UK in 1982 it was defined as 'a person's sensitivity to and conscious awareness of the nature of language and its role in human life' (Donmall 1985: 7). Van Lier (1995: xi) defines it similarly as 'an understanding of the human faculty of language and its role in thinking, learning and social life'. These definitions are quite broad and accommodate various interpretations and practices. In this review I look at the most common ways in which language awareness has been understood in the past, and the ways in which it is currently being interpreted, practised, and promoted.

Background

The concept of language awareness is not new. Van Essen (1997) points to a long tradition in several European countries; see *Language Awareness*, 1990, 1(1). In van Lier (1996), I refer to the 1930s in the Netherlands, noting distinctions made at the time between 'language understanding' (*taalbegrip*), 'language feeling' (*taalgevoel*) and 'language insight' (*taalinzicht*). Even though grammar translation was dominant in teaching and learning languages up to the 1960s, there have long been strong critiques against prescriptive approaches from applied linguists, including Otto Jespersen, Harold Palmer and Charles Fries (see Howatt 1984). Language awareness proponents have always firmly opposed a view of language learning (both first and second) that focuses on prescriptive instruction and is concerned primarily with correctness, and only secondarily with understanding, appreciation and creative expression.

In the US, language awareness, especially in the English-language (first language) education of college students, has been conducted through the study of texts examining language from a variety of perspectives, including literary, political, cultural and everyday uses. This perspective is illustrated in collections of readings such as Goshgarian (1997) and Eschholz *et al.* (1990). In more recent years the term has been used in the US in two added contexts, language across the curriculum (related curricular efforts are reading across the curriculum and writing across the curriculum, mostly at the undergraduate level) and brief introductory overview courses in several foreign languages at the junior secondary level (sometimes called 'taster courses'). Finally, language awareness as a pedagogical approach is closely related to the whole language movement which started in the US in the 1970s, led by Kenneth and Yetta Goodman (Goodman 1997). However, whole language has generally been limited to early literacy in the early grades of elementary school, and has hardly played a role in the higher grades, in adult education or in foreign language teaching.

Current interest in language awareness stems largely from three sources: first, a practical, pedagogically oriented language awareness such as that of the language awareness movement in the UK; second, a more psycholinguistic focus on consciousness-raising and explicit attention to language form; and, third, a critical, ideological perspective that looks at language and power, control and emancipation.

THE LANGUAGE AWARENESS MOVEMENT IN THE UK

The language awareness movement of the early 1980s in the UK followed a period of intense debate about the role of language in education, spurred on by the influential report of a national commission (Department of Education and Science 1975), and the work of linguists and educators including Douglas Barnes, Michael Halliday, Lawrence Stenhouse and Harold Rosen.

In 1982 the National Council on Language in Education (NCLE) set up a Language Awareness Working Party, which formulated the definition mentioned in the introduction. The NCLE initiative, chaired by John Trim and later John Sinclair, led to several developments. In 1986 a National Consortium of centres for Language Awareness (NCcLA) was set up by Gillian Donmall which promoted a range of innovative activities. In 1992 an Association for Language Awareness was founded that has since had conferences in Wales, England, Ireland and Canada, and produced an international journal called *Language Awareness*.

A number of publications have established language awareness as an active area in educational linguistics. Some of these publications are discussed in the next section, but it is worth mentioning the pioneering work of Eric Hawkins (1987a, 1987b). Hawkins also produced a series of booklets for secondary school students (described in Hawkins 1987a). A more overtly critical language awareness stance is illustrated in a series of small secondary school books published in South Africa (Janks 1993), and in a resource book produced for students and teachers in multilingual and multiethnic schools in London (ILEA 1990).

Another major initiative was the Language in the National Curriculum (LINC) project directed by Professor Ronald Carter, which produced materials for teacher education and was commissioned by the British government, only to be rejected as soon as it was completed for not sufficiently addressing basic grammar and correctness. It took a critical approach to language which displeased the then Conservative government. Nevertheless, the materials have had a significant impact as a publication of the University of Nottingham (Carter 1990, 1997; Donmall-Hicks 1997).

CONSCIOUSNESS-RAISING, FOCUS ON FORM AND VARIOUS APPROACHES TO EXPLICIT TEACHING AND METALINGUISTIC AWARENESS

Many researchers and teachers argue that awareness, attention and noticing particular features of language adds to learning. In 1981, Sharwood Smith published an influential article proposing that the teaching of formal aspects of language need not necessarily proceed by rules and drills, but can be done by judiciously highlighting relevant aspects of language (Sharwood Smith 1981, 1994).

Second language (L2) learners regularly have misconceptions about the target language; e.g. they may misuse a lexical item due to its similarity to their first language (L1) or because of the context in which they learned the word. By making explicit this problem, L2 learners' knowledge of their own language can be similarly used to raise conscious awareness about features of the target language.

Language awareness assumes that some form or level of awareness about linguistic use, knowledge and learning is beneficial for learners. There are widely varying opinions of how such awareness can be brought about. At the traditional end this might include explicit teaching of form, metalinguistic rules and terminology. However, most advocates of language awareness question the effectiveness of the explicit teaching of prescriptive grammar and warn against a return to 'the ghost of grammar past' (Donmall 1985). Currently, more inductive and implicit ways of focusing on form are generally preferred, and it is usually regarded as essential that a focus on form must derive from a focus on meaning and context. In this sense, Long (1996) distinguishes a focus on *form* within a meaningful context from a focus on *forms* when teaching is driven by grammatical items.

CRITICAL PERSPECTIVES ON LANGUAGE AND DISCOURSE

According to Clark and Ivanič, the purpose of critical language awareness is to 'present the view that language use is part of a wider social struggle, and that language education has the opportunity to raise learners' awareness of this' (1997: 220). As such, the target audiences of critical work in classrooms are often discriminated minorities or otherwise disenfranchised populations, i.e. 'children from oppressed social groupings' (as put by Fairclough 1989: 239; see also Freire 1970 [1996]). However, Janks (1997: 246) points to a frequent 'slippage' from awareness or critical literacy to 'emancipation', and warns that claims for the empowerment of learners need to be further researched. In addition, both learners from privileged and oppressed backgrounds need a critical perspective on the circumstances and mechanisms of inequality.

Research

The approaches to language awareness discussed above have led to a variety of research efforts, although researchers active in this field agree that solid evidence of the success of language awareness is rather scarce. Garrett and James report a number of classroom-based studies illustrating diverse aspects of language awareness, but few report solid research findings. Indeed, Garrett and James's chief message is a call for research showing evidence of the benefits of language awareness. They discuss the research agenda in terms of five interdependent domains: *affective* (including attention and curiosity), *social*, *power*, *cognitive* and *performance* domains (Garrett and James 1991: 310).

In the realm of affective and other individual factors, researchers have looked at attention and focusing (Schmidt 1995; N. Ellis 1995a), and the relationships between implicit and explicit learning (N. Ellis 1994). Schmidt (1994b) reviews much of the experimental research in this area, and concludes that attention to input is a necessary condition of learning, at the very least for explicit learning, and probably also for implicit learning, i.e. learning that occurs unconsciously and automatically. However, the articles collected in Schmidt (1995) and N. Ellis (1994) show that the controversies between implicit and explicit learning, instruction and knowledge (R. Ellis 1997), and the necessity of noticing, are far from settled. Krashen (1994) continues to insist that there is little or no evidence available that successfully counters his strong hypothesis that comprehensible input is all that is needed. On the other hand, classroom-based studies such as Brooks *et al.* (1997) and Doughty and Varela (1998) suggest that learners in their collaborative work, and teachers in subject-matter interactions with students, can successfully focus on formal aspects of language (for more detailed reviews on these issues, see Long 1996 and Gass 1997). Case studies of successful learners in various settings also show a significant role for focusing and noticing, including attending to form (Schmidt and Frota 1986; Ioup *et al.* 1994).

One of the claims of proponents of language awareness is that drawing attention to and working with interesting and meaningful manifestations of language enhances motivation and positive attitudes to language and language learning. So far the evidence for this is largely anecdotal, based on reports of action research in elementary schools (Bain *et al.* 1992) and teacher development (van Lier 1996; Wright and Bolitho 1997). Similarly, the reasonable expectation that a greater awareness of language fosters a better understanding of speakers of other languages and dialects, and thus might enhance inter-group relations, awaits confirmation by research studies (Wolfram 1993).

In critical language awareness and discourse analysis, as in other areas of language awareness, there is much theoretical and some practical work, but little in the way of tangible research results. As Janks points out, 'So far what we have are largely descriptive accounts, journal studies, interviews' (1997: 247). She calls particularly for detailed classroom observation studies and reports of pre-service and in-service teacher development (on the latter, see also Brumfit 1997; Wright and Bolitho 1997). The new research practices proposed by discursive social psychologists may become a promising force to move this area of research forward (Potter and Wetherell 1987; Kalaja and Leppänen 1998).

For cognitive research one can point to the area of metacognitive strategies and autonomy (O'Malley and Chamot 1990; Wenden 1991), though this does not specifically address the issue of language awareness. A significant recent study is Alderson *et al.* (1997), which reports little or no connection between metalinguistic knowledge and language proficiency among learners of French as a foreign language in the United Kingdom. Of course, language awareness and metalinguistic knowledge may be two quite separate things (van Lier 1998b), and reliable conclusions are still some distance away. Studies by Doughty (1991), Fotos and Ellis (1991), Slimani (1989) and Sorace (1985), among others, show the complexities within the area of metalinguistic work and explicit instruction. However, as Long has argued on several occasions, the value of instruction and the importance of a focus on form are quite well established (see, e.g., Long 1996; see also Doughty and Williams 1998a; van Lier and Corson 1997).

Finally, how might language awareness improve performance in an L2? We are all familiar with arguments that performance in complex skills (riding a bicycle, playing a musical instrument, typing, etc.) rely largely on automatised actions, and that focusing explicit attention while performing such skills tends to destroy their smooth performance. However, the feeling among learners and teachers alike persists that practice makes perfect, and that conscious effort and reflection on practice are essential components of learning. One route to investigating such issues is the assessment of studies of automatisation and control from an information-processing or constructivist perspective (Bialystok 1990; Sharwood Smith 1994). An alternative route is that of social constructionism or sociocultural theory, in which interaction in context is examined to find out how proficiency is collaboratively constructed or appropriated within and through practical activity (Lave and Wenger 1991; Donato 1994; van Lier and Matsuo 1999).

Practice

The preceding section was dominated by the familiar theme in our field that 'further research is needed.' Fortunately, the teacher interested in the practical side of language awareness can find a large number of useful tips, examples and descriptive accounts. In this section some of the resources that are available are introduced without distinguishing between different age or proficiency levels, nor between formal, ludic (playful) or critical language awareness work. The interested teacher or teacher educator can use published examples as ideas for the development of suitable activities for specific classes and contexts. In addition, there are many ideas available outside educational settings that can be enormously productive, such as puzzle and word-game publications available at news stands.

The first source are published books in language awareness. Among these, I have already mentioned the series of booklets by Hawkins (for a description, see Hawkins 1987a), and the critical language awareness series by Janks (1993). Both series contain numerous ideas for activities, and in their contrast they show the differences between a 'straight' and a 'critical' approach. Other published resources include Papaefthymiou-Lytra 1987; Tinkel 1988; ILEA 1990; Burrell 1991; Andrews 1993; Wright 1994; van Lier 1995. A book of considerable interest is

MacAndrew (1991), which shows, through activities and quizzes, the discrepancies between English as spoken by native speakers in the media and the prescriptive rules laid down in grammar books. Of practical use for teachers in elementary schools is Bain *et al.* (1992), a collection of action research reports from teachers working in the LINC project.

A number of journals have published articles detailing language awareness work, often with practical examples of tasks (Fotos and Ellis 1991; Wright and Bolitho 1993; in general, see also the journal *Language Awareness*).

Most work in language awareness is inductive. This means that, using data provided or collected, learners observe and analyse patterns of interest and come up with descriptions or tentative rules, usually in group work. In most cases the data are from authentic sources, the learners' environment, the internet or elsewhere. In my own work I have used field work conducted by learners as data, e.g. by asking learners to bring examples of target language use to class, written down on 3 x 5 cards that I collected as 'entry tickets' (van Lier 1996). Although field work and data collection are easiest in L2 environments, most foreign-language environments should also allow for such work, particularly if the internet and its inexhaustible resources are used well. Teachers can also use concordancers with authentic texts in order to raise awareness of grammatical, stylistic and lexical features (Johns and King 1991).

Awareness-raising itself is not sufficient. It must be integrated with action/collaboration and with reflection/interpretation/analysis. Thus, one possible approach is a progression from perception to (inter)action to interpretation and so on, in cyclical and spiral fashion.

Current and future trends and directions

There is a perpetual tension in language teaching between form (or structure) and meaning (or function), and the pendulum swings back and forth. Thus, the recommendations made by the LINC project in the UK were soon followed by a call for a return to teaching proper (i.e. prescriptive) grammar. Similarly, the enthusiasm for the whole language approach to literacy in the US has recently been replaced by a backlash demanding a phonics approach (Goodman 1997), and in some school districts in California even calling for an explicit ban on the use of whole language methodology.

There is no reason to expect that this pattern will disappear at the start of the twenty-first century, although one hopes that certain gains will endure. An increasingly important role for perception (including awareness, attention and focusing) in language learning is predicted along with a realisation that perception and action go hand in hand. The use of authentic resources will continue to favour inductive approaches to the integration of formal and functional aspects of language.

In terms of research there is likely to be a growing role for contextualised research such as case studies, action research and classroom observation studies. A number of researchers are now looking at complexity theory for ideas to develop rigorous procedures for researching learning processes in intact complex settings (Larsen-Freeman 1997b; van Lier 1998a).

In the last two decades, language awareness has created an identity that assures it a place within educational linguistics. The variety of approaches and opinions within language awareness are a strength rather than a weakness, since they allow for healthy debate and act as incentives to explore different options, methods and directions. Two particular areas that should gain in strength are concerted and integrative approaches to language awareness across the curriculum, and a strong push for language awareness in teacher education.

Key readings

Doughty and Williams (1998a) *Focus on Form in Classroom Second Language Acquisition*
Fairclough (1992) *Critical Language Awareness*
James and Garrett (1991) *Language Awareness in the Classroom*
Schmidt (1995) *Attention and Awareness in Foreign Language Learning*
van Lier (1995) *Introducing Language Awareness*
van Lier and Corson (1997) *Knowledge About Language*

CHAPTER 24

Language learning strategies

Rebecca L. Oxford

Introduction

This chapter reviews theory and research in the realm of language learning strategies and provides implications for teaching and future research. Learning strategies are 'operations employed by the learner to aid the acquisition, storage, retrieval and use of information, specific actions taken by the learner to make learning easier, faster, more enjoyable, more self-directed, more effective and more transferable to new situations'.

Background

This section offers a conceptual background for understanding language learning strategies, summarising common features of these strategies and then delineating six types of strategies.

COMMON FEATURES OF LANGUAGE LEARNING STRATEGIES

All language learning strategies are related to the features of control, goal-directedness, autonomy and self-efficacy.

Goals are the engine that fires language learning action and provides the direction for the action (Dörnyei and Ottó 1998, after Locke and Latham 1994); examples of goals are to use English fluently and accurately in business, to order meals, to ask directions, etc. Using learning strategies does not instantly propel language learners to attain such goals. They are usually fulfilled by aiming for smaller short-term language goals – or **proximal subgoals** (Dörnyei and Ottó 1998: 60) – linked to specific language tasks.

For instance, the aim of rapidly but accurately reading many English-language journal articles can be addressed by reading and understanding one such article per week until good comprehension is matched by speed. Relevant learning strategies for accomplishing this weekly task include scheduling time to read articles, skimming for main ideas, noting key vocabulary and guessing from the context, all of which might be called a **strategy chain**: a set of interlocking, related and mutually supportive strategies.

Learning strategies help learners become more autonomous. Autonomy requires conscious control of one's own learning processes. For discussions of autonomous language learning, see Holec 1981, 1985; Allwright 1990; Wenden 1991; Cotterall 1995; Dam 1995. Learning strategies also enhance **self-efficacy**, individuals' perception that they can successfully complete a task or series of tasks (Bandura 1997).

TYPES OF LANGUAGE LEARNING STRATEGIES AND THEIR BACKGROUND

Major varieties of language learning strategies are cognitive, mnemonic, metacognitive, compensatory (for speaking and writing), affective and social. Theoretical distinctions can be made among these six types; however, the boundaries are fuzzy, particularly since learners sometimes employ more than one strategy at a given time.

Cognitive strategies

Cognitive strategies help learners make and strengthen associations between new and already-known information (O'Malley and Chamot 1990; Oxford 1990, 1996) and facilitate the mental restructuring of information (Iran-Nejad *et al.* forthcoming). Examples of cognitive strategies are: guessing from context, analysing, reasoning inductively and deductively, taking systematic notes and reorganising information.

A different theory of language learning is the **tapestry approach** (Scarcella and Oxford 1992), which reflects work of Vygotsky (1978, 1986). Vygotsky emphasised that learning occurs in interaction with other people (social learning), especially with the help of a 'more capable other', often a teacher. The teacher provides scaffolding, or assistance given to the learner, which is gradually pulled away when the learner no longer needs it (Williams and Burden 1997). In these approaches teachers can help students develop cognitive learning strategies (known as **higher thinking skills**), such as analysing, synthesising and reasoning. Cognitive strategies usually involve hypothesis testing, such as searching for clues in surrounding material and one's own background knowledge, hypothesising the meaning of the unknown item, determining if this meaning makes sense and, if not, repeating at least part of the process.

Mnemonic strategies

Mnemonic strategies help learners link a new item with something known. These devices are useful for memorising information in an orderly string (e.g. acronyms) in various ways; examples are: by sounds (e.g. rhyming), by body movement (e.g. total physical response, in which the teacher gives a command in English and learners physically follow this) or by location on a page or blackboard (the locus technique). Theoretical and empirical justification exists for separating mnemonic strategies from cognitive strategies. In contrast to cognitive strategies, mnemonic strategies do not typically foster deep associations but instead relate one thing to another in a simplistic, stimulus–response manner. Even with their limitations, mnemonic strategies are often the first step in learning vocabulary items or grammar rules.

Metacognitive strategies

Metacognitive strategies help learners manage: (1) themselves as learners, (2) the general learning process and (2) specific learning tasks. Several varieties exist. One group of metacognitive strategies helps individuals know themselves better as language learners. Self-knowledge strategies include identifying one's own interests, needs and learning style preferences. **Learning styles** are the broad approaches that each learner brings to language learning or to solving any problem. Examples of learning styles include visual vs. auditory vs. kinesthetic, global vs. analytic, concrete-sequential vs. intuitive-random, and ambiguity-tolerant vs. ambiguity-intolerant (Ely 1989; Oxford and Ehrman 1995; Reid 1995a; Dreyer and Oxford 1996). Knowledge of learning styles helps learners choose strategies that comfortably fit with their learning styles, although using and learning others is obviously useful.

Another set of metacognitive strategies relates to managing the learning process in general and includes identifying available resources, deciding which resources are valuable for a given task, setting a study schedule, finding or creating a good place to study, etc. This set also includes establishing general goals for language learning. Language learning may be hindered if goals are unclear or in conflict.

Other metacognitive strategies also help learners deal effectively with a given language task, not just with the overall process of language learning. This set of metacognitive strategies includes, among other techniques, deciding on task-related (as opposed to general) goals for language learning, paying attention to the task at hand, planning for steps within the language task, reviewing relevant vocabulary and grammar, finding task-relevant materials and resources, deciding which other strategies might be useful and applying them, choosing alternative strategies if those do not work and monitoring language mistakes during the task.

Compensatory strategies for speaking and writing

Compensatory strategies for speaking and writing help learners make up for missing knowledge when using English in oral or written communication, just as the strategy of guessing from the context while listening and reading compensates for a knowledge gap. Compensatory strategies (or communication strategies) for speaking include using synonyms, circumlocution and gesturing to suggest the meaning. Compensatory strategies for writing encompass some of the same actions, such as synonym use or circumlocution.

Cohen (1997) asserts that communication strategies are intended only for language use, not for language learning, and that such strategies should therefore not be considered language learning strategies. However, Little (1999) and Oxford (1990) contend that compensatory strategies, even when employed for language use, simultaneously aid language learning: each instance of language use provides an immediate opportunity for 'incidental learning'. Incidental learning is one of the most important but least researched areas in language learning (Schmidt 1994a).

Affective strategies

Affective strategies include identifying one's feelings (e.g. anxiety, anger and contentment) and becoming aware of the learning circumstances or tasks that evoke them (see Arnold 1999). Using a language learning diary to record feelings about language learning can be very helpful, as can 'emotional checklists' (see Oxford 1990). However, the acceptability or viability of affective strategies is influenced by cultural norms. Some cultures do not encourage individuals to probe or record their own feelings in relation to learning.

Language learning anxiety – which has received an abundance of attention in the last decade (Horwitz and Young 1991; Young 1998) – is usually related to fear of communicating in English (or, indeed, the native language) when a judgement of performance is anticipated. In some individuals anxiety can sorely sabotage the language learning process (Young 1998). Certain affective strategies can help learners deal with anxiety through actions such as deep breathing, laughter, positive self-talk ('I know I can do it!', 'I know more than I did before') and praising oneself for performance. Corno (1993) suggests additional strategies, including generating useful diversions or visualising success and feeling good about it.

Negative attitudes and beliefs can reduce learners' motivation and harm language learning, while positive attitudes and beliefs can do the reverse. Using the affective strategy to examine beliefs and attitudes is therefore useful for, e.g., learning any language, the native speaker, the teacher and the language classroom.

Social strategies

Social strategies facilitate learning with others and help learners understand the culture of the language they are learning. Examples of social strategies are asking questions for clarification or confirmation, asking for help, learning about social or cultural norms and values and studying together outside of class. Cognitive information-processing theory tends to downplay social strategies in favour of cognitive and metacognitive strategies (O'Malley and Chamot 1990); however, social strategies are nevertheless crucial for communicative language learning.

Research

We first present tools for assessing use of language learning strategies and then address three areas of strategy research: the 'good language learner', strategy instruction research and influences on strategy choice.

ASSESSING STRATEGY USE

Rubin (1975) originally used observation to assess language learning strategy use. Some strategies – such as asking questions for clarification, taking notes and making outlines – are directly observable. However, other strategies – such as using inductive logic to determine a grammar rule or making mental associations between a new word and known concepts – are not. Other techniques are therefore used, including interviews, verbal reports while doing a task ('think aloud' procedures), strategy diaries, and strategy questionnaires such as the **Strategy Inventory for Language Learning** (**SILL**; Oxford 1990). Cohen and Scott (1996) discuss the purposes and limitations of each technique.

THE 'GOOD LANGUAGE LEARNER'

Studies in the mid-1970s focused on characteristics of the 'good language learner'. Rubin (1975) identifies the following characteristics of the good language learner; he or she:

* is a willing and accurate guesser;

* has a strong drive to communicate;

* is uninhibited and willing to make mistakes;

* focuses on form by looking at patterns and using analysis;

* takes advantage of all practice opportunities;

* monitors his or her own speech and that of others;

* pays attention to meaning.

Naiman *et al.* (1975) added that good language learners learn to think in the language and deal with affective aspects of language learning. Although tantalising, 'good language learner' studies are sometimes interpreted as being a little too prescriptive and not always open to multiple ways of language learning. Such studies led to investigations comparing more successful language learners with less successful peers. At first it was thought that the former, compared with the latter, employed more strategies and did so with greater frequency, more awareness and better ability to describe their strategy use.

However, none of these factors consistently distinguished between more and less effective language learners. It was observed that more successful learners typically understand which strategies fitted the particular language tasks they were attempting. Moreover, more effective learners are better at combining strategies as needed (Abraham and Vann 1987).

Relationships between strategy use and language proficiency

Research shows that greater strategy use is often related to higher levels of language proficiency (O'Malley and Chamot 1990; Oxford and Ehrman 1995; Oxford 1996; Cohen 1997). Many predictive studies (Dreyer and Oxford 1996) about the relationship between strategy use and language proficiency have employed SILL. In these predictive studies, strategy use explained from 21 per cent to 61 per cent of the variability or differences in English proficiency scores.

It was found that reported strategy use does not totally predict (or perfectly correlate with) language proficiency. However, strategy use clearly contributes to language learning, and in many studies the contribution is substantial. If strategy use and language proficiency are related, how can we improve learners' strategy use? Strategy instruction offers interesting possibilities.

STRATEGY INSTRUCTION RESEARCH

Learning strategies are teachable, and positive effects of strategy instruction emerged for proficiency in listening (Johnson 1999), speaking (Dadour and Robbins 1996; Varela 1999), reading (Park-Oh 1994) and writing (Sano 1999). In various language learning investigations, strategy instruction led to greater strategy use and self-efficacy (Chamot *et al.* 1996), anxiety reduction (Johnson 1999), and to increased motivation, strategy knowledge and positive attitudes (Nunan 1997).

Effectiveness of strategy instruction appears to relate partially to cultural background and beliefs (O'Malley *et al.* 1985) as well as to the content and presentation of the instruction. According to research, strategy instruction should address affective and learning-style issues, deal with strategies students really need to know, be authentic and relevant, and be woven into regular language instruction (Chamot and O'Malley 1996b; Oxford and Leaver 1996; Cohen and Weaver 1998; Ehrman 1999). Furthermore, research suggests that, to improve language learning proficiency, strategy instruction should be explicit. The term **fully informed strategy-plus-control instruction** (Brown *et al.* 1980; Oxford 1990) expresses the main thrust of such instruction, which can be introduced into every language lesson (Chamot and O'Malley 1996b; Green 1999).

Much of the research cited above cautions that strategy instruction should not occur in *ad hoc* sessions, and should be integrated only as part of the regular language class. However, note that Feyten and Flaitz' (1996) well-controlled study showed that a one-time-only strategy-awareness workshop resulted in higher final grades in language courses for participants than for comparable non-participants. Positive results about strategy instruction are pleasing; however, we might not have the complete picture because educational studies reporting ineffective treatments are rarely published. A different problem (noted by Nyikos 1999) is that many language teachers feel ill-equipped to conduct strategy instruction because they have not had the chance to see or participate in such instruction themselves (for recommendations, see 'Practice' below).

INFLUENCES ON STRATEGY CHOICE

According to language learning studies, many factors influence strategy use.

- *Motivation* was an important influence on strategy use (Oxford and Nyikos 1989; Oxford *et al.* 1993; Oxford and Ehrman 1995; Chamot *et al.* 1996), with greater motivation related to higher frequencies of strategy use. As Dörnyei and Ottó (1998) explained, learning strategies as goal-directed behaviours inherently indicate the presence of motivation.

- The *language learning environment* affected strategy use, with students in ESL environments using strategies more frequently than those in EFL environments.

- *Learning style and personality type* influenced strategy use; Schmeck 1988; Ely 1989; Reid 1995a, 1998.

- *Gender* has frequently been associated with strategy use; with some variation across studies, females usually report greater strategy use than males; Oxford *et al.* 1988; Oxford and Nyikos 1989; Oxford *et al.* 1993; Zoubir-Shaw and Oxford 1999. However, the reverse was true in two Middle Eastern cultures (Dadour and Robbins 1996) and among Serbo-Croatian refugees in Sweden (Nordin-Eriksson 1999). Results suggest that gender–role socialisation might be a factor in these differences.

- *Culture or national origin* had a strong effect on how students learn, according to general research (Hofstede 1986) and language learning strategy research (Bedell and Oxford 1996; Gopal 1999; Nordin-Eriksson 1999).

- *Career orientation* also has an influence on strategy use, as reflected in major academic field or educational/career aspirations; Politzer and McGroarty 1985; Oxford and Nyikos 1989; Nyikos 1999.

- *Age* affected the kinds of strategies students reported (Bialystok 1981; Gunning 1997), but even young children were able to identify and describe their language learning strategies (Chamot 1999).

- The *nature of the language task* was an influence on strategy choice in many studies; Bialystok 1981; O'Malley and Chamot 1990; Gopal 1999.

Practice

The research given in this chapter has implications for classroom practice in several related areas: assessing strategy use, attuning instruction to learners' needs, considering formats for strategy instruction and conducting strategy instruction in the language classroom.

- Assessing strategy use: ESL or EFL classrooms can benefit from the assessment of learners' strategy use. Strategy assessment, particularly when discussed openly, can lead to greater understanding of learning strategies by learners and teachers alike. Practical, realistic means – such as questionnaires, interviews, learner diaries and classroom observations – exist to conduct strategy assessment.

- Attuning instruction to learners' needs: The more teachers know about their students' current learning strategy preferences (as well as favoured learning styles), the more effectively they can attune instruction and to the specific needs of students. For example, one student might benefit from more visually presented rather than auditorally presented material. Such knowledge helps teachers systematically to initiate strategy instruction and improve language instruction.

- Considering formats for strategy instruction: Teachers should consider conducting strategy instruction in their classrooms. Some researchers and teachers successfully base their whole language programmes on strategies, while others use strategy instruction in more limited but useful ways. In considering strategy instruction formats, helpful steps include taking teacher development courses, finding relevant information in published material and making contact with strategy specialists.

- Conducting strategy instruction: There is growing evidence that strategy instruction can be valuable to many students, although the jury is still out on optimal ways to conduct strategy instruction for different age groups and cultural settings. Language teachers can conduct strategy instruction in their own classrooms. It is probably advisable to start with small strategy interventions rather than full-scale strategies-based language instruction.

In evaluating the success of any form of strategy instruction, language teachers should consider the progress of each individual, both those with the greatest need for strategy assistance and those needing merely to sharpen their strategy use. Evaluation should involve checking the frequency of using language learning strategies, the task appropriateness of the strategies the learner selects and the effects on language proficiency. In most cases, progress occurs incrementally rather than rapidly.

Current and future trends and directions

Future research on language learning strategy use must deal with a number of key issues. First, it is crucial to learn how to help language teachers become aware of the importance of language learning strategies. Second, we must discover how to teach strategies effectively in both linguistically diverse and linguistically homogenous classrooms. Third, there must be a focus on the degree of success of various forms of strategy instruction for ESL or EFL students of different ages, cultural backgrounds and career orientations. Fourth, researchers must study the effects of learner motivation, institutional practices and cultural beliefs on the success of strategy instruction. Fifth, the frequent gender differences in ESL/EFL strategy research deserve further investigation. Sixth, if certain learning strategies conflict with cultural norms, we must learn how far to push students to use them, especially strategies that involve co-operative practice and active communication. Finally, research needs to show the extent to which individuals can successfully challenge their culture's values in using particular learning strategies.

Research is burgeoning in the area of language learning strategies. Teachers could conduct 'action research' within their own classrooms in order to know their students better and provide strategy instruction that students need. In larger-scale, multi-classroom studies, within every study investigators could regularly examine multiple factors, such as motivation, age, gender, cultural background, learning environment, home language, prior language learning and prior travel. If this were done, research results would become more comparable, and we would be able to understand more about strategies and how they operate for different individuals and groups.

Key readings

Dickinson (1987) *Self-Instruction in Language Learning*
Ellis and Sinclair (1989) *Learning to Learn English* (course material)
Holec (1981) *Autonomy and Foreign Language Learning*
O'Malley and Chamot (1990) *Learning Strategies in Second Language Acquisition*
Oxford (1990) *Language Learning Strategies*
Wenden (1991) *Learner Strategies for Learner Autonomy*

CHAPTER 25

Task-based language learning

Dave Willis and Jane Willis

Introduction

Most approaches to language teaching can be described as 'form-based'. Such approaches analyse the language into an inventory of forms which can then be presented to the learner and practised as a series of discrete items. There is an assumption that there is a direct relationship between 'input' and 'intake', that what is presented can be mastered directly and will, as a result of that mastery, become a part of the learner's usable repertoire. But second language acquisition (SLA) research (see Chapter 12) shows quite clearly that there is no such direct relationship between input and intake. If language learning did work in this way, we would reasonably expect learners to acquire language as a series of successive structures and so to build up the language system in an orderly progression, moving from mastery of one sentence form to mastery of the next and so on, until the language was acquired in all its complexity. But this does not happen. Since the work of Corder (1967), Selinker (1972) and other interlanguage theorists, it has been clear that we cannot predict how input will affect the learner's language development. There is clear evidence that intake does not equal input. Effective learning is constrained by natural developmental processes. What is consciously learned is not necessarily incorporated into spontaneous language production.

In contrast to form-based approaches, **task-based learning** (TBL) involves the specification not of a sequence of language items, but of a sequence of communicative tasks to be carried out in the target language. Central to the notion of a communicative task is the exchange of meanings. Nunan (1993) defines a communicative task as 'a piece of classroom work which involves learners in comprehending, manipulating, producing or interacting in the target language while their attention is principally focused on meaning rather than form'. J. Willis (1996) defines a task as an activity 'where the target language is used by the learner for a communicative purpose (goal) in order to achieve an outcome'. Here the notion of meaning is subsumed in 'outcome'. Language in a communicative task is seen as bringing about an outcome through the exchange of meanings. One obvious outcome is the exchange of information in spoken or written form. But there are other possible outcomes to which the exchange of information may be contributory but subsidiary. We may ask learners to exchange and carry out instructions, or to solve a problem, or to entertain one another with anecdotes, spoken or written. All of these activities have a goal which is independent of the language used to achieve that goal.

The use of the word 'task' is sometimes extended to include 'metacommunicative tasks', or exercises with a focus on language form, in which learners manipulate language or formulate generalisations about form (see Chapter 22). But a definition of task which includes an explicit focus on form seems to be so all-embracing as to cover almost anything that might happen in a classroom. We therefore restrict our use of the term task to communicative tasks and exclude metacommunicative tasks from our definition.

One feature of TBL, therefore, is that learners carrying out a task are free to use any language they can to achieve the outcome: language forms are not prescribed in advance. As language users, human beings have an innate capacity to work out ways of expressing meanings. Learners do not simply take note of new language input and attempt to reproduce it. As soon as they put language to use by attempting purposeful communication, they begin to adjust and adapt input to enable them to create new meanings. They are not aiming to reproduce a series of language forms in conformity with target norms. Their aim in language use is to create a meaning system which they can operate rapidly and efficiently in real time. In order to achieve this goal they will use and develop language forms to which they have been recently exposed, but they will also adopt strategies which sometimes lead them to ignore grammatical niceties and to create for themselves forms which are not sanctioned by the target norms. The purpose of a communicative task, therefore, is to encourage learners to develop towards the creation of a meaning system. Different learners adopt different strategies and different language forms in the achievement of the goal, depending on their stage of language development, their degree of involvement with the task, the cognitive challenge the task presents and a host of other factors.

In task-based approaches, therefore, language development is prompted by language use, with the study of language form playing a secondary role. Recent research, however, suggests that while communicative language use is the driving force for language acquisition we also need to focus at some point on language form if acquisition is to be maximally efficient. Skehan (1996), e.g., argues that unless we encourage a focus on form, learners will develop more effective strategies for achieving communicative goals without an accompanying development of their language system. They will develop a 'classroom dialect', which enables them to exchange meanings in spite of the shortcomings of their language. As a result they may fossilise at a relatively low level of language development. Skehan (1992) suggests that learning is prompted by the need to communicate, but argues that learning will be more efficient if:

1. There is a need to focus on accuracy within a task-based methodology.
2. There is a critical focus on language form within the task-based cycle.

The challenge for TBL, therefore, is to devise a methodology which affords learners the freedom to engage natural learning processes in the creation of a meaning system, but which also provides them with incentives to 'restructure' their system in the light of language input.

Background

TBL grows out of the more general notion of **communicative language teaching (CLT)**. Hymes' (1971 [1972, 1979]) notion of communicative competence encouraged a more critical look at language and sharpened awareness of the need to make language relevant to students' needs and to provide opportunities for language use in the classroom. There were two strands to CLT. The first was to do with syllabus specification (see Wilkins 1976; see also Chapter 22 of this volume). Instead of specifying a syllabus in terms of grammar and lexis, the 'communicative syllabus' specified an inventory of notions and functions, identifying the semantic and pragmatic needs of the learners and proposing ways of meeting these needs as efficiently as possible. Instead of specifying items like 'the present perfect' or 'the definite article' syllabuses began by specifying items like 'making requests' and 'talking about the future'. However, although the communicative syllabus claimed to specify notions and functions, it in fact specified linguistic realisations of those notions and functions. The syllabus was still a series of language patterns, albeit patterns linked to semantic and pragmatic values.

The second strand in CLT was methodological. There was an emphasis on language use in the classroom, and this was seen as a rehearsal for language use in the real world. But in general the communicative approach adopted in the classroom was a 'weak form' (Littlewood 1981) of the approach. There was still a powerful tendency to see the study of language form as prior to language use. Tasks were used to assist 'free' production at the end of a controlled form-based teaching cycle. The stimulus to learning was still provided by the identification of a new structure or pattern. Language use was seen as subsidiary to the study of language form. TBL, on the other hand, sees language use as the driving force in language learning, with the task itself central to both syllabus planning and methodology. The study of language itself may enhance effective learning, but it is subsidiary to language use.

One of the first to argue for the effectiveness of tasks as a stimulus to learning was Allwright (1981) who questioned the need for language instruction and emphasised the need for language use. The best documented application of a task-based approach is probably Prabhu's procedural syllabus (Prabhu 1987). Prabhu headed a project in schools in South India in which learners were simply presented with a series of problems and information/opinion gap activities which were solved under teacher guidance through the medium of English. Prabhu argued that a focus on language form actually inhibited language learning. Language development was seen as the outcome of natural processes. Evaluation of this project (Beretta and Davies 1985) suggests that Prabhu's learners were more successful than their counterparts who were taught in a more traditional way; it is, of course, notoriously difficult to provide conclusive evaluation of a project of this kind.

An approach similar in some ways to Prabhu's is put forward by Breen (1987) and Candlin (1987) in their advocacy of a *process* syllabus. Breen and Candlin agree with Prabhu in that they see the basic unit of syllabus design and classroom methodology as an activity of some kind, which is to be mediated through the use of language, rather than as a language item (see Chapter 22). The process syllabus differs from the procedural syllabus in two ways:

- The role of the teacher is not to determine unilaterally how learning will be organised and sequenced, but to consult learners and help them realise their own learning plan.

- Prabhu's procedural approach deliberately avoids all focus on language. Students operating with the process syllabus, however, may choose for themselves to focus explicitly on language form.

Long and Crookes (1992) have criticised the procedural and process syllabuses on three grounds. Such syllabuses offer no procedures for basing task selection on an analysis of learners' needs; they offer no criteria for task sequencing; and they make no allowance for a systematic focus on form, although the process syllabus may focus on form in response to learner initiative. Long and Crookes argue that classroom or pedagogic tasks should be systematically linked to communicative tasks that the learners will be likely to perform outside the classroom. Communicative needs should be identified and expressed in terms of meanings and outcomes. These meanings and outcomes should then be incorporated in pedagogic tasks. The problem of task sequencing, however, is more difficult, and is the focus of much of current research. Similarly there are no clear conclusions on how best to incorporate a focus on form into a task-based approach.

Research

As set out in the introduction, TBL rests initially on the findings of SLA research as summarised in Chapter 12 – taking what R. Ellis (2000) terms the 'psycholinguistic perspective'. The work of Long (1983a, 1998), Doughty and Pica (1986) and Swain (1995) shows that the interaction generated in language use does lead learners to modify and develop their language system even without the intervention of instruction. This is reinforced by the findings of Skehan (1992), Foster

(1996) and Bygate (1996). When faced with the need to interpret language and encode meanings for themselves, learners adopt new forms and refashion their language system to meet the new demands placed upon it. The implication of this is that if we can provide learners with a series of tasks which involve both the comprehension and the production of language with a focus on meaning this will prompt language development.

Researchers are now beginning to look at the nature and content of tasks themselves. The work of Pica *et al.* (1993) identifies variables that generate more negotiation of meaning; these included two-way rather than one-way information flows, closed rather than open outcomes, narrative rather than expository discourse domains. A major problem, however, is that these and similar studies have been carried out under pseudo-laboratory conditions far removed from classrooms (Foster 1998), and using decontextualised tasks.

There has been very little formal research into TBL in classrooms, where a host of different variables come into play. The 'same' task might be done quite differently according to where it comes in the teaching cycle, the role taken by the teacher, the learners' interpretations of what is expected, the learners' previous experience of the task type and the topic or content matter and other implementation variables, such as time limit, group size and participant roles. R. Ellis (2000) exemplifies the effects of some of these factors when examining task use from a 'sociocultural perspective', arising out of the theories of Vygotsky (1986) and Lantolf (2000). The focus here is on how participants 'co-construct the activity they engage in, in accordance with their own sociohistory and locally determined goals' (R. Ellis 2000).

In one of the few classroom-based studies (see Foster 1996, 1998) Skehan and Foster looked at the influence of affording learners time to plan a task before they carry it out, and also of the effect of teacher guidance upon that planning. Three classes were recorded doing three different types of task under varying conditions, and the resulting interactions were transcribed and compared. There were many interesting and sometimes unexpected findings, but generally learners who had planning time produced a richer and longer discourse than those with no planning time, as well as generally showing a stronger engagement with the task itself.

Finally there is research on form-focused instruction. Doughty and Williams (1998b) provide a summary. At one extreme Long (1998) sees an effective focus on form as necessarily incidental, that is as arising in the course of a communicative task and as a necessary part of the successful achievement of such a task. At the other extreme De Keyser (1998) and Lightbown (1998) allow for an explicit focus on form abstracted from immediate engagement with meaning. All agree, however, that forms will not be processed to become a part of the learners' grammar unless learners are allowed to engage with meaningful use of those forms while the explicit focus is held in short term memory. Other researchers stress the importance of intellectual effort in the study of form.

Practice

In practice, most teachers use coursebooks as a basis for their teaching, and then supplement the coursebook (see Chapter 9 of this volume). Commercially produced teaching materials are understandably packaged to reach as wide an audience as possible. Many coursebooks produced since the 1970s described themselves as 'communicative' irrespective of whether or not they were based on communicative principles. There is a danger that the label 'task-based' will now be exploited in the same way. TBL like CLT rests on broad principles rather than precise recommendations or prescriptions. The first principle of TBL is that units of syllabus organisation should be tasks which define what outcomes can be achieved through language, rather than linguistic items as such. The second principle is that learning will be effective only if it is related closely to language use and involves relating form and meaning. When choosing a text book that claims to contain 'tasks' or to follow a TBL approach, it is worth looking closely at what kind of activities bear the label 'task' and at whether the course design follows the principles above.

If we are to see tasks as units of syllabus design we need criteria for sequencing tasks. Candlin (1987), Stern (1992) and Skehan (1996, 1998) offer such criteria, taking account of both linguistic and cognitive complexity. At first sight these criteria are difficult to apply, but if they are seen as parameters of task design the problem is less intractable. Any task will be made simpler if, for example, learners first work through a parallel task under teacher guidance, or if they are first given a chance to rehearse the mental operations involved into achieving a successful outcome. Similarly, a task will be simpler if it is one of a sequence interwoven in the syllabus so that learners have rehearsed some of the linguistic and cognitive complexities before they are asked to carry out a particular task. Perhaps more work is needed looking at basic task types and seeing how these may be linked into sequences with one task building on another.

As we have seen, Long and Crookes argue for a specification of the task-based syllabus in terms of pedagogic tasks derived from real world tasks. Working with relatively advanced learners whose needs can be clearly defined, it is certainly possible to offer pedagogic tasks which relate immediately and directly to real world tasks. Most learners, however, are at a much lower level and have diffuse and heterogeneous needs. With such learners it is necessary to devise tasks which will build up gradually to something which reflects more directly the complexities of the real world. With this in mind a number of researchers offer general typologies of tasks as a starting point for task design.

Prabhu (1987) identified three broad task types: information gap, reasoning gap and problem-solving. Stern (1992) offers a similarly useful typology. Learners can be asked to:

- give and follow instructions;
- gather and exchange information;
- solve problems;
- give informal talks in the classroom;
- take part in role play and drama activities.

Some writers, however (see, e.g., D. Willis 1990), are doubtful about the value of role play. If a role play involves problem-solving then it involves genuine language use; but a role play in which learners are simply required to act out a situation merely simulates language use, and there is no outcome except for the performance itself. In this situation learners are displaying rather than using language.

J. Willis (1996) offers another classification of tasks which subsumes the above types and is intended as a generative pedagogic tool. She suggests that we first draw up a series of topics (e.g. families) suited to our learners. She then identifies a number of operations, based on a chosen topic to be carried out in the target language. These operations are: listing; ordering and sorting; comparing; problem-solving; sharing personal experiences; creative tasks.

These operations may be combined in a number of ways. If, for example, we start with the topic 'films', learners might be asked to work in a group to name their five favourite films and justify their choice. This would involve listing, sequencing (ordering and sorting) and sharing personal experiences. Given a list of topics these operations seem to yield a rich variety of tasks. Similarly, tasks may be built around a written text, asking students to predict the development of a story, for example, or to compare their knowledge of the world with the way things are presented in a text. Recordings of fluent speakers doing such tasks generally yield an interaction rich in features typical of everyday language use and provide accessible and natural input for learners to process.

The need for a focus on form within a task-based methodology may be met in part by manipulating the circumstances of communication in the classroom. Tasks carried out orally in groups or pairs demand a relatively low level of accuracy. Tasks which involve a presentation to the class as a whole, or the preparation of written output, demand a higher level of accuracy. This is in line with natural language use. We are more conscious of language form in public presentation than in private use. Willis and Willis (1987, 1996) offer a detailed rationale for these procedures, a framework involving a pre-task phase followed by a task-planning report cycle, in which learners move from pair discussion of a task to a public report of their findings.

A three-part task cycle is central to this methodology. At the task stage, learners – working in twos or threes – are encouraged to use whatever language they can recall to fulfil the task outcome; the teacher stands back, but encourages all attempts at communication. Following the task there is a planning stage, where the teacher helps learners plan a public presentation of their task findings in preparation for the report to the class. It is at the planning stage that a focus on form is natural and teacher advice and correction is likely to be of most use, since learners, faced with a wider audience, will naturally want to present as accurately and fluently as they can. At the report phase, the teacher simply acts as chair, commenting on the content and summing up at the end. After the task cycle, a 'Language Focus' phase allows time for deeper and more systematic study of the language arising out of the task cycle, from the text or task recording; this can also incorporate examples from tasks and texts used in previous lessons.

A critical focus on language form may be achieved through consciousness-raising techniques which encourage learners to reflect on language and to observe recurrent and typical patternings (see, e.g., Sharwood Smith 1981; Rutherford 1987; Skehan 1998). Consciousness-raising activities help the learner to notice a specific feature of language in context as a first step towards its acquisition (Schmidt 1990). Such activities, then, encourage the learner to make hypotheses and further generalisations about the language which contribute to present or future learning. R. Ellis (1992) and T.F. Johns (1991a, 1991b) offer examples of such procedures. We can make no predictions about what will be learned. We can, however, be reasonably confident that procedures of this kind will develop and sharpen learning strategies in a way which enhances language development.

Current and future trends and directions

In the past, tasks have been used for two distinct purposes: for research and pedagogy; the former to generate learner language data to allow investigation into interlanguage development, and the latter to give learners opportunities to use language freely to express their meanings. More recently there has been an increasing interest in classroom-based research, examining, for example, the quality and quantity of the interaction produced by learners doing tasks in different circumstances. Small-scale research projects carried out by teachers also shed light on aspects of TBL and help us to create better conditions for learning through the use of tasks. Topics investigated informally include:

- the relationship between task and interaction: What roles do speakers adopt? How do task instructions affect these roles?

- allocating roles within tasks: How does it affect the interaction if one student is given the role of, for example, chairing or providing a written record of the task?

- differences between first performance of a task, often in a small group, and subsequent performances, often to the class as a whole: Are there differences in lexis and syntax between the two modes? Are there different levels of accuracy?

- acceptability of TBL: How comfortable do learners feel with a particular approach to TBL? How can the approach be adapted to make it more acceptable?

- differences over time: Students have been encouraged to record themselves on task or to keep records of written tasks and compare performances over the course of a term's work.

- imposing extra constraints on task performance: What difference does it make if a time limit is imposed? What if a written record must be kept?

It is important that teachers question for themselves the principles and procedures which inform

TBL. Formal research may identify and refine questions to do with classroom practice and provide experimental findings which are indicative of answers to some of those questions, but it is important to test these findings through critical observation (often self-observation) of classroom practice.

Conclusion

SLA research suggests overwhelmingly that language learning is a developmental process, which cannot be consciously controlled or predicted by teachers or learners. It seems that language learning – in the sense of acquiring the ability to use the language spontaneously – is powerfully driven by natural processes. But it also seems that these processes can be sharpened and rendered more efficient by an appropriate focus on form. TBL represents an attempt to harness natural processes and to provide language focus activities based on consciousness-raising which will support these processes. The crucial challenges for TBL, therefore, are to do with the design and sequencing of tasks, and the determination of how best to encourage learners to focus on language form in a way which prompts language development while, at the same time, recognising that there is no direct relationship between language instruction and language learning.

Key readings

Crookes and Gass (1993a) *Tasks in a Learning Context*
Doughty and Williams (1998a) *Focus on Form in Classroom Second Language Acquisition*
Long (1983a) Does second language instruction make a difference?
Long and Crookes (1992) Three approaches to task-based syllabus design
Nunan (1989a) *Designing Tasks for the Communicative Classroom*
Prabhu (1987) *Second Language Pedagogy*
Skehan (1998) *A Cognitive Approach to Language Learning*
Willis (1996) *A Framework for Task-Based Learning*
Willis and Willis (1996) *Challenge and Change in Language Teaching*

CHAPTER 26

Literature in the language classroom

Alan Maley

Introduction

Literature in language teaching has a long pedigree. It was a fundamental part of foreign language teaching in the 'classical humanist' paradigm, where an understanding of the high culture and thought expressed through literature took precedence over mere competence in using the language. Indeed, in the teaching of European classical languages, such as Greek and Latin, the literature was virtually all that remained of the language.

This central role of literature was carried over into TESL/TEFL in the early part of the twentieth century. In many parts of the world, such as India, it remains integral to the teaching of the language to this day. However, as the TESL/TEFL profession developed a more sophisticated understanding of how languages are learned, and as the demand for English shifted its focus from the small-scale production of scholarly elites to the mass production of large numbers of functionally competent users of the language, literature came to be regarded as, at best, an irrelevance and, at worst, positively harmful.

Among other things, this resulted in an unproductive debate between the 'ancients', staunch supporters of Literatures (with a capital L), and the 'moderns', devotees of linguistic structures, functions and the like, who would have no truck with literature. To some extent this divide continues, especially at the college/university level. In more recent times, however, there has been a gradual rehabilitation of literature and its value for language teaching. Nonetheless, the role of literature in language teaching remains contentious, owing to widespread differences in interpretation of the precise nature of that role. It is to these differing interpretations that I turn my attention in the next section.

Background

Discussion focuses on two sets of issues: 'What is literature?' and 'What do we mean by the teaching of literature?'

WHAT IS LITERATURE?

The answer would seem to be self-evident, yet the question gives rise to continuing debate. Traditionally, Literature (with a large L) has tended to be thought of as the 'best' writing produced in a given language or society, and this collection of 'approved' works has constituted the literary canon deemed by authority to be fit to study. The syllabuses of many institutions still confine themselves to the Beowulf to Virginia Woolf parade of great writers, with Shakespeare, the Metaphysical poets, Jane Austen, Dickens and the rest featured prominently, and often excluding any writer who is not yet safely dead.

In the post-modern, deconstructionist age, however, the classical canon has been under attack as a bastion of power and privilege. The definition of what constitutes literature worthy of study has been widened to include feminist and gay writing, genres such as detective fiction and horror, and – most notably – the new literatures developing in countries such as India and Singapore, where English has been grafted on to cultures and societies far removed from the metropolis.

A further enlargement of the field has taken place through the recognition of the widespread occurrence of literary devices – such as parallelism, rhyme, rhythm and metaphor – in texts which were not even written as literary texts – such as advertising copy, graffiti and public notices.

The debate about what constitutes literature is relevant to the claims literature has on the language classroom since it broadens the range of texts which may be considered for treatment. Classical texts are often burdened with linguistic, historical and cultural baggage which come in the way of their usefulness as exemplars of contemporary usage. Contemporary quasi-literary texts – such as advertising texts – come without this baggage and are perceived as more immediately relevant by students.

WHAT DO WE MEAN BY THE TEACHING OF LITERATURE?

Literature is used and studied in many different ways and different contexts. The following are the most common emphases:

1. focus on teaching language vs. focus on teaching literature;
2. language learning purpose (pragmatic focus) vs. academic/analytical purpose (intellectual focus);
3. linguistic orientation (stylistics) vs. literary critical orientation (the new criticism, post-modernism, etc.);
4. learning how to study literature vs. studying literature.

Considering each of these in turn, in (1) there is a clear difference of objective. At one end of the scale we find literary texts being used as just one among many other kinds of texts. At the other end, literary texts alone are the object of study, and they are studied for their literary qualities.

In (2) the difference is equally clear, as between a primarily pragmatic learning purpose and a primarily studial, academic analysis of literary texts. Note that such an analysis can be either linguistically or aesthetically motivated; see (3) below.

Point (3) refers to the type of analysis which is carried out: whether this is primarily stylistic, seeking to understand the ways in which language is deployed to achieve aesthetic effects, or primarily literary-critical, using aesthetic criteria (most recently with a heavy ideological focus). Generally, linguistic analysis would be thought of (by linguists at least!) as an objective process, whereas literary criticism is almost inevitably tarred with the subjective brush.

In (4) I make the distinction between learning how to study literature and actually studying it. Widdowson (1975, 1992), among many others, has made the point that students are frequently exposed to literary texts as if they already knew how to tackle them. This often results in demotivation and a kind of pseudo-literary competence, with students merely parroting ideas based upon received opinion. By contrast, students can be progressively introduced and sensitised to the devices through which literature achieves its special effects before they embark upon a fully-fledged study of particular literary works.

In practice, of course, the situation is not as simple as that. With rare exceptions, what we find are complex combinations of the above emphases. And the specific approach adopted depends on factors such as language level, type of institution, examination requirements and students' cultural orientation. However, given that the main emphasis of this book is on language teaching, I focus my attention on that area, recognising that the use of literary texts to teach language can often also open the way for an enlargement of literary understanding and sensitivity.

A RATIONALE FOR INTEGRATING LITERARY TEXTS IN LANGUAGE TEACHING

An early writer on language teaching made the following case for using literature in the form of poetry:

> To leave poetry out of a language course . . . is to renounce an extremely effective and labour-saving method of absorbing useful language. It is also to abandon opportunities to humanize and warm what may also be a very dry and chilly traffic in words and information. It is to renounce the hope of delivering us from the pedestrian writing – if not platitudes – of the textbook writer. It is to neglect an important and powerful aid in establishing in the pupils' mind a favourable mental set. It is to stop short of what might be most rewarding in the pupil's experience of the language.
> (Billows 1961: 238)

Billows puts his finger on two, if not all three, of the reasons usually given for the teaching of literature: the cultural model, the language model and the personal growth model.

> Teaching literature within a cultural model enables students to understand and appreciate cultures and ideologies different from their own in time and space, and to come to perceive traditions of thought, feeling and artistic form within the heritage the literature of such cultures endows.
> (Carter and Long 1991: 2)

In the language model, the text may be used as an example of certain types of pattern and structure. A more important aim may be to help students find independent ways into a text in a systematic manner. The personal growth model stresses the personal enjoyment and emotional gain students can procure by engaging with such texts.

A number of writers (e.g. McRae 1991; Kramsch 1993) have stressed the difference between referential texts, which are essentially vehicles for conveying information, and representational texts, which require the reader to re-create in his or her own terms the imaginative world of the text. Kramsch also stresses that the reading process itself is different from 'efferent' reading, where the reader simply carries away information, and 'aesthetic' reading, where the reader interacts emotionally and experientially with the text.

Maley and Duff (1989) draw attention to the motivating power of literary texts in terms of their universality and their non-triviality, echoing Billow's comments on the texts usually found in textbooks. They also stress how literary texts invite multiple interpretation, thus providing ready-made material for discussion.

The rationale for incorporating literature is thus well established, even if it does not go entirely uncontested. Edmondson (1997) has argued that many of the assumptions which underpin the use of literary texts in language teaching cannot be sustained. Many also argue against the use of such texts on the grounds of linguistic complexity and cultural remoteness from the learners using them.

Research

I have already drawn attention above to the relative paucity of empirical research in the field. The work that exists tends to fall into one of three main categories:

- theoretical debate, in which the author typically puts forward a set of assertions about what literature (and/or literature teaching) is, or ought to be: Hall (1999: 3) is a good example of the genre, as is Edmondson (1997). These contributions to the debate are frequently ideologically motivated, and may even be intentionally polemical. Nonetheless, they generally rest on assertion and argument rather than on empirically based investigation. This is not to say that they have no value, although it has to be said that they are often couched in language which puts them beyond the range of most classroom practitioners.

- practical demonstration, in which the author presents a possible set of practical classroom activities based on his or her own experience of, and beliefs about, the use of literary texts in language teaching. An excellent example of the genre is Philip Chan's detailed description of activities based on Catherine Lim's short story 'The teacher' (Chan 1999). Such practically oriented contributions are usually set in the context of a particular rationale: theory with a small 't'.

- empirical research, which is usually small-scale and oriented to particular classroom contexts; very often these are action research projects forming part of an MA or PhD study. As such, they are relatively rarely published and, therefore, tend to be somewhat inaccessible. Most of these research projects are qualitative and ethnographic in their approach. They are welcomed for their focus on specific, local contexts. Although this makes their conclusions difficult to generalise with confidence, they nonetheless offer suggestive avenues for application and variation in other specific contexts.

One area of investigation which merits more attention is the evaluation and testing of teaching through literature. The main work in this area has been undertaken by Spiro (1992). In developing new-style test items, she is concerned to draw on a range of stimulating and fresh material, to allow scope for personal response and creativity and to encourage empathy with the text.

Practice

In general, the literature teaching approach has shown a preference for practical exploration in the classroom rather than for empirical research. This may in part be a legacy of literary criticism, which is prone to assertion rather than proof. This notwithstanding, there is now a large body of published materials on all aspects of using literature to teach language.

At the advanced level there are a number of books offering useful activities to develop literary sensitivity through greater linguistic awareness (Short 1986; Carter and Long 1987; Birch 1989; Carter and Nash 1990; Durant and Fabb 1990; Widdowson 1992; G. Cook 1994). Useful collections of mainly practically oriented articles include Carter et al. (1989) and Carter and McRae (1996). Both these collections would serve as an invaluable introduction to the area for trainee teachers or the uninitiated.

At intermediate level the variety of resources is considerable (Maley and Duff 1982, 1989; Maley and Moulding 1986; Collie and Slater 1987; Tomlinson 1987; Greenwood 1989; Maley 1989, 1994; Duff and Maley 1990; McRae and Pantaleoni 1990; Carter and Long 1991; McRae 1991, 1992; Bassnet and Grundy 1993; Lazar 1993, 1999; McRae and Vethamani 1999). All these titles offer the teacher texts and activities for immediate classroom use, with only minimal reference to theory.

For the most part, activities fall into one of two categories: those that focus on the linguistic analysis of the text, and those in which the text acts as a springboard for a variety of language activities, including discussion and writing. Not surprisingly, the kinds of activities in the second category in particular draw heavily on techniques developed as part of the communicative approach in general. They tend to utilise generalisable categories such as comparison, completion, re-ordering, matching, extension and reformulation (for a useful taxonomy of these categories, see Maley 1994). Techniques such as opinion and information gap, problem-solving and role-play/ simulation are also in widespread use, as well as a variety of activities to promote students' creative writing.

Other heuristics used to generate activities include the 'what, how, who, when/where, why' model. For any text, it is possible to examine:

- what it contains: language features, information, emotions, as well as what associations and personal feelings it arouses;

- how it works: repetition, rhyme, rhythm, metaphor, parallelism;

- who wrote it, and who it was addressed to;

- when/where it was written: background information on the sociocultural and personal context against which it was written;

- why it was written; why certain choices were made (e.g. why a poem not a pamphlet? why this word and not that? why the omission of some information?).

All these questions have the potential to generate interactive language work which is meaningful and stimulating.

Clearly, the appropriacy of the texts selected for a particular class remains a crucial factor in the success of the approach. Texts which tend to be chosen are those that are not too long, not too complex linguistically, not too far removed from the world knowledge of the students, and not too anachronistic (for criteria for selecting texts, see Hill 1992). Above everything else, however, the text has to have the capacity to engage the interest of the student.

Current and future trends and directions

The following areas are of particular interest and will doubtless continue to grow.

- Interest in oral literature, and in particular story-telling, has been revived. The work of Andrew Wright – who through his story-telling workshops has virtually single-handedly stimulated interest – is especially noteworthy (Wright 1996, 1997). Interest has been further fuelled by the immense growth of demand for English among young learners worldwide, and the corresponding demand for suitable materials (Ellis and Brewster 1991). Story-telling is not, of course, confined to children: Dufeu (1994) has drawn extensively on a range of cultural traditions in story-telling, and Rinvolucri and Morgan (1990) offer a range of approaches to the genre.

- Reading literary texts aloud in performance also attracts favourable attention. This is a far cry from the enfeebling practice of 'reading round the class' of earlier days. The advantages of scripting prose text for performance or orchestrating verse or dramatic texts are considerable (Maley 1998a, 1999b; Cazden 1992; Kramsch 1993).

- Length and linguistic difficulty have always counted among the major problems in using literary texts. Materials writers tend to select short extracts from longer texts to circumvent the problem of length, and to rely on simplified readers to deal with the linguistic difficulty. Relatively little work has been published on using longer complete texts (for exceptions, however, see Collie and Slater 1987; Rossner 1988; Greenwood 1989; Lazar 1990). There is, however, renewed interest in developing readers. Up to now these have tended to be pale shadows of classic texts. While the simplification or abridgement of published literature remains an option, there is now a new generation of readers written as originals, specifically for the foreign language learning market (Maley 1997, 1999a; Prowse 1999). This new genre of writing can be seen as authentic in its own right rather than derivative at several removes from classic texts. Most major publishers of ELT materials now incorporate such original readers in their lists, and the Cambridge English Readers list is composed exclusively of originals. It is likely that the demand for this new genre of writing will grow.

- The growth of strong local literatures in English has triggered a corresponding interest in incorporating such texts into language teaching materials (McRae and Vethamani 1999). As these literatures grow in confidence and acceptability, there is likely to be further growth in this area too.

- The new literatures will also continue to fuel interest in using literary texts for cross-cultural exploration. Literature is reflective of cultural presuppositions and practices. As such it lends itself well to investigating similarities and differences between self and others, and to an awareness and understanding of 'the other' (Kramsch 1993; see also Chapter 29).

- In an age of critical theory, it is unsurprising that literature can also form the basis for a critical analysis of the distribution of power, not least as reflected in issues such as the role of men and women in society, the consumerist agenda and the unequal distribution of wealth and poverty. The recent growth of interest in global issues and globalisation will find a rich source to draw upon in literary texts.

Conclusion

In this chapter I trace the development of a renewed interest in literature as one source of input to language learning, offering a rationale for incorporating literature and drawing attention to useful resources for teachers to access. It may seem anomalous in a market-oriented world of supply and demand and cost–benefit calculation that there is still a place for literature. Perhaps the growing interest in literature is one manifestation of the spread of parallel notions such as 'emotional intelligence'.

Key readings

Carter and McRae (1996) *Language, Literature and the Learner*
Carter *et al*. (1989) *Literature and the Learner*
Kramsch (1993) *Context and Culture in Language Teaching*
Lazar (1993) *Literature and Language Teaching*
Maley and Duff (1989) *Poetry in the Language Classroom*
McRae (1991) *Literature with a Small 'l'*
Widdowson (1992) *Practical Stylistics*

CHAPTER 27

Genre

Jennifer Hammond and Beverly Derewianka

Introduction

The term **genre** is used in various educational contexts to refer to the recognisable and recurring patterns of everyday, academic and literary texts that occur within particular cultures. Those working with the notion of genre share a belief in the importance of cultural and social contexts of language use. They also share a concern with ways of assisting students, through effective engagement with texts, to become active and participating members of the cultures in which those texts play a part.

Background

The term **genre** has a long history, dating back to ancient Greeks and their study of rhetorical structure in different categories of the epic, lyric and dramatic. For many years the term has been commonly used to refer to particular kinds of literature or other media of creative expression (e.g. art or film). More recently, however, it has been used in a range of educational contexts to refer not only to types of literary texts, but also to the predictable and recurring texts that are part of everyday life (e.g. work, study). As Bakhtin (translation 1986) has argued, learning genres is a fundamental part of language development, and it is our ability to predict the compositional structure and length of genres that enables us to communicate.

The impact of genre in educational contexts is evident primarily in three major areas (Hyon 1996; Johns 2000): **English for specific purposes (ESP)**, **New Rhetoric** studies and **systemic functional linguistics**. Although the boundaries between these areas are often blurred, distinctions are useful as they serve to highlight similarities and differences of how the notion of genre has been adopted as a theoretical construct and as a basis for practical teaching strategies.

The overall concern of **ESP** is to assist students to gain access to the English language demands they encounter in their studies or professions, i.e. to assist them in recognising and learning the patterns of language required in various academic and professional contexts (Swales 1990a; A. Johns 1991; Bhatia 1993; Dudley-Evans and St John 1998). ESP scholars' focus lies in analysing communicative purpose and formal language features of genres in these contexts (see Chapter 19).

New Rhetoric work on genre is particularly associated with developments in North America, although some scholars from the UK, Australia and elsewhere also locate their work under this general heading. While genre work in ESP focuses primarily in descriptions of genres in professional and academic settings, the focus of New Rhetoric work lies in more detailed analyses of the social and cultural contexts in which genres occur, with an emphasis on social purposes, or actions, that these genres fulfil. For example, Miller (1984), in an article that is central to this work, argues that a rhetorically sound definition of genre must be centred not on the substance or the form of the discourse but on the action it is used to accomplish. Freedman and Medway (1994a: 1) argue that the term genre has been able to 'connect a recognition of regularities in discourse types with a broader social and cultural understanding of language in use'. Within this tradition, then, genres are seen as actions within particular social and historical contexts, and are seen 'not just as text types but as typical ways of engaging rhetorically with recurring situations' (Freedman and Medway 1994b: 2). Indeed, Freedman and Macdonald (1992: 7) argue that 'the very best work on genre simply assumes the category and puts it to work'. The emphasis is on the fluid and dynamic character of genres, and how they evolve and change over time.

Unlike ESP scholars, who locate their work broadly within the field of discourse analysis, those whose work fits under the umbrella of New Rhetoric draw on studies of rhetoric, composition studies and professional writing (Freedman and Medway 1994a; Berkenkotter and Huckin 1995). Rather than attempting linguistic analysis for descriptions of genres, they draw on ethnographic methods of analysis, resulting in detailed descriptions of the academic and professional contexts surrounding genres, and of the actions that texts perform within these contexts. As Hyon (1996: 698) remarks, their concern is less with the potential of genre for teaching patterns of text organisation and language, and more with helping university students understand the social functions of genres and the contexts in which they are used.

Work on genre drawing from **systemic functional linguistics** has developed primarily in Australia. This work incorporates a number of features that are central to systemic function linguistic theory (Halliday and Hasan 1976, 1985; Halliday 1978, 1994). Such features include a functional perspective in the study of language; a focus on the interrelationship between language texts and the context in which those texts occur; analytic tools deriving from the descriptions of discourse and language resources of English; and a focus on the interrelationship between spoken and written modes of English. These features provide a means of studying the organisation, development and cohesion of spoken and written texts used by people in a variety of contexts. The term genre is used to refer to the relationship between social function and the predictable patterning of language. Genres in this sense have been described as 'staged, goal-oriented social processes; in which language plays a significant role' (Martin *et al.* 1987).

The systemic linguistic approach to genre theory and the related genre-based approach to language education developed in the 1980s primarily in the context of school education. Its impetus was a concern that prevailing educational practices were not adequately assisting young students develop control of the range of literary and factual genres demanded of them in primary and secondary school. The argument – developed initially by Martin and Rothery (1980, 1981) – was that in teaching writing, attention needs to be paid not only to the processes of composing texts but to the nature of texts that students write. In addition, they argued, literacy programmes should include some active teaching about genres. Such arguments have remained a central feature of this genre-based approach to language teaching. The term **genre-based approach** here refers to an approach to language and literacy education that incorporates an understanding of the notion of genre, and of teaching about genres, into educational programmes.

As shown above, there are important commonalities, as well as differences, in how genre has been theorised in ESP, New Rhetoric and systemic functional linguistics. This is also the case in the areas of proposed pedagogical practices. In part the differences can be related to differences in the audience in each area. ESP students are generally adult non-native university or business students (typically highly educated and literate in their mother tongues). New Rhetoric students are generally also highly educated university students, many of whom are native English speakers. Students who are the focus of genre work in systemic functional linguistics, however, are primarily 'disadvantaged' school and adult students, i.e. students from diverse and minority cultural and

Move 1	**Establishing a territory**
Step 1	Claiming centrality
	and/or
Step 2	Making topic generalisations
	and/or
Step 3	Reviewing items of previous research
Move 2	**Establishing a niche**
Step 1A	Counter-claiming
	or
Step 1B	Indicating a gap
	or
Step 1C	Question-raising
	or
Step 1D	Continuing a tradition
Move 3	**Occupying the niche**
Step 1A	Outlining purposes
	or
Step 1B	Announcing present research
Step 2	Announcing principal findings
Step 3	Indicating research paper structure

Figure 27.1 CARS model of article introductions
Source: Swales 1993:141

linguistic backgrounds who traditionally do not achieve high levels of academic success in mainstream education. The nature of research and pedagogical practices associated with each of the areas reflect these differences.

Research

Research and teaching practices associated with ESP and systemic linguistics – with their more explicit proposals for the analysis and teaching of genres – have had the most direct impact on TESOL education. Consequently, we focus below on research and pedagogical practices associated with these genres. (For further background on New Rhetoric, see especially Freedman and Medway 1994a, 1994b.)

Research in ESP has been motivated by the potential of genre as a tool for analysing and teaching the language required of non-native speakers in academic and professional settings (Hyon 1996: 695). In this context Swales' (1981, 1990a) research on the introductory stage of academic articles has been especially influential. Swales' concern was to address the difficulties faced by many students, as well as more experienced writers, in getting started on academic articles. From analyses of examples of academic articles, he developed the Create a Research Space (CARS) model. This model summarises structural moves and steps to identify the regular and predictable ways in which introductions of academic articles are organised. Swales' (1993: 141) CARS model of article introductions is presented in Figure 27.1.

The obvious implications of Swales' research for EAP (English for academic purposes) teaching inspired research into other sections of research papers, including research, discussion of results and abstract. Swales' model has been further extended to account for longer and more complex studies (i.e. academic dissertations; Dudley-Evans 1994a) and grant proposals (Connor

1996). While overall this line of research has been influential in EAP, Dudley-Evans and St John (1998: 90) note that it has encountered difficulties with less predictable genres such as academic essays.

Swales' work has also influenced research in the broader area of ESP. For example, Bhatia (1993) has drawn on Swales' techniques for analysis of academic texts in his research on business letters and legal documents. Working with the interests of non-native English speakers in mind, Bhatia (1993: 22–36) proposes a sequence of seven steps that, he argues, are necessary to undertake a comprehensive investigation of any genre. These steps are:

- placing the given genre-text in a situational context;
- surveying existing literature;
- refining the situational/contextual analysis;
- selecting corpus;
- studying the institutional context;
- (deciding on) levels of linguistic analysis;
- (checking against) specialist information in genre analysis.

Bhatia then applies this framework in his research to patterns of moves in sales promotion letters, job application letters and legal cases. Bhatia argues that communicative purpose is crucial for identification of genre. To support this he shows through linguistic analysis that apparently different communicative events from the business world (sales promotion and job application letters) are, in fact, instances of the same genre.

Research in systemic linguistics and genre studies in Australia has been extensive in the last 10 to 15 years, having considerable impact on language and literacy education at state and national level. Such research is not widely known internationally. The research focuses primarily on the identification of the language demands in the educational contexts of primary and secondary schooling and in adult ESL education; on analysis of texts within these contexts; and on the development of related teaching practices (Derewianka 1990; Hammond *et al.* 1992; Cope and Kalantzis 1993; Martin 1993; Christie 1995a).

Early influential research was carried out by Martin and Rothery (1980, 1981, 1986). In the 1980s they collected some hundreds of written texts from primary and secondary schools in order to focus on the kinds of writing that students produce at school. Their research indicated that, at the time, a very narrow range of genres was encouraged in primary schools; these were primarily personal response genres – observation/comments; personal recounts; some narratives – and a smattering of factual genres. The study highlighted a hidden curriculum operating in most schools, where teachers (unwilling to encroach on the students' creativity and ownership) gave little guidance regarding the communicative purposes and the nature of texts that they were trying to write. The researchers found that students who were unable to intuit the teacher's implicit agenda, or who were unfamiliar with different school genres, were ultimately penalised on reaching secondary school where their writing was judged as inadequate or inappropriate. The study also found that teachers were generally unaware of the different genres employed across the curriculum and that they lacked a language for talking about language with their students. It was therefore difficult for students to discover why their writing was judged as poor and to determine how to improve it.

While the early work of Martin and Rothery contributed to the development and description of a taxonomy of educational genres, other research has focused more directly on the significance of the specific context in which students learn to write. For example, Christie's research (1995b) explores the relationship between classroom discourse and students' writing. Through a close analysis of morning 'show and tell' sessions in primary school classes, this research traces the impact of recurring patterns of classroom interaction on young students' writing. Her research (see also research by Gray and Cazden 1992; Macken-Horarik 1996), emphasising the socially constructed nature of language and learning, has had a considerable impact on literacy pedagogy in Australia. It has also challenged long-held assumptions about what is 'natural' in the writing development of both native and non-native English-speaking students.

Practice

Genre pedagogy typically includes the following kinds of teaching tasks: exploring the cultural context, analysing the target situation, analysing models of specific genres and identification of grammatical patterns.

EXPLORING THE CULTURAL CONTEXT

Students are typically assisted to explore the relationship between use of genre and the cultural context in which the genre is located; i.e. they are encouraged to see genres as social processes existing in specific cultural contexts and fulfilling specific communicative purposes. For example, Swales (1990a) suggests that EAP students interview expert informants of a particular discourse community in order to better understand their values, interests, concerns and expectations. Hammond and Macken-Horarik (1999) describe a unit of work on human sexual reproduction in which secondary school students are encouraged to explore the (sometimes controversial) role of science in society.

ANALYSING THE TARGET SITUATION

Teacher and students together analyse the language demands of situations relevant to students' lives or their educational goals. Hammond *et al.* (1992) outline a unit of work developed for adult migrant students facing problems with rented accommodation and negotiations with real estate agents. The unit assisted students to write letters of request and complaint to estate agents.

ANALYSING MODELS OF SPECIFIC GENRES

In genre pedagogy students are typically offered opportunities to analyse examples of the genre that they will later attempt to write themselves. For inexperienced students in particular, opportunities to study models of the target genre and identify rhetorical patterns assist them in developing a clearer sense of what to aim for in their own writing. Such analysis is central to pedagogical practices associated with systemic functional linguistics where students are typically encouraged to engage in detailed and explicit discussion of specific genres (e.g. Callaghan and Rothery 1988; Derewianka 1990; Martin 1993; Christie 1995a). Such analysis is also common in ESP; e.g. Bhatia's (1997) models identifying rhetorical stages.

IDENTIFICATION OF GRAMMATICAL PATTERNS

In addition to analysing the rhetorical patterns of a target genre, students are generally assisted to identify grammatical patterns characterising the particular genre; i.e. they are encouraged to focus on how grammatical patterns vary between genres. Detailed analyses of language features are again characteristic of pedagogy associated with Australian work on genre. This work draws more generally on systemic linguistic descriptions of register and functional grammar (e.g. Halliday 1994). Analysis of the language features of genres is also central to ESP pedagogy; e.g. Swales and Feak (1994) identify the need for students to be able to use the grammar of definitions and generalisations when working with particular stages of academic texts; Bhatia (1997) also addresses genre-specific syntactic forms.

Additionally, Australian genre pedagogy typically begins with an emphasis on developing a knowledge base before focusing on any targeted genre. Since the audience is typically school students or adult migrant students, this emphasis is important. It is frequently argued that students cannot be expected to write about a topic unless they know something about it. Consequently, units of work in this field that draw on the notion of genre typically emphasise the development of content knowledge, talk about that content, and reading (and learning to read), as well as the tasks described above. This pedagogy also typically includes collaborative writing where teacher and students together write an example of the target genre following analysis of model genres. The advantage of this shared and collaborative writing is that students actively participate by providing the content, or subject matter, while at the same time being guided and supported by the teacher in the construction of an effectively organised text. Such guidance and support is designed to ensure that the student writer will be more confident and successful when they write independently (Cope and Kalantzis 1993).

Current and future trends and directions

In the 1990s genre studies emerged as a robust field of inquiry. This is evident in the substantial number of publications addressing issues of theory and practice (e.g. Swales 1990a; Bhatia 1993; Cope and Kalantzis 1993; Freedman and Medway 1994a, 1994b; Christie and Martin 1997). As with other emerging fields of study, genre studies are marked by ongoing debates, which have addressed similarities and differences in ways of theorising genre and also differences in pedagogical practices associated with genre in various educational contexts. Debates about pedagogical practices in particular have implications for TESOL education, as they raise questions central to issues about what constitutes effective language teaching.

The most intense debates centre around the following issues:

- the value of detailed analyses of genres;

- the extent to which it is possible (and useful) to teach explicitly about genres;

- the value of developing a language shared between teachers and students for talking about language (a metalanguage);

- the most effective ways of assisting students develop systematic knowledge about language; and

- the extent to which explicit focus on the linguistic resources deployed in the construction of specific texts is necessary for the development of 'critical language studies' and 'critical literacy'.

Due to the different audiences in New Rhetoric studies, systemic functional linguistic studies and ESP, these issues are approached from different perspectives. For example, proponents of New Rhetoric studies are critical of detailed analyses of genres, which, they argue, serve to 'freeze frame' (Luke 1994: viii) something which is dynamic and constantly evolving. Generally they are reluctant to provide specific descriptions of genres or explicit suggestions for teaching about genres. For example, Freedman (1993) argues that much of genre knowledge can be acquired tacitly as students are exposed to genres in their course readings and given contexts that lead them to write in appropriate text types. This reluctance to engage with specific pedagogical practices means that New Rhetoric studies have had less direct impact on language teaching that other areas of genre study.

In ESP and systemic linguistic genre studies, ongoing tensions exist regarding explicit pedagogy. Those working in these areas are centrally concerned with language teaching. Thus, while on the one hand they recognise the complexities involved in developing theoretically valid notions of genre, on the other hand they recognise that students need descriptions of specific genres that are explicit and (at least temporarily) 'fixed' if they are to be assisted to develop control of the genres relevant to their educational goals. While ESP proponents caution against prescriptiveness in genre teaching (e.g. Swales 1990a), they also propose explicit strategies for assisting students (e.g. Bhatia 1997). While those working in systemic genre studies propose explicit pedagogical practices that have had a significant impact on language teaching in Australia, debates continue about the dangers of such practices becoming overly prescriptive and reductive.

Further debates raise questions regarding the extent to which students are enabled/encouraged to take a 'critical' stance in relation to the genres they are studying. For example, Benesch (1996), while not exclusively targeting genre-based ESP/EAP programmes, criticises curriculum development in this field as being primarily descriptive and based on 'neutral discovery of elements of the (students') target situation'. She argues that such programmes ignore broader social and political issues that impact on students' academic lives, and function to reify dominant academic discourses and practices (see also Hammond and Macken-Horarik 1999).

More research is required to explore further these questions and the issues that they raise. However, the questions themselves are important ones that have implications for current and future trends and directions in TESOL education.

Despite differences and debates in the field of genre studies, there are also important commonalities. These include a shared theoretical perspective that views the role of language not just as transmitting meaning but as being itself constitutive of meaning. Thus, genre theorists share the view that language is a system for making meaning – a social semiotic system (Halliday 1978). Associated with this theoretical perspective is a recognition of the importance of locating language study within social and cultural contexts of language use, and the importance of focusing on language at the text level (i.e. of focusing on the recurring and predictable patterns of texts), as well as at the sentence level.

The emphasis on context and on text-level study has profound implications for TESOL education. To date this emphasis has been primarily directed to raising students' awareness of rhetorical text-level patterns of genres relevant to the particular context being studied. However, the importance of the emphasis on context goes beyond work that deliberately introduces students to specific genres: it also has implications for all English language teaching (ELT). Many ELT programmes and textbooks do not take adequate account of the ways in which people use language in real contexts. By taking context seriously, we not only need to include a focus on relevant genres but, as Celce-Murcia (1997: 185) argues, we need to undertake a re-analysis of virtually all of English grammar at discourse levels in order to be able to teach rules of grammar that serve students effectively. Such arguments suggest the need for considerable rethinking of ways in which English language has traditionally been taught, and substantial rewriting of many ELT coursebooks.

Conclusion

In this short chapter much is inevitably left out. The complexities of theorising genre have not been fully explored. Developments within genre studies have been only briefly introduced, much work on research and practice has not been included, and the complexities of debates amongst genre proponents have only been touched upon. However, we hope that this chapter provides a taste of the dynamic and exciting nature of this field of study, and a sense of its far-reaching implications for ELT.

Key readings

Berkenkotter and Huckin (1995) *Genre Knowledge in Disciplinary Communication*
Bhatia (1993) *Analysing Genre: Language Use in Professional Settings*
Christie (1995a) Genre-based approaches to teaching literacy
Christie and Martin (1997) *Genre and Institutions*

Cope and Kalantzis (1993) *A Genre Approach to Teaching Writing*
Derewianka (1990) *Exploring How Texts Work*
Dudley-Evans and St John (1998) *Developments in English for Specific Purposes*
Freedman and Medway (1994a) *Genre and the New Rhetoric*
Freedman and Medway (1994b) *Learning and Teaching Genre*
Hyon (1996) Genre in three traditions: implications for ESL
Martin (1993) Genre and literacy: modelling context in educational linguistics
Swales (1990a) *Genre Analysis: English in Academic and Research Settings*

CHAPTER 28

Programme management

Ron White

Introduction

A programme of study typically refers to the organised components which make up a specified set of content and activities over a defined period of time, while programme management involves organising available resources – materials, human skills and time – for the efficient and effective delivery of the programme. Programme management includes identifying teaching and learning goals; establishing standards of performance; identifying and deploying resources (including financial and human); implementing the delivery of the programme within a budget; monitoring actual performance; comparing actual achievement against planned targets (both learning and financial); taking corrective action to align goals and performance, and developing insights into and understandings of the delivery and management of the programme with a view to continuing improvement.

Background

Educational management has long been a significant field, with its own body of theory and research (see, e.g., Musgrave 1968; Houghton *et al.* 1975; Goulding *et al.* 1984; Bush 1985), as well as being concerned with issues such as managing ethics (Bottery 1992), change (see Fullan 1982, 1991; Newton and Tarrant 1992), schools (e.g. Glatter *et al.* 1988; Everard and Morris 1996), teams (e.g. Bell 1992), quality (e.g. Murgatroyd and Morgan 1992) and marketing (e.g. Stott and Parr 1991). Until the late 1980s, TESOL remained relatively isolated from this body of principles and practices and – with the occasional exception of articles on project management (e.g. Bowers 1983; Woods 1988) and languages for specific purposes (see Robinson 1988b) – even the accounts of the former were largely concerned with matters of language content (Smith 1998: 35).

In fact, despite the recent development of a management culture in TESOL, there is a dearth of empirical research of the kind that characterises second language acquisition (SLA), with virtually no articles on management appearing in flagship journals like *Applied Linguistics* (however, on managing innovation, see Stoller 1994), *TESOL Quarterly* (however, on EFL teachers' working lives, see Johnston 1997) and *System* (however, on pedagogical efficiency and cost-effectiveness, see Wigzell 1992; on language teaching in the post-Fordist era, see Tuffs 1995). Currently, TESOL professionals with an interest in management have only the IATEFL ELT Management Special Interest Group and the TESOL Program Administration Interest Section newsletters as sources for ideas on practice rather than research.

Discussions of TESOL curriculum management, such as that provided by Johnston and Peterson (1994), offer sequences of stages which represent an idealisation of the process:

- stage;
- processes;
- planning;
- finding out about the learners and their needs;
- designing a syllabus;
- selecting content;
- implementing (e.g. using materials based on the syllabus);
- evaluating: formative evaluation (e.g. monitoring materials in use, amount of learning, speed of progress);
- developing the programme, using feedback from formative evaluation;
- revision;
- evaluation: summative–formal, involving various elements of the programme;
- re-planning: redesigning on the basis of formative evaluation;
- re-implementing (compare initial implementation).

Although this sequence incorporates management processes such as planning, implementing, monitoring and evaluating, the main concern is pedagogical. The major participants are cast in the roles of teachers and learners, and their relationship is defined in pedagogical and professional terms. However, in programme management the focus shifts, and curriculum management is simply one part of a service supported by management processes (such as planning and budgeting, decision-making and information systems), even though, as Robinson (1988b: 146) points out, its aim is the effective realisation of pedagogy.

MANAGEMENT PRINCIPLES

It is now recognised that teaching and learning take place in organisations operating in contexts which involve factors outside the teaching–learning situation itself. Likewise, it is accepted that TESOL programme management occurs within an open system (Mullins 1999) dependent on the environment in which it operates, and to which it contributes, while TESOL programme management involves groups of individuals who are directly or indirectly affected by an organisation's pursuit of its goals, i.e. its stakeholders (Stoner and Freeman 1995).

The external environment includes indirect-action elements such as the technology, economy and policies of a society. These affect the climate in which an organisation operates and have the potential to become direct-action elements (Stoner *et al.* 1995: 63). Direct-action elements include the stakeholders, who are themselves of two kinds: internal and external. The former are the stakeholders found in most models of curriculum development, such as that proposed by Johnson (1989: 15): policy makers, needs analysts, methodologists, materials writers, teacher trainers, teachers and learners. The external stakeholders – who are members of the open system – include parents, sponsors, advisers, the relevant ministry of education, employers, publishers, examination boards and various commercial interests.

Stakeholders have different motives and interests in their attempts to influence the process of curriculum development, programme management and evaluation (compare Weir and Roberts 1994: 19f.). Consequently, programme managers may find themselves thrust into maintaining a balance and even adjudicating between competing interests which – as exemplified by many contemporary curriculum reforms – can be a source of political conflict. Stakeholders' influence depends on where they fit into the system, and the amount of direct or indirect authority and power they command. For example, part-time teachers, even though they are important internal stakeholders, may be restricted by time, opportunity and commitment in exercising authority, whereas 'controlling authorities' (Johnston and Peterson 1994), such as members of an examinations board, although very remote from the individuals concerned with delivering a programme, may exercise considerable power, even at local level.

The interdependence of stakeholders in Johnson's scheme is exemplified by how policy decisions at each stage are shown to impact on other decisions at successive stages. Implementation is affected by pragmatic constraints such as the political, economic, social and technical (PEST) factors which are taken into account in SWOT analysis of strengths, weaknesses, opportunities and threats in strategic market planning (White *et al.* 1991: 231f.). In addition, there are also human resource constraints such as the knowledge, attitude and skills of syllabus and materials writers and teachers, which can impact on the implementation of change (compare Fullan 1982, 1991).

Johnson (1989) contrasts process and product at each stage. He identifies process decisions as being concerned with answering questions such as:

- Who will be involved?
- What are their powers and terms of reference?
- What resources will they have available to them?
- What constraints will they be under?
- What procedures will they follow?

At the end of each decision-making process there is a 'product', i.e. a policy document, a syllabus, a set of teaching materials, a teacher-training programme, and teaching and learning acts. Although various stakeholders can contribute to the decision-making process, only designated individuals can deliver particular stages of the products; e.g. teaching acts can typically only be performed by people certified or designated to do so.

Curriculum management occurs in an organisational context. Dawson (1996: xxii) defines organisations as:

> collections of people joining together in some formal association in order to achieve group or individual objectives. At least one set of objectives of any organisation will relate to the production and output of specified goods and services to individuals, groups and other organisations.
>
> (Dawson 1996: xxii)

During the 1980s and 1990s, there was an increasing awareness that in focusing on the professional and pedagogical aspects of programme management, the equally significant managerial requirements of producing and delivering 'specified services' to clients and customers had been overlooked. This 'post-Fordist' development (Tuffs 1995: 495) coincided with a change in the outlook and practices of both publicly and privately funded education, in which market forces and issues of accountability became increasingly prominent (Weir and Roberts 1994: 13). However, such a change is not without controversy, and many educationists are critical of a market-driven approach to education which:

- defines 'teaching and teachers as products';
- fails 'to be sensitive to teaching as a process and to teachers engaged in a process' (Slater 1985: 19); and
- complains about theorising as though it were a waste of time (Swanick 1990: 96).

Such caveats need to be borne in mind in the account of programme management which follows. This market-driven approach has seen a rise in the power of stakeholders, who have begun to assert increasingly direct influence on the curriculum, in addition to exercising more stringent

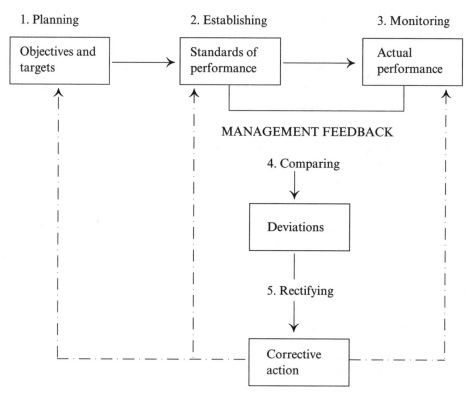

Figure 28.1 Five essential stages of management control
Source: Mullins 1993: 547

controls over funding. At the same time, stakeholders have become concerned with verifying the range of skills and competencies acquired during the teaching process. In other words, they want to know what value has been added. Not surprisingly, these influences have affected both school and programme management, with education and training in all sectors increasingly assuming the characteristics of a service industry in which students assume the role of customers or clients receiving a range of services, of which language instruction is one of a number of components.

The stages and processes involved in programme management are not substantially different from those for curriculum development summarised above; this is clear from Mullins' figure (1999: 547) shown in Figure 28.1. The fundamental difference between the curriculum-management and programme-management models is that the latter is associated with roles and functions within an organisational structure (Robbins 1998: 478f.), and the carrying-out of specific arrangements by designated individuals so as to ensure the smooth and effective delivery of the service. The management-control model is recursive, with corrective action modifying objectives, standards of performance and actual performance in a continuous cycle, as indicated in Figure 28.1.

MANAGEMENT PRACTICE

Programme management involves responsibility for cost-effectiveness and the efficient deployment of resources in pursuit of customer satisfaction. Whereas in pedagogically focused planning the cost of resourcing the programme is a separate issue, in management planning this is an integral part of the process, which means that at the planning stage two sets of objectives and targets are defined: those concerned with learning outcomes (the pedagogical goals) and those concerned with resources and finances (the managerial targets). Programme managers have to calculate the cost of planning and preparation as well as 'delivery' (or teaching) time, since all have to be paid for, while they will also have to cost resources in terms of the number (and quality) of teaching and support staff, materials and facilities. Increasingly, they will also have to demonstrate what value is being added for the client; in other words, to show what transferable benefits or skills have been acquired (Pepitone 1995). The financial calculations may then have to be evaluated in the light of factors such as price (what the client or customer will pay) and profitability, or, for the public sector, in comparison with a budget specified by a funding authority.

In a pedagogical model, standards of performance are concerned with teacher and learner performance evaluated against projected learning outcomes. In a management model, standards of performance additionally include considerations of productivity, the efficient use of resource inputs and customer satisfaction. In turn, these considerations impact on matters such as the number of hours required for preparation, marking and contact, the size of classes, and the quantity and quality of facilities.

The monitoring of performance in a pedagogical model should take into account learner and teacher development (which is also a component of a management model, since auditing the motivation and performance of personnel is part of human resource management). While the programme-management model has organisations' interests at heart, these cannot be divorced from those of their clients and stakeholders. This means that observing learning outcomes is just one aspect of the monitoring process, since the manager is now accountable for efficient resource utilisation and the achievement of performance objectives, as well as customer satisfaction, staff morale and motivation, and quality assurance.

Where a mismatch is discovered between required standards and performance, corrective action is required. Pedagogically, this might require changes to various aspects of the programme. What the programme manager has to decide is whether such changes or additions are feasible within existing resources, whether there is a need to increase provision (which may mean an increase in cost), and what effects such changes may have on staff commitment and motivation. In turn, this may mean balancing various issues such as efficient allocation of resources and consultation with stakeholders (compare Weir and Roberts 1994: 82f.).

An important aspect of programme management is the concern with quality (Tuffs 1995: 496), and there are three ways of looking at quality in the management of TESOL programmes:

- Fitness for purpose: This involves how standards are related to the defined objectives of a course. This involves the explicit specification of skills and abilities as objectives, with assessment being concerned with the performance of specified competencies to a defined level of skill.

- Value for money: This means maintaining or improving pedagogical outcomes for the same (or declining) unit of resource. Students and other stakeholders are seen as 'paying customers'. In short, the concern is with the efficient delivery of a service.

- Transformation: Quality is defined as a process of change which adds value to students through their learning experience. Students are provided with enhanced skills and abilities that empower them to continue to learn and to engage effectively with the complexities of the 'outside' world.

Clarifying how quality is to be defined and realised requires the programme manager continually to enquire about the needs of stakeholders. It is also important for stakeholders to see that their ideas, concerns and suggestions are implemented on a regular basis (Murgatroyd and Morgan 1992: 50).

The programme manager may also be accountable to standards which are codified and evaluated by objective criteria, and which are set by external experts. This involves all or some of the following methods: self-assessment, inspection, formal evaluation and examination. Quality assurance (QA) schemes may take 'best practice' as the criterion for measuring standard. Typical of such schemes is the English Language Schools Recognition Scheme (British Council 1996: 20), in which academic management is one of six categories for inspection, focusing on the following:

- Course design: Appropriate objectives and syllabus content are established for all courses. Appropriate materials and methodology are identified to achieve the objectives. There should be evidence that courses develop as appropriate in response to feedback and changing needs.

- Students' progress: There should be satisfactory systems for the correct placement of students, for monitoring their progress, for diagnosing their problems and language needs and for providing guidance and support. Where appropriate, special attention is paid to the implications of continuous enrolment.

- Teaching standards: Lesson content and classroom performance is monitored, guidance offered, and appropriate resources and practical support provided for teachers.

- Resources management: There should be appropriate systems for access to all teaching and learning resources and for their effective maintenance, together with a policy for continuing review and development.

- Examinations management: Where public examinations and examination training are offered, staffing and resources should be appropriate. Students should be guided to select the examinations and examination training best suited to their needs and interests.

- Management of the teaching team: Teacher responsibilities should be clearly specified and supervised. Adequate channels of communication should be maintained amongst teachers, between teachers and the academic manager or director of studies, and between teachers and senior management. Special attention should be paid to the resources provided for teacher induction, monitoring, in-service development and general support.

Current and future trends and directions

TESOL operates in a volatile and changing world (Graddol 1997), involving the continued expansion of knowledge-based industries in which new knowledge is created, applied and adapted to changing circumstances. As part of this expansion, TESOL will be affected by two trends:

- the replacing of bureaucratic hierarchies by more informal, self-organised forms of co-ordination, i.e. networks (Fukuyama 1999); and

- the growth of high performance work systems (Nadler *et al.* 1992) in which organisations bring together work, people, technology and information in a way that optimises the fit among them so as to respond effectively to customers' requirements and other demands and opportunities in the environment.

Conclusion

In this chapter, I outline an approach to programme management which is based on principles and practices largely drawn from business management, in which market forces and accountability are prominent. The growth of a management culture in TESOL has yet to be accompanied by a body of published empirical research and the development of a TESOL management literature. In the meantime, existing management models and processes have been appropriated, providing a basis for the development of effective and responsive programme management.

Key readings

Atrill and McLaney (1997) *Accounting and Finance for Non-specialists*
Barnes (1993) *Practical Marketing for Schools*

Cooper and Agyris (1998) *The Concise Blackwell Encyclopaedia of Management*
Davies (1998) *Understanding Marketing*
Dessler (1999) *Essentials of Human Resource Management*
Everard and Morris (1996) *Effective School Management*
Garratt (2000) *The Twelve Organizational Capabilities*
Handy (1999) *Understanding Organizations*
Impey and Underhill (1994) *The ELT Manager's Handbook*
Johnston and Peterson (1994) The program matrix: a conceptual framework for language programs
Markee (1997) *Managing Curricular Innovation*
Mead (1998) *International Management: Cross Cultural Dimensions*
Mullins (1999) *Management and Organisational Behaviour*
Murgatroyd and Morgan (1992) *Total Quality Management and the School*
Robbins (1998) *Organizational Behavior*
Stoner *et al.* (1995) *Management*
White *et al.* (1991) *Management in English Language Teaching*

CHAPTER 29

Intercultural communication

Claire Kramsch

Introduction

Intercultural or cross-cultural communication is an interdisciplinary field of research that studies how people understand each other across group boundaries of various sorts: national, geographical, ethnic, occupational, class or gender. In the United States it has traditionally been related to the behavioural sciences, psychology and professional business training; in Europe it is mostly associated with anthropology and the language sciences. Researchers generally view intercultural communication as a problem created by differences in behaviours and world views among people who speak different languages and who belong to different cultures. However, these problems may not be very different from those encountered in communication among people who share the same national language and culture.

Background

TESOL has always had as its goal the facilitation of communication among people who do not share the same language and national culture. But before the Second World War, the term 'culture' meant knowledge about great works of literature, social institutions and historical events, acquired through the translation of written texts. The rise of linguistics and of the social sciences after the Second World War, and the demands of market economies, gave prominence to spoken language and to communication across cultures in situations of everyday life.

While the term 'intercultural communication' became prominent in TESOL only in the 1980s, as the necessary supplement to communicative language teaching first developed in Europe in the early 1970s, the field itself can be traced to the work in the 1950s of Georgetown University linguist Robert Lado and of anthropologist and US Foreign Service Institute (FSI) officer Edward T. Hall. Lado's *Linguistics Across Cultures* (1957) was the first attempt to link language and culture in an educationally relevant way; Lado had an enormous influence on the teaching of English around the world. In *The Silent Language* (1959), Hall showed the complex ways in which 'culture is communication and communication is culture' (1959: 191). The principles of intercultural communication developed by Hall and his colleagues in the Foreign Service were used by the Peace Corps, founded in the early 1960s. They gave rise to simulation games, studies of 'critical incidents' where miscommunication occurred, and comparative studies of Asian and American cultures, especially Japan (see, e.g., Brislin 1981; Hofstede 1983; Brislin *et al.* 1986; Thiagarajan and Steinwachs 1990). In the 1970s these studies were employed by the international business community and applied to the training of salespeople and corporate executives. In the 1980s, following the Civil Rights Movement and the demands for cultural recognition by ethnic groups and minorities, intercultural communication became relevant also to ethnically diverse groups within one and the same country and was used by social workers and educators.

In sum, the field of intercultural communication grew out of the practical, competitive needs of post-Second World War American international diplomacy and business, and was only later applied to interethnic conflicts within the United States. Influenced by research in areal linguistics during the Second World War, and in business organisational management after the Second World War, its foundational disciplines were, besides linguistics, the behavioural sciences, especially psychology and social psychology.

By contrast, the field of intercultural communication in Europe was a direct outcome of the social and political upheavals created by the large scale immigrations into the industrialised countries. It has therefore been much more closely linked to fields such as anthropology, sociolinguistics, pragmatics and discourse analysis (see, e.g., Barth 1969; Blommaert and Verschueren 1991; Dahl 1995) even though behavioural training is also part of the field in Europe. It is worth noting that intercultural communication studies have not drawn to any notable extent on humanistic disciplines like semiotics, hermeneutics or cultural studies (see, however, Byram 1989).

Some of the major facets of human interaction that intercultural communication has helped to define are:

- the situation of communication itself; e.g. the socially conventionalised roles adopted by participants, their expected norms of interaction and interpretation, the way they construct a shared sense of reality;
- the stereotypes they entertain of each other, as individuals and as members of a social group;
- their non-verbal and paraverbal behaviour;
- the way they save their own and each other's face;
- the way they structure their discourse to meet their communicative goals;
- the attitudes, values and beliefs (called also 'discourses') they share with the social group they belong to;
- the way their language reflects these deeper discourses;
- the way members of different groups realise various speech acts (like making compliments, requests or apologies).

Intercultural communication training and research takes place in the US at centres such as the East–West Center in Honolulu, Hawai'i which was founded in the early 1960s to ameliorate deteriorating East–West relations. Other centres include: the Intercultural Communication Institute in Portland, Oregon and three National Foreign Language Centers with specialisation in some aspect of intercultural communication at the University of Hawai'i at Manoa, at San Diego State University and at the University of Minnesota. The need to co-ordinate the business, governmental, private consulting and training, religious and academic organisations involved in intercultural education led in 1974 to the creation of the Society for Intercultural Education, Training and Research (SIETAR), which now has affiliates in France, Germany, the Netherlands and Japan, among others. In Europe, towards the end of the 1970s, a project on intercultural education initiated by the Council of Europe led to the founding of the International Association of Intercultural Education within the larger International Communication Association (ICA). Major journals in the field are: *International Journal of Intercultural Relations*; *Journal of Cross-Cultural Psychology*; *Multilingua: Journal of Cross-Cultural and Interlanguage Communication*; *Journal of Multilingual and Multicultural Development*; *Language, Culture and Curriculum*; *Cross-Cultural Research*.

Teachers of English are, however, encouraged to look beyond professional organisations and research journals explicitly dedicated to 'intercultural communication' and to acquaint themselves with academic research conducted within a cross-cultural framework in the general fields of applied linguistics, pragmatics, discourse analysis, linguistic anthropology, ethnography and cultural studies.

Research

One of the major concerns in the beginnings of the field was how to help FSI officers interact with people in the foreign countries to which they were dispatched. Thus, in *The Silent Language* (1959), Hall studied particularly the 'out-of-awareness' aspects of communication – the paralanguage of pitch, rhythm and intonation, the 'silent language' of gestures and movements (kinesics), and the use of time (chronemics). In his next book, *The Hidden Dimension* (Hall 1966), he studied the use of space (proxemics) and found, e.g., that Anglo-Americans establish a greater distance between face-to-face interlocutors than, say, Japanese or Arabs. In *Beyond Culture* (Hall 1981), he discussed the concepts of 'high-context communication', where most of the information is implicit because it is located in the physical context or part of a shared world view, and 'low-context communication', where the bulk of the information is to be found in the words uttered. The latter, he claimed, is more typical of Northern European style communication, whereas high-context communication is particularly characteristic of Chinese speakers.

Many intercultural researchers were influenced by work in cross-cultural psychology: Segall (1979) identified human universals in visual perception and cognitive processing of which each culture showed specific variations. Triandis (1995) – drawing on Hofstede (1983) – propagated the concepts of individualistic vs. collectivist cultures (e.g. American or Germany vs. Brazil or Japan). Some attempted to build an intercultural communication theory with a broad interdisciplinary base (Kroeber and Kluckhohn 1952; Condon and Yousef 1975; Gudykunst 1983). Because studies in intercultural communication are often spurred by a perceived sense of inferiority vis-à-vis a foreign country or by a desire to open up that country's markets, there has been a flurry of comparative studies of American and Japanese interactional practices (e.g. Barnlund 1975; Gudykunst 1993). Today, many studies in cross-cultural psychology seem simplistic because they ignore the cultural diversity within a given nation-state and the increasing potential for change within a global economy.

Besides these psychological studies, linguistics entered the field with Kaplan's (1966) contrastive study of the various rhetorical patterns found in the writing of ESL learners. This study illustrated the different ways various cultures have of expressing themselves. 'Westerners' were claimed to prefer a direct mode of expression; 'Semitics' and 'Latin-Americans' to use a more loop-like way of argumentation, and 'Orientals' were said to favour digression and 'beating around the bush'. Today, such characterisations sound dangerously ethnocentric. They show the difficulty of expressing one culture in terms of another without sounding critical or condescending.

Since the 1980s, the field has been broadened to include sociolinguistics and linguistic anthropology. The most prominent work here is that of Ron and Suzanne Scollon. In their first book *Narrative, Literacy and Face in Interethnic Communication* (Scollon and Scollon 1981) they document the different nature and value attributed to literacy and orality practices among Anglo-Americans and Athabaskans. In the way they told stories, their own three-year-old daughter, Rachel, and her ten-year-old Athabaskan friend, Big Sister, were differentially literate. Even before she could read and write, Rachel told stories she made up according to a tripartite pattern (orientation–complication–resolution) familiar to her from the English bedtime stories she was read by her parents. By contrast, Big Sister's spoken and written stories conformed to a four-part, repetitive pattern favoured by members of her culture.

In their second book *Intercultural Communication* (Scollon and Scollon 1995), the Scollons focus on the professional discourse between Americans and East Asians, especially Chinese. They draw on classical work in sociolinguistics and linguistic anthropology: Hymes' (1974) work on the ethnography of communication, Gumperz' (1982) investigation of the link between discourse and social identity, Tannen's (1984a) exploration of cultural differences in conversation, Brown and Levinson's (1987) pioneering study on politeness and face and Blum-Kulka *et al.*'s (1989) studies in cross-cultural pragmatics. The Scollons pass in review the parameters of intercultural speech situations, the strategies of politeness and power, the conversational inferences, topics and face systems that regulate cross-cultural communication, and the realisation of speech acts across cultures. They also extend the usual boundaries of intercultural communication by discussing the discourse systems (or discourses, ideologies and stereotypes) that underlie the way people talk and interact with one another; examples of such systems are corporate discourses, professional discourses, generational discourses and gender discourses.

As intercultural communication moves into a critical examination of systems of thought, the work of linguists like Gee and Pennycook have yielded important insights into intercultural communication in recent years. Cultural differences are often of political importance and are linked to issues of power and control. For example, Gee (1990) shows how our autonomous concept of literacy is a Western construct, favouring the academic-essay type of literacy and the individual literate performance over more creative and community-based uses of the written language. Gee's work has far-reaching implications for the teaching of English reading and writing to members of cultures that have a view of literacy different from Western ones. Pennycook (1994) adds an important dimension to intercultural communication by problematising the field itself. He debunks the idea that the spread of English around the world is a natural, culturally neutral and necessarily beneficial phenomenon. Like Phillipson (1992) he argues that it is the result of a complex conjuncture of historical circumstances (e.g. the colonial legacy of the British Commonwealth, the victory of the English-speaking allies in the Second World War), American advances made in information technologies, purposeful language policies by government agencies like the United States Information Service (USIS) and the British Council, worldwide immigration patterns and the globalisation of the world economy. Certain uses of the English language bear traces of a colonial past that teachers of English should be critically aware of. Moreover, the spread of English and the concomitant globalisation of a certain kind of consumer culture are raising fears that they might displace local languages and cultures, or reinforce the gap between the international culture of the upwardly mobile, internet-connected elite and the geographically rooted, traditional local cultures.

Practice

The insights gained by research in intercultural communication have made English teachers aware of the cultural dimensions of language as social interaction. While literature and 'high' culture waned in importance, the small 'c' culture of attitudes and mind-sets, lifestyles and interactional styles became crucially important to successful communication in EFL. Success in business transactions and diplomatic negotiations is not dependent on grammar alone; one has to know how to say what to whom at the right time in the right place. Thus, many cross-cultural simulation games, case studies of miscommunication, culture capsules and handbooks of cross-cultural communication flooded the professional market in the 1970s and 1980s. They were mostly directed at English speakers learning about foreign cultures, but TESOL textbooks also focused explicitly on pragmatic strategies for effective behavioural training and on the realisation of speech functions in authentic situations with the help of role play and videotape observation. With the end of the Cold War a flurry of educational materials advocating the teaching of language and culture and the teaching of language as culture were introduced in the late 1980s and the 1990s (Valdes 1986; Byram 1989; Harrison 1990; Kramsch 1993; Heusinkveld 1996; Fantini 1997). TESOL now has a Special Interest Group in Intercultural Communication and an Intercultural Communication column editor in *TESOL Matters*.

Until recently, teaching intercultural communication in a TESOL class has been pretty much a one-way street, i.e. transmitting information about English-speaking countries and training non-English speakers to adopt the behaviours of English speakers. Because the student body in most ESL classes is multilingual and multicultural, any comparison between the target English-speaking culture and any one native culture has seemed futile. However, the pedagogy of intercultural communication is currently shifting from teaching accurate facts and culturally appropriate behaviours to teaching the social and historical contexts that have given present cultural phenomena their meaning within larger cross-cultural networks. In this regard, authentic texts lend themselves to being put in relation to other texts of various kinds – visual, musical, oral or written – in order to identify the social position of the non-native speaker vis-à-vis native speakers (see, e.g., Rampton 1990; Kramsch and Lam 1998), or to explore what a non-native perspective can add to the international culture of English as an international language (Widdowson 1990; Kramsch 1993).

Current and future trends and directions

The field of intercultural communication in the US has traditionally been a relatively apolitical field of research, grounded primarily in psychology and the behavioural sciences. With the increased importance it has gained in recent years because of world-scale geopolitical, economic and demographic changes, European and American research efforts in intercultural communication are converging to include other disciplines that pay more attention to the sociological, anthropological, discursive and symbolic dimensions of language and culture (see, e.g., Geertz 1973; Bourdieu 1991; Shore 1996). In addition, the rise of cultural studies and critical pedagogy has brought issues of conflict, power and control within the scope of intercultural communication as a field of research (see Kramsch 1998). For example, the spread of English as the world's lingua franca is often seen as displacing other national or regional languages and cultures. Thus, the notion of linguistic rights – officially proclaimed in the Universal Declaration of Linguistic Rights at an international conference in Barcelona in 1996 (Skutnabb-Kangas and Phillipson 1994) – has recently been joined by that of 'intercultural rights' and 'intercultural linguistics' (Gomes de Matos 1997) as a way of integrating a human rights' philosophy into the research and practice of language teaching.

At the beginning of the twenty-first century, the essentialisation of national traits and cultural characteristics – i.e. the comparison of differences between one native and one foreign culture, seen as stable spaces on the map and permanent in time – seems too reductionist. Such a view of intercultural communication research doesn't reflect the complexities of a post-colonial, global age in which people live in multiple, shifting spaces and partake of multiple identities often in conflict with one another, and where the possibility for one individual to better his or her chances of success are not as clear as was once believed (in part, because the notion of 'success' itself is not universally shared). In a few years, the traditional binary tradition of Us vs. Them in intercultural communication will be replaced by the notion that in a networked, interdependent world the Other is in Us and We are in the Other. Intercultural communication will have to deal with shifting identities and cross-cultural networks rather than with autonomous individuals located in stable and homogeneous national cultures.

For the English teacher, new directions include looking at the social and historical conditions of teaching intercultural communication through English. New questions will be asked; not only 'How can I teach English more effectively, so that the people of the world can be "empowered" by knowing English?', but also:

- How does the teaching of English change the balance of the haves and the have-nots in local cultures around the world?

- What kinds of identities does the teaching of English create and promote in an international playing field that will never be level?
- How does our enabling individuals to speak English and pass TOEFL tests enhance world peace and harmony?; and, finally
- How can we train those who move back and forth over cross-cultural borders – i.e. diplomats, lawyers and English teachers – to foster intercultural rights and responsibilities?

These are momentous questions which the field of intercultural communication is only starting to address.

Key readings

Barth (1969) *The Social Organization of Cultural Differences*
Byram (1989) *Cultural Studies and Foreign Language Education*
Geertz (1973) *The Interpretation of Cultures*
Gumperz (1982) *Language and Social Identity*
Hall (1959) *The Silent Language*
Kramsch (1998) *Language and Culture*
Lado (1957) *Linguistics Across Cultures*
Pennycook (1994) *The Cultural Politics of English as an International Language*
Scollon and Scollon (1995) *Intercultural Communication*
Shore (1996) *Cognition, Culture, and the Problem of Meaning*

CHAPTER 30

On-line communication

Mark Warschauer

Introduction

The term **on-line communication** refers to reading, writing and communication via networked computers. It encompasses:

- synchronous computer-mediated communication, whereby people communicate in real time via chat or discussion software, with all participants at their computers at the same time;
- asynchronous computer-mediated communication, whereby people communicate in a delayed fashion by computer, e.g. by email; and
- the reading and writing of on-line documents via the internet.

Second language (L2) researchers are interested in two overlapping issues related to on-line communication:

- How do the processes which occur in on-line communication assist language learning in a general sense (i.e. on-line communication for language learning)?; and
- What kinds of language learning need to occur so that people can communicate effectively in the on-line realm (i.e. language learning for on-line communication)?

Background

On-line communication dates back to the late 1960s, when US researchers first developed protocols that allowed the sending and receiving of messages via computer (Hafner and Lyon 1996). The ARPANET, launched in 1969 by a handful of research scientists, eventually evolved into the internet, bringing together some 200 million people around the world at the start of the twenty-first century. On-line communication first became possible in educational realms in the 1980s, following the development and spread of personal computers. The background to on-line communication in language teaching and research can be divided into two distinct periods, marked by the introduction of computer-mediated communication in education in the mid-1980s and the emergence of the world wide web in the mid-1990s.

COMPUTER-MEDIATED COMMUNICATION

In the first period, dating from the mid-1980s, language educators began to discover the potential of computer-mediated communication for language teaching (Cummins 1986). The integration of computer-mediated communication in the classroom itself divided into two paths: some educators began to use email to set up long-distance exchanges, while other educators began to use synchronous software programs – in particular Daedalus Interchange (Daedalus 1989) – to allow computer-assisted conversation in a single classroom.

Long-distance exchanges and computer-assisted conversation had overlapping, but distinctive, justifications. Both types of activities were seen to shift the focus from language form to language use in a meaningful context (e.g. Kelm 1992; Meskill and Krassimira 2000), and thereby increase student motivation (e.g. Warschauer 1996b; Meunier 1998). In addition, long-distance exchanges were viewed as bringing about increased cultural knowledge from communication with native-speaking informants (e.g. Soh and Soon 1991; Kern 1995a), and making reading and writing more authentic and collaborative (e.g. Tella 1992b). Those implementing computer-assisted conversation emphasised the linguistic benefits which could be achieved from rapid written interaction, such as better opportunities to process and try out new lexical or syntactic patterns as compared to oral interaction (e.g. Ortega 1997; Warschauer 1999).

THE WORLD WIDE WEB

The world wide web is an international on-line database that allows the sharing of linked multimedia documents. These documents can be authored in a non-linear, layered and linked format, which is referred to as hypertext or hypermedia. The development and spread of the world wide web, or the internet, in the 1990s marked a second period in the use of on-line communication in language teaching. On the one hand, the web allows additional modes of computer-mediated communication through web-based chat rooms, bulletin boards and discussion forums, thus making even more popular the kind of long-distance exchanges and computer-assisted conversation activities described above. In addition, the internet adds a new dimension to on-line communication and learning by allowing students to find and read on-line documents on a variety of topics from throughout the world and to author and publish similar documents to share with others.

Some researchers have viewed the web as an extension of an L2 culture or society; by engaging in web-based activities, students can gradually become members of the community of English language speakers, in the same way that they might through other forms of immersion in a culture (Zhao 1996). Others view the internet as an extension of a CD-ROM, i.e. a good environment to create multimedia language learning materials with the added advantage of allowing student interactivity (Chun and Plass 2000). Others view the web as an extension of (and alternative to) print, i.e. as a major new medium of literacy that needs to be mastered on its own terms for success in twenty-first century life (Warschauer 1999; Shetzer and Warschauer 2000). Since the web is a vast and diverse environment – encompassing a huge variety of on-line documents and an array of evolving communications tools – it is perhaps overreaching to seek a single unitary framework to motivate its integration in the classroom.

Research

Research on on-line communication and L2 learning has focused on three general topic areas: interaction; reading and writing; and affect.

INTERACTION

Computer-mediated communication, which allows the recording of all messages for *post hoc* analysis, provides a wealth of easily accessible data for language researchers studying interaction. Studies of L2 computer-mediated interaction have thus far looked at the linguistic characteristics of computer-mediated messages, the types of negotiation and linguistic modification that occur, and the patterns of participation that emerge.

• Linguistic characteristics: An important question facing both first language (L1) and L2 researchers is whether computer-mediated communication has its own distinctive linguistic features. L2 research has found that computer-assisted conversation is syntactically more complex and lexically more dense than face-to-face conversation (Warschauer 1996a). In a comparative study of two modes of student–teacher dialogue, it has also been shown that L2 students' writing via email is more informal and conversational than their writings via pencil and paper (Wang 1993). These studies support prior claims that computer-mediated communication tends to fall in the middle of the continuum of more formal communication (as often featured in writing) and informal communication (as often featured in speech). The studies suggest that computer-mediated communication can help serve as a useful bridge between speaking and writing by facilitating L2 interaction that is linguistically complex yet informal and communicative.

• Negotiation and linguistic modification: One of the most important domains of L2 research is that of negotiation and modification, i.e. how L2 learners modify their communication in negotiation and interaction with others (see Pica 1994). Several studies have shown extensive incorporation of new syntactical patterns or lexical chunks during computer-mediated interaction and have concluded that the on-line medium facilitates such incorporation by allowing greater opportunity to study incoming messages and carefully to plan responses (e.g. St John and Cash 1995; Pelletieri 2000). Research also indicates that the types of tasks and topics chosen have an important affect on the nature of computer-mediated negotiation, with substantial benefits found from conversational tasks which are goal-oriented and encourage learners to reflect on their own use of language (Lamy and Goodfellow 1999; Pelletieri 2000).

• Patterns of participation: L1 research has shown that computer-mediated communication tends to feature more balanced participation than face-to-face conversation, with less dominance by outspoken individuals (for a summary of research, see Sproull and Kiesler 1991). Studies of L2 classroom discourse have validated this finding. First, it has been shown that student participation (in contrast to teacher participation) increases dramatically in computer-mediated communication (e.g. Kern 1995b; Warschauer 1999). Second, it has been found that students themselves participate more equally in computer-mediated communication, and it is precisely those students who participate least in face-to-face conversation who increase their participation most when changing to a computer medium (Warschauer 1996a). Third, it has been found that in mixed L2–L1 classrooms, L2 students are more likely to participate in computer-mediated than in face-to-face conversation (Warschauer 1999). These findings suggest that computer-mediated communication can be a useful tool for encouraging greater participation of quiet or shy students and for creating alternatives to the traditional 'IRF' (teacher initiation, student response and teacher follow-up) discourse pattern which dominates most classrooms.

READING AND WRITING

A second line of research has investigated the types of reading and writing processes that occur in on-line environments. Qualitative studies in several on-line classrooms have described how students' reading and writing processes become more collaborative and purposeful as students engage in project-oriented research and writing for a real audience (Tella 1992b; Barson *et al.* 1993; Warschauer 1999; Meskill and Krassimira 2000). These benefits occur both during email exchanges (e.g. Kern 1996) and, especially, when students publish their work on the internet, as the act of public display encourages them to make their writing more 'reader-centred' (i.e. written with the audience in mind; see Warschauer 1999). These changes in reading and writing processes have been reported only in those classrooms where the internet is integrated by teachers into collaborative, content-focused project work, and not in situations characterised by a high amount of teacher control and a focus on the mechanics of writing (see Warschauer 1998).

AFFECT

A third area of research has been on the affective impact of on-line learning and particularly whether opportunities for on-line communication increase students' motivation. Research to date suggests that on-line learning activities are generally quite motivating for language learners, in part because learners feel they are gaining technical skills which will prove beneficial in the future (Warschauer 1996b). Learners are also motivated by the opportunity to publish their own work, communicate with distant partners, work collaboratively in groups and create their own projects that reflect their own interests (Tella 1992a; Barson *et al.* 1993; Warschauer 1999). However, learners lose motivation if they don't understand or agree with the purpose of technology-based activities and feel that that such activities are interfering with their language-learning goals (Pinto 1996; Warschauer 1998).

Research to date, although still in its infancy, indicates that on-line activities can support a number of important language learning objectives if the activities are implemented in a well-planned and purposeful manner. Planning should include the establishment of topics, tasks, projects and organisation that exploit the value of the internet for goal-oriented communication, research and publication.

Practice

The internet is, by its nature, a dynamic and interactive medium that requires a high degree of flexibility and interaction. Research indicates that on-line communication activities which are too highly restrictive, which focus on form to the exclusion of content, which insist on a high degree of teacher control or which fail to allow students to pursue their own initiatives or interests are likely to cause frustration and demotivation (Warschauer 1998). At the same time, the highly decentralised and diverse nature of the internet can make it a confusing and even chaotic medium for learners of English, especially those at beginners' level. Simply leaving learners to their own devices on the internet is unlikely to bring satisfying results, as beginners drop out in frustration and more advanced learners stagnate at the level of conversational chatting or superficial 'net-surfing'.

Best on-line teaching practices take the contradictory nature of the internet into account. Internet-based activities should be complex enough to allow for the kinds of interaction, collaboration and autonomous decision-making that are well supported by the medium. The activities should also be sufficiently structured to allow learners to achieve objectives without floundering or getting lost. These two points, taken together, mean that internet-based projects and activities are likely to be most successful when they reflect in-depth planning and integration. As Roberts, one of the co-ordinators of International Email Classroom Connections stated:

> There is a significant difference in educational outcome depending on whether a teacher chooses to incorporate email classroom connections as (1) an *add-on* process, like one would include a guest speaker, or (2) an *integrated* process, in the way one would include a new textbook. The email classroom connection seems sufficiently complex and time consuming

that if there are goals beyond merely having each student send a letter to a person at a distant school, the *add-on* approach can lead to frustration and less-than-expected academic results – the necessary time and resources come from other things that also need to be done. On the other hand, when the email classroom connection processes are truly integrated into the ongoing structure of homework and student classroom interaction, then the results can be educationally transforming.   (Warschauer 1995a: 95)

On-line communication thus fits especially well with a structured, project-based approach that allows learners to engage in increasingly complex tasks throughout a course, in collaboration with partners in the same class or in other locations, and with appropriate scaffolding from the teacher or from other sources (including on-line resources). The types of projects which can be organised are varied, and may incorporate the following elements:

- Interviews and surveys: Students work in teams to design, conduct, and interpret surveys or interviews of distant partners on social, cultural or other issues (see Ady 1995; Kendall 1995).

- On-line research: Students learn to conduct research on-line to answer questions selected by the teacher or to investigate matters of their own choosing (see Lixl-Purcell 1995).

- Comparative investigations: Students work in teams to investigate social, cultural or economic conditions in their locality and to compare the results on line (see Livesy and Tudoreanu 1995).

- Simulations: Students work in teams on projects such as a model United Nations, business simulations or contests to find the best solution to a real-world problem (see Feldman 1995; Vilmi 1995).

- On-line publication: Students work in teams to publish on-line newsletters, magazines or documentary reports (Jor 1995; Barson and Debski 1996).

Such long-term projects can provide a meaningful and motivating context to frame learning activities throughout a teaching term or semester. Within the context of the project, specific language-focused activities can be included, such as those related to reading, writing, research, vocabulary, grammar and other skill areas. Classroom discussions, planning meetings and oral presentations can help students develop aural–oral skills to complement the reading and writing skills which may be the focus of their on-line work.

Current and future trends and directions

Beginning in the late 1990s, there has been a gradual shift from seeing on-line communication as a tool to promote language learning towards seeing the mastery of on-line communication as a valuable end in itself. This reflects the increased prominence of on-line communication in society, with email surpassing telephone conversation and even face-to-face conversation as a frequent tool of communication among some occupational groups (American Management Association International 1998) and with the internet rapidly expanding its presence and impact in fields ranging from academia to entertainment to marketing. Thus, an important new future direction in both research and practice focuses on integrating the teaching of language skills and new 'electronic literacies' (Warschauer 1999).

Shetzer and Warschauer (2000) have categorised electronic literacies in three areas:

- communication, involving internet-based activities which allow people to converse with individuals and groups, and involving mastering the pragmatics of various forms of synchronous and asynchronous communication, both in one-to-one interaction and 'many-to-many' electronic discussion forums;

- construction, involving the ability to work individually or collaboratively to write and publish information on the internet, and including mastery of hypermedia authoring (i.e. making a point effectively while combining texts with graphics or other media, all packaged in a non-linear, linked 'hypertextual' format); and

• research, encompassing a range of navigation, reading and interpretation skills, including how to search the internet effectively, how to evaluate information found, and how critically to consider multimedia information.

In summary, electronic literacies will be important in many languages, but in none more so than English since an estimated 85 per cent of the electronically-stored information in the world is in the English language (Crystal 1997). Several approaches for the development of electronic literacies are emerging. These include the fuller integration of electronic literacy skills in the 'traditional' ESL classroom as well as the establishment of special content-based courses that are specifically based on combining a focus on language and technology.

Conclusion

On-line communication is a new phenomenon, having first come into existence towards the end of the twentieth century. It is growing at one of the fastest rates of any new form of communication in human history, and its long-term impact is expected to be substantial. A not uncommon and, in my eyes, justifiable view is that on-line communication represents the most important development in human communication and cognition since the development of the printing press (Harnad 1991).

During the early years of the internet, teachers began to think about how they could exploit on-line communication to promote language learning, and this effort will surely continue. However, it is increasingly clear that on-line communication represents for the field of TESOL much more than a useful pedagogical tool. Rather, on-line communication is a major new medium of English-language communication and literacy in its own right, and one that is likely to affect the development of TESOL in important ways that we cannot yet predict. Both researchers and language teachers will do well to play close attention to the expanding and evolving role of on-line communication as it relates to the teaching, learning and use of English.

Key readings

Cummins and Sayers (1995) *Challenging Cultural Illiteracy through Global Learning Networks*
Debski *et al.* (1997) *Language Learning Through Social Computing*
Ortega (1997) Processes and outcomes in networked classroom interaction
Tella (1992b) *A Thematic and Linguistic Analysis of Electronic Mail Communication*
Warschauer (1995b) *Online Activities and Projects for Networking Language Learners*
Warschauer (1997) Computer-mediated collaborative learning
Warschauer (1999) *Language, Culture, and Power in Online Education*
Warschauer and Kern (2000) *Network-Based Language Teaching*
Warschauer *et al.* (2000) *Internet for English Teaching*

Postscript: The ideology of TESOL

Jack C. Richards

Note: The references in this concluding chapter are to contributions in the volume.

The present volume seeks to provide snapshots of significant issues and trends that have shaped language teaching in the recent past and to highlight the current state of our understanding of these issues. Collectively the chapters can be seen to reflect the current underlying ideology of TESOL, that is, the beliefs and principles held by scholars and TESOL leaders that have determined the issues and priorities characterising the recent history of the subject. It is instructive therefore to conclude this collection of articles with a statement of what these beliefs and principles are. In order to do so I present in what follows a summary of the recurring themes I have identified in this book. Some are stated explicitly by the authors, and others are inferred from the accounts given. Despite the wide range of topics covered in the collection, a core set of assumptions can be identified. These can be thought of as constituting the underlying ideology of TESOL.

The contexts of teaching and learning play an important role in shaping processes and in determining learning outcomes

English is learned and taught in a variety of individual and social contexts, and these contexts (i.e. the settings, participants, purposes and transactions that characterise a language learning situation) play a crucial role in shaping the processes and outcomes of learning. The distinction between **English as a second language (ESL)** and **English as a foreign language (EFL)** seeks to reflect some of these contextual differences, although it is too crude to capture the full complexity of contextual factors (Carter and Nunan). Contexts can affect such issues as the roles English plays in learners' lives, i.e.:

- whether it serves primarily interactional or transactional functions;
- the role of English in relation to other languages in the community and in the learner's speech repertoire;
- the extent to which learners focus on accuracy or fluency as learning goals;
- whether learners seek to acquire a native speaker or non-native speaker variety of English;
- whether learners seek to acquire a standard or a non-standard pronunciation (Seidlhofer); and
- the type of language input learners receive.

The classroom is the major learning context for many learners, and it creates its own norms for language use and interaction (Tsui). Classroom language use is often characterised by recurring task types, patterns of interaction, question-and-answer routines and turn-taking, and the quality of language data students are exposed to is often dependent upon the extent to which the classroom can become a context for authentic or semi-authentic language use (Bailey).

Learners shape the process of learning in powerful ways

Whereas traditional transmission-oriented methods of teaching viewed learners as passive recipients of the teacher's methodology, learning is today seen from a constructivist perspective. The underlying systems which learners employ are viewed as something which learners construct for themselves. Learners are seen as building up a series of approximations to the target language, through trial and error, hypothesis testing and creative representations of input. This has led to a reassessment of the role of errors and a recognition of the systematic nature of learners' interlanguage (Nunan, Silberstein).

Second language (L2) learners are also viewed as starting not with a blank slate but are already in possession of a unique human ability: the ability to use language. Learners bring a diversity of literacy and other language contact experiences to learning, and these can influence their approaches to L2 learning (Wallace). The learner is therefore on the way to becoming bilingual or multilingual, and previous learning will inform new learning in many different ways (Lam). These include transfer not only at the linguistic level but also at the level of pragmatic, cultural and sociolinguistic competence. Learning a new language may also involve acquiring a new identity – a new set of beliefs and values – without necessarily requiring the abandonment of first culture/language values and norms (Silberstein, Kramsch).

Learning is also an active process. The successful language learner is a manager of strategies. These are used to monitor learning, to plan goals and to assess outcomes. Language teaching involves the teaching of strategies and developing awareness of the nature and role of strategies in successful language learning. Learners can be made aware of their own learning processes and can be shown how to organise and structure their own learning (Oxford).

Learning is facilitated by exposure to authentic language and through using language for genuine communication

This principle permeates the entire spectrum of TESOL; e.g. it is seen in:

- approaches to grammar teaching which move from sentence-based instruction to the study of discourse and text (McCarthy);
- use of authentic spoken and written texts, including literature (Maley);
- sources for reading, writing and other language learning activities;
- use of corpora of authentic language as a basis for understanding lexical and grammatical usage (Carter); and
- focus on communicative methodologies, such as communicative language teaching (CLT) and task-based approaches (Willis and Willis).

Opportunities provided by technology (particularly computers in general, and use of the internet, email, etc.) are providing new scope for learners to use English for meaningful communication. They are also creating new types of interaction (Hanson-Smith, Warschauer).

A corollary to the above principle is the assumption that the style of communication within the language classroom must be as close as possible to the style of communication that occurs in natural settings outside the classroom. This has prompted close examination of the structure of classroom interaction and classroom discourse, leading to the development of teaching strategies such as the use of tasks and information-exchange activities that seek to create authentic use of language. This is believed to provide optimum conditions for learning (Nunan, Willis and Willis).

Language teaching is informed by an understanding of language processes

Crucial to the development of teaching approaches is an understanding of the underlying cognitive, psycholinguistic, social and linguistic processes involved in language use, i.e. in listening, speaking, reading and writing (Scovel). In describing language comprehension, these include both top-down processes (those driven by background knowledge, expectations, etc.) as well as bottom-up processing (those which make use of syntactic clues and systems in reading and understanding) (Rost). In describing language use they include on-line processes involved in the planning, articulation and editing of spoken language in real time. The processes involved in understanding and producing utterances in an L2 are active and creative, and are central to L2 learning (Bygate). There is therefore a need to better understand these processes as the basis for developing appropriate methodology.

TESOL is shaped by an informed understanding of the nature of language and of the English language in particular

Since the subject matter of TESOL is English, the study of English plays a central role in the development of the field and in the education of teachers. Such study needs to incorporate both the study of sentences (grammar) as well as texts (van Lier). It needs to include both the study of spoken and written texts. The role of corpora of authentic language use is important in understanding how language is used in authentic contexts, and such corpora can also be used as teaching resources and in the development of teaching materials (Carter, McCarthy, Larsen-Freeman).

The nature of grammatical competence is crucial, and appropriate theories of grammar are needed to inform both second language acquisition (SLA) research as well as classroom practice. Both formal and functional approaches to the study of grammar can inform TESOL grammatical theory, but TESOL depends more on the development of appropriate pedagogical grammars (those designed to support language teaching) rather than those which serve a primarily explanatory purpose (Hammond and Derewianka). The study of grammar should also include the study of vocabulary and lexical units and must move the level of analysis beyond the level of the sentence to focus on discourse and spoken language.

At the same time, language teaching goals are often seen to go beyond the teaching of language. A critical pedagogy informs TESOL professional practice. Learners and teachers need to develop a critical awareness of how language is used to create and maintain power (van Lier, Kramsch). In many cases the teaching of English is not a neutral activity. Teachers need to ask whose interests are served by their curriculum and classroom practices. In some cases the learning of English may be the key to economic mobility. In others it may be part of a process of social and economic marginalisation (Carter and Nunan).

Research and theory have an important role to play in TESOL

The field of TESOL is informed by theory, research and practice. TESOL is primarily a practical activity but practice on its own can only be understood and improved when it is systematically examined and explored. Hence, research is seen as a testing ground for the beliefs and assumptions on which practice is based and also as a source for new practices. There should not be a dichotomy between theory and practice. While there is both applicable as well as inapplicable theory and research, what defines the research basis of TESOL is the focus on the theoretical foundations of TESOL practices as well as the significance of theory for successful practice.

The status of the disciplines supporting TESOL is impartial. Their status changes, however, as new theories and research clarify understanding of the nature of language, of language learning and of language use. Such theory and research contributes to our knowledge of how language is used, the nature of L2 performance, the development of ability and skill in language use, the effects of different instructional strategies, etc. The insights gained from the observation and study of good teaching practice also serve to generate new theories and understanding of the nature of L2 teaching and learning.

Research in TESOL has a broad agenda, seeking to:

- understand and describe the processes of L2 teaching and learning;
- develop theories of learning to explain research findings;
- describe and document teaching and learning practices;
- identify psychological and social factors that affect language learning;
- understand the role of factors that impede or facilitate successful learning;
- describe differences between strategies and processes employed by learners at different proficiency levels (elementary, intermediate, advanced) and in relation to different modes of language use (reading, writing, speaking);
- clarify teaching and learning problems and suggest strategies to address them;
- identify significant instructional variables in teaching, and understanding the role of factors such as practice, tasks, interaction and feedback;
- validate more effective ways of teaching languages.

Research is moving away from a narrow focus on SLA (the development of L2 proficiency, particularly with reference to spoken-language competence) to encompass a broader range of issues across different skills areas, including lexis and phonology. A range of research strategies is needed to address these issues, including 'experimental research' as well as classroom research and teacher action research.

TESOL is an autonomous discipline

L2 learning and teaching needs to be understood in its own terms rather than approached via something else. While much can be learned by applying to TESOL insights gained from such fields as first language acquisition, educational theory, the psychology of learning and so on, increasingly TESOL seeks to establish its own theoretical foundations and research agenda rather than being seen as an opportunity to test out theories developed elsewhere and for different purposes. Thus, while approaches to the teaching of L2 writing in the 1970s and 1980s often reflected preoccupations and interests in first language writing (hence the focus on process writing in the 1970s and genre theory in the 1980s and 1990s), L2 writing specialists now seek to understand L2 writing processes and teaching practices in their own terms (Reid). Similarly, while early models of SLA compared L2 acquisition with native speaker norms, later there was a movement to try to understand L2 developing systems as autonomous systems (Nunan).

Successful language teaching assumes a high level of professional expertise and skill on the part of language teachers

Language teachers are viewed throughout this book as highly skilled professionals. Although language teachers may vary according to language proficiency and level of experience and training, effective language teaching depends upon teachers who have a high degree of professional expertise and knowledge (Freeman).

Teachers are expected to draw upon their knowledge of the subject matter as well as their knowledge of learners and of teaching in order to diagnose problems, to adapt and apply theories, and to prepare appropriate teaching and assessment materials (Brindley, Genesee). They need to be familiar with technology, particularly computer-based technology. The teacher is not simply a consumer of other people's materials but also needs to be able to plan and develop syllabuses, curriculums and materials, carry out needs analyses and course evaluations, as well as monitor learners' use of strategies, skills, etc. (Tomlinson, Breen). The language teacher is not simply a consumer of theory, but is a generator of theories and hypotheses based on his or her professional knowledge and ongoing reflection of classroon teaching.

The learning of teaching occurs in a variety of ways, including activities that involve both teacher training and teacher education. Teacher-training activities focus on the development of classroom skills and techniques, while teacher-education activities involve longer term development resulting from reflection and critical awareness. The teacher's role is not limited to teaching language. He or she is also often expected to empower learners, e.g. to furnish them with skills to enable them to confront injustices they may encounter in their lives.

Successful L2 learning is dependent upon effective instruction and the use of sound instructional systems

Good teaching involves many different dimensions, including:

- well-trained and well-educated teachers (Freeman);
- opportunities for classroom observation and other forms of teacher development and appraisal (Bailey, Tsui);
- instructional materials that are informed by theory and reflect sound pedagogical principles (Tomlinson);
- needs-based syllabuses and curriculums: these will typically be multi-skilled and communicative. The curriculum should prepare learners to be able to use the range of genres found in their learning contexts (Hammond and Derewianka). In ESP/EAP this involves a focus on the types of texts used in different discourse communities (Hamp-Lyons, Dudley-Evans);
- a communicative methodology: this will be interpreted by teachers according to learners' needs and programme factors. Communicative methodologies are recommended that are compatible with SLA theory (Nunan, Willis and Willis);
- appropriate use of technology, particularly computers (Hanson-Smith, Warschauer);
- appropriate measures of assessment and evaluation. These will be both formative and summative (Brindley, Genesee);
- not only sound pedagogical practices, but support from institutional systems that reflect good management principles (White).

Glossary

Note: This glossary is not a comprehensive glossary of the terms used in TESOL but refers to the terms most frequently used in the chapters in this book.

AAVE: see **African American Vernacular English**

accent: social and/or regional variety of a language which differs from others in pronunciation

achievement: the extent to which a student has learned the content or objectives of a particular curriculum or course of instruction

additive bilingualism: **bilingualism** which occurs when becoming bilingual helps learners to develop positive attitudes to their native languages and themselves

African American Vernacular English (AAVE): a language variety historically associated with and serving as a sociolinguistic marker for African Americans, variously termed **Black English**, **Black English Vernacular (BEV)** and **Ebonics** (from *ebony + phonics*). See also **Ebonics**

allophones: different realisations of one phoneme in speech (which make no difference to the meaning); observe, e.g., the shape of your lips when you pronounce the initial sound of the word '*tea*' as compared to '*toe*'

aphasia: language loss due to brain damage to a certain part of the brain (a term used by neurolinguists)

articulatory phonetics: the branch of phonetics which studies and describes the way in which sounds are formed with the speech organs

articulatory setting: the overall posture of the organs of speech typical of a particular language or dialect

assessment: the act of collecting information on individual learners' proficiency or achievement

assimilation: a process of simplification by which a speech sound is influenced by the surrounding sounds (usually the sound following it) to make them more alike, e.g. when /n/ the last sound in 'ten' becomes /m/ in the pronunciation of 'ten minutes'

asynchronous computer-mediated communication: communication via computer that is not simultaneous, but delayed, as with email

backchannelling: providing feedback from the listener to show that the speaker is being attended to and is encouraged to continue. In English this includes phrases such as *I see, uhhu, mm* and so on. Also called **listenership cues**

balanced bilingual: a person who is equally good at both languages he or she knows

bidialectalism: the phenomenon of competence and communication in two dialects of the same language

bilingualism: the phenomenon of competence and communication in two languages

biscripturalism: the phenomenon of competence in reading and writing two scripts of the same language

Black English and **Black English Vernacular**: see **African American Vernacular English**

bottom-up processing: processing using phonological and verbal cues from the input to attend to micro-features of text such as the form of individual words and grapheme/phoneme connections

CA: see **contrastive analysis**

CALL: the use of computer technology to assist processes of language learning

CALLA: see **Cognitive Academic Language Learning Approach**

care-taker speech: speech produced by care-takers when they talk to young children. To help young children to understand them, care-takers typically use simplified syntactic structures, exaggerated pronunciation and a slow rate of speech

categorical perception: the ability of native speakers to very rapidly and accurately listen to a wide range of sounds and hear them as a single phoneme in their mother tongue

child-directed speech (CDS): the special register of speech used by care-takers which assists infants and young children in their attempts to learn their mother tongue

classroom-based evaluation: the purposeful collection of information about teaching and learning in the classroom in order to plan and deliver instruction that is optimally suitable for meeting the goals and language learning needs of ESL/EFL students

CLT: see **communicative language teaching**

CMC: see **computer-mediated communication**

code-switching: the phenomenon of switching from one language to another in the same discourse

Cognitive Academic Language Learning Approach (CALLA): language learning which emphasises awareness of learning strategies and the need for student structuring of their own learning

collaborative evaluation: the assessment and evaluation of a curriculum or programme that is carried out jointly by classroom teachers, researchers or other trained educational experts

communicative competence: the ability to use language appropriate to the social context in order to accomplish one's goals

communicative language teaching (CLT): an approach to the teaching of language which emphasises the uses of language by the learner in a range of contexts and for a range of purposes; CLT emphasises speaking and listening in real settings and does not only prioritise the development of reading and writing skills; methodologies for CLT tend to encourage active learner involvement in a wide range of activities and tasks and strategies for communication

competency statements: written descriptions of what a student is able to do with the language, usually in terms of target language performance

complexity theory: a scientific theory (related to chaos theory) dedicated to the study of complex systems that are non-linear, self-organising and often include unpredictable processes and outcomes

comprehensible input: spoken language that can be understood by the listener even though some structures and vocabulary may not be known

computer-assisted conversation: written discussion that takes place via computer networks

computer assisted language learning: see **CALL**

computer-mediated communication (CMC): communication that takes place over computer networks

concordancer: computer software that searches for words or phrases in text files and displays targets in a list with surrounding context

concordancing: the study through the use of a computer-based corpus of the context in which a lexical item occurs

connected speech: spoken language when analysed as a continuous sequence as opposed to the analysis of individual sounds or words in isolation

consciousness-raising: often synonymous with **language awareness**, but emphasising the cognitive processes of noticing input or making explicit learners' intuitive knowledge about language, in the belief that an awareness of form will contribute to more efficient acquisition

consonant: a speech sound produced by creating an obstruction to the air-stream during articulation, e.g. /p/, /v/

contact zones: social spaces, including classrooms, where disparate cultures come together, often in contexts of asymmetrical power relations

contrastive analysis (CA): the analysis of differences between languages which can be used to explain a language learner's developmental errors and **interlanguage** competence

contrastive rhetoric: a field of study that investigates the linguistic, rhetorical, and situational differences in the ways written ideas are presented in English and in other languages/cultures

corpus data: samples of language use normally recorded from real situations. The samples are collated for easy access by researchers and materials developers who want to know how the language is used and are usually stored electronically

corpus linguistics: a new discipline in which large-scale computer-based language corpora (mainly extensive collections of spoken and written texts) are utilised by means of sophisticated **concordancing** programmes for purposes of language analysis

creolisation: a process through which speakers of a pidgin (a simplified code developed to allow communication among speakers of diverse languages in contact) evolve a fully elaborated code that can accommodate the full range of life's needs

criterion-referenced assessment: the interpretation of a learner's performance in relation to explicitly stated goals or standards

critical language awareness: an approach to **language awareness** that emphasises the ideological aspects of language use, and the ways in which language relates to social issues, such as power, inequality and discrimination

critical pedagogy: a way of teaching that strives not only to transmit linguistic knowledge and cultural information, but also to examine critically both the conditions under which the language is used, and the social, cultural and ideological purposes of its use

critical period: a time during early childhood (approximately the first decade of life) when language can be acquired natively. Language learned after this period invariably exhibits non-native features

critical reading: a reading practice which attends to the ideological underpinning of text, as signalled not so much by what a writer chooses as a topic but how people, places and events are talked about

critical theory: an approach to the study of society (including literature) which questions things which we have come to take for granted. In so doing it seeks to unmask the ways in which power is exercised by one group to the disadvantage of other groups

cross-cultural pragmatics: the study of similarities and differences in cultural norms for expressing and understanding messages

crossing: the phenomenon of switching to the non-hereditary language forms used by those with whom one has contact, e.g. the use of Punjabi by Anglo and Afro-Caribbean adolescents in the UK

cultural studies: an academic field that studies the conditions under which individuals are invested with or divested of social and historical identities (their 'culture') through the use of various symbolic systems, e.g. language

culture: membership in a social group that defines itself by its national, ethnic, professional, gender or other characteristics. The term encompasses both the 'high' culture of literature and the arts, and the small 'c' culture of attitudes, values, beliefs and everyday lifestyles

curriculum: the aims, content, methodology and evaluation procedures of a particular subject or subjects taught in a particular institution or school system

data triangulation: see **triangulation**

de-construction: a critical technique designed to reveal that there is no single meaning in a text but that each reader constructs variant interpretations

decreolisation: a gradual process by which creole speakers respond to pressure to 'standardise', incorporating forms from a socially dominant norm external to that speech community

descriptive grammar: a presentation of what grammarians observe; a presentation of the grammatical system that speakers employ. See also **prescriptive grammar**

dialogue journals: written (electronically or by hand) or orally-recorded discussions between students and teachers about school-related or other topics of interest to students. Journals can provide information about students' writing/speaking skills and about their communication strategies, interests, attitudes or background – all of which can be useful for understanding students' performance in class and planning instruction to meet their individual needs, goals and styles

diglossic/diglossia: the situation/phenomenon in which two languages or varieties of languages exist side by side and are used for different purposes, or for formal vs. informal uses

discourse: the organisation of language beyond the level of the sentence and the individual speaking turn, whereby meaning is negotiated in the process of interaction. The study of discourse is called **discourse analysis**

discourse community: a group of people involved in a particular disciplinary or professional area that communicate with each other and have therefore developed means of doing so

drill-and-grill software: computer applications that present material and then test, usually in simple multiple-choice formats allowing little interactivity

Ebonics: from *ebony* + *phonics* (meaning 'black sounds'), a term used to refer to the speech of African Americans. Ebonics has also been used as a superordinate term to refer generally to West African–European language mixtures with **USEB** (**United States Ebonics**) referring specifically to US language varieties. See also **African American Vernacular English**

editing: the practices, in L2 composition classes, that students engage in to correct discrete language errors in their writing, i.e. errors in grammar, vocabulary, sentence structure, spelling, etc. See also **revision**

electronic discussion: on-line forums, such as bulletin boards, mailing lists or real-time conversation; most provide a written record of all correspondents' contributions

electronic literacies: reading and writing practices in on-line environments

elision: processes in connected speech by which a **consonant** sound is left out in order to make articulation easier, e.g. when the /t/ in 'must' is left out in the pronunciation of 'must be'

essentialisation: a process by which individuals are reduced to one of their many identities (e.g. a Chinese, a woman, a student) and stereotyped accordingly

ethnography of speaking/communication: the study of the range of knowledge necessary to use language appropriately and effectively

evaluation: a purposeful, cyclical process of collecting, analysing and interpreting relevant information in order to make educational decisions. Evaluation may focus on the quality, appropriateness, worth or relevance of teachers, students, classroom instruction, instructional materials and activities, or whole courses or programmes of instruction

explicit learning: learning that occurs as a result of specifically targeting the subject matter to be learned

explicit teaching: an approach in which information about a language is given to the learners directly by the teacher or the textbook

explicit vocabulary learning: the learning of vocabulary by means of overt and intentional strategies, such as techniques of memorisation

expressive approach: a teaching approach in which L2 composition students focus on personal writing and development. See also **product writing, process writing, sociocognitive approach**

focus on form: within a communicative approach, referring to learners and teachers addressing formal features of language that play a role in the meanings that are being negotiated. This is contrasted with a **focus on forms**, which emphasises formal aspects rather than meaningful activities

formal grammars: these investigate grammatical structures as 'primitives' or universal features to be explained in terms of their contribution to the systematic nature of language. See also **functional grammars**

formal syllabus: aims and content of teaching that focus upon systems and rules of phonology, morphology, vocabulary, grammar and upon discourse and genres as text. Also referred to as structural, grammatical, lexical, genre-based syllabuses

formative evaluation: the collection and interpretation of information about TESOL students or programmes in order to fine-tune instruction to meet students' needs better and to modify programmes to work more effectively. Formative evaluation occurs on a periodic basis during the course of instruction and is intended to enhance educational success and effectiveness

functional grammars: these focus upon language use in order to explain how grammatical structures are employed to produce meaningful and appropriate communication. See also **formal grammars**

functional load: the use made of a linguistic contrast in the sound system: the more minimal pairs a contrast between two phonemes distinguishes, the greater its functional load

functional syllabus: aims and contents of teaching that focus upon the purposes of language use, from specific speech acts within conversation to larger texts such as particular genres serving specific social functions

grammar: the subconscious internal system of the language user; linguists' explicit codification of this system to reflect the structural organisation of language, normally up to the level of the sentence. See also **descriptive grammar, formal grammars, functional grammars, prescriptive grammar**

grammar clusters: the co-occurrence of certain grammatical forms within a specific genre (type) of writing; e.g. chronological transitions, the use of personal pronouns and specific uses of present, past and past progressive verb forms often re-occur in narrative writing

implicit meaning: an approach in which the learners gain awareness of a language through experience of the language in use

implicit vocabulary learning: the learning of vocabulary primarily by incidental means, such as unconscious exposure to and experience of using words

innateness: evidence that strongly suggests that a substantial part of language learning in humans is genetically programmed or 'hard-wired'

intake: vocabulary, grammar and expressions that are understood and subsequently acquired by the learner

intercultural communication: an interdisciplinary field of research that studies how people understand each other across group boundaries of various sorts: national, geographical, linguistic, ethnic, occupation, class or gender

interdiscourse communication: communications that take place across boundaries of groups or discourse systems, such as a corporate culture, a professional group, a gender discourse system, a generational discourse system

interlanguage: the systematic language a learner constructs, conceived of as a continuum between a learner's L1 and L2

intonation: the use of **pitch** to convey different kinds of meaning in discourse

intonation groups: see **meaning units**

IRF (initiation, response, follow-up): a common pattern of classroom discourse based on a teacher's initiation move, a student's response and a teacher's follow-up. Also called **IRE (initiation, response, evaluation)**

language awareness: an understanding of the human faculty of language and its role in thinking, learning and social life. See also **consciousness-raising**

language proficiency: ability to use the target language for communicative purposes

learning strategies: techniques used by learners to help make their learning be more effective and to increase their independence and autonomy as learners. Strategies can be employed by learners to assist with the storage of information, to help with the construction of language rules and to help with an appropriate attitude towards the learning situation

lexical approach: an approach to language teaching and learning which stresses the importance of learning 'lexical chunks', i.e. whole, communicatively significant phrases

lexical corpus: a collection of words for purposes of language analysis. Most modern lexical corpora run to millions of words and are normally computationally retrievable

lexical phrases: recurrent phrases and patterns of language which have become institutionalised through frequent use. Phrases such as 'Can I help you?' or 'Have you heard the one about . . .?' are lexical phrases

lexical syllabus: a syllabus which makes the learning of frequent vocabulary central to the content of a language course

lexico-grammar: the relationship between vocabulary and grammar. These forms of language organisation are normally studied separately but, increasingly, lexico-grammatical patterns are being seen as central to language description and learning

lexicography: the art and science of dictionary making. Foreign language lexicography involves the creation of bilingual dictionaries for language learners

lingua franca: a language for routine communication between (groups of) people who have different L1s

linguistic environment: the spoken language surrounding the learner (in both educational and social settings) that serves as potential listening input

linguistic relativity: the popular belief that differences in the structures of languages also reflect or create differences in the way people perceive or think about the world around them. Also called **Sapir–Whorf hypothesis**

listenership cues: see **backchannelling**

listening strategy: a conscious plan to deal with incoming speech, particularly when the listener experiences problems due to incomplete understanding, such as a clarification strategy

literacy practices: culture-specific ways of utilising literacy in everyday life, related to our social roles and identities

look-and-say methods: reading methods which ask learner readers to learn a large sight vocabulary, often through words presented on flash cards. See also **phonics**

macro-sociolinguistics: sociolinguistic research with a sociological or social psychological slant, focusing on what entire societies do with language, including such topics as language maintenance and language loss. See also **micro-sociolinguistics**

materials evaluation: the process of measuring the value of learning materials. This can be predictive (**pre-use evaluation**), ongoing (**whilst-use evaluation**) or retrospective (**post-use evaluation**)

meaning units: chunks of spoken discourse which serve listeners as signals of organisation and are characterised by pitch change on the most important syllable. Also called **intonation groups**, **sense groups** or **tone units**

metalinguistic knowledge: explicit, formal knowledge about language that can be verbalised, usually including metalinguistic terminology, such as 'present tense', 'indefinite article', etc.

methods triangulation: see **triangulation**

micro-sociolinguistics: sociolinguistic research with a linguistic slant often focusing on dialect and stylistic/register variation, including how language use correlates with social attributes such as class, sex and age. See also **macro-sociolinguistics**

minimal pairs: pairs of words distinguished by one phoneme only, e.g. *pin* – *b*in; frequently used for practising sound contrasts in a foreign language

miscue analysis: the manner of evaluating how a reader draws on syntactic, graphophonemic and semantic knowledge in his or her sampling of text with a view to establishing reader strengths and weaknesses

modification: an attempt by a speaker to simplify or elaborate a normal discourse pattern in order to make a message more accessible to a listener

MOO (multi-user object-oriented) environment: software that allows multiple users to interact in real time on the internet. Users may exchange virtual 'objects', hyperlink to maps or games, create password-secured private spaces, etc.

morphology: the study of the smallest units of grammar that have meaning, i.e. morphemes

needs analysis: analysis to determine what students need to be able to do in English in their educational or professional situation

norm-referenced assessment: the interpretation of a learner's performance in relation to the performance of other learners. See also **criterion-referenced assessment**

observation: in language classrooms, the purposeful examination of teaching and/or learning events through systematic processes of data collection and analysis

observation schedules: analytic instruments (documents) used to record observable behaviours in classrooms, either as events occur ('real-time coding') or with electronically recorded data

participant observation: observation conducted by a member of the group under investigation, e.g. the teacher or a student in the classroom

performance standards: statements that specify how students will demonstrate their knowledge and skills in language as well as the level at which they must perform in order to be considered to have met the standard

phoneme: a speech sound which is distinctive within the sound system of a particular language and so makes contrasts in meaning. See also **minimal pairs**

phonemic script: a set of symbols for the transcription of spoken language, usually based on the conventions of the International Phonetic Alphabet (IPA)

phonetics: the study of human speech sounds, describing the wide range of sounds humans can produce

phonics: reading methods which emphasise sound–symbol relationships in written language by, e.g., asking learner readers to match up letters in words to a sound equivalent. See also **look-and-say methods**, **whole-word methods**

phonology: the study of the distinctive speech sounds (**phonemes**) and the patterns they form in particular languages

pidginisation: a process by which speakers of two or more unintelligible languages create a simplified code through which trading and other basic needs can be met

pitch: voice height, which depends on the frequency of vibrations of the vocal cords. Every person has an individual pitch range. Relative pitch and pitch movement (**tone**) are central to changes in use of in **intonation**. See also **suprasegmentals**

post-use evaluation: see **materials evaluation**

pragmalinguistic failure: a communicative failure that occurs when the pragmatic force of a message is misunderstood, e.g. if an intended apology were to be interpreted solely as an excuse. See also **sociopragmatic failure**

pragmatics: the study of how people typically convey meanings in context

preferred strategies: the most efficient strategies for speech processing of a particular language, utilising the phonological and metrical rules of the language

prescriptive grammar: normative rules of correctness indicating how the writer of these rules considers the language should be used. See also **descriptive grammar**

pre-use evaluation: see **materials evaluation**

procedural syllabus: a syllabus consisting of a series of tasks sequenced in order of difficulty with learners acquiring language by negotiating these tasks under teacher guidance and with no focus on language form. The syllabus was developed in Bangalore, South India by a team led by N.S. Prabhu

process syllabus: a framework for classroom decision-making based upon negotiation among teacher and students applied to any chosen aspect of the curriculum

process writing: a teaching approach in which L2 composition students focus on fluency and self-development by focusing on expressive, rather than persuasive, steps ('processes') in their writing. See also **expressive approach**, **product writing**, **sociocognitive approach**

product writing: a teaching approach in which L2 composition students focus on accuracy and rhetorical principles, rather than personal steps ('processes') in their writing. See also **expressive approach**, **process writing**, **sociocognitive approach**

programme management: an approach which involves identifying teaching and learning goals, establishing standards of performance, identifying and deploying resources (both financial and human), monitoring performance and taking corrective action as and if necessary

prominence: the placement of stress in discourse by the speaker. Also called **sentence stress**

prosody: see **suprasegmentals**

reader-based writing: writing in which L2 composition students write for an external audience rather than for themselves. Contrasted with **writer-based writing**

reading skills: sets of abilities which are specifically and sequentially taught, on the basis that there are particular kinds of knowledge which learners need to acquire in advance of access to continuous text

reading strategies: ways of accessing text meaning which are employed flexibly and selectively in the course of reading. In teaching, attention is paid to the manner in which the reader is able to draw effectively on existing linguistic and background knowledge

real-time coding: assigning events to analytic categories as the events happen (in contrast to analysing audio- or video-recorded data)

reliability: the extent to which a test or assessment procedure measures consistently

researcher triangulation: see **triangulation**

restructuring: the internal reorganisation of the learner's grammar to facilitate rapid deployment of language in real time

revision: the practices in L2 composition classes in which students 'look again' at their writing holistically in order to improve areas such as organisation, adequate use of evidence, focus, etc. See also **editing**

rhetoric: the study of how texts are effective in persuading readers or listeners to accept the arguments presented

rhythm: the sequence of strong and weak elements in language, such as the patterns made up by stressed and unstressed syllables. See also **suprasegmentals**

Sapir–Whorf hypothesis: see **linguistic relativity**

scaffolding: the support given to language learners to enable them to perform tasks and construct communications which are at the time beyond their capability

segmental sounds: individual sounds (**consonants** and **vowels**). Compare **suprasegmentals**

selective listening: attending to specific information that had been signalled prior to listening

self-monitoring: one of the final stages of speech (or writing) which demonstrates the important role feedback plays in language production

semi-lingualism: a person's inability to develop to his or her full linguistic potential as a result of imperfect learning in both languages he or she is exposed to

sense groups: see **meaning units**

sentence stress: see **prominence**

sequencing (grading): how areas of knowledge and particular skills and abilities are organised within a syllabus or within teaching materials so that they represent a path of progression and development

silent language: the non-verbal and paraverbal dimensions of language, i.e. the gestures and body movements whose display and timing may reveal information about an individual's culture

simulations: software using large databases to present information in a simulated environment where learner input changes outcomes, e.g. controlling variables in an ecosystem

simultaneous bilingualism: the acquisition of two languages at the same time both as L1s, i.e. by the time a child is, say, three years old

slips of the tongue: performance mistakes all speakers make (especially when speaking or writing under pressure) which help psycholinguists identify different levels of language production

social identity: the way we categorise ourselves and others in relation to an identifiable social group. This categorisation can be at any level, e.g. the level of nation-state, gender, ethnicity, class, profession, etc.

sociocognitive approach: a teaching approach in which students focus on the needs and expectations of the audience and the situation for their writing. See also **expressive approach**, **product writing**, **process writing**

sociolinguistic marker: a linguistic feature that marks the speaker as a member of a social group and to which social attitudes are attached, e.g. absence of postvocalic /r/ in the speech of some New Yorkers (this absence is stigmatised) and some British speakers, for example those speaking Received Pronunciation (for whom the absence is not stigmatised)

sociopragmatic failure: a communicative failure that occurs when one does not know what to say to whom, e.g. which questions are appropriately asked of guests.

speech act: a type of verbal action, such as promising, apologising, inviting

speech community: speakers who share communicative norms and who are affiliated by features such as geography, profession, ethnicity

speech processing: the perception of sounds, the recognition of words and the parsing of grammatical structures in speech

speech recognition: computer software that allows the computer to receive audio input rather than input via the keyboard or mouse

stakeholders: all the people who have an interest in an organisation (e.g. a school) and who may influence its activities or be affected by its activities. Stakeholders can be internal (e.g. employer, students) or external (e.g. parents, employers, pressure groups)

stress: referring to a syllable which is pronounced with greater energy, greater length and (possibly) higher pitch to make it prominent. Contrasted with **unstress**. See also **suprasegmentals**

stylistics: the study of texts which is preceded by a careful analysis of how the language devices used (e.g. repetition, parallelism, etc.) achieve their effects on the reader

submersion model: a model of education in which a non-dominant language in a community is not used as a medium of instruction which results in children who speak the non-dominant language as their L1 following an educational programme in the dominant language of the community

subtractive bilingualism: **bilingualism** which occurs when learners develop negative attitudes towards their own languages in the process of becoming bilingual

successive bilingualism: the acquisition of an L2 after competence in the L1 has been established to some extent, i.e. by the time a child is, say, three years old

summative evaluation: evaluation of student performance or the effectiveness of a TESOL programme in order to decide on the status of the student or programme. In the case of students, summative evaluation is linked through decisions about pass–failure or admissions–rejection to a particular course or programme of study. In the case of programmes, summative evaluation is undertaken to make decisions to continue or discontinue particular programmes. Summative evaluation usually occurs at the end of an extended period of instruction or learning

suprasegmentals: features of speech stretching over more than one sound or segment, usually including whole utterances and taking into account **pitch**, **rhythm**, **stress**, **tempo**, **voice quality**. Also called **prosody**

syllabus: the selected and organised content (areas of knowledge and particular skills and abilities) appropriate to the particular aims of a course

synchronous computer-mediated communication: communication via computer networks which takes place in real time, such as on-line chat

syntax: the structural organisation of language at the sentence level, e.g. word order

target language: the language or variety of language to which teaching and learning is principally directed

target situation: the situation in which the ESP student has to use English, e.g. in a study or work situation

task: an activity in the classroom which involves language use to achieve a communicative purpose

task-based syllabus: aims and contents of teaching focusing upon the creation and interpretation of meaning and organised on the basis of appropriate sequences and permutations of communicative tasks and metacommunicative (form-focused or learning-focused) tasks

tempo: the speed at which speech takes place. See also **suprasegmentals**

test: a method of eliciting a sample of an individual's language behaviour under standardised conditions

theory triangulation: see **triangulation**

tone: the pitch level or pitch movement of a syllable. See also **pitch**

tone units: see **meaning units**

top-down processing: using background knowledge and expectations about what is being said or written to understand a message

transitional bilingualism: a bilingual education model in which a non-dominant language in a community is used as a medium of instruction for a period but is not ultimately highly valued as a target language

triangulation: ethnographic processes of verification which give us confidence in our observations. There are four different kinds of triangulation: **data triangulation**, in which different sources of data (teachers, students, parents, etc.) contribute to an investigation; **theory triangulation**, when various theories are brought to bear in a study; **researcher triangulation**, in which more than one researcher contributes to the investigation; and **methods triangulation**, which entails the use of multiple methods (e.g. interviews, questionnaires, observation schedules, test scores, field notes, etc.) to collect data

unstress: see **stress**

USEB: see **Ebonics**

validity: the extent to which a test or assessment procedure measures what it claims to measure

voice quality: permanent features which characterise a person's voice (e.g. high or low), as well as temporary vocal effects produced by a speaker to communicate a particular emotional state (e.g. joy or anger). See also **suprasegmentals**

voicing: the vibration of the vocal cords to produce a voiced (contrasted with voiceless) **vowel** or **consonant**. All vowels are voiced; consonants may be either voiced or unvoiced

vowel: speech sound where the air-stream escapes evenly over the tongue, e.g. /e/ in the word 'well' or 'bed'

whilst-use evaluation: see **materials evaluation**

whole-word methods: an approach to literacy that stresses meaning and the experience of creating and understanding text. Proponents of **phonics** often argue that whole language neglects accuracy and encourages sloppy language use. See also **phonics**

writer-based writing: see **reader-based writing**

writing modes: a teaching approach in which L2 composition students write paragraphs and essays whose primary purpose is to focus on such organisational models ('modes') as definition, comparison-contrast, classification and cause–effect

References

Abbs, B. and M. Sexton (1978) *Challenges*. London: Longman.

Abraham, R.G. and R. Vann (1987) Strategies of two language learners: A case study. In A.L. Wenden and J. Rubin (eds) *Learner Strategies in Language Learning*. New York: Prentice Hall, pp. 85–102.

ACTFL (1986) *ACTFL Proficiency Guidelines*. Hastings-on-Hudson, NY: American Council on the Teaching of Foreign Languages.

ACTFL (1996) Standards for foreign language learning: preparing for the twenty-first century. Yonkers, NY: American Council on the Teaching of Foreign Languages.

Adams, M.J. (1990) *Beginning to Read*. Cambridge: MIT Press.

Ady, J. (1995) Survey across the world. In M. Warschauer (ed.) *Virtual Connections: Online Activities and Projects for Networking Language Learners*. Honolulu, HI: University of Hawai'i, Second Language Teaching and Curriculum Center, pp. 101–103.

Aitchison, J. (1994) *Words in the Mind*. 2nd edn. Oxford: Blackwell.

Aitchison, J. (1996) *The Seeds of Speech: Language Origin and Evolution*. Cambridge: Cambridge University Press.

Alatis, J.E. and J.J. Staczek (eds) (1985) *Perspectives on Bilingualism and Bilingual Education*. Washington, DC: Georgetown University Press.

Alderson, J.C. (1984) Reading: A language problem or a reading problem? In J.C. Alderson and A.H. Urquhart (eds) *Reading in a Foreign Language*. London: Longman.

Alderson, J.C. (ed.) (1985) *Lancaster Practical Papers in English Language Education, Vol. 6: Evaluation*. Oxford: Pergamon.

Alderson, J.C. and A.H. Urquhart (eds) (1984) *Reading in a Foreign Language*. London: Longman.

Alderson, J.C. and D. Wall (1993) Does washback exist? *Applied Linguistics* 14(2), 115–129.

Alderson, J.C., C. Clapham and D. Steel (1997) Metalinguistic knowledge, language aptitude and language proficiency. *Language Teaching Research* 1(2), 93–121.

Alexander, L.G. (1967) *New Concept English: First Things First*. London: Longman.

Allen, J.P.B. and H.G. Widdowson (1974) Teaching the communicative use of English. *International Review of Applied Linguistics* 12, 1–20.

Allen, J.P.B., M. Fröhlich and N. Spada (1984) The communicative orientation of language teaching: An observation scheme. In J. Handscombe, R.A. Orem and B. Taylor (eds) *On TESOL 1983: The Question of Control*. Washington, DC: TESOL, pp. 231–252.

Allison, D. (1996) Pragmatist discourse and English for academic purposes. *English for Specific Purposes* 15(1), 85–103.

Allison, D. (1998) Response to Pennycook: Whether, why and how. *English for Specific Purposes* 17(3), 313–316.

Allwright, D. (1980) Turns, topics and tasks: Patterns of participation in language learning and teaching. In D. Larsen-Freeman (ed.) *Discourse Analysis in Second Language Research*. Rowley, MA: Newbury House, pp. 165–187.

Allwright, D. (1981) What do we need teaching materials for? *ELT Journal* 36(1), 5–18.

Allwright, D. (1984) Why don't learners learn what teachers teach? The interaction hypothesis. In D. Singleton and D. Little (eds) *Language Learning in Formal and Informal Contexts*. Dublin: IRAL.

Allwright, D. (1988) *Observation in the Language Classroom*. London: Longman.

Allwright, D. (1990) *Autonomy in Language Pedagogy*. CRILE Working Paper 6. Centre for Research in Education, University of Lancaster, UK.

Allwright, D. and K. Bailey (1991) *Focus on the Language Classroom: An Introduction to Classroom Research for Language Teachers*. New York: Cambridge University Press.

Altmann, G. (1997) *The Ascent of Babel: An Exploration of Language, Mind, and Understanding*. Oxford: Oxford University Press.

American Management Association International (AMAI) (1998) E-mail tops telephone, say HR execs at 69th annual human resources conference. New York: AMAI.

Anderson, A. and T. Lynch (1988) *Listening* (*Language Teaching: A Scheme for Teacher Education*). Oxford: Oxford University Press.

Anderson, J. (1982) Acquisition of cognitive skill. *Psychological Review* 89, 369–406.

Anderson, R. (ed.) (1983) *Pidginization and Creolization as Language Acquisition*. Rowley, MA: Newbury House.

Anderson-Hsieh, J. (1992) Using electronic visual feedback to teach suprasegmentals. *System* 20(1), 51–62.

Andrews, L. (1993) *Language Exploration and Awareness*. White Plains, NY: Longman.

Appel, R. and P. Muysken (1987) *Language Contact and Bilingualism*. London: Edward Arnold.

Arnberg, L. (1987) *Raising Children Bilingually: The Pre-school Years*. Clevedon: Multilingual Matters.

Arnold, J. (ed.) (1999) *Affect in Language Learning*. Cambridge: Cambridge University Press.

Atkinson, J. and J. Heritage (eds) (1984) *Structures of Social Action*. Cambridge: Cambridge University Press.

Atrill, P. and E. McLaney (1997) *Accounting and Finance for Non-Specialists*. 2nd edn. London: Prentice Hall.

Auerbach, E. (1986) Competency-based ESL: One step forward or two steps back? *TESOL Quarterly* 20(3), 411–429.

Auerbach, E. (1993) Examining English only in the ESL classroom. *TESOL Quarterly* 27, 9–32.

Auerbach, E. (1994) What's critical in teaching writing to adults? *Prospect* 9(3), 54–58.

Averill, J., C. Chambers and M. Dantas-Whitney (2000) OSU-ELI: An investment in people, not just flashy gadgets. In E. Hanson-Smith (ed.) *Technology-Enhanced Learning Environments*. Alexandria, VA: TESOL.

Avery, P. and S. Ehrlich (1992) *Teaching American English Pronunciation*. Oxford: Oxford University Press.

Bachman, L.F. (1990) *Fundamental Considerations in Language Testing*. Oxford: Oxford University Press.

Bachman, L.F. and A.D. Cohen (eds) (1998) *Interfaces between Second Language Acquisition and Language Testing Research*. Cambridge: Cambridge University Press.

Bachman, L.F. and D.R. Eignor (1997) Recent advances in quantitative test analysis. In C. Clapham and D. Corson *Encyclopedia of Language and Education, Vol. 7: Language Testing and Assessment*. Dordrecht: Kluwer Academic, pp. 227–242.

Bachman, L.F. and A.S. Palmer (1989) The construct validation of self-ratings of communicative language ability. *Language Testing* 6(2), 14–25.

Bachman, L.F. and A.S. Palmer (1996) *Language Testing in Practice*. Oxford: Oxford University Press.

Bachman, L.F., F. Davidson, K. Ryan and I.-C. Choi (1995) *An Investigation into the Comparability of Two Tests of English as a Foreign Language*. Cambridge: Cambridge University Press.

Bacon, S.M. and M.D. Finnemann (1990) A study of the attitudes, motives and strategies of university foreign language students and their disposition to authentic oral and written input. *Modern Language Journal* 74(4), 459–473.

Baetens Beardsmore, H. (1982) *Bilingualism: Basic Principles*. Clevedon: Tieto.

Baetens Beardsmore, H. (1993) *European Models of Bilingual Education*. Clevedon: Multilingual Matters.

Bailey, K. (1990) The use of diary studies in teacher education programs. In J.C. Richards and D. Nunan (eds) *Second Language Teacher Education*. Cambridge: Cambridge University Press, pp. 215–226.

Bailey, K. (1998) *Learning about Language Assessment*. Pacific Grove, CA: Heinle and Heinle.

Bailey, K. and D. Nunan (eds) (1996) *Voices from the Language Classroom*. Cambridge: Cambridge University Press.

Bailey, K. and L. Savage (eds) (1994) *New Ways in Teaching Speaking*. Alexandria, VA: TESOL.

Bailey, N., C. Madden and S. Krashen (1974) Is there a 'natural sequence' in adult second language learning? *Language Learning* 21, 235–243.

Bailey, K. *et al.* (1996) The language learners' autobiography: Examining the apprenticeship of observation. In D. Freeman and J.C. Richards (eds) *Teacher Learning in Language Teaching*. New York: Cambridge University Press, pp. 11–29.

Bain, R., B. Fitzgerald and M. Taylor (eds) (1992) *Looking into Language: Classroom Approaches to Knowledge About Language*. London: Hodder and Stoughton.

Baker, C. (1988) *Key Issues in Bilingualism and Bilingual Education*. Clevedon: Multilingual Matters.

Bakhtin, M. (1986) *Speech Genres and Other Late Essays*. Edited by C. Emerson and M. Holquist (eds) Austin, TX: University of Texas Press.

Balan, R., M. Carianopol, S. Colibaba, C. Coser, V. Focseneanu, V. Stan and R. Vulcanescu (1998) *English News and Views 11*. Bucharest: Oxford University Press.

Bandura, A. (1997) *Self-Efficacy: The Exercise of Control*. New York: Freeman.

Bardovi-Harlig, K. and B. Hartford (1993) Learning the rules of academic talk: A longitudinal study of pragmatic change. *Studies in Second Language Acquisition* 15, 279–304.

Barnes, C. (1993) *Practical Marketing for Schools*. Oxford: Blackwell.

Barnes, D. (1969) Language in the secondary classroom. In D. Barnes, J. Britton and H. Rosen (eds) *Language, the Learner and the School*. London: Penguin, pp. 11–77.

Barnlund, D.C. (1975) *Private and Public Self in Japan and the United States*. Tokyo: Simul Press.

Barrs, M. (1992) The Primary Language Record: What we are learning in the UK. In C. Bouffler (ed.) *Literacy Evaluation: Issues and Practicalities*. Sydney: Primary English Teaching Association, pp. 53–62.

Barson, J. and R. Debski (1996) Calling back CALL: Technology in the service of foreign language learning based on creativity, contingency and goal-oriented activity. In M. Warschauer (ed.) *Telecollaboration in Foreign Language Learning*. Honolulu, HI: University of Hawai'i, Second Language Teaching and Curriculum Center, pp. 49–68.

Barson, J., J. Frommer and M. Schwartz (1993) Foreign language learning using e-mail in a task-oriented perspective: Interuniversity experiments in communication and collaboration. *Science Education and Technology* 4(2), 565–584.

Barth, F. (ed.) (1969) *Ethnic Groups and Boundaries: The Social Organization of Cultural Differences*. Bergen-Oslo: Universitetsforlaget.

Barton, D. and R. Ivanič (eds) (1991) *Writing in the Community*. London: Sage.

Bassnet, S. and P. Grundy (1993) *Language Through Literature: Creative Language Teaching Through Literature*. London: Longman.

Bates, L., J. Lane and E. Lange (1993) *Writing Clearly: Responding to ESL Compositions*. Boston, MA: Heinle and Heinle.

Bates, M. and T. Dudley-Evans (eds) (1976–85) *Nucleus*. Series of books. London: Longman.

Batstone, R. (1995) Grammar in discourse: attitude and deniability. In G. Cook and B. Seidlhofer (eds) *Principle and Practice in Applied Linguistics: Studies in Honour of H.G. Widdowson*. Oxford: Oxford University Press, pp. 197–213.

Baynham, M. (1995) *Literacy Practices: Investigating Literacy in Social Contexts*. London: Longman.

Beaugrande, R. de and W. Dressler (1981) *Introduction to Text Linguistics*. London: Longman.

Beauvois, M.H. (1998) E-talk: computer-assisted classroom discussion: Attitudes and motivation. In J. Swaffar, S. Romano, P. Markley and K. Arens (eds) *Language Learning Online: Theory and Practice in the ESL and L2 Computer Classroom*. Austin, TX: Labyrinth Publications/Daedalus Group, pp. 99–120.

Bedell, D. and R.L. Oxford (1996) Cross-cultural comparisons of language learning strategies in the People's Republic of China and other countries. In R. Oxford (ed.) *Language Learning Strategies Around the World: Cross-Cultural Perspectives*. Manoa, HI: University of Hawai'i Press, pp. 47–60.

Belcher, D. (1994) The apprenticeship approach to advanced academic literacy: Graduate students and their mentors. *English for Specific Purposes* 13(1), 23–34.

Belcher, D. and G. Braine (eds) (1995) *Academic Writing in a Second Language: Essays on Research and Pedagogy*. Norwood, NJ: Ablex.

Bell, J. and R. Gower (1998) Writing course materials for the world: A great compromise. In B. Tomlinson (ed.) *Materials Development for Language Teaching*. Cambridge: Cambridge University Press, pp. 116–129.

Bell, L. (1992) *Managing Teams in Secondary Schools*. London: Routledge.

Bellack, A., H. Kliebard, R.T. Hyman and F.L. Smith (1966) *The Language of the Classroom*. New York: Teachers College Press.

Benesch, S. (1996) Needs Analysis and Curriculum Development in EAP: An Example of a Critical Approach. *TESOL Quarterly* 30(4), 723–738.

Benesch, S. (1999) Rights analysis: studying power relations in an academic setting. *English for Specific Purposes*, 18, 313–327.

Benson, P. and P. Voller (eds) (1997) *Autonomy and Independence in Language Learning*. London: Longman.

Beretta, A. and A. Davies (1985) Evaluation of the Bangalore Project. *ELT Journal* 39(2), 121–127.

Bergvall, V.L., J.M. Bing and A.F. Freed (1996) *Rethinking Language and Gender Research: Theory and Practice*. London: Longman.

Berkenkotter, C. and T. Huckin (1995) *Genre Knowledge in Interdisciplinary Communication*. Hillsdale, NJ: Lawrence Erlbaum.

Berlin, J.A. (1988) Rhetoric and ideology in the writing class. *College English* 50, 477–494.

Berliner, D. (1986) In pursuit of expert pedagogue. *Educational Researcher* 15(7), 5–13.

Bernhardt, E. and J. Hammadou (1987) A decade of research in foreign language teacher education. *Modern Language Journal* 71, 291–299.

Bernstein, B. (1971) *Class, Codes and Control*. London: Routledge and Kegan Paul.

Bhatia, T.K. and W.C. Ritchie (1996) Bilingual language mixing, universal grammar, and second language acquisition. In W.C. Ritchie and T.K. Bhatia (eds) *Handbook of Second Language Acquisition*. San Diego, CA: Academic Press, pp. 627–688.

Bhatia, V.K. (1993) *Analyzing Genre: Language Use in Professional Settings*. London: Longman.

Bhatia, V.K. (1997) Applied Genre Analysis and ESP. In T. Miller (ed.) *Functional Approaches to Written Text: Classroom Applications*. Washington, DC, English Language Programs, United States Information Agency.

Bialystok, E. (1981) The role of conscious strategies in second language proficiency. *Modern Language Journal* 65, 24–35.

Bialystok, E. (1990) *Communication Strategies*. Oxford: Blackwell.

Bialystok, E. (ed.) (1991) *Language Processing in Bilingual Children*. Cambridge: Cambridge University Press.

Biber, D. (1988) *Variation Across Speech and Writing*. Cambridge: Cambridge University Press.

Biber, D., S. Conrad and R. Reppen (1998) *Corpus Linguistics: Investigating Language Structure and Use*. Cambridge: Cambridge University Press.

Biber, D. *et al.* (1999) *Longman Grammar of Spoken and Written English*. London: Longman.

Billows, F.L. (1961) *The Techniques of Language Teaching*. London: Longman.

Birch, D. (1989) *Language, Literature and Critical Practice: Ways of Analyzing Text*. London: Routledge.

Birdsong, D. (1999) *Second Language Acquisition and the Critical Period Hypothesis*. Mahwah, NJ: Lawrence Erlbaum.

Bitzer, D. (1960) PLATO [Computer software]. Urbana, IL: University of Illinois, Urbana-Champaign.

Blanche, P. and B. Merino (1989) Self-assessment of foreign-language skills: Implications for teachers and researchers. *Language Learning* 39(3), 313–340.

Bley-Vroman, R., S. Felix and G. Ioup (1988) The accessibility of Universal Grammar in adult language learning. *Second Language Research* 4, 1–32.

Block, D. (1996) A window on the classroom: Classroom events viewed from different angles. In K. Bailey and D. Nunan (eds) *Voices from the Language Classroom: Qualitative Research in Second Language Education*. Cambridge: Cambridge University Press, pp. 168–194.

Block, E. (1986) The comprehension strategies of second language readers. *TESOL Quarterly* 20(3), 463–492.

Blommaert, J. and J. Verschueren (eds) (1991) *The Pragmatics of Intercultural and International Communication*. Amsterdam: John Benjamins.

Bloomfield, L. (1942) *Outline Guide for the Practical Study of Foreign Languages*. Baltimore, MD: Linguistic Society of America.

Blue, G. (1988) Individualising academic writing tuition. In P. Robinson (ed.) *Academic Writing: Process and Product*. ELT Documents 129. London: Modern English Publications / Macmillan / The British Council.

Blue, G. (1994) Self-assessment of foreign language skills: Does it work? *CLE Working Papers* 3, 18–35.

Blum-Kulka, S., J. House and G. Kasper (ed.) (1989) *Cross-Cultural Pragmatics: Requests and Apologies*. Norwood, NJ: Ablex.

Blyth, C.S. (1999) *Untangling the Web: Nonce's Guide to Language and Culture on the Internet*. New York: Nonce.

Boden, D. and D.H. Zimmerman (eds) (1991) *Talk and Social Structure: Studies in Ethnomethodology and Conversation Analysis*. Cambridge: Polity Press.

Bogaards, P. (1996) Dictionaries for learners of English. *International Journal of Lexicography* 9(4), 277–320.

Bolitho, R. and B. Tomlinson (1995) *Discover English*. 2nd edn. Oxford: Heinemann.

Borg, S. (1998) Teachers' pedagogical systems and grammar teaching: A qualitative study. *TESOL Quarterly* 32, 9–38.

Borg, S. (1999) The use of grammatical terminology in the second language classroom: A qualitative study of teachers' practices and cognitions. *Applied Linguistics* 20, 95–126.

Boswood, T. (ed.) (1999) *New Ways of Using Computers in Language Teaching*. Alexandria, VA: TESOL.

Bottery, M. (1992) *The Ethics of Educational Management*. London: Cassell.

Bottomley, Y., J. Dalton and C. Corbel (1994) *From Proficiency to Competencies: A Collaborative Approach to Curriculum Innovation*. Sydney: National Centre for English Language Teaching and Research, Macquarie University.

Bourdieu, P. (1991) *Language and Symbolic Power*. Cambridge: Harvard University Press.

Bowen, T. and J. Marks (1992) *The Pronunciation Book. Student-Centred Activities for Pronunciation Work*. London: Longman.

Bowers, R. (1983) Project planning and performance. In C.J. Brumfit (ed.) *Language Teaching Projects for the Third World*. ELT Documents 116. London: Pergamon / The British Council.

Bowler, B. and S. Cunningham (1991) *Headway Pronunciation: Upper-Intermediate*. Oxford: Oxford University Press.

Bradford, B. (1988) *Intonation in Context*. Cambridge: Cambridge University Press.

Braine, G. (1997) Beyond word processing: Networked computers in ESL writing classes. *Computers and Composition* 14(1), 45–58.

Brazil, D. (1994) *Pronunciation for Advanced Learners of English*. Cambridge: Cambridge University Press.

Brazil, D. (1995) *A Grammar of Speech*. Oxford: Oxford University Press.

Brazil, D. (1997) *The Communicative Value of Intonation in English*. Cambridge: Cambridge University Press.

Brazil, D., M. Coulthard and A. Johns (1980) *Discourse Intonation and Language Teaching*. London: Longman.

Breen, M.P. (1984) Process syllabuses for the language classroom. In C.J. Brumfit (ed.) *General English Syllabus Design*. Oxford: Pergamon / The British Council.

Breen, M.P. (1987) Contemporary paradigms in syllabus design, Parts 1 and 2. *Language Teaching* 20(3), 81–92; 20(4), 156–174.

Breen, M.P. and C.N. Candlin (1980) The essentials of a communicative curriculum for language teaching. *Applied Linguistics* 1(2), 89–112.

Breen, M.P. and C.N. Candlin (1987) Which materials? A consumer's and designer's guide. In L.E. Sheldon (ed.) *ELT Textbooks and Materials: Problems in Evaluation and Development*. ELT Documents 126. London: Modern English Publications / The British Council, pp. 13–28.

Breen, M.P. and A. Littlejohn (eds) (2000) *Classroom Decision-Making: Negotiation and Process Syllabuses in Practice*. Cambridge: Cambridge University Press.

Breen, M.P., C.N. Candlin and A. Waters (1979) Communicative materials design: Some basic principles. *RELC Journal* 10(2), 1–13.

Bremer, K., C. Roberts, M. Vasseur, M. Simonot and P. Broeder (1996) *Achieving Understanding: Discourse in Intercultural Encounters*. London: Longman.

Brett, P. (1994) A genre analysis of the results section of sociology articles. *English for Specific Purposes* 13(1), 47–60.

Brindley, G. (1989) *Assessing Achievement in the Learner-Centred Curriculum*. Sydney: National Centre for English Language Teaching and Research, Macquarie University.

Brindley, G. (1995) Competency-based assessment in second language programs. In G. Brindley (ed.) *Language Assessment in Action*. Sydney: New South Wales Adult Migrant Education Service.

Brindley, G. (1998a) Outcomes-based assessment and reporting in second language programmes: A review of the issues. *Language Testing* 15(1), 45–85.

Brindley, G. (1998b) Assessing listening abilities. *Annual Review of Applied Linguistics* 18, 171–191.

Brinton, D. and C. La Belle (1997) Using internet resources to teach pronunciation. *Speak Out! (Journal of the IATEFL Pronunciation Special Interest Group)* 21, 54–60.

Brinton, D., M.A. Snow and M.J. Wesche (1989) *Content-Based Second Language Instruction*. New York: Newbury House.

Brislin, R.W. (1981) *Cross-Cultural Encounters*. Elmsford, NY: Pergamon.

Brislin, R.W., K. Cushner, C. Cherrie, M. Yong (1986) *Intercultural Interactions: A Practical Guide*. London: Sage.

British Council (1996) *English Language Schools Recognition Scheme: Handbook*. Manchester: The British Council.

Britton, J. (1970) *Language and Learning*. London: Penguin.

Brock, C.A. (1986) The effects of referential questions on ESL classroom discourse. *TESOL Quarterly* 20, 47–59.

Brock, M.N. and L. Walters (eds) (1993) *Teaching Composition Around the Pacific Rim: Politics and Pedagogy*. Clevedon: Multilingual Matters.

Brooks, F.B., R. Donato and J.V. McGlone (1997) When are they going to say 'it' right? Understanding learner talk during pair-work activity. *Foreign Language Annals* 30(4), 524–541.

Brown, A. (1991a) Functional load and the teaching of pronunciation. In A. Brown (ed.) *Teaching English Pronunciation: A Book of Readings*. London: Routledge.

Brown, A. (ed.) (1991b) *Teaching English Pronunciation: A Book of Readings*. London: Routledge.

Brown, G. (1994) Dimensions of difficulty in listening comprehension. In D. Mendelsohn and J. Rubin (eds) *A Guide for the Teaching of Second Language Listening*. San Diego, CA: Dominie Press.

Brown, J.B. (1997) Textbook evaluation form. *The Language Teacher* 21(10), 15–21.

Brown, J.D. (1989) Language program evaluation: A synthesis of existing possibilities. In R.K. Johnson (ed.) *The Second Language Curriculum*. Cambridge: Cambridge University Press, pp. 222–241.

Brown, J.D. (1995) *The Elements of Language Curriculum: A Systematic Approach to Program Development*. Boston, MA: Heinle and Heinle.

Brown, J.D. (1996) *Testing in Language Programs*. Upper Saddle River, NJ: Prentice Hall Regents.

Brown, J.D. (1997) Computers in language testing: present research and some future directions. *Language Learning and Technology* 1(1), 44–59.

Brown, P. and S. Levinson (1987) *Politeness: Universals in Language Usage*. Cambridge: Cambridge University Press.

Brown, R. (1973) *A First Language: The Early Stages*. Cambridge, MA: Harvard University Press.

Brown, T.S. and F.L. Perry Jr (1991) A comparison of three learning strategies for ESL vocabulary acquisition. *TESOL Quarterly* 25, 655–670.

Brumfit, C.J. (1981) Language variation and the death of language teaching. *British Association for Applied Linguistics Newsletter* 13.

Brumfit, C.J. (1984a) *Communicative Methodology in Language Teaching*. Cambridge: Cambridge University Press.

Brumfit, C.J. (ed.) (1984b) *General English Syllabus Design*. ELT Documents 118. Oxford: Pergamon / The British Council.

Brumfit, C.J. (1997) The teacher as educational linguist. In L. van Lier and D. Corson, (eds) *Encyclopedia of Language and Education, Vol. 6: Knowledge About Language*. Dordrecht: Kluwer Academic, pp. 163–172.

Brumfit, C.J. and K. Johnson (eds) (1979) *The Communicative Approach to Language Teaching*. Oxford: Oxford University Press.

Bullough, R. (1989) *First-Year Teacher: A Case Study*. New York: Teachers College Press.

Bunton, D. (1999) The use of higher-level metatext in PhD theses. *English for Specific Purposes* 18, S41–S56 (supplementary issue).

Burns, A. (1996a) Collaborative research and curriculum change: Australian Adult Migrant English Program, *TESOL Quarterly* 30, 591–597.

Burns, A. (1996b) Starting all over again: From teaching adults to teaching beginners. In D. Freeman and J.C. Richards (eds) *Teacher Learning in Language Teaching*. New York: Cambridge University Press, pp. 154–177.

Burrell, K. (1991) *Knowledge About Language*. Walton-on-Thames: Nelson.

Burstein, J., L. Frase, A. Ginther and L. Grant (1996) Technologies for language assessment. *Annual Review of Applied Linguistics* 16, 240–260.

Bush, T. (1985) *Theories of Educational Management*. London: Harper Education Series.

Butler, M. and G. Keith (1999) *Language, Power and Identity*. London: Hodder and Stoughton.

Bygate, M. (1987) *Speaking*. Oxford: Oxford University Press.

Bygate, M. (1996) Effects of task repetition: Appraising learners' performances on tasks. In D. Willis and J. Willis *Challenge and Change in Language Teaching*. London: Heinemann.

Bygate, M. (1999) Task as context for the framing, reframing and unframing of language. *System* 27, 33–48.

Bygate, M., A. Tonkyn and E. Williams (eds) (1994) *Grammar and the Language Teacher*. London: Prentice Hall.

Byram, M. (1989) *Cultural Studies in Foreign Language Education*. Clevedon: Multilingual Matters.

Byram, M. (1998) Cultural identities in multilingual classrooms. In J. Cenoz and F. Genesee (eds) *Beyond Bilingualism: Multilingualism and Multilingual Education*. Clevedon: Multilingual Matters, pp. 96–116.

Byrd, P. (1995) *Material Writers Guide*. New York: Newbury House.

Byrd, P. (1998) Rethinking grammar at the various proficiency levels: implications of various materials for the EAP curriculum. In P. Byrd and J. Reid *Grammar in the Composition Classroom*. Boston, MA: Heinle and Heinle, pp. 69–67.

Callaghan, M. and J. Rothery (1988) *Teaching Factual Writing: A Genre Based Approach*. Report of the Disadvantaged Schools Program Literacy Project. Metropolitan East Region, Sydney, NSW Department of Education.

Canagarajah, A.S. (1999) *Resisting Linguistic Imperialism in English Teaching*. Oxford: Oxford University Press.

Canale, M. (1983) From communicative competence to communicative language pedagogy. In J.C. Richards and R. Schmidt (eds) *Language and Communication*. London: Longman, pp. 2–27.

Canale, M. and M. Swain (1980) Theoretical bases of communicative approaches to second language teaching and testing. *Applied Linguistics* 1(1), 1–47.

Candland, D. (1993) *Feral Children and Clever Animals: Reflections on Human Nature*. Oxford: Oxford University Press.

Candlin, C.N. (1984) Syllabus design as a critical process. In C.J. Brumfit (ed.) *General English Syllabus Design*. Oxford: Pergamon / The British Council.

Candlin, C.N. (1987) Towards task-based language learning. In C.N. Candlin and D. Murphy (eds) *Lancaster Practical Papers in English Language Education, Vol. 7*. Englewood Cliffs, NJ: Prentice Hall.

Candlin, C.N. and M.P. Breen (1979) *Practical Papers in English Language Education, Vol. 2: Evaluating and*

Designing Language Teaching Materials. Lancaster: Institute for English Language Education, University of Lancaster.

Candlin, C.N. and D. Murphy (eds) (1987) *Lancaster Practical Papers in English Language Education, Vol. 7: Language Learning Tasks.* Englewood Cliffs, NJ: Prentice Hall.

Cantoni-Harvey, G. (1987) *Content-Area Language Instruction: Approaches and Strategies.* Reading, MA: Addison-Wesley.

Caplan, D. (1987) *Neurolinguistics and Linguistic Aphasiology: An Introduction.* Cambridge: Cambridge University Press.

Carrasco, R.L. (1981) Expanded awareness of student performances: A case study in applied ethnographic monitoring in a bilingual classroom. In H.T. Trueba, C.P. Guthrie and H.P. Au (eds) *Culture and the Bilingual Classroom: Studies in Classroom Ethnography.* Rowley, MA: Newbury House, pp. 153–177.

Carrell, P. (1983) Some issues in studying the role of schemata, or background knowledge, in second language comprehension. *Reading in a Foreign Language* 1, 81–92.

Carrell, P., J. Devine and D. Eskey (eds) (1988) *Interactive Approaches to Second Language Reading.* Cambridge: Cambridge University Press.

Carroll, D. (1994) *Psychology of Language.* 2nd edn. Pacific Grove, CA: Brooks/Cole.

Carroll, S. and M. Swain (1993) Explicit and implicit negative feedback: An empirical study of the learning of linguistic generalizations. *Studies in Second Language Acquisition* 15, 357–386.

Carter, R.A. (ed.) (1990) *Knowledge About Language and the Curriculum.* London: Hodder and Stoughton.

Carter, R.A. (1997) *Investigating English Discourse: Language, Literacy and Literature.* London: Routledge.

Carter, R.A. (1998) *Vocabulary: Applied Linguistic Perspectives.* 2nd edn. London: Routledge.

Carter, R.A. and M.N. Long (1987) *The Web of Words: Exploring Literature Through Language.* Cambridge: Cambridge University Press.

Carter, R.A. and M.N. Long (1991) *Teaching Literature.* London: Longman.

Carter, R.A. and M.J. McCarthy (1988) *Vocabulary and Language Teaching.* London: Longman.

Carter, R.A. and M.J. McCarthy (1995) Grammar and the spoken language. *Applied Linguistics* 16(2), 141–158.

Carter, R.A. and M.J. McCarthy (1997) *Exploring Spoken English.* Cambridge: Cambridge University Press.

Carter, R.A. and J. McRae (eds) (1996) *Language, Literature and the Learner: Creative Classroom Practice.* London: Longman.

Carter, R.A. and W. Nash (1990) *Seeing Through Language: A Guide to Styles of English Writing.* Oxford: Blackwell.

Carter, R.A., R. Hughes and M.J. McCarthy (1998) Telling tails: Grammar, the spoken language and materials development. In B. Tomlinson (ed.) *Materials Development for Language Teaching.* Cambridge: Cambridge University Press, pp. 67–86.

Carter, R.A., R. Walker and C.J. Brumfit (eds) (1989) *Literature and the Learner: Methodological Approaches.* ELT Documents 130. London: Modern English Publications / Macmillan / The British Council.

Casanave, C. (1990) The role of writing in socializing graduate students into an academic discipline in the social sciences. Unpublished PhD dissertation, Stanford University.

Catford, J.C. (1987) Phonetics and the teaching of pronunciation: A systematic description of English phonology. In J. Morley (ed.) *Current Perspectives on Pronunciation: Practices Anchored in Theory.* Washington, DC: TESOL.

Catford, J.C. (1988) *A Practical Introduction to Phonetics.* Oxford: Oxford University Press.

Cauldwell, R.T. (1996) Stress-timing: observations, beliefs, and evidence. *Eger Journal of English Studies* 1, 33–48.

Cazden, C. (1992) Performing expository texts in the foreign language classroom. In C.J. Kramsch and S. McConnell-Ginet (eds) *Text and Context: Cross-Disciplinary Perspectives on Language Study.* Lexington, MA: D.C. Heath.

CCED (1995) *Collins COBUILD English Dictionary.* Glasgow and London: HarperCollins.

CCELD (1987) *Collins COBUILD English Language Dictionary.* Glasgow: Collins.

Celce-Murcia, M. (1991a) Discourse analysis and grammar instruction. *Annual Review of Applied Linguistics* 11, 135–151.

Celce-Murcia, M. (1991b) Grammar pedagogy in second and foreign language teaching. *TESOL Quarterly* 25(3), 459–480.

Celce-Murcia, M. (1997) Describing and Teaching English Grammar with Reference to Written Discourse. In T. Miller (ed.) *Functional Approaches to Written Text: Classroom Applications.* Washington, DC: English Language Programs, United States Information Agency.

Celce-Murcia, M. and D. Larsen-Freeman (1999) *The Grammar Book: An ESL/EFL Teacher's Course.* 2nd edn. Boston, MA: Heinle and Heinle.

Celce-Murcia, M., D. Brinton and J. Goodwin (1996) *Teaching Pronunciation: A Reference for Teachers of English to Speakers of Other Languages.* Cambridge and New York: Cambridge University Press.

Celce-Murcia, M., Z. Dörnyei and S. Thurrell (1997) Direct approaches in L2 instruction: A turning point in communicative language teaching? *TESOL Quarterly* 31(1), 141–152.

Cenoz, J. and F. Genesee (eds) (1998) *Beyond Bilingualism: Multilingualism and Multilingual Education.* Clevedon: Multilingual Matters.

Chafe, W. (ed.) (1980) *The Pear Stories: Cognitive, Cultural, and Linguistic Aspects of Narrative Production.* Norwood, NJ: Ablex.

Chafe, W. (1982) Integration and involvement in speaking, writing and oral literature. In D. Tannen (ed.) *Spoken and Written language: Exploring Orality and Literacy.* Norwood NJ: Ablex, 35–54.

Chalhoub-Deville, M. (1995) Deriving oral assessment scales across different tasks and rater groups. *Language Testing* 12(1), 16–33.

Chalhoub-Deville, M., C. Alcaya and V.M. Lozier (1997) Language and measurement issues in developing computer-adaptive tests of reading ability: The University of Minnesota model. In A. Huhta, V. Kohonen, L. Kurki-Suonio and S. Luoma (eds) *Current Developments and Alternatives in Language Assessment.* Jyväskylä: Centre for Applied Language Studies, University of Jyväskylä, pp. 545–588.

Chambers, F. (1980) A re-evaluation of needs analysis. *ESP Journal* 1, 25–33.

Chamot, A.U. (1999) Learning strategies of immersion students. In R. Oxford (ed.) *Language Learning Strategies in the Context of Autonomy: Strategy Research Compendium: Proceedings of the First Annual Strategy Research Symposium, Teachers College.* New York: Columbia University, pp. 12–13.

Chamot, A.U. and J.M. O'Malley (1996a) The Cognitive Academic Language Learning Approach: A model for linguistically diverse classrooms. *Elementary School Journal* 96(3), 259–273.

Chamot, A.U. and J.M. O'Malley (1996b) Implementing the Cognitive Academic Language Learning Approach (CALLA). In R. Oxford (ed.) *Language Learning Strategies Around the World: Cross-Cultural Perspectives.* Manoa, HI: University of Hawai'i Press, pp. 167–184.

Chamot, A.U., S. Barnhardt, P. El-Dinary and J. Robbins (1996) Methods for teaching learning strategies in the foreign language classroom. In R. Oxford (ed.) *Language Learning Strategies Around the World: Cross-Cultural Perspectives.* Manoa, HI: University of Hawai'i Press, pp. 175–188.

Chan, P.K.W. (1999) Literature, language awareness and ELT. Special issue of *Language Awareness* 8(1), 38–50.

Channell, J. (1990) The student-tutor relationship. In M. Kinnell (ed.) *The Learning Experiences of Overseas Students.* The Society for Research into Higher Education. Milton Keynes: Open University Press.

Chapelle, C.A. (1990) The discourse of computer-assisted language learning: Toward a context for descriptive research. *TESOL Quarterly* 24(2), 199–225.

Chapelle, C.A. (1997) CALL in the year 2000: Still in search of research paradigms? *Language Learning and Technology* 1(1), 19–43. Available: http://llt.msu.edu/vol1num1 [2000, Nov 3].

Chapelle, C.A. (2001) *Computer Applications in Second Language Acquisition: Foundations for Teaching, Testing and Research.* Cambridge: Cambridge University Press.

Chapman, J. (1983) *Reading Development and Cohesion.* London: Heinemann Educational.

Charles, M. (1994) Layered negotiations in business: interdependencies between discourse and the business relationship. Unpublished PhD thesis, University of Birmingham.

Charles, M. (1996) Business negotiations: Interdependence between the discourse and the business relationship. *English for Specific Purposes* 15, 19–36.

Chaudron, C. (1988) *Second Language Classrooms: Research on Teaching and Learning.* New York: Cambridge University Press.

Chick, K. (1996) Safetalk: Collusion in apartheid education. In H. Coleman (ed.) *Society and the Language Classroom.* Cambridge: Cambridge University Press.

Chomsky, N. (1957) *Syntactic Structures.* The Hague: Mouton.

Chomsky, N. (1959) Review of 'Verbal behavior'. *Language* 35, 26–58.

Chomsky, N. (1965) *Aspects of a Theory of Syntax.* Cambridge, MA: MIT Press.

Chomsky, N. (1968) *Language and Mind.* New York: Harcourt Press.

Chomsky, N. (1980) On cognitive structures and their development: A reply to Piaget. In M. Piattelli-Palmarini (ed.) *Language and Learning: The Debate Between Jean Piaget and Noam Chomsky.* Cambridge, MA: Harvard University Press, pp. 35–52.

Chomsky, N. (1995) *The Minimalist Program.* Cambridge, MA: MIT Press.

Christie, F. (1992) Literacy in Australia. In W. Grabe *et al.* (eds) *Annual Review of Applied Linguistics* 8, 142–155. Also published in *Annual Review of Applied Linguistics* 12, 142–155.

Christie, F. (1995a) Genre-based approaches to teaching literacy. In M.L. Tickoo (ed.) *Reading and Writing: Theory into Practice.* Singapore: SEAMEO, Regional English Language Centre.

Christie, F. (1995b) Pedagogic Discourse in the Primary School. *Linguistics and Education* 7(3), 221–242.

Christie, F. and J.R. Martin (eds) (1997) *Genre and Institutions: Social Processes in the Workplace and School.* London: Cassell.

Chun, D.M. and J.L. Plass (1997) Research on text comprehension in multimedia environments. *Language Learning and Technology* 1(1), 60–81. Available: http://llt.msu.edu/vol1num1 [2000, Nov 3].

Chun, D.M. and J.L. Plass (2000) Networked multimedia environments for second language acquisition. In M. Warschauer and R. Kern (eds) *Network-Based Language Teaching: Concepts and Practice*. New York: Cambridge University Press.

Churchill, S. (1986) *The Education of Linguistic and Cultural Minorities in the OECD Countries*. Clevedon: Multilingual Matters.

CIDE (1995) *Cambridge International Dictionary of English*. Cambridge: Cambridge University Press.

Clandinin, D.J. (1986) *Classroom Practice: Teacher Images in Action*. London: Falmer Press.

Clapham, C. and J.C. Alderson (eds) (1996) *IELTS Research Reports 3: Constructing and Trialling the IELTS Test*. Cambridge: University of Cambridge Local Examinations Syndicate.

Clapham, C. and D. Corson (eds) (1997) *Encyclopedia of Language and Education, Vol. 7: Language Testing and Assessment*. Dordrecht: Kluwer Academic.

Clark, C.M. and P.L. Peterson (1986) Teachers' thought processes. In M.C. Wittrock (ed.) *Handbook of Research on Teaching*. New York: Macmillan, pp. 255–296.

Clark, E. (1998) The design solution: Systems thinking. *Encounter* 11(1).

Clark, H. (1996) *Using Language*. Cambridge: Cambridge University Press.

Clark, H. and E. Clark (1977) *Psychology and Language: An Introduction to Psycholinguistics*. Fort Worth, TX: Harcourt Brace Jovanovich.

Clark, J. (1987) *Curriculum Renewal in School Foreign Language Learning*. Oxford: Oxford University Press.

Clark, J. and C. Yallop (1990) *An Introduction to Phonetics and Phonology*. Oxford: Blackwell.

Clark, R. and R. Ivanič (1997) Critical discourse analysis and educational change. In L. van Lier and D. Corson, (eds) *Encyclopedia of Language and Education, Vol. 6: Knowledge About Language*. Dordrecht: Kluwer Academic, pp. 217–227.

Clyne, M. (1997) Multilingualism. In F. Coulmas (ed.) *Handbook of Sociolinguistics*. Oxford: Blackwell, pp. 301–314.

Coady, J. and T. Huckin (eds) (1997) *Second Language Vocabulary Acquisition*. Cambridge: Cambridge University Press.

Coates, J. (1993) *Women, Men and Language*. 2nd edn. London: Longman.

Coates, J. and D. Cameron (eds) (1988) *Women in their Speech Communities: New Perspectives on Language and Sex*. New York: Longman.

Cohen, A.D. (1994) *Assessing Language Ability in the Classroom*. Boston, MA: Heinle and Heinle.

Cohen, A.D. (1996) Speech acts. In S.L. McKay and N.H. Hornberger (eds) *Sociolinguistics and Language Teaching*. Cambridge: Cambridge University Press, pp. 383–420.

Cohen, A.D. (1997) Language learning strategies and language use strategies. Lecture, Strategies-Based Instruction Workshop, University of Minnesota, Minneapolis, MN.

Cohen, A.D. and K. Scott (1996) A synthesis of approaches to assessing language learning strategies. In R. Oxford (ed.) *Language Learning Strategies Around the World: Cross-Cultural Perspectives*. Manoa, HI: University of Hawai'i Press, pp. 89–106.

Cohen, A.D. and S.J. Weaver (1998) Strategies-based instruction for second language learners. In W.A. Reyandya and G.M. Jacobs (eds) *Learners and Language Learning*. Anthology Series 39. Singapore: SEAMEO Regional Language Center, pp. 1–25.

Collentine, J. (2000) Insights into the construction of grammatical knowledge provided by user-behavior tracking technologies. *Language Learning and Technology* 3(2), 44–57. Available: http://llt.msu.edu/vol3num2 [2000, Nov 3].

Collie, J. and S. Slater (1987) *Literature in the Language Classroom*. Cambridge: Cambridge University Press.

Condon, J.C. and F. Yousef (1975) *An Introduction to Intercultural Communication*. Indianapolis, IN: Bobbs-Merrill.

Conklin, N.F. and M.A. Lourie (1983) *A Host of Tongues: Language Communities in the United States*. New York: Free Press.

Connor, U. (1987) Research frontiers in writing analysis. *TESOL Quarterly* 21(4), 677–696.

Connor, U. (1996) *Contrastive Rhetoric: Cross-Cultural Aspects of Second Language Writing*. New York: Cambridge University Press.

Connor, U. and R.B. Kaplan (eds) (1987) *Writing Across Languages: Analysis of L2 Texts*. Reading, MA: Addison-Wesley.

Cook, G. (1989) *Discourse*. Oxford: Oxford University Press.

Cook, G. (1994) *Discourse and Literature*. Oxford: Oxford University Press.

Cook, V. (1994) Universal Grammar and the learning and teaching of second languages. In T. Odlin (ed.) *Perspectives on Pedagogical Grammar*. Cambridge: Cambridge University Press, pp. 25–48.

Cooper, C.L. and C. Agyris (eds) (1998) *The Concise Blackwell Encyclopaedia of Management*. Oxford: Blackwell.

Cope, B. and M. Kalantzis (eds) (1993) *The Powers of Literacy: A Genre Approach to Teaching Writing*. London: Falmer Press.

Cope, W. and M. Kalantzis (eds) (2000) *Multiliteracies: Literacy Learning and the Design of Social Futures*. London: Routledge.

Corder, S.P. (1967) The significance of learners' errors. *International Review of Applied Linguistics* 5, 161–170. Reprinted in S.P. Corder (1981) *Error Analysis and Interlanguage*. Oxford: Oxford University Press.

Corno, L. (1993) The best-laid plans: Modern conceptions of volition and educational research. *Educational Researcher* 22, 14–22.

Cotterall, S. (1995) Developing a course strategy for learner autonomy. *ELT Journal* 49, 219–227.

Coulmas, F. (ed.) (1997) *The Handbook of Sociolinguistics*. Oxford: Blackwell.

Coulthard, R.M. (1985) *An Introduction to Discourse Analysis*. 2nd edn. London: Longman.

Council of Europe (1971) *Linguistic Content, Means of Evaluation and their Interaction in the Teaching and Learning of Modern Languages in Adult Education*. Strasbourg: Council of Europe.

Couper-Kuhlen, E. (1993) *English Speech Rhythm: Form and Function in Everyday Verbal Interaction*. Amsterdam: John Benjamins.

Coupland, N. and A. Jaworski (eds) (1997) *Sociolinguistics: A Reader*. Basingstoke: Macmillan.

Cowan, N. (1995) *Attention and Memory: An Integrated Framework*. Oxford: Oxford University Press.

Cowie, A.P. and J.B. Heaton (eds) (1977) *English for Academic Purposes*. Reading: The British Association of Applied Linguistics.

A Cow's Head and Other Tales (1996). West Taegu, South Korea: West Taegu Secondary Education Association for English Language Teaching Research.

Craik, F.I.M. and R.S. Lockhart (1972) Levels of processing: A framework for memory record. *Journal of Verbal Learning and Verbal Behaviour* 11, 671–684.

Cram, B. (1995) Self-assessment: from theory to practice. Developing a workshop guide for teachers. In G. Brindley (ed.) *Language Assessment in Action*. Sydney: National Centre for English Language Teaching and Research, Macquarie University, pp. 271–305.

Criper, C. and A. Davies (1988) *ELTS Validation Project Report*. Research Report 1(1). London and Cambridge: The British Council and University of Cambridge Local Examinations Syndicate.

Crompton, P. (1997) Hedging in academic writing: Some theoretical problems. *English for Specific Purposes* 16(4), 271–288.

Crookall, D. and R. Oxford (eds) (1990) *Simulation, Gaming, and Language Learning*. New York: Newbury House.

Crookes, G. and S. Gass (eds) (1993a) *Tasks in a Learning Context: Integrating Theory and Practice*. Clevedon: Multilingual Matters.

Crookes, G. and S. Gass (eds) (1993b) *Tasks in a Pedagogical Context: Integrating Theory and Practice*. Clevedon: Multilingual Matters.

Crow, J.T. and J.R. Quigley (1985) A semantic field approach to passive vocabulary acquisition for reading comprehension. *TESOL Quarterly* 19, 497–513.

Crystal, D. (1997) *English as a Global Language*. Cambridge: Cambridge University Press.

Cumming, A. (1997) Theoretical perspectives on writing. *Annual Review of Applied Linguistics* 18, 61–78.

Cummins, J. (1984) Bilingualism and cognitive functioning. In S. Shapson and V. D'oyley (eds) *Bilingual and Multilingual Education: Canadian Perspectives*. Clevedon: Multilingual Matters, pp. 55–67.

Cummins, J. (1986) Cultures in contact: Using classroom microcomputers for cultural exchange and reinforcement. *TESL Canada Journal / Revue TESL du Canada* 3(2), 13–31.

Cummins, J. and D. Sayers (1995) *Brave New Schools: Challenging Cultural Illiteracy through Global Learning Networks*. New York: St Martin's Press.

Cummins, J. and M. Swain (1986) *Bilingualism in Education: Aspects of Theory, Research and Practice*. London: Longman.

Cunningsworth, A. (1984) *Evaluating and Selecting EFL Teaching Material*. London: Heinemann.

Cunningsworth, A. (1996) *Choosing Your Coursebook*. Oxford: Heinemann.

Cutler, A. (1997) The comparative perspective on spoken language processing. *Speech Communication* 21, 3–15.

Dadour, E.S. and J. Robbins (1996) University-level studies using strategy instruction to improve speaking ability in Egypt and Japan. In R. Oxford (ed.) *Language Learning Strategies Around the World: Cross-Cultural Perspectives*. Manoa, HI: University of Hawai'i Press, pp. 157–166.

Daedalus (1989) *Daedalus Integrated Writing Environment*. Austin, TX: The Daedalus Group.

Dahl, O. (ed.) (1995) *Intercultural Communication and Contact*. Stavanger: Misjonshogskolens Forlag.

Dai, Q.-X., X. Teng, X.-Q. Guan and Y. Dong (1997) *Zhongguo Xiaoshu Minzu Shuangyu Jiaoyu Gailun* (Introduction to Bilingual Education for China's Ethnic Minorities) Shenyang: Liaoning Nationalities.

Dalton, C. and B. Seidlhofer (1994) *Pronunciation (Language Teaching: A Scheme for Teacher Education)*. Oxford: Oxford University Press.

Dam, L. (1995) *Learner Autonomy 3: From Theory to Classroom Practice*. Dublin: Authentik.

Daneš, F. (1974) Functional sentence perspective and the organisation of the text. In F. Daneš (ed.) *Papers on Functional Sentence Perspective*. Prague: Academia.

Danesi, J. (1993) Whither contrastive analysis? *Canadian Modern Language Review* 51, 37–46.

Daniels, H. (1997) Psycholinguistic, psycho-affective and procedural factors in the acquisition of authentic L2 phonology. In A. McLean (ed.) *SIG Selections 1997 Special Interests in ELT*. Whitstable, Kent: IATEFL.

Dauer, R. (1983) Stress-timing and syllable-timing reanalyzed. *Journal of Phonetics* 11, 51–62.

Davies, F. (1995) *Introducing Reading*. London: Penguin.

Davies, M. (1998) *Understanding Marketing*. London: Prentice Hall.

Davis, P. and M. Rinvolucri (1995) *More Grammar Games*. Cambridge: Cambridge University Press.

Dawson, S. (1996) *Analyzing Organizations*. Basingstoke: Macmillan.

Day, R. (1984) Student participation in the ESL classroom or some imperfections in practice. *Language Learning* 34(3), 69–102.

Day, R. (1990) Teacher observation in second language teacher education. In J.C. Richards and D. Nunan (eds) *Second Language Teacher Education*. Cambridge: Cambridge University Press, pp. 43–61.

Day, R. and J. Bamford (1998) *Extensive Reading in the Second Language Classroom*. Cambridge: Cambridge University Press.

de Bot, K. (1992) A bilingual production model: Levelt's 'speaking' model adapted. *Applied Linguistics* 13, 1–24.

De Keyser, R. (1995) Learning second language grammar rules: An experiment with miniature linguistic systems. *Studies in Second Language Acquisition* 17, 379–410.

De Keyser, R. (1998) Beyond focus on form: Cognitive perspectives on learning and practising second language grammar. In C. Doughty and J. Williams (eds) *Focus on Form in Classroom Second Language Acquisition*. Cambridge: Cambridge University Press.

Debski, R., J. Gassin and M. Smith (eds) (1997) *Language Learning Through Social Computing*. Melbourne: Applied Linguistics Association of Australia.

Denzin, N.K. (ed.) (1970) *Sociological Methods: A Source Book*. Chicago, IL: Aldine.

Department of Education and Science (DES) (1975) *A Language for Life*. London: HMSO.

Derewianka, B. (1990) *Exploring How Texts Work*. Sydney: Primary English Teaching Association.

Dessler, G. (1999) *Essentials of Human Resource Management*. Englewood Cliffs, NJ: Prentice Hall.

Dewey, J. (1938) *Experience and Education*. New York: Macmillan.

DIALANG (1997) DIALANG: A new European system for diagnostic language assessment. *Language Testing Update* 21, 38. See also: www.sprachlabor.fu-berlin.de/dialang/ [2000, Nov 3].

Dickerson, W.B. (1991) Orthography as a pronunciation resource. In A. Brown *Teaching English Pronunciation: A Book of Readings*. London: Routledge. Originally published 1987.

Dickerson, W.B. (1994) Empowering students with predictive skills. In J. Morley (ed.) *Pronunciation Pedagogy and Theory: New Views, New Directions*. Alexandria, VA: TESOL.

Dickins, P. and E. Woods (1988) Some criteria for the development of communicative grammar tasks. *TESOL Quarterly* 22(3), 623–646.

Dickinson, L. (1987) *Self-Instruction in Language Learning*. Cambridge: Cambridge University Press.

Dijkstra, T. and K. de Smelt (eds) (1996) *Computational Psycholinguistics: AI and Connectionist Models of Human Language Processing*. London: Taylor and Francis.

Dik, S. (1991) Functional grammar. In F. Droste and J. Joseph (eds) *Linguistic Theory and Grammatical Description*. Amsterdam/Philadelphia, PA: John Benjamins, pp. 247–274.

Dingwall, W. (1993) The biological bases of human communicative behavior. In J. Berko-Gleason and N. Ratner (eds) *Psycholinguistics*. Fort Worth, TX: Harcourt Brace Jovanovich.

DiPardo, A. (1993) *A Kind of Passport: A Basic Writing Adjunct Program and the Challenge of Student Diversity*. Urbana, IL: NCTE.

DiPietro, R.J. (ed.) (1982) *Linguistics and the Professions*. Norwood, NJ: Ablex.

Dobinson, T. (1996) The recall and retention of new vocabulary from second language classrooms. Unpublished MA dissertation, Edith Cowan University, Australia.

Donato, R. (1994) Collective scaffolding in second language learning. In J.P. Lantolf and G. Appel (eds) *Vygotskian Approaches to Second Language Research*. Norwood, NJ: Ablex, pp. 33–56.

Dong, Y.-R. (1998) Non-native graduate students thesis/dissertation writing in science: Self reports by students and their advisers from two institutions. *English for Specific Purposes* 17(4), 369–390.

Donmall, B.G. (ed.) (1985) *Language Awareness*. NCLE Papers and Reports 6. London: Centre for Information on Language Teaching and Research.

Donmall-Hicks, B.G. (1997) The history of language awareness in the United Kingdom. In L. van Lier and D. Corson, (eds) *Encyclopedia of Language and Education, Vol. 6: Knowledge About Language*. Dordrecht: Kluwer Academic, pp. 21–30.

Donovan, P. (1998) Piloting: A publisher's view. In B. Tomlinson (ed.) *Materials Development for Language Teaching*. Cambridge: Cambridge University Press, pp. 149–190.

Dooling, D. and R. Lachman (1971) Effects of comprehension on retention of prose. *Journal of Experimental Psychology* 88, 216–222.

Dopke, S. (1992) *One Parent, One Language: An Interactional Approach*. Amsterdam: John Benjamins.

Dörnyei, Z. and J. Kormos (1998) Problem solving mechanisms in L2 communication: A psycholinguistic perspective. *Studies in Second Language Acquisition* 20, 349–385.

Dörnyei, Z. and I. Ottó (1998) Motivation in action: A process model of L2 motivation. *Working Papers in Applied Linguistics* 4, 43–69.

Dörnyei, Z. and S. Thurrell (1992) *Conversation and Dialogues in Action*. New York: Prentice Hall.

Doughty, C. (1991) Second language instruction does make a difference. *Studies in Second Language Acquisition* 13, 431–469.

Doughty, C. and T. Pica (1986) 'Information gap' tasks: Do they facilitate second language acquisition? *TESOL Quarterly* 20, 305–325.

Doughty, C. and E. Varela (1998) Communicative focus on form. In C. Doughty and J. Williams (eds) *Focus on Form in Classroom Second Language Acquisition*. Cambridge: Cambridge University Press, pp. 114–138.

Doughty, C. and J. Williams (eds) (1998a) *Focus on Form in Classroom Second Language Acquisition*. Cambridge: Cambridge University Press.

Doughty, C. and J. Williams (1998b) Issues and Terminology. In C. Doughty and J. Williams (eds) *Focus on Form in Classroom Second Language Acquisition*. Cambridge: Cambridge University Press.

Doughty, C. and E. Varela (1998) Communicative focus on form. In C. Doughty and J. Williams (eds) *Focus on Form in Classroom Second Language Acquisition*. Cambridge: Cambridge University Press, pp. 114–138.

Doughty, C. and J. Williams (eds) (1998a) *Focus on Form in Classroom Second Language Acquisition*. Cambridge: Cambridge University Press.

Doughty, C. and J. Williams (1998b) Issues and Terminology. In C. Doughty and J. Williams (eds) *Focus on Form in Classroom Second Language Acquisition*. Cambridge: Cambridge University Press.

Douglas, D. (1995) Developments in language testing. *Annual Review of Applied Linguistics* 15, 167–187.

Dreyer, C. and R. Oxford (1996) Learning strategies and other predictors of ESL proficiency among Afrikaans-speakers in South Africa. In R. Oxford (ed.) *Language Learning Strategies Around the World: Cross-Cultural Perspectives*. Manoa, HI: University of Hawai'i Press.

Dubin, F. and E. Olshtain (1986) *Course Design*. New York: Cambridge University Press.

Dudley-Evans, T. (1991) Socialization into the academic community: linguistic and stylistic expectations of a PhD thesis as revealed by supervisor comments. In P. Adams, B. Heaton and P. Howarth (eds) *Socio-Cultural Issues in English for Academic Purposes: Developments in ELT*. London: Macmillan, pp. 41–51.

Dudley-Evans, T. (1993) Variation in discourse patterns between discourse communities: The case of highway engineering and plant biology. In G.M. Blue (ed.) *Language, Learning and Success: Studying through English. Developments in ELT*. London: Phoenix ELT.

Dudley-Evans, T. (1994a) Genre Analysis: an approach to text analysis for ESP. In M. Coulthard (ed.) *Advances in Written Text Analysis*. London: Routledge.

Dudley-Evans, T. (1994b) Variations in the discourse patterns favoured by different disciplines and their pedagogical implications. In J. Flowerdew (ed.) *Academic Listening: Research Perspectives*. Cambridge: Cambridge University Press.

Dudley-Evans, T. (1995) Variations in the discourse patterns favoured by different disciplines and their pedagogical implications. In J. Flowerdew (ed.) *Academic Listening: Research Perspectives*. Cambridge: Cambridge University Press, pp. 146–158.

Dudley-Evans, T. (1997) Genre: How far can we, should we, go? *World Englishes* 16(13), 351–358.

Dudley-Evans, T. and W. Henderson (1990a) *The Language of Economics: The Analysis of Economics Discourse*. ELT Documents 134. London: Modern English Publications / Macmillan / The British Council.

Dudley-Evans, T. and W. Henderson (1990b) The organisation of article introductions: evidence of change in economics writing. In T. Dudley-Evans and W. Henderson (eds) *The Language of Economics: The Analysis of Economics Discourse*. ELT Documents 134. London: Modern English Publications / Macmillan / The British Council.

Dudley-Evans, T. and M.J. St John (1998) *Developments in English for Specific Purposes: A Multi-disciplinary Approach*. Cambridge: Cambridge University Press.

Dufeu, B. (1994) *Teaching Myself*. Oxford: Oxford University Press.

Duff, A. and A. Maley (1990) *Literature*. Oxford: Oxford University Press.

Duff, P.A. (1993) Tasks and interlanguage performance: An SLA research perspective. In G. Crookes and S.M. Gass (eds) *Tasks and Language Learning: Integrating Theory and Practice*. Clevedon: Multilingual Matters.

Dulay, H. and M. Burt (1973) Should we teach children syntax? *Language Learning* 23.

Dulay, H. and M. Burt (1974) You can't learn without goofing. In J.C. Richards (ed.) *Error Analysis*. London: Longman.

Dulay, H. and M. Burt and S. Krashen (1982) *Language Two*. Oxford: Pergamon.

Dunkel, P.A. (1999) Considerations in developing or using second/foreign language proficiency computer-adaptive tests. *Language Learning and Technology* 2(2), 77–93. Available: http://llt.msu.edu/vol2num2 [2000, Nov 3].

Dunkin, M. and B. Biddle (1974) *The Study of Teaching*. New York: Holt, Rinehart and Winston.

Durant, A. and N. Fabb (1990) *Literary Studies in Action*. London: Routledge.

Dynamic English (1997) [Computer software] (Version 2.3). Foster City, CA: DynEd.

Eckert, P. (1997) Age as a linguistic variable. In F. Coulmas (ed.) *Handbook of Sociolinguistics*. Oxford: Blackwell, pp. 151–167.

Edge, J. and K. Richards (eds) (1993) *Teachers Develop Teachers Research*. Oxford: Heinemann.

Edmondson, W. (1997) The role of literature in foreign language learning and teaching: Some valid assumptions and invalid arguments. *AILA Review* 12, 42–55.

Educational Testing Service (1998) *TOEFL 1998–99*. Information bulletin for computer-based testing. Princeton, NJ: Educational Testing Service.

Edwards, J. and M.D. Lampert (1993) *Talking Data: Transcription and Coding in Discourse Research*. Hillsdale, NJ: Lawrence Erlbaum.

Egbert, J. and E. Hanson-Smith (1999) *CALL Environments: Research, Practice and Critical Issues*. Alexandria, VA: TESOL.

Eggins, S. and D. Slade (1997) *Analyzing Casual Conversation*. London: Cassell.

Ehrman, M. (1999) Bringing strategies to the student: The FSI Language Learning Consultation Service. In R. Oxford (ed.) *Language Learning Strategies in the Context of Autonomy: Strategy Research Compendium: Proceedings of the First Annual Strategy Research Symposium, Teachers College*. New York: Columbia University, pp. 19–21.

Ehsani, F. and E. Knodt (1998) Speech technology in computer-aided language learning: Strengths and limitations of a new CALL paradigm. *Language Learning and Technology* 2(1), 45–60. Available: http://llt.msu.edu/vol2num1 [2000, Nov 3].

Eiler, M.A. (1986) Thematic distribution as a heuristic for written discourse function. In B. Coutoure (ed.) *Functional Approaches to Writing Research Perspectives*. London: Frances Pinter.

Eisenstein Ebsworth, M. and C.W. Schweers (1997) What teachers say and practitioners do: Perspectives on conscious grammar instruction in the ESL classroom. *Applied Language Learning* 8, 237–260.

Elbaz, F. (1983) *Teacher Thinking: A Study of Practical Knowledge*. London: Crown Helm.

Elley, W. (1989) Tailoring the evaluation to fit the context. In R.K. Johnson (ed.) *The Second Language Curriculum*. Cambridge: Cambridge University Press, pp. 270–285.

ELLIS (1998) [Computer software] (Mastery Series). American Fork, UT: CALI.

Ellis, G. and J. Brewster (1991) *The Story-Telling Handbook for Primary Teachers*. London: Penguin.

Ellis, G. and B. Sinclair (1989) *Learning to Learn English: A Course in Learner Training*. Cambridge: Cambridge University Press.

Ellis, N. (1993) Rules and instances in foreign language learning: Interactions of implicit and explicit knowledge. *European Journal of Cognitive Psychology* 5, 280–319.

Ellis, N. (ed.) (1994) *Implicit and Explicit Learning of Languages*. London: Academic Press.

Ellis, N. (1995a) Consciousness in second language acquisition: A review of field studies and laboratory experiments. *Language Awareness* 4(3), 123–146.

Ellis, N. (1995b) Vocabulary acquisition: Psychological perspectives and pedagogical implications. *The Language Teacher* 19(2), 12–16.

Ellis, N. (1996) Sequencing in SLA: Phonological memory, chunking, and points of order. *Studies in Second Language Acquisition* 18(1), 91–126.

Ellis, N. (1998) Emergentism, connectionism, and language learning. *Language Learning* 48, 631–664.

Ellis, N. and R. Schmidt (1997) Morphology and longer-distance dependencies: Laboratory research illuminating the A in SLA. *Studies in Second Language Acquisition* 19, 145–171.

Ellis, R. (1988) *Classroom Second Language Development*. New York: Prentice Hall.

Ellis, R. (1992) *Second Language Acquisition and Language Pedagogy*. New York: Multilingual Matters.

Ellis, R. (1993) The structural syllabus and second language acquisition. *TESOL Quarterly* 27, 91–113.

Ellis, R. (1994) *The Study of Second Language Acquisition*. Oxford: Oxford University Press.

Ellis, R. (1995) Interpretation tasks for grammar teaching. *TESOL Quarterly* 29(1), 87–105.

Ellis, R. (1997) Explicit knowledge and second language pedagogy. In L. van Lier and D. Corson, (eds)

Encyclopedia of Language and Education, Vol. 6: Knowledge About Language. Dordrecht: Kluwer Academic, pp. 109–118.

Ellis, R. (1998a) The evaluation of communicative tasks. In B. Tomlinson (ed.) *Materials Development for Language Teaching*. Cambridge: Cambridge University Press, pp. 217–238.

Ellis, R. (1998b) Teaching and research: Options in grammar teaching. *TESOL Quarterly* 32(1), 39–60.

Ellis, R. (1999) Input-based approaches to teaching grammar: A review of classroom-oriented research. *Annual Review of Applied Linguistics* 19, 64–80.

Ellis, R. (2000) Task-based research and language pedagogy. *Language Teaching Research*. Special issue on tasks in language pedagogy 4(3), 193–220.

Elman, J., E. Bates, M. Johnson, A. Karmiloff-Smith, D. Parisi and K. Plunkett (1996) *Rethinking Innateness: A Connectionist Perspective on Development*. Cambridge, MA: MIT Press.

Elson, N. (1992) Unintelligibility and the ESL learner. In P. Avery and S. Ehrlich *Teaching American English Pronunciation*. Oxford: Oxford University Press.

Ely, C.M. (1989) Tolerance of second language learning and use of language learning strategies. *Foreign Language Annals* 22, 437–445.

English Language Centre (1997) Materials development for real outcomes: A course proposal. Unpublished institutional document, English Language Centre, Durban.

English Language Services (1964) *English 900*. New York: Collier Macmillan.

Ervin, S. and C. Osgood (1965) Second language learning and bilingualism. In C.E. Osgood and T.A. Sebeok (eds) *Psycholinguistics: A Survey of Theory and Research Problems*. Bloomington, IN: Indiana University Press, pp. 139–146.

Eschholz, P., A. Rosa and V. Clark (1990) *Language Awareness*. New York: St Martin's Press.

Eskenazi, M. (1999) Using automatic speech processing for foreign language pronunciation tutoring: Some issues and a prototype. *Language Learning and Technology* 2(2), pp. 62–76. Available: http://llt.msu.edu/vol2num2 [2000, Nov 3].

Eskey, D. (1988) Holding in the Bottom: An interactive approach to the language problems of second language learners. In P. Carrell, J. Devine and D. Eskey (eds) *Interactive Approaches to Second Language Reading*. Cambridge: Cambridge University Press.

Esling, J.H. (1994) Some perspectives on accent: range of voice quality variation, the periphery, and focusing. In J. Morley (ed.) *Pronunciation Pedagogy and Theory: New Views, New Directions*. Alexandria, VA: TESOL.

Esling, J.H. and R.F. Wong (1991) Voice quality settings and the teaching of pronunciation. In A. Brown *Teaching English Pronunciation: A Book of Readings*. London: Routledge. Originally published 1983.

Eubank, L. (ed.) (1991) *Point Counterpoint*. Amsterdam/Philadelphia, PA: John Benjamins.

Evans, K. and J. King (1994) Research on OBE: What we know and what we don't know. *Educational Leadership* 51(6), 12–17.

Everard, K.B. and G. Morris (1996) *Effective School Management*. 3rd edn. London: Paul Chapman.

Ewer, J.R. and G. Latorre (1969) *A Course in Basic Scientific English*. London: Longman.

Færch, K. and G. Kasper (eds) (1987) *Introspection in Second Language Research*. Clevedon: Multilingual Matters.

Fairclough, N. (1989) *Language and Power*. London: Longman.

Fairclough, N. (ed.) (1992) *Critical Language Awareness*. London: Longman.

Fairclough, N. (1995) *Critical Discourse Analysis*. London: Longman.

Fairclough, N. (1997) Discourse across disciplines: discourse analysis in researching social change. *AILA Review* 12, 3–17.

Falsetti, J. (1998) *Welcome to schMOOze University*. Available: http://schmooze.hunter.cuny.edu [2000, Nov 3].

Falsetti, J. and E. Schweitzer (1995) schMOOze University: A MOO for ESL/EFL students. In M. Warschauer (ed.) *Virtual Connections: On-line Activities and Projects for Networking Language Learners*. Honolulu: University of Hawai'i, Second Language Teaching and Curriculum Center.

Fan, Shen (1989) The classroom and the writer culture: Identity as a key to learning English composition. *College Composition and Communication* 40, 459–466.

Fanselow, J.F. (1977) Beyond 'Rashomon': conceptualizing and describing the teaching act. *TESOL Quarterly* 11, 17–39.

Fantini, A.E. (ed.) (1997) *New Ways in Teaching Culture*. Alexandria, VA: TESOL.

Fasold, R. (1984) *An Introduction to Sociolinguistics, Vol. 1: The Sociolinguistics of Society*. Oxford: Blackwell.

Fasold, R. (1990) *An Introduction to Sociolinguistics, Vol. 2: The Sociolinguistics of Language*. Oxford: Blackwell.

Feldman, M. (1995) Import/export e-mail business simulation. In M. Warschauer (ed.) *Virtual Connections:*

Online Activities and Projects for Networking Language Learners. Honolulu, HI: University of Hawai'i, Second Language Teaching and Curriculum Center, pp. 216–217.

Ferguson, C.A. (1959 [1996]) Diglossia. In T. Huebner (ed.) (1996) *Sociolinguistic Perspectives: Papers on Language in Society 1959–1994*, pp. 25–39. Reprinted from *Word* (1959) 15, 325–340.

Ferris, D. (1995) Student reactions to teacher response in multiple-draft composition classrooms. *TESOL Quarterly* 29, 33–53.

Ferris, D. (1997) The influence of teacher commentary on student revision. *TESOL Quarterly* 31(2), 315–339.

Ferris, D. and J. Hedgcock (1998) *Teaching ESL Composition: Purpose, Process, and Practice*. Mahwah, NJ: Lawrence Erlbaum.

Firth, J.R. (1957) *Papers in Linguistics 1934–1951*. Oxford: Oxford University Press.

Fishman, J.A. (1967a) Bilingualism with and without diglossia; diglossia with and without bilingualism. *Journal of Social Issues* 32, 29–38.

Fishman, J.A. (1967b [1970]) Societal bilingualism: stable and transitional. In J.A. Fishman (1970) *Socio-linguistics: A Brief Introduction*. Rowley, MA: Newbury House, pp. 78–89. Reprinted from Bilingualism with and without diglossia: diglossia with and without bilingualism. *Journal of Social Issues* (1967) 23, 29–38.

Fishman, J.A. (1997) Language and ethnicity: The view from within. In F. Coulmas (ed.) *Handbook of Sociolinguistics*. Oxford: Blackwell, pp. 327–343.

Flaitz, J. and Feyten, C. (1996) A two-phase study involving consciousness raising and strategy use for foreign language learners. In R.L. Oxford (ed.) *Language Learning Strategies Around the World*. Manoa: University of Hawai'i Press, pp. 211–226.

Flanders, N. (1970) *Analyzing Teaching Behavior*. Reading, MA: Addison-Wesley.

Flowerdew, J. (1993) An educational, or process, approach to the teaching of professional genres. *ELT Journal* 47, 305–316.

Flowerdew, J. (1994a) *Academic Listening: Research Perspectives*. Cambridge: Cambridge University Press.

Flowerdew, J. (1994b) Research related to second language lecture comprehension: An overview. In J. Flowerdew (ed.) *Academic Listening: Research Perspectives*. Cambridge: Cambridge University Press.

Flowerdew, J., T. Brock and S. Hsia (eds) (1992) *Perspectives on Second Language Teacher Education*. City Polytechnic of Hong Kong: Hong Kong.

Flynn, S. (1989) The role of the head-initial/head-final parameter in the acquisition of English relative clauses by adult Spanish and Japanese speakers. In S. Gass and J. Schachter (eds) *Linguistic Perspectives on Second Language Acquisition*. Cambridge: Cambridge University Press, pp. 89–108.

Foll, D. (1990) *Contrasts Developing Text Awareness*. London: Longman.

Foster, P. (1996) Doing the task better: How planning time influences students' performance. In J. Willis and D. Willis (eds) *Challenge and Change in Language Teaching*. London: Heinemann.

Foster, P. (1998) A classroom perspective on the negotiation of meaning. *Applied Linguistics* 19(1), 1–23.

Foster, P. and P. Skehan (1996) The influence of planning on performance in task-based learning. *Studies in Second Language Acquisition* 18, 299–324.

Fotos, S. and R. Ellis (1991) Communicating about grammar: A task-based approach. *TESOL Quarterly* 25(4), 605–628.

Fox, G. (1998) Using corpus data in the classroom. In B. Tomlinson (ed.) *Materials Development for Language Teaching*. Cambridge: Cambridge University Press, pp. 25–43.

Fox, H. (1994) *Listening to the World: Cultural Issues in Academic Writing*. Urbana, IL: NCTE.

Fradd, S.H. and P.L. McGee (1994) *Instructional Assessment: An Integrative Approach to Evaluating Student Performance*. Reading, MA: Addison-Wesley.

Francis, G. (1993) A corpus-driven approach to grammar: Principles, methods and examples. In M. Baker *et al.* (eds) *Test and Technology*. Amsterdam: Benjamin, pp. 137–156.

Frank, C., M. Rinvolucri and M. Berer (1982) *Challenge to Think*. Oxford: Oxford University Press.

Freedman, A. (1993) Show and tell? The role of explicit teaching in the learning of new genres. *Research in the Teaching of English* 27, 222–251.

Freedman, A. and A. Macdonald (1992) *What is this thing called 'genre'?* Brisbane: Boombana.

Freedman, A. and P. Medway (1994a) (eds) *Genre and the New Rhetoric*. London: Taylor and Francis.

Freedman, A. and P. Medway (1994b) *Learning and Teaching Genre*. Portsmouth, NH: Boynton/Cook.

Freeman, D. (1982) Observing teachers: Three approaches to in-service training and development. *TESOL Quarterly* 16(1), 21–28.

Freeman, D. (1989) Teacher training, development, and decision-making: A model of teaching related strategies for language teacher education. *TESOL Quarterly* 23(1), 27–45.

Freeman, D. (1991) 'To make the tacit explicit': Teacher education, emerging discourse, and conceptions of teaching. *Teaching and Teacher Education* 7(5 and 6), 439–454.

Freeman, D. (1994) Knowing into doing: Teacher education and the problem of transfer. In D.C.S. Li,

D. Mahoney, J.C. Richards (eds) *Exploring Second Language Teacher Development*. City Polytechnic of Hong Kong: Hong Kong.

Freeman, D. (1996a) Redefining the relationship between research and what teachers know. In K. Bailey and D. Nunan (eds) *Voices from the Language Classroom*. New York: Cambridge University Press, pp. 88–115.

Freeman, D. (1996b) The 'unstudied problem': Research on teacher learning in language teaching. In D. Freeman and J.C. Richards (eds) *Teacher Learning in Language Teaching*. New York: Cambridge University Press, pp. 351–378.

Freeman, D. and K. Johnson (1998) Reconceptualizing the knowledge-base of language teacher education. *TESOL Quarterly* 32(3), 397–417.

Freeman, D. and J.C. Richards (eds) (1996) *Teacher Learning in Language Teaching*. New York: Cambridge University Press.

Freeman, R. and B. McElhinny (1996) Language and gender. In S.L. McKay and N.H. Hornberger (eds) *Sociolinguistics and Language Teaching*. Cambridge: Cambridge University Press, pp. 218–280.

Freeman, Y.S. and D.E. Freeman (1993) *Whole Language for Second Language Learners*. Portsmouth, NH: Heinemann.

Freire, P. (1970 [1996]) *Pedagogy of the Oppressed*. New York: Seabury Press. 2nd edn published 1996. London: Penguin.

Fries, C.C. (1952) *The Structure of English: An Introduction to the Structure of English Sentences*. New York: Harcourt Brace.

Fries, P. (1983) On the status of theme in English: arguments from discourse. In J.S. Petöfi and E. Sözer (eds) *Micro and Macro Connexity of Texts*. Hamburg: Helmut Baske.

Fromkin, V. (1993) Speech production. In J. Berko-Gleason and N. Ratner (eds) *Psycholinguistics*. Fort Worth, TX: Harcourt Brace Jovanovich.

Fukuyama, F. (1999) *The Great Disruption: Human Nature and the Reconstitution of Social Order*. Ascot, Berks: Profile Books.

Fulcher, G. (1996a) Testing tasks: Issues in task design and the group oral. *Language Testing* 13(1), 23–52.

Fulcher, G. (1996b) Does thick description lead to smart tests? A data-based approach to rating scale construction. *Language Testing* 13(2), 208–238.

Fullan, M. (1982) *The Meaning of Educational Change*. New York: Teachers College Press.

Fullan, M. (1991) *The New Meaning of Educational Change*. 2nd edn. London: Cassell.

Fullan, M. (1993) *Change Forces: Probing the Depths of Educational Reform*. New York: Falmer Press.

Furneaux, M., G. Locke, P. Robinson and A. Tonkyn (1991) Talking heads and shifting bottoms: The ethnography of academic seminars. In P. Adams, B. Heaton and P. Howarth (eds) *Socio-Cultural Issues in English for Academic Purposes. Developments in ELT*. London: Phoenix ELT.

Gaer, S. (2000) *E-mail Projects Home Page* [Online] (1997) Staff Development Institute (SDI) and the Outreach Technical Assistance Network (OTAN). Available: www.otan.dni.us/webfarm/emailproject/email.htm [2000, Nov 3].

Garcez, P. (1993) Point-making styles in cross-cultural business communication: A microethnographic study. *English for Specific Purposes* 12, 103–120.

Garratt, R. (2000) *The Twelve Organizational Capabilities*. London: HarperCollins Business.

Garrett, P. and C. James (1991) Language awareness: A way ahead. In C. James and P. Garrett (eds) *Language Awareness in the Classroom*. London: Longman, pp. 306–318.

Gass, S. (1982) From theory to practice. In M. Hines and W. Rutherford (eds) *On TESOL 1981*, 129–139. Washington, DC: TESOL.

Gass, S. (1988) Integrating research areas: A framework for second language studies. *Applied Linguistics* 9(2), 198–217.

Gass, S. (1997) *Input, Interaction and the Second Language Learner*. Mahwah, NJ: Lawrence Erlbaum.

Gasser, M. (1990) Connectionism and universals of second language acquisition. *Studies in Second Language Acquisition* 12, 179–199.

Gatbonton, E. and N. Segalowitz (1988) Creative automatization: Principles for promoting fluency within a communicative framework. *TESOL Quarterly* 22(3), 473–492.

Gathercole, S., C. Frankish, S. Pickering and S. Peaker (1999) Phonotactic influences on short-term memory. *Journal of Experimental Psychology* 25, 84–95.

Gebhard, J. (1996) *Teaching English as a Second or Foreign Language: A Self-Development and Methodology Guide*. Ann Arbor, MI: University of Michigan Press.

Geddes, M. (1986) *Fast Forward 3*. Oxford: Oxford University Press.

Geddes, M. and G. Sturtridge (1979) *Listening Links*. London: Heinemann.

Gee, J. (1990) *Social Linguistics and Literacies: Ideology in Discourses*. Bristol, PA: Falmer Press.

Geertz, C. (1973) *The Interpretation of Cultures*. New York: Basic Books.

Genburg, V. (1992) Patterns and organizing perspectives: A view of expertise. *Teaching and Teacher Education* 8(5 and 6), 485–496.

Genesee, F. (1984) French immersion programs. In S. Shapson and V. D'oyley (eds) *Bilingual and Multilingual Education: Canadian Perspectives*. Clevedon: Multilingual Matters.

Genesee, F. and J. Upshur (1996) *Classroom-Based Evaluation in Second Language Education*. Cambridge: Cambridge University Press.

Geoghegan, G. (1983) *Non-Native Speakers of English at Cambridge University*. Cambridge: Bell Educational Trust.

Gilbert, J.B. (1993) *Clear Speech: Pronunciation and Listening Comprehension in American English*. 2nd edn. Cambridge: Cambridge University Press.

Gilbert, J.B. (1994) Intonation: A navigation guide for the listener. In J. Morley (ed.) *Pronunciation Pedagogy and Theory: New Views, New Directions*. Alexandria, VA: TESOL.

Gilbert, J.B. (1995) Pronunciation practice as an aid to listening comprehension. In D. Mendelsohn and J. Rubin (eds) *A Guide for the Teaching of Second Language Listening*. San Diego, CA: Dominie Press. 97–112.

Giroux, H.A. (1994) Literacy and the politics of difference. In C. Lankshear and P. McLaren (eds) *Critical Literacy: Politics, Praxis and the Postmodern*. Albany, NY: State University of New York Press, pp. 367–378.

Giroux, H.A. and P. McLaren (eds) (1994) *Between Borders: Pedagogy and the Politics of Cultural Studies*. New York: Routledge.

Givón, T. (1993) *English Grammar: A Function-Based Introduction*. Amsterdam/Philadelphia, PA: John Benjamins.

Glatter, R., M. Preedy, C. Riches and M. Masterston (eds) (1988) *Understanding School Management*. Milton Keynes: Open University.

Glatthorn, A. (1993) Outcome-based education: Reform and the curriculum process. *Journal of Curriculum and Supervision* 8, 354–363.

Gledhill, C. (2000) The discourse function of collocation in research article introductions. *English for Specific Purposes* 19, 115–136.

Glendinning, E. and B. Holmstrom (1992) *Study Reading*. Cambridge: Cambridge University Press.

Goldstein, L. and S. Conrad (1990) Student input and the negotiation of meaning in ESL writing conferences. *TESOL Quarterly* 24, 443–460.

Golombek, P. (1998) A study of language teachers' personal practical knowledge. *TESOL Quarterly* 32(3), 447–464.

Gomes de Matos, F. (1997) Teachers' intercultural rights: A plea. *FIPLV World News*. October, 1–2.

Goodman, K. (1967) Reading: A psycholinguistic guessing game. *Journal of the Reading Specialist* 6(4), 126–135.

Goodman, K. (1997) Whole language: The whole story. In L. van Lier and D. Corson (eds) *Encyclopedia of Language and Education, Vol. 6: Knowledge About Language*, pp. 87–97. Dordrecht: Kluwer Academic.

Gopal, R.N. (1999) Learning strategies of Malaysian ESL learners. In R. Oxford (ed.) *Language Learning Strategies in the Context of Autonomy: Strategy Research Compendium: Proceedings of the First Annual Strategy Research Symposium, Teachers College*. New York: Columbia University, pp. 26–27.

Goshgarian, G. (1997) *Exploring Language*. 8th edn. New York: Addison-Wesley.

Goss, N., Z. Ying-Hua and J. Lantolf (1994) Two heads may be better than one: Mental activity in second-language grammaticality judgements. In E. Tarone, S. Gass and A.D. Cohen (eds) *Research Methodology in Second Language Acquisition*. Hillsdale, NJ: Lawrence Erlbaum, pp. 263–286.

Goulding, S., J. Bell, T. Bush, A. Fox and J. Goodey (eds) (1984) *Case Studies in Educational Management*. London: Harper Education Series.

Grabe, W. and R.B. Kaplan (eds) (1996) *Theory and Practice of Writing: An Applied Linguistics Perspective*. New York: Longman.

Grabe, W. and R.B. Kaplan (1997) The writing course. In K. Bardovi-Harlig and B. Hartford (eds) *Beyond Methods: Components of Second Language Teacher Education*. New York: McGraw Hill, pp. 172–197.

Graddol, D. (1997) *The Future of English?* London: The British Council.

Graddol, D. and J. Swann (1989) *Gender Voices*. Oxford: Blackwell.

Graham, C. (1978) *Jazz Chants*. Oxford: Oxford University Press.

Gray, B. and C. Cazden (1992) Concentrated Language Encounters: The International Biography of a Curriculum Concept. Joint Plenary, 26th Annual TESOL Convention, Vancouver, BC.

Green, C. (1999) Strategy development in Reading Recovery. In R. Oxford (ed.) *Language Learning Strategies in the Context of Autonomy: Strategy Research Compendium: Proceedings of the First Annual Strategy Research Symposium, Teachers College*. New York: Columbia University, pp. 28–29.

Greenwood, J. (1989) *Class Readers*. Oxford: Oxford University Press.

Gregory, E. (1996) *Making Sense of a New World: Learning to Read in a Second Language*. London: Paul Chapman.

Grellet, F. (1996) *Writing for Advanced Learners*. Cambridge: Cambridge University Press.

Grimes, J. (1975) *The Thread of Discourse*. The Hague: Mouton.

Grosjean, F. (1992) Another view of bilingualism. In R.J. Harris (ed.) *Cognitive Processing in Bilinguals*. Amsterdam: North-Holland, pp. 51–62.

Grossman, P. (1990) *The Making of A Teacher: Teacher Knowledge and Teacher Education*. New York: Teachers College Press.

Grozdanova, L., M. Georgieva, M. Nedkova, N. Mladenova and D. Veselinova (1996) *A World of English*. Sofia: Lettera.

Gruba, P. and C. Corbel (1997) Computer-based testing. In C. Clapham and D. Corson (eds) (1997) *Encyclopedia of Language and Education, Vol. 7: Language Testing and Assessment*. Dordrecht: Kluwer Academic, pp. 141–149.

Grundy, P. (1993) Student and supervisor perceptions of the role of English in academic success. In G.M. Blue (ed.) *Language, Learning and Success: Studying through English: Review of ELT 3(1)*. London: Phoenix ELT.

Gudykunst, W.B. (ed.) (1983) *Intercultural Communication Theory*. Beverly Hills, CA: Sage.

Gudykunst, W.B. (1993) *Communication in Japan and the United States*. Albany: SUNY Press.

Guiora, A. (1972) Construct validity and transpositional research: toward an empirical study of psycho-analytic concepts. *Comprehensive Psychiatry* 13(2), 139–150.

Guiora, A., R. Brannon and C. Dull (1972) Empathy and second language learning. *Language Learning* 22, 111–130.

Gumperz, J.J. (ed.) (1982) *Language and Social Identity*. Cambridge: Cambridge University Press.

Gumperz, J.J. and D. Hymes (eds) (1972) *Directions in Sociolinguistics: The Ethnography of Communication*. New York: Rinehart and Winston.

Gumperz, J.J. and S.C. Levinson (eds) (1996) *Re-thinking Linguistic Relativity*. Cambridge: Cambridge University Press.

Gunning, P. (1997) The learning strategies of beginning ESL learners at the primary level. Unpublished Master's thesis, Concordia University, Montreal.

Hadfield, J. and C. Hadfield (2000) *Simple Writing*. Oxford: Oxford University Press.

Hafner, K. and M. Lyon (1996) *Where Wizards Stay Up Late: The Origins of the Internet*. New York: Simon and Schuster.

Hale, G., C. Taylor, B. Bridgeman, J. Carson, B. Kroll and R. Kantor (1996) *A Study of Writing Tasks Assigned in Academic Degree Programs*. TOEFL Research Report 54. Princeton, NJ: Educational Testing Service.

Hall, D. (1995) Materials production: theory and practice. In A.C. Hidalgo, D. Hall and G.M. Jacobs (eds) *Getting Started: Materials Writers on Materials Writing*. Singapore: SEAMEO Regional Language Centre, pp. 8–24.

Hall, E.T. (1959) *The Silent Language*. New York: Doubleday.

Hall, E.T. (1966) *The Hidden Dimension*. Garden City, NY: Doubleday.

Hall, E.T. (1981) *Beyond Culture*. Garden City, NY: Anchor Books.

Hall, G.M. (1999) Awareness, response and what might lie beyond: A critical linguistic perspective on literature as a social practice and the implications of this perspective for the use of literature in education. Special issue of *Language Awareness* 8(1), 3–14.

Halliday, M.A.K. (1978) *Language as Social Semiotic: The Social Interpretation of Language and Meaning*. London: Edward Arnold.

Halliday, M.A.K. (1994) *An Introduction to Functional Grammar*. 2nd edn. London: Edward Arnold.

Halliday, M.A.K. and R. Hasan (1976) *Cohesion in English*. London: Longman.

Halliday, M.A.K. and R. Hasan (1985) *Language, Context and Text: Aspects of Language in a Social Semiotic Perspective*. Geelong, Victoria: Deakin University Press.

Hamayan, E. (1995) Approaches to alternative assessment. *Annual Review of Applied Linguistics* 15, 212–226.

Hamers, J.F. and M. Blanc (2000) *Bilinguality and Bilingualism*. 2nd edn. 1st edn published 1989. 1st published in French 1983. Cambridge: Cambridge University Press.

Hammersley, M. (1986) Revisiting Hamilton and Delamont: A cautionary note on the relationship between 'systematic observation' and ethnography. In M. Hammersley (ed.) *Controversies in Classroom Research*. Milton Keynes: Open University Press, pp. 44–48.

Hammersley, M. (1990) *Classroom Ethnography*. Milton Keynes: Open University Press.

Hammond, J. and M. Macken-Horarik (1999) Critical literacy: Challenges for ESL classrooms. *TESOL Quarterly* 33(3), 528–544.

Hammond, J., A. Burns, H. Joyce, D. Brosnan and L. Gerot (1992) *English for Social Purposes: A Handbook for Teachers of Adult Literacy*, Sydney: National Centre for English Language Teaching and Research, Macquarie University.

Hamp-Lyons, E. (ed.) (1991) *Assessing Second Language Writing in Academic Contexts*. Norwood, NJ: Ablex.

Hamp-Lyons, E. (1994) Emerging academic literacy: exclusions and solutions. In *Prospect: Journal of Australian TESOL* 9(3), 58–62.

Hamp-Lyons, E. (1995) Rating non-native writing: The trouble with holistic scoring. *TESOL Quarterly* 29, 759–762.

Hamp-Lyons, E. (1996) Applying ethical standards to portfolio assessment of writing in English as a second language. In M. Milanovich and N. Saville, *Studies in Language Tests 3: Performance Testing, Cognition, and Assessment*. Cambridge: Cambridge University Press.

Hamp-Lyons, E. (1997) The challenges of second-language writing assessment. In E. White, W. Lutz and S. Kamasukiri (eds) *The Politics and Policies of Assessment in Writing*. New York: Modern Language Association, pp. 226–240.

Hamp-Lyons, E. (1998) Ethics in language testing. In C. Clapham and D. Corson (eds) (1997) *Encyclopedia of Language and Education, Vol. 7: Language Testing and Assessment*. Dordrecht: Kluwer Academic, pp. 323–333.

Hamp-Lyons, E. and B. Heasley (1987) *Study Writing*. Cambridge: Cambridge University Press.

Hamp-Lyons, E. and B. Kroll (1996) Issues in ESL writing assessment: An overview. *College ESL* 6, 52–72.

Hamp-Lyons, E. and B. Kroll (1997) *TOEFL 2000 Writing: Composition, Community, and Assessment*. TOEFL Monographic Series MS-5. Princeton, NJ: Educational Testing Service.

Hancock, M. (1996) *Pronunciation Games*. Cambridge: Cambridge University Press.

Hancock, M. (1997) Behind classroom code switching: Layering and language choice in L2 learner interaction. *TESOL Quarterly* 31(2), 217–235.

Handy, C. (1999) *Understanding Organizations*. 4th edn. London: Penguin.

Hanson-Smith, E. (1997a) Multimedia projects for EFL/ESL students. *CAELL Journal* 7(4), 3–12.

Hanson-Smith, E. (1997b) *Technology in the Classroom: Practice and Promise in the Twenty-first Century*. TESOL Professional Papers 2. Alexandria, VA: TESOL.

Hanson-Smith, E. (ed.) (2000) *Technology-Enhanced Learning Environments*. Alexandria, VA: TESOL. Available: www.tesol.edu

Harding, E. and P. Riley (1986) *The Bilingual Family: A Handbook for Parents*. Cambridge: Cambridge University Press.

Harley, B. (1988) Effects of instruction on SLA: Issues and evidence. *Annual Review of Applied Linguistics* 9, 165–178.

Harley, B., P. Allen, J. Cummins and M. Swain (1990) *The Development of Bilingual Proficiency*. Cambridge: Cambridge University Press.

Harley, T. (1995) *The Psychology of Language: From Data to Theory*. East Sussex: Psychology Press.

Harnad, S. (1991) Post-Gutenberg galaxy: The fourth revolution in the means of production and knowledge. *Public-Access Computer Systems Review* 2(1), 39–53.

Harris, J. (1993) *Introducing Writing*. London: Penguin.

Harris, R.J. (ed.) (1992) *Cognitive Processing in Bilinguals*. Amsterdam: North-Holland Elsevier.

Harrison, B. (ed.) (1990) *Culture and the Language Classroom*. London: British Council.

Hasan, R. (1984) Coherence and cohesive harmony. In J. Flood (ed.) *Understanding Reading Comprehension*. Newark, Delaware: International Reading Association, 181–219.

Hasan, R. (1985) The structure of a text. In M.A.K. Halliday and R. Hasan *Language, Context and Text: Aspects of Language in a Social-Semiotic Perspective*. Oxford: Oxford University Press, 52–69.

Hasan, R. (1996) Literacy, everyday talk and society. In R. Hasan and G. Williams (eds) *Literacy in Society*. London: Longman.

Hasan, R. and J. Martin (eds) (1989) *Language Development: Learning Language, Learning Culture*. Norwood, NJ: Ablex.

Hatch, E. (1978) Discourse analysis in second language acquisition. In E. Hatch (ed.) *Second Language Acquisition: A Book of Readings*. Rowley, MA: Newbury House, pp. 402–435.

Hatch, E. (1992) *Discourse and Language Education*. Cambridge: Cambridge University Press.

Hatch, T. (1998) The differences in theory that matter in the practices of school improvement. *American Educational Research Journal* 35(1), 3–31.

Hawkins, E. (1987a) *Awareness of Language: An Introduction*. 2nd edn. Cambridge: Cambridge University Press.

Hawkins, E. (1987b) *Modern Languages in the Curriculum*. 2nd edn. Cambridge: Cambridge University Press.

Heath, S.B. (1983) *Ways with Words: Language, Life and Work in Communities and Classrooms*. Cambridge: Cambridge University Press.

Heath, S.B. (1993) Inner city life through drama: Imagining the language classroom. *TESOL Quarterly* 27, 177–192.

Heath, S.B. (1998) Interpreting interpretation: New perspectives on bilingualism, culture and cognition. Plenary address delivered at the annual AAAL Conference, Seattle, WA.

Hedgcock, J. and N. Lefkowitz (1996) Some input on input: Two analyses of student response to expert feedback in L2 writing. *Modern Language Journal* 80, 287–308.

Hedge, T. (1988) *Writing*. Oxford: Oxford University Press.

Heinemann International Guide for Writers (1991) Oxford: Heinemann.

Helgesen, M., S. Brown and J. Kahny (1999) *English Firsthand: Gold Edition*. London: Longman.

Henderson, W., T. Dudley-Evans and R. Backhouse (1993) *Economics and Language*. Cambridge: Cambridge University Press.

Henry, A.R. (1993) *Second Language Rhetorics in Process: A Comparison of Arabic, Chinese, and Spanish*. New York: Peter Lang.

Herbst, T. (1996) On the way to the perfect learners' dictionary: A first comparison of OALD5, LDOCE3, COBUILD2 and CIDE. *International Journal of Lexicography* 9(4), 321–357.

Heritage, J. and D. Watson (1979) Formulations as conversational objects. In G. Psathas (ed.) *Everyday Language*. New York: Irvington Press, 123–162.

Heron, J. (1988) Assessment revisited. In D. Boud (ed.) *Developing Student Autonomy in Learning*. New York: Kogan Page, pp. 77–90.

Heusinkveld, P.R. (ed.) (1996) *Pathways to Culture. Readings on Teaching Culture in the Foreign Language Class*. Intercultural Press.

Hewings, M. (1993) *Pronunciation Tasks*. Cambridge: Cambridge University Press.

Hidalgo, A.C., D. Hall and G.M. Jacobs (eds) (1995) *Getting Started: Materials Writers on Materials Writing*. Singapore: SEAMEO Regional Language Centre.

Higgins, J. and T. Johns (1984) *Computers in language learning*. London: Collins ELT and Addison-Wesley.

Hill, C. and K. Parry (eds) (1994) *From Testing to Assessment: English as an International Language*. London: Longman.

Hill, R. (1992) Criteria for the selection of literary texts. In D.A. Hill (ed.) *The State of the Art*. London: Modern English Publications / The British Council.

Hoey, M. (1983) *On the Surface of Discourse*. London: Allen and Unwin.

Hoey, M. (1991) Some properties of spoken discourses. In R. Bowers and C.J. Brumfit (eds) *Applied Linguistics and English Language Teaching*. London: Modern English Publications / Macmillan / The British Council, pp. 65–84.

Hoffman, C. (1991) *An Introduction to Bilingualism*. New York: Longman.

Hofstede, G. (1983) Dimensions of national culture in 50 countries and three regions. In J.B. Deregowski, S. Dziurawiec and R.C. Annis (eds) *Explications in Cross-Cultural Psychology*. Lisse: Swets and Zeitlinger.

Hofstede, G. (1986) Cultural differences in learning and teaching. *International Journal of Intercultural Relations* 10, 301–320.

Holec, H. (1981) *Autonomy and Foreign Language Learning*. Oxford: Pergamon.

Holec, H. (1985) On autonomy: Some elementary concepts. In P. Riley (ed.) *Discourse and Learning*. New York: Longman.

Holley, F. and J.K. King (1974) Imitation and correction in foreign language learning. In J.H. Schumann and N. Stenson (eds) *New Frontiers in Second Language Learning*: Rowley, MA: Newbury House, pp. 81–89.

Holliday, A. (1994) *Appropriate Methodology*. Cambridge: Cambridge University Press.

Holliday, A. and T. Cooke (1982) An ecological approach to ESP. *Lancaster Practical Papers in English Language Education, Vol. 5: Issues in ESP*. Lancaster: English Language Research, University of Lancaster.

Holliday, L. (1993) Negotiations as a source of positive data for acquisition of L2 syntax. Paper presented at The Second Language Acquisition Forum, Pittsburgh, PA.

Holliday, L. (1995) International ESL/EFL email student discussion lists for language practice with a purpose and a peer audience. Paper presented at the Thai TESOL Fifteenth Annual convention, Bangkok, Thailand.

Holliday, L. (1998) The grammar of second language learners of English email messages. In J. Nerbonne (ed.) *Proceedings of Language Teaching and Language Technology Conference*. Groningen: Swets and Zeitlinger.

Holliday, L. (1999) Theory and research: Input, interaction and CALL. In J. Egbert and E. Hanson-Smith (eds) *CALL Environments: Research, Practice and Critical Issues*. Alexandria, VA: TESOL, pp. 181–188.

Holmes, J. (1992) *An Introduction to Sociolinguistics*. London: Longman.

Honikman, B. (1991) Articulatory settings. In A. Brown (ed.) *Teaching English Pronunciation: A Book of Readings*. London: Routledge. Originally published 1964.

Hopper, P. and S. Thompson (1980) Transitivity in grammar and discourse. *Language* 56, 251–299.

Horwitz, E. and D. Young (eds) (1991) *Language Anxiety: From Theory and Research to Classroom Implications*. Englewood Cliffs, NJ: Prentice Hall.

Horwitz, E., M. Horwitz and J. Cope (1991) Foreign language classroom anxiety. In E. Horwitz and D. Young (eds) *Language Anxiety: From Theory and Research to Classroom Implications*. Englewood Cliffs, NJ: Prentice Hall.

Hosenfeld, C. (1977) A preliminary investigation of the reading strategies of successful and non-successful second language learners. *System* 5, 110–123.

Hosenfeld, C. (1984) Case Studies of ninth grade readers. In J.C. Alderson and A.H. Urquhart (eds) *Reading in a Foreign Language*. London: Longman.

Houghton, V., R. McHugh and C. Morgan (eds) (1975) *Management in Education*. London: Ward Lock.

Howatt, A.P.R. (1984) *A History of English Language Teaching*. Oxford: Oxford University Press.

Hozayen, G. (1994) A study of the discussion section of the medical research article: A genre based approach to text analysis. Unpublished PhD thesis, University of Birmingham.

Huberman, M. (1993) *The Lives of Teachers*. New York: Teachers College Press.

Huckin, T., M. Haynes and J. Coady (eds) (1993) *Second Language Reading and Vocabulary Learning*. Norwood, NJ: Lawrence Erlbaum.

Hudelson, S. and J. Lindfors (eds) (1993) *Delicate Balance: Collaborative Research In Language Education*. Urbana, IL: National Council of Teachers of English.

Hudson, R.A. (1996) *Sociolinguistics*. 2nd edn. Cambridge: Cambridge University Press.

Hughes, A. (1989) *Testing for Language Teachers*. Cambridge: Cambridge University Press.

Hughes, R. and M.J. McCarthy (1998) From sentence to discourse: Discourse grammar and English language teaching. *TESOL Quarterly* 32, 263–287.

Hulstijn, J. (1992) Retention of inferred and given word meanings: Experiments in incidental vocabulary learning. In P. Arnaud and H. Béjoint (eds) *Vocabulary and Applied Linguistics*. Basingstoke: Macmillan, pp. 113–125.

Hulstijn, J.H. (2000) The use of computer technology in experimental studies of second language acquisition: A survey of some techniques and ongoing studies. *Language Learning and Technology* 3(2), 32–43. Available: http://llt.msu.edu/vol3num2 [2000, Nov 3].

Hunston, S., G. Francis and E. Manning (1997) Grammar and vocabulary: showing the connections. *ELT Journal* 51(3), pp. 208–216.

Hutchinson, T. (1997) *Lifelines Pre-Intermediate*. Oxford: Oxford University Press.

Hutchinson, T. and E. Torres (1994) The textbook as agent of change. *ELT Journal* 48(4), 315–328.

Hutchinson, T. and A. Waters (1987) *English for Specific Purposes*. Cambridge: Cambridge University Press.

Hyland, F. (1998) The impact of teacher-written feedback on individual writers. *Journal of Second Language Writing* 7(3), 255–286.

Hyland, K. (1994) Hedging in academic writing and EAP textbooks. *English for Specific Purposes* 13(3), 239–256.

Hyland, K. (1998) *Hedging in Scientific Research Articles*. Amsterdam: Benjamins.

Hyland, K. (2000) Disciplinary discourses: Writer stance in research articles. In C.N. Candlin and K. Hyland (eds) *Writing: Texts, Processes and Practices*. London: Longman.

Hymes, D. (1962 [1968]) The ethnography of speaking. In J.A. Fishman (ed.) (1968) *Readings in the Sociology of Language*. The Hague: Mouton, pp. 99–138. Reprinted from T. Gladwin and W.C. Sturtevant (eds) (1962) *Anthropology and Human Behavior*. Washington, DC: Anthropology Society of Washington, pp. 13–53.

Hymes, D. (1964) Towards ethnographies of communication. In J.J. Gumperz and D. Hymes (eds) *The Ethnography of Communication. American Anthropologist* 66(6), 1–34.

Hymes, D. (1971 [1972, 1979]) *On Communicative Competence*. Philadelphia, PA: University of Pennsylvania Press. Also published as On communicative competence. In J.B. Pride and J. Holmes (eds) *Sociolinguistics: Selected Readings*. London: Penguin Books, pp. 269–293. Also in C.J. Brumfit and K. Johnson (eds) *The Communicative Approach to Language Teaching* (1979). Oxford: Oxford University Press, pp. 5–26.

Hymes, D. (1974) *Foundations in Sociolinguistics: An Ethnographic approach*. Philadelphia, PA: University of Pennsylvania Press.

Hyon, S. (1996) Genre in three traditions: Implications for ESL. *TESOL Quarterly* 30(4), 693–722.

ILEA (1990) *Language and Power: Afro-Caribbean Language and Literacy Project in Further and Adult Education*. London: Harcourt Brace Jovanovich.

Impey, G. and N. Underhill (1994) *The ELT Manager's Handbook*. Oxford: Heinemann.

Ioup, G. and S. Weinberger (eds) (1987) *Interlanguage Phonology: The Acquisition of a Second Language Sound System*. Cambridge, MA: Newbury House.

Ioup, G., E. Boustagui, M. El Tigi and M. Moselle (1994) Reexamining the critical period hypothesis. *Studies in Second Language Acquisition* 16, 73–98.

Iran-Nejad, A., R. Oxford and Y. Kawai (forthcoming) Sources of internal self-regulation with a focus on language learning. *Journal of Mind and Behavior*, special issue 'Knowledge and Self-Regulation'.

Ivanič, R. (1998) *Writing and Identity: The Discoursal Construction of Identity in Academic Writing*. Amsterdam: John Benjamins.

Jacobs, B. and J. Schumann (1992) Language acquisition and the neurosciences: Towards a more integrative perspective. *Applied Linguistics* 13(3), 282–301.

Jaeglin, C. (1998) Learners' and instructors' attitudes towards computer-assisted class discussion. In J. Swaffar, S. Romano, P. Markley and K. Arens (eds) *Language learning online: Theory and practice in the ESL and L2 computer classroom*. Austin, TX: Labyrinth Publications/Daedalus Group, pp. 121–138.

Jakobsdottir, S. and S. Hooper (1995) Computer-assisted foreign language learning: Effects of text, context, and gender on listening comprehension and motivation. *Educational Technology Research and Development* 43(4), 43–59. Also available as ERIC Document EJ 516544.

Jakobson, R. (1931) Über die phonologischen Sprachbunde. *Travaux du Cercle Linguistique de Prague* 4, 234–240.

James, C. and P. Garrett (eds) (1991) *Language Awareness in the Classroom*. London: Longman, pp. 306–318.

Janks, H. (1993) *Critical Language Awareness Series*. Johannesburg: Hodder and Stoughton and Wits University Press.

Janks, H. (1997) Teaching language and power. In R. Wodak and D. Corson (eds) *Encyclopedia of Language and Education, Vol. 1: Language Policy and Political Issues in Education*. Dordrecht: Kluwer Academic, pp. 241–251.

Janzen, J. and F. Stoller (1998) Integrating strategic reading in L2 instruction. *Reading in a Foreign Language* 12(1), 251–269.

Jarvis, J. and M. Robinson (1997) Analysing educational discourse: An exploratory study of teacher response and support to pupils' learning. *Applied Linguistics* 18(2), 212–228.

Jefferson, G. (1978) Sequential aspects of storytelling in conversation. In J. Schenkein (ed.) *Studies in the Organisation of Conversational Interaction*. New York: Academic Press, 219–248.

Jenkins, J. (1998) Which pronunciation norms and models for English as an International Language? *ELT Journal* 52(2), 119–126.

Jenkins, J. (2000) *The Phonology of English as an International Language*. Oxford: Oxford University Press.

Johns, A. (1991) English for specific purposes: Its history and contributions. In M. Celce-Murcia (ed.) *Teaching English as a Second or Foreign Language*. Boston, MA: Heinle and Heinle.

Johns, A. (1992) Toward developing a cultural repertoire: A case study of Lao freshmen. In D. Murray (ed.) *Diversity as a Resource: Redefining Cultural Literacy*. Arlington, VA: TESOL, pp. 183–201.

Johns, A. (1997) *Text, Role and Context*. New York: Cambridge University Press.

Johns, A. (ed.) (2000) *Genre in the Classroom*. Hillsdale, NJ: Lawrence Erlbaum.

Johns, A. and T. Dudley-Evans (1993) English for specific purposes: International in scope, specific in purpose. *TESOL Quarterly* 25, 297–314.

Johns, A. and P. King (eds) (1991) Classroom concordancing. *English Language Research Journal* 4, 1–16.

Johns, T.F. (1991a) From Printout to Handout: Grammar and Vocabulary Teaching in the Context of Data-driven Learning. In T.F. Johns and P. King (eds) *Birmingham University English Language Research Journal, Vol. 4: Classroom Concordancing*. Birmingham: University of Birmingham.

Johns, T.F. (1991b) Should you be persuaded: Two examples of data-driven learning. In T.F. Johns and P. King (eds) *Birmingham University English Language Research Journal, Vol. 4: Classroom Concordancing*. Birmingham: University of Birmingham.

Johnson, D.W. and R. Johnson (eds) (1998) *Encyclopaedic Dictionary of Applied Linguistics*. London: Blackwell.

Johnson, K. (1988) Mistake correction. *ELT Journal* 42(2), 89–96.

Johnson, K. (1989) A decision-making framework for the coherent language curriculum. In R.K. Johnson (ed.) *The Second Language Curriculum*. Cambridge: Cambridge University Press, pp. 1–23.

Johnson, K. (1995) *Understanding Communication in Second Language Classrooms*. New York: Cambridge University Press.

Johnson, K. (1996a) Cognitive apprenticeship in second language teacher education. In G. Sachs, M. Brock and R. Lo (eds) *Directions in Second Language Teacher Education*. City University of Hong Kong: Hong Kong, pp. 23–36.

Johnson, K. (1996b) *Skill Learning and Language Teaching*. Oxford: Blackwell.

Johnson, K. (1996c) The vision vs. the reality: The tensions of the TESOL practicum. In D. Freeman and J.C. Richards (eds) *Teacher Learning in Language Teaching*. New York: Cambridge University Press, pp. 30–49.

Johnson, K. (1999) *Understanding Language Teaching: Reasoning in Action*. Boston, MA: Heinle and Heinle.

Johnson, K. and G. Johnson (1999) *Teachers Understanding Teaching*. Boston, MA: Heinle and Heinle.

Johnson, S. and U.H. Meinhof (eds) (1997) *Language and Masculinity*. Oxford: Blackwell.

Johnston, B. (1997) Do EFL teachers have careers? *TESOL Quarterly* 31(4), 681–712.

Johnston, B. and S. Peterson (1994) The program matrix: A conceptual framework for language programs. *System* 22(1), 63–80.

Johnston, M. and K. Goettsch (1999) In search of the knowledge base of language teaching: Explanations by experienced teachers. Paper presented at the American Association of Applied Linguistics, Stamford, CT, March.

Jolly, D. and R. Bolitho (1998) A framework for materials writing. In B. Tomlinson (ed.) *Materials Development for Language Teaching*. Cambridge: Cambridge University Press, pp. 90–115.

Jor, G. (1995) Web newsletter 1995: A collaborative learning project for technical writing instruction. In M. Warschauer (ed.) *Virtual Connections: Online Activities and Projects for Networking Language Learners*. Honolulu, HI: University of Hawai'i, Second Language Teaching and Curriculum Center, pp. 368–374.

Jordan, R.R. (1997) *English for Academic Purposes: A Guide and Resource Book for Teachers*. Cambridge: Cambridge University Press.

Joseph, F. and T. Travers (1996) *Candidate for CAE*. London: Phoenix ELT.

Journal of Second Language Writing. Norword, NJ: Ablex.

Joyce, B. and B. Showers (1982) The coaching of teaching. *Educational Leadership* 40(1), 4–8, 10.

Joyce, B. and B. Showers (1987) Low-cost arrangements for peer-coaching. *Journal of Staff Development* 8(1), 22–24.

Jusczyk, P. (1997) *The Discovery of Spoken Language*. Cambridge, MA: MIT Press.

Kachru, B. (1990) *The Alchemy of English*. Urbana, IL: University of Illinois Press.

Kalaja, P. and S. Leppänen (1998) Towards discursive social psychology of second language learning: The case of motivation. In J. Fisiak (ed.) *Festschrift for Kari Sajavaara on his sixtieth birthday*. Poznan: Studia Anglica Posananiensia 33, pp. 165–180.

Kaplan, R.B. (1966) Cultural thought patterns in intercultural education. *Language Learning* 16(1), 1–20.

Kaplan, R.B. (1988) Contrastive rhetoric and second language learning: Notes toward a theory of contrastive rhetoric. In A. Purves (ed.) *Writing Across Languages and Cultures*, pp. 275–304. Newbury Park, CA: Sage.

Kaplan, R.B. and W. Grabe (1996) *Theory and Practice of Writing*. London: Longman.

Kasper, G. (1984) Pragmatic comprehension in learner-native speaker discourse. *Language Learning* 34, 1–20.

Katzner, K. (1986) *The Languages of the World*. 2nd edn. London: Routledge.

Keatley, C.W. (1992) History of bilingualism research in cognitive psychology. In R.J. Harris (ed.) *Cognitive Processing in Bilinguals*. Amsterdam: North-Holland Elsevier, pp. 15–49.

Keenan, E.O. (1974) Norm-makers, norm-breakers: Uses of speech by men and women in a Malagasy community. In R. Bauman and J. Sherzer (eds) *Explorations in the Ethnography of Speaking*. Cambridge: Cambridge University Press, pp. 125–143.

Kelm, O. (1992) The use of synchronous computer networks in second language instruction: A Preliminary Report. *Foreign Language Annals* 25(5), 441–454.

Kemmis, S. and R. McTaggart (1988) *The Action Research Planner*. Geelong, Victoria: Deakin University Press.

Kendall, C. (1995) Cyber-surveys. In M. Warschauer (ed.) *Virtual Connections: Activities and Projects for Networking Language Learners*. Honolulu, HI: University of Hawai'i, Second Language Teaching and Curriculum Center, pp. 97–100.

Kennedy, C. (1983) Exploiting a text. In S. Holden (ed.) *Second Selections from Modern English Teacher*. London: Longman, pp. 65–67.

Kennedy, M. (1990) *A Survey of Recent Literature on Teachers' Subject Matter Knowledge*. East Lansing, MI: National Center for Research on Teacher Learning.

Kennedy, M. (1991) *An Agenda for Research on Teacher Learning*. East Lansing, MI: National Center for Research on Teacher Learning.

Kenworthy, J. (1987) *Teaching English Pronunciation*. London: Longman.

Kern, R. (1995a) Découvrir Berkeley: Students' representation of their world on the world wide web. In M. Warschauer (ed.) *Virtual Connections: Activities and Projects for Networking Language Learners*. Honolulu, HI: University of Hawai'i, Second Language Teaching and Curriculum Center, pp. 355–356.

Kern, R. (1995b) Restructuring classroom interaction with networked computers: Effects on quantity and quality of language production. *Modern Language Journal* 79(4), 457–476.

Kern, R. (1996) Computer-mediated communication: Using e-mail exchanges to explore personal histories in two cultures. In M. Warschauer (ed.) *Telecollaboration in Foreign Language Learning*. Honolulu, HI: University of Hawai'i, Second Language Teaching and Curriculum Center, pp. 105–119.

Kesner Bland, S. (1988) The present progressive in discourse: Grammar versus usage revisited. *TESOL Quarterly* 22(1), 53–68.

Kim, H.-Y. (1995) Input from the speech stream: Speech elements that learners attend to. In R. Schmidt (ed.) *Attention and Awareness in Foreign Language Learning*. Honolulu, HI: University of Hawai'i Press.

Kleinsasser, R. and S. Savignon (1992) Linguistics, language pedagogy, and teachers' technical cultures. In J.E. Alatis (ed.) *Linguistics and Language Pedagogy: The State of the Art*. Georgetown University Roundtable on Languages and Linguistics: Georgetown University Press, pp. 289–301.

Klippel, F. (1984) *Keep Talking*. Cambridge: Cambridge University Press.

Kormos, J. (1999) Monitoring and self-repair in L2. *Language Learning* 49, 303–342.

Kramsch, C.J. (1993) *Context and Culture in Language Teaching*. Oxford: Oxford University Press.

Kramsch, C.J. (1998) *Language and Culture*. Oxford Introductions to Language Study. Oxford: Oxford University Press.

Kramsch, C.J. and W.-S.E. Lam (1998) Textual identities: The importance of being non-native. In G. Braine (ed.) *Non-Native Educators in English Language Teaching*. Mahwah, NJ: Lawrence Erlbaum, pp. 57–72.

Krashen, S. (1982) *Principles and Practice in Second Language Acquisition*. Oxford: Pergamon.

Krashen, S. (1985) *The Input Hypothesis*. Oxford: Oxford University Press.

Krashen, S. (1988) *Second Language Acquisition and Second Language Learning*. 2nd edn. Oxford: Prentice Hall / Pergamon.

Krashen, S. (1989) We acquire vocabulary and spelling by reading: Additional evidence for the input hypothesis. *Modern Language Journal* 73, pp. 445–464.

Krashen, S. (1992) Formal grammar instruction: An educator comments. *TESOL Quarterly* 26, 409–411.

Krashen, S. (1994) The input hypothesis and its rivals. In N. Ellis (ed.) (1994) *Implicit and Explicit Learning of Languages*. London: Academic Press, pp. 45–77.

Krashen, S. and T. Terrell (1983) *The Natural Approach*. Oxford: Pergamon.

Kress, G. (1990) Critical discourse analysis. *Annual Review of Applied Linguistics* 11, 84–99.

Kress, G. (1994) *Learning to Write*. 2nd edn. London: Routledge.

Kroeber, A.L. and C. Kluckhohn (1952) *Culture: A Critical Review of Concepts and Definitions*. New York: Vintage Books.

Kroll, B. (ed.) (1990) *Second Language Writing: Research Insights for the Classroom*. Cambridge: Cambridge University Press.

Kroll, B. (1998) Assessing writing abilities. *Annual Review of Applied Linguistics* 18, 219–240.

Kunnan, A. (1997) Connecting fairness with validation in language assessment. In A. Huhta, V. Kohonen, L. Kurki-Suonio and S. Luoma (eds) *Current Developments and Alternatives in Language Assessment*. Jyväskylä: Centre for Applied Language Studies, University of Jyväskylä, pp. 85–106.

Kuo, C.H. (1993) Problematic issues in EST materials development. *English for Specific Purposes* 12, 171–181.

Labov, W. (1966) *The Social Stratification of English in New York City*. Washington, DC: Center for Applied Linguistics.

Labov, W. (1972a) *Language in the Inner City*. Philadelphia, PA: University of Pennsylvania Press.

Labov, W. (1972b) Some principles of linguistic methodology. *Language in Society* 1, 97–120.

Labov, W. (1972c [1963]) The social motivation of a sound change. In W. Labov, *Sociolinguistic Patterns*. Philadelphia, PA: University of Pennsylvania Press, pp. 1–42. Reprinted from *Word* (1963) 19, 273–309.

Labov, W. (1972d) *Sociolinguistic Patterns*. Philadelphia, PA: University of Pennsylvania Press, pp. 122–159.

Labov, W. (1982) Objectivity and commitment in linguistic science: The case of the Black English trial in Ann Arbor. *Language in Society* 11, 165–201.

Lackstrom, J.E., L. Selinker and L. Trimble (1973) Technical rhetorical principles and grammatical choice. *TESOL Quarterly* 7, 127–136.

Ladefoged, P. (1993) *A Course in Phonetics*. 3rd edn. Fort Worth: Harcourt Brace College.

Lado, R. (1957) *Linguistics Across Cultures*. Ann Arbor, MI: University of Michigan Press.

Lakoff, R. (1975) *Language and Women's Place*. New York: Harper and Row.

Lam, A. (1997) Biscriptural reading in Chinese. Paper presented at the International Symposium on Cognitive Processes of the Chinese Language, Hong Kong.

Lam, A., C.A. Perfetti and L. Bell (1991) Automatic phonetic transfer in bidialectal reading. *Journal of Applied Psycholinguistics* 12, 299–311.

Lambert, W.E., J. Havelka and C. Crosby (1958) The influence of language-acquisition contexts on bilingualism. *Journal of Abnormal Psychology* 56, 239–244.

Lamy, M.-N. and R. Goodfellow (1999) 'Reflective Conversation' in the Virtual Language Classroom. *Language* 2(2), 43–61. Available: http://llt.msu.edu/vol2num2 [2000, Nov 3].

Lankshear, C., J.P. Gee, M. Knobel and C. Searle (1997) *Changing Literacies*. Buckingham: Open University Press.

Lantolf, J. (2000) *Sociocultural and Second Language Learning*. Oxford: Oxford University Press.

Laroy, C. (1995) *Resource Books for Teachers: Pronunciation*. Oxford: Oxford University Press.

Larsen-Freeman, D. (1983) Training teachers or educating a teacher? In J.E. Alatis, H.H. Stern and P. Strevens (eds) *Georgetown University Roundtable on Languages and Linguistics 1983*. Washington, DC: Georgetown University, pp. 264–274.

Larsen-Freeman, D. (1991a) Second language acquisition research: Staking out the territory. *TESOL Quarterly* 25, 315–350.

Larsen-Freeman, D. (1991b) Teaching grammar. In M. Celce-Murcia (ed.) *Teaching English as a Second or Foreign Language*. 2nd edn. New York: Newbury House / HarperCollins, pp. 279–296.

Larsen-Freeman, D. (1992) On the teaching and learning of grammar: Challenging the myths. In F. Eckman, D. Highland, P. Lee, J. Milehamand, R. Rutkowski Weber (eds) *Second Language Acquisition Theory and Pedagogy*. Mahwah, NJ: Lawrence Erlbaum, pp. 131–150.

Larsen-Freeman, D. (1997a) *Grammar Dimensions: Form, Meaning, and Use*. 2nd edn. Boston, MA: Heinle and Heinle.

Larsen-Freeman, D. (1997b) Chaos/Complexity science and second language acquisition. *Applied Linguistics* 18, 141–165.

Larsen-Freeman, D. (2001) *Teaching Language: From Grammar to Grammaring*. Boston, MA: Heinle and Heinle.

Larsen-Freeman, D. and M.H. Long (1991) *An Introduction to Second Language Acquisition Research*. London: Longman.

Latour, B. and S. Woolgar (1986) *Laboratory Life: The Construction of Scientific Facts*. Princeton, NJ: Princeton University Press.

Lauffer, B. and M. Hill (2000) What lexical information do L2 learners select in a CALL dictionary and how does it affect word retention? *Language Learning and Technology* 3(2), 58–76. Available: http://llt.msu.edu/vol3num2 [2000, Nov 3].

Lave, J. and E. Wenger (1991) *Situated Learning: Legitimate Peripheral Participation*. New York: Cambridge University Press.

Laver, J. (1980) *The Phonetic Description of Voice Quality*. Cambridge: Cambridge University Press.

Lazar, G. (1990) Using novels in the language learning classroom. *ELT Journal* 44(3), 204–214.

Lazar, G. (1993) *Literature and Language Teaching: A Guide for Teachers and Trainers*. Cambridge: Cambridge University Press.

Lazar, G. (1999) *A Window on Literature*. Cambridge: Cambridge University Press.

Lazaraton, A. (1996) Interlocutor support in oral proficiency interviews: The case of CASE. *Language Testing* 13(2), 151–172.

LDAE (1997) *Longman Dictionary of American English*. London: Longman.

LDOCE (1995) *Longman Dictionary of Contemporary English*. 3rd edn. London: Longman.

Leather, J. and A. James (eds) (1997) *Second-Language Speech. Structure and Process*. Berlin and New York: Mouton de Gruyter.

Lee, I. (1997) ESL learners' performance in error correction in writing: Some implications for teaching. *System* 25, 465–477.

Lee, J. and van Patten, B. (1995) *Making Communicative Language Teaching Happen*. New York: McGraw-Hill.

Leech, G., G. Myers and J. Thomas (eds) (1995) *Spoken English on Computer*. London: Longman.

Leki, I. and J. Carson (1997) 'Completely different worlds': EAP and the writing experiences of ESL students in university courses. *TESOL Quarterly* 31, 39–69.

Lenneberg, E. (1967) *Biological Foundations of Language*. New York: John Wiley and Sons.

Levelt, W.J.M. (1989) *Speaking: From Intention to Articulation*. Cambridge, MA: MIT Press.

Levinson, S. (1983) *Pragmatics*. Cambridge: Cambridge University Press.

Levis, J. (1999) Variations in pronunciation and ESL teacher training. *TESOL Matters* 9(3), 16.

Lewis, M. (1993) *The Lexical Approach: The State of ELT and a Way Forward*. Hove: Language Teaching Publications.

Lewis, M. (1997) *Implementing the Lexical Approach*. Hove: Language Teaching Publications.

Li, D.C.S., D. Mahoney, J.C. Richards (eds) (1994) *Exploring Second Language Teacher Development*. City Polytechnic of Hong Kong: Hong Kong.

Lieberman, P. (1991) *Uniquely Human: The Evolution of Speech, Thought, and Selfless Behavior*. Cambridge, MA: Harvard University Press.

Lightbown, P. (1998) The importance of timing in focus on form. In C. Doughty and J. Williams (eds) *Focus on Form in Classroom Second Language Acquisition*. Cambridge: Cambridge University Press, pp. 177–196.

Lightbown, P. and N. Spada (1993) *How Languages are Learned*. Oxford: Oxford University Press.

Linguistic Minorities Project (1988) Linguistic minorities and the mother-tongue debate in England. In C.B.

Paulston (ed.) *International Handbook of Bilingualism and Bilingual Education*. New York: Greenwood Press, pp. 225–246.

Linn, R. and E. Burton (1994) Performance-based assessment: implications for task specificity. *Educational Measurement: Issues and Practice* 13(1), 5–15.

Liou, H.-C. (1995) Assessing learner strategies using computers: New insights and limitations. Paper presented at the Annual Meeting of the American Association for Applied Linguistics. ERIC Document ED 386 948. Long Beach, CA.

Lipp, E. and D. Davis-Ockey (1997) Praise-question-encourage: Guidelines for writing teacher-comments between essay drafts. *English Teaching Forum* 38(19), 12–15, 36–37.

Little, B.L., S. Devitt and D. Singleton (1994) Authentic texts, pedagogical grammar and language awareness in foreign language learning. In C. James and P. Garrett (eds) *Language Awareness in the Classroom*. London: Longman, pp. 123–132.

Little, D. (1999) Developing learner autonomy in the foreign language classroom: A social-interactive view of learning and three fundamental pedagogical principles. *Evaluación e Intervención Psicoeducativa: Revista Interuniversitaria de Psicologa de la Educación*, 3.

Littlefair, A. (1991) *Reading All Types of Writing*. Buckingham: Open University Press.

Littlejohn, A. (1998) *Writing 1, 2, 3, 4*. Cambridge: Cambridge University Press.

Littlejohn, A. (1992) Why are ELT materials the way they are? Unpublished PhD thesis, University of Lancaster.

Littlejohn, A. (1998) The analysis of language teaching materials: inside the Trojan Horse. In B. Tomlinson (ed.) *Materials Development for Language Teaching*. Cambridge: Cambridge University Press, pp. 190–216.

Littlewood, W. (1981) *Communicative Language Teaching: An Introduction*. Cambridge: Cambridge University Press.

Livesy, R. and E. Tudoreanu (1995) 'What's yours like? Ours is . . .' A motivating e-mail project for TESL. In M. Warschauer (ed.) *Virtual Connections: Online Activities and Projects for Networking Language Learners*. Honolulu, HI: University of Hawai'i, Second Language Teaching and Curriculum Center, pp. 137–138.

Livia, A. and K. Hall (eds) (1997) *Queerly Phrased: Language, Gender and Sexuality*. New York: Oxford.

Lixl-Purcell, A. (1995) German area studies on the net. In M. Warschauer (ed.) *Virtual Connections: Online Activities and Projects for Networking Language Learners*. Honolulu, HI: University of Hawai'i, Second Language Teaching and Curriculum Center, pp. 292–294.

LLA (1994) *Longman Language Activator*. London: Longman.

Lock, G. (1996) *Functional English Grammar*. Cambridge: Cambridge University Press.

Locke, E.A. and G.P. Latham (1990) *A Theory of Goal Setting and Task Performance*. Englewood Cliffs, NJ: Prentice Hall.

Locke, E.A. and G.P. Latham (1994) Goal setting theory. In H.F. O'Neil, Jr and M. Drillings (eds) *Motivation: Theory and Research*. Hillsdale, NJ: Lawrence Erlbaum.

Long, M.H. (1981) Input, interaction and second language acquisition. In H. Winitz (ed.) *Native Language and Foreign Language Acquisition: Annals of the New York Academy of Sciences* 379. New York: New York Academy of Sciences, pp. 259–278.

Long, M.H. (1983a) Does second language instruction make a difference? A review of research. *TESOL Quarterly* 20(1), 9–26.

Long, M.H. (1983b) Native-speaker/non-native-speaker conversation and the negotiation of comprehensible input. *Applied Linguistics* 4, 126–141.

Long, M.H. (1985a) Input and second language acquisition theory. In S. Gass and C. Madden (eds) *Input in Second Language Acquisition*. Rowley, MA: Newbury House, pp. 377–393.

Long, M.H. (1985b) A role for instruction in second language acquisition: Task-based language teaching. In K. Hyltenstan and M. Pienemann (eds) *Modelling and Assessing Second Language Acquisition*. Clevedon: Multilingual Matters.

Long, M.H. (1988) Instructed interlanguage development. In L. Beebe (ed.) *Issues in Second Language Acquisition: Multiple Perspectives*. Rowley, MA: Newbury House, pp. 115–141.

Long, M.H. (1991) Focus on form: A design feature in language teaching methodology. In K. de Bot, R. Ginsberg and C.J. Kramsch (eds) *Foreign Language Research in Cross-Cultural Perspective*. Amsterdam/Philadelphia, PA: John Benjamins, pp. 39–52.

Long, M.H. (1996) The role of the linguistic environment in second language acquisition. In W. Ritchie and T.K. Bathia (eds) *Handbook of Second Language Acquisition*. San Diego, CA: Academic Press.

Long, M.H. (1998) Focus on Form: Theory, Research and Practice. In C. Doughty and J. Williams (eds) *Focus on Form in Classroom Second Language Acquisition*. Cambridge: Cambridge University Press.

Long, M.H. (in press) *Task-Based Language Teaching*. Oxford: Blackwell.

Long, M.H. and G. Crookes (1992) Three approaches to task-based syllabus design. *TESOL Quarterly* 26(1), 27–56.

Long, M.H. and P. Porter (1985) Group Work, interlanguage talk and second language acquisition. *TESOL Quarterly* 19, 207–228.

Long, M.H. and C. Sato (1983) Classroom foreigner talk discourse: forms and functions of teachers' questions. In H.W. Seliger and M.H. Long (eds) *Classroom-Oriented Research in Second Language Acquisition*. Rowley, MA: Newbury House, pp. 268–285.

Long, M.H., L. Adams, M. McLean and F. Castaños (1976) Doing things with words: Verbal interaction in lockstep and small group classroom situations. In J.F. Fanselow and R. Crymes (eds) *On TESOL 1976*. Washington, DC: TESOL, pp. 137–153.

Longacre, R. (1983) *The Grammar of Discourse*. New York: Plenum.

Lortie, D. (1975) *Schoolteacher: A Sociological Study*. Chicago, IL: University of Chicago Press.

Loschky, L. and R. Bley-Vroman (1993) Grammar and task-based methodology. In G. Crookes and S. Gass (eds) *Tasks and Language Learning: Integrating Theory and Practice*. Clevedon: Multilingual Matters, pp. 123–167.

Luke, A. (1994) Introduction to A. Freedman and P. Medway (1994a) (eds) *Genre and the New Rhetoric*. London: Taylor and Francis.

Luke, A. (1996) Genres of power? Literacy education and the production of capital. In R. Hasan and G. Williams (eds) *Literacy in Society*. London: Longman, pp. 308–338.

Lunzer, E. and K. Gardner (eds) (1979) *The Effective Use of Reading*. London: Heinemann.

Lynch, A. and K. Anderson (1992) *Study Speaking*. Cambridge: Cambridge University Press.

Lynch, B. and T. McNamara (1998) Using G-theory and Many-facet Rasch measurement in the development of performance assessments of the ESL speaking skills of immigrants. *Language Testing* 15(2), 158–180.

Lynch, T. (1983) *Study Listening*. Cambridge: Cambridge University Press.

Lynch, T. (1996) *Communication in the Language Classroom*. Oxford: Oxford University Press.

Lyster, R. and L. Ranta (1997) Corrective feedback and learner uptake: Negotiation of form in communicative classrooms. *Studies in Second Language Acquisition* 19, 37–66.

Macken-Horarik, M. (1996) Literacy and learning across the curriculum: Towards a model of register for secondary school teachers. In R. Hasan and G. Williams (eds) *Literacy in Society*. New York: Longman.

Mackey, W.F. (1965) *Language Teaching Analysis*. London: Longman.

Magiste, E. (1985) Development of intra- and interlingual inference in bilinguals. *Journal of Psycholinguistic Research* 14, 137–154.

Major, R.C. (1987) A model for interlanguage phonology. In G. Ioup and S. Weinberger (eds) *Interlanguage Phonology: The Acquisition of a Second Language Sound System*. Cambridge, MA: Newbury House.

Malderez, A. and C. Bod'Oczky (1999) *Mentor Courses: A Resource Book for Teacher Trainers*. Cambridge: Cambridge University Press.

Maley, A. (1989) Down from the pedestal: Literature as resource. In R.A. Carter, R.J. Walker and C.J. Brumfit (eds) *Literature and the Learner: Methodological Approaches*. ELT Documents 130. London: Modern English Publications / Macmillan / The British Council.

Maley, A. (1994) *Short and Sweet*. London: Penguin.

Maley, A. (1997) *Musical Cheers and Other Very Short Stories*. London: Penguin.

Maley, A. (1998a) Making the text speak. In J. Kahny (ed.) *LIOJ 30th Anniversary Volume*. Odawara, Japan: LIOJ.

Maley, A. (1998a) Squaring the circle: reconciling materials as constraint with materials as empowerment. In B. Tomlinson (ed.) *Materials Development for Language Teaching*. Cambridge: Cambridge University Press, pp. 279–294.

Maley, A. (1999a) *He Knows Too Much*. Cambridge English Readers. Cambridge: Cambridge University Press.

Maley, A. (1999b) Choral speaking. *English Teaching Professional* 12, 9–11.

Maley, A. and A. Duff (1982) *Drama Techniques in Language Teaching*. Cambridge: Cambridge University Press.

Maley, A. and A. Duff (1989) *The Inward Ear: Poetry in the Language Classroom*. Cambridge: Cambridge University Press.

Maley, A. and S. Moulding (1981) *Learning to Listen: Tasks for Developing Listening Skills*. Cambridge: Cambridge University Press.

Maley, A. and S. Moulding (1986) *Poem into Poem*. Cambridge: Cambridge University Press.

Maley, A., A. Duff and F. Grellet (1980) *In the Mind's Eye*. Cambridge: Cambridge University Press.

Malinowitz, H. (1995) *Textual Orientations: Lesbian and Gay Students and the Making of Discourse Communities*. Portsmouth, NH: Heinemann.

Mann, W. and S. Thompson (1988) Rhetorical structure theory: Toward a functional theory of text organization. *Text* 8(3), 243–281.

Mariani, L. (1983) Evaluating and supplementing coursebooks. In S. Holden (ed.) *Second Selections from Modern English Teacher*. London: Longman, pp. 127–130.

Markee, N. (1997) *Managing Curricular Innovation*. Cambridge: Cambridge University Press.

Martin, J. (1989) *Factual Writing: Exploring and Challenging Social Reality*. Oxford: Oxford University Press.

Martin, J. (1993) Genre and literacy: modelling context in educational linguistics. *Annual Review of Applied Linguistics* 13, 141–172.

Martin, J. and J. Rothery (1980) Writing Project Report 1. *Working Papers in Linguistics*, Linguistics Department, University of Sydney.

Martin, J. and J. Rothery (1981) Writing Project Report 2. *Working Papers in Linguistics*, Linguistics Department, University of Sydney.

Martin, J. and J. Rothery (1986) Writing Project Report 4. *Working Papers in Linguistics*, Linguistics Department, University of Sydney.

Martin, J., F. Christie and J. Rothery (1987) Social processes in education. In I. Reid (ed.) *The Place of Genre in Learning*. Centre for Studies in Literacy Education. Geelong, Victoria: Deakin University Press.

Martyn, E. (1996) The influence of task type on the negotiation of meaning in small group work. Paper presented at the Annual Pacific Second Language Research Forum, Auckland, New Zealand.

Master, P. (1991) Active verbs with inanimate subjects in scientific prose. *English for Specific Purposes* 10(1), 15–34.

Masuhara, H. (1998) What do teachers really want from coursebooks? In B. Tomlinson (ed.) *Materials Development for Language Teaching*. Cambridge: Cambridge University Press, pp. 239–260.

Masuku, N. (1996) A lexicogrammatical approach to the analysis of rhetorical goals in professional academic writing in the social sciences. Unpublished PhD thesis, University of Birmingham.

Matalene, C. (1985) Contrastive rhetoric: An American teacher in China. *College English* 47(8), 789–808.

Mauranen, A. (1993) *Cultural Differences in Academic Rhetoric*. Frankfurt-am-Main: Peter Lang.

MacAndrew, R. (1991) *English Observed*. Hove: Language Teaching Publications.

McCarthy, M.J. (1990) *Vocabulary*. Oxford: Oxford University Press.

McCarthy, M.J. (1991) *Discourse Analysis for Language Teachers*. Cambridge: Cambridge University Press.

McCarthy, M.J. and R.A. Carter (1994) *Language as Discourse: Perspectives for Language Teaching*. London: Longman.

McCarthy, M.J. and R.A. Carter (1995) Spoken grammar: What is it and how can we teach it? *ELT Journal* 49(3), 207–218.

McClelland, J. (1987) The case of interactionism in language processing. In M. Coltheart (ed.) *Attention and Performance, Vol. 12: The Psychology of Reading*. London: Earlbaum.

McDiarmid, G.W., D. Ball and C.W. Anderson (1989) Why staying one chapter ahead doesn't really work: subject specific pedagogy. In M. Reynolds (ed.) *The Knowledge-Base for Beginning Teachers*. Elmsford, NY: Pergamon. 193–206.

McDonough, J. and C. Shaw (1993) *Materials and Methods in ELT: A Teachers Guide*. London: Blackwell.

McEnery, T. and A. Wilson (1996) *Corpus Linguistics*. Edinburgh: Edinburgh University Press.

McGhan, B. (1994) The probable outcomes of outcome-based education. *Educational Leadership* 51(6), 70–72.

Mackay, D., B. Thompson and P. Schaub (1970) *Breakthrough to Literacy Teachers' Manual: The Theory and Practice of Teaching Initial Reading and Writing*. London: Longman.

McKay, P. (1995) Developing ESL proficiency descriptions for the school context: The NLLIA bandscales. In G. Brindley (ed.) *Language Assessment in Action*. Sydney: National Centre for English Language Teaching and Research, Macquarie University, pp. 31–64.

Mackay, R. and A. Mountford (1978) *English for Special Purposes*. London: Longman.

McKay, S.L. and N.H. Hornberger (eds) (1995) *Sociolinguistics and Language Teaching*. Cambridge: Cambridge University Press.

McKenna, E. (1987) Preparing foreign students to enter discourse communities in the US. *English for Specific Purposes* 6(2), 187–202.

McLaughlin, B. (1982) Second-language learning and bilingualism in children and adults. In S. Rosenberg (ed.) *Handbook of Applied Psycholinguistics: Major Thrusts of Research and Theory*. Hillsdale, NJ: Lawrence Erlbaum, pp. 217–256.

McNamara, T. (1996) *Measuring Second Language Performance*. London: Longman.

McRae, J. (1991) *Literature with a Small 'l'*. London: Modern English Publications / Macmillan.

McRae, J. (1992) *Wordsplay*. London: Macmillan.

McRae, J. and L. Pantaleoni (1990) *Chapter and Verse*. Oxford: Oxford University Press.

McRae, J. and E.M. Vethamani (1999) *Now Read On*. London: Routledge.

McVicker, J. (1995). NewReader [Computer software]. Athens, OH: Hyperbole Software. Demonstration available from mcvicker@ohiou.edu

MacWhinney, B. (1997) Second language acquisition and the competition model. In A. de Groot and J. Kroll (eds) *Tutorials in Bilingualism: Psycholinguistic Perspectives*. Hillsdale, NJ: Lawrence Erlbaum, pp. 113–144.

Mead, R. (1998) *International Management: Cross Cultural Dimensions*. 2nd edn. Oxford: Blackwell.

Meara, P. (1996) The dimensions of lexical competence. In G. Brown, K. Malmkjaer and J. Williams (eds) *Performance and Competence in Second Language Acquisition*. Cambridge: Cambridge University Press, pp. 35–53.

Meara, P. (1997) Towards a new approach to modelling vocabulary acquisition. In N. Schmitt and M.J. McCarthy (eds) *Vocabulary: Description, Acquisition and Pedagogy*. Cambridge: Cambridge University Press, pp. 109–121.

Medgyes, P. (1994) *The Non-Native Teacher*. Basingstoke: Macmillan.

Mellor, B., J. Hemming and J. Legget (1984a) *Changing Stories*. London: the English Centre.

Mellor, B., M. Raleigh and P. Ashton (1984b) *Making Stories*. London: the English Centre.

Mendelsohn, D. (1998) Teaching listening. *Annual Review of Applied Linguistics* 18, 81–101.

Mendelsohn, D. and J. Rubin (1995) *A Guide for the Teaching of Second Language Listening*. San Diego, CA: Dominie Press.

Meskill, C. and R. Krassimira (2000) Curriculum innovation in TEFL: Technologies supporting socio-collaborative language learning in Bulgaria. In M. Warschauer and R. Kern (eds) *Network-Based Language Teaching: Concepts and Practice*. New York: Cambridge University Press.

Messick, S. (1980) Test validity and the ethics of assessment. *American Psychologist* 35, 1012–1027.

Messick, S. (1989) Validity. In R. Linn (ed.) *Educational Measurement*. New York: Macmillan, pp. 13–103.

Meunier, L. (1998) Personality and motivational factors in electronic networking. In J. Muyskens (ed.) *New Ways of Learning and Teaching: Focus on Technology and Foreign Language Education. AAUSC Series: American Association of University Supervisors, Coordinators, and Directors of Foreign Language Programs*. Boston, MA: Heinle and Heinle, pp. 63–126.

Meyer, L. (1996) The contribution of genre theory to theme-based EAP: Navigating foreign fiords. *TESOL Canada Journal* 13(2), 33–44.

Milanovic, M., N. Saville, A. Pollitt and A. Cook (1996) Developing rating scales for CASE: Theoretical concerns and analyses. In A. Cumming and R. Berwick (eds) *Validation in Language Testing*. Clevedon, Avon: Multilingual Matters, pp. 15–38.

Miller, C. (1984) Genre as Social Action. *Quarterly Journal of Speech* 70, 151–167.

Mills, D. (2000) Enthusiasm, experience and collaboration: Technology in the IEI at UIUC. In E. Hanson-Smith (ed.) *Technology-Enhanced Learning Environments*. Alexandria, VA: TESOL.

Mills, D. and Salzmann, A. (1998) *Grammar Safari* [Online]. Intensive English Institute, DEIL LinguaCenter, University of Illinois, IL. Available: http://deil.lang.uiuc.edu/web.pages/grammarsafari.html [2000, Nov 3].

Milroy, L. and P. Muysken (eds) (1995) *One Speaker, Two Languages: Cross-Disciplinary Perspectives on Code-Switching*. Cambridge: Cambridge University Press.

Mingucci, M. (1999) Action research in ESL staff development. *TESOL Matters* 9(2), 16.

Mitchell, T.F. (1957) The language of buying and selling in Cyrenaica: A situational statement. *Hespéris* 44, 31–71.

Morley, J. (1984) *Listening and Language Learning in ESL: Developing Self-Study Activities for Listening Comprehension*. Orlando: HBJ.

Morley, J. (1991) The pronunciation component in teaching English to speakers of other languages. *TESOL Quarterly* 25, 481–520.

Morley, J. (1994) A multidimensional curriculum design for speech-pronunciation instruction. In J. Morley *Pronunciation Pedagogy and Theory: New Views, New Directions*. Alexandria, VA: TESOL.

Morton, J., D. Williams and G. Wigglesworth (1997) Approaches to the evaluation of interviewer behaviour in oral tests. In G. Brindley and G. Wigglesworth (eds) *Access: Issues in Language Test Design and Delivery*. Sydney: National Centre for English Language Teaching and Research, Macquarie University, pp. 175–196.

Moskowitz, G. (1967) The FLint system: An observational tool for the foreign language classroom. In A. Simon and E.G. Boyer (eds) *Mirrors for Behavior: An Anthology of Classroom Observation Instruments*. Philadelphia, PA: Center for the Study of Teaching at Temple University, Section 15, pp. 1–15.

Moskowitz, G. (1968) The effects of training foreign language teachers in Interaction Analysis. *Foreign Language Annals* 1(3), 218–235.

Moskowitz, G. (1971) Interaction Analysis: A new modern language for supervisors. *Foreign Language Annals* 5, 211–221.

Moskowitz, G. (1976) The classroom interaction of outstanding foreign language teachers. *Foreign Language Annals* 9, 125–43 and 146–157.

Mullins, J.J. (1999) *Management and Organisational Behaviour*. 5th edn. London: Pitman.

Mumby, J. (1978) *Communicative Syllabus Design*. Cambridge: Cambridge University Press.

Munro, M.J., J.E. Flege and I.R.A. Mackay (1996) The effects of age of second language learning on the production of English vowels. *Applied Psycholinguistics* 17(3), 313–334.

Murgatroyd, S. and C. Morgan (1992) *Total Quality Management and the School*. Buckingham: Open University Press.

Murphy, D. and J. Cooper (1995) *Getting the Message*. Cambridge: Cambridge University Press.

Murphy-Judy, K.A. (ed.) (1998) *NEXUS: The convergence of language teaching and researching using technology*. CALICO Monograph Series, 4. San Marcos, TX: CALICO Publications.

Murray, D. (1998) Ebonics: A case study in language, power and pedagogy. *TESOL Quarterly* 32, 144–146.

Musgrave, P.W. (1968) *The School as an Organisation*. London: Macmillan.

Muysken, P. (1995) Code-switching and grammatical theory. In L. Milroy and P. Muysken (eds) *One Speaker, Two Languages: Cross-Disciplinary Perspectives on Code-Switching*. Cambridge: Cambridge University Press, pp. 177–198.

Myers, G. (1990) Making a discovery: Narratives of split genes. *Applied Linguistics* 10, 1–35.

Myers-Scotton, C. (1993) *Duelling Languages: Grammatical Structure in Code-Switching*. Oxford: Clarendon Press.

Myers-Scotton, C. (1995) A lexically based model of code-switching. In L. Milroy and P. Muysken (eds) *One Speaker, Two Languages: Cross-Disciplinary Perspectives on Code-Switching*. Cambridge: Cambridge University Press, pp. 233–256.

Myers-Scotton, C. (1997) Code-switching. In F. Coulmas (ed.) *Handbook of Sociolinguistics*. Oxford: Blackwell, pp. 217–237.

Nadler, D.A., M.S. Gerstein, R.B. Shaw *et al.* (1992) *Organizational Architecture: Designs for Changing Organizations*. San Francisco, CA: Jossey-Bass.

Naiman, N., M. Fröhlich, H.H. Stern and A. Todesdo (1975) *The Good Language Learner*. Toronto: Ontario Institute for Studies in Education.

Nash, W. and D. Stacey (1997) *Creating Texts: An Introduction to the Study of Composition*. London: Longman.

Nation, I.S.P. (1990) *Teaching and Learning Vocabulary*. Boston, MA: Heinle and Heinle.

Nation, I.S.P. (2001) *Learning Vocabulary in Another Language*. Cambridge: Cambridge University Press.

Nattinger, J. and J. DeCarrico (1992) *Lexical Phrases and Language Teaching*. Oxford: Oxford University Press.

Naustdal Fenner, A. and G. Nordal-Petersen (1997) *Search 8*. Oslo: Gyldendal.

Negretti, R. (1999) Web-based activities and SLA: A conversation analysis research approach. *Language Learning and Technology* 3(1), 75–87. Available: http://llt.msu.edu/vol3num1 [2000, Nov 3].

Nelson, C. (1999) Sexual identities in ESL: Queer theory and classroom inquiry. *TESOL Quarterly* 33, 371–391.

Nelson, G. and J. Carson (1998) ESL students' perceptions of effectiveness in peer response groups. *Journal of Second Language Writing* 7, 113–131.

Neu, J. (1986) American-English business negotiations: training for non-native speakers. *English for Specific Purposes* 5, 41–57.

Newton, C. and T. Tarrant (1992) *Managing Change in Schools*. London: Routledge.

Nichols, P. (1976) Black women in the rural South: conservative and innovative. In B.L. Dubois and I. Crouch (eds) *Papers in Southwest English IV: Proceedings of the Conference on the Sociology of the Language of American Women*. San Antonio, TX: Trinity University, pp. 103–114. Revised and reprinted as Linguistic options and choices for Black women in the rural South. In B. Thorne, C. Kramerae and N. Henley (eds) (1983) *Language, Gender and Society*. Rowley, MA: Newbury House, pp. 54–68.

Nilsen, D. and A.P. Nilsen (1971) *Pronunciation Contrasts in English*. New York: Regents.

Nordin-Eriksson, S. (1999) Learner training, learning strategies, and attitudes among adult immigrants and refugees learning Swedish as a second language. In R. Oxford (ed.) *Language Learning Strategies in the Context of Autonomy: Strategy Research Compendium: Proceedings of the First Annual Strategy Research Symposium, Teachers College*. New York: Columbia University, pp. 49–50.

Norman, K. (1992) *Thinking Voices*. London: Hodder and Stoughton.

Norton, B. (1997) Accountability in language assessment. In C. Clapham and D. Corson (eds) *Encyclopedia of Language and Education, Vol. 7: Language Testing and Assessment*. Dordrecht: Kluwer Academic, pp. 313–322.

Norton Peirce, B. (1993) Language learning, social identity and immigrant women. Unpublished PhD dissertation, University of Toronto.

Norton Peirce, B. (1995) Social identity, investment and language learning. *TESOL Quarterly* 29, 9–31.

Nunan, D. (1988a) *The Learner Centred Curriculum*. Cambridge: Cambridge University Press.

Nunan, D. (1988b) *Syllabus Design*. Oxford: Oxford University Press.

Nunan, D. (1989a) *Designing Tasks for the Communicative Classroom*. Cambridge: Cambridge University Press.

Nunan, D. (1989b) *Understanding Language Classrooms*. London: Prentice Hall.

Nunan, D. (1991) *Language Teaching Methodology*. London: Prentice Hall.

Nunan, D. (1992) *Research Methods in Language Learning*. Cambridge: Cambridge University Press.

Nunan, D. (1993) *Introducing Discourse Analysis*. London: Penguin.

Nunan, D. (1995a) *Atlas 2*. Boston, MA: Heinle and Heinle.

Nunan, D. (1995b) Closing the gap between learning and instruction. *TESOL Quarterly* 29, 33–58.

Nunan, D. (ed.) (1995c) *New Ways in Teaching Listening*. Washington, DC: TESOL.

Nunan, D. (1996) Hidden voices: insiders' perspective on classroom interaction. In K. Bailey and D. Nunan (eds) *Voices from the Language Classroom*. New York: Cambridge University Press, pp. 41–56.

Nunan, D. (1997) Does learner strategy training make a difference? *Lenguas Modernas* 24, 123–142.

Nunan, D. (1999) *Second Language Teaching and Learning*. Boston, MA: Heinle and Heinle.

Nunan, D. and A. Lam (1998) Teacher education for multilingual contexts: Models and issues. In J. Cenoz and F. Genesee (eds) *Beyond Bilingualism: Multilingualism and Multilingual Education*. Clevedon: Multilingual Matters, pp. 117–140.

Nunan, D. and C. Lamb (eds) (1995) *The Self-Directed Teacher*. New York: Cambridge University Press.

Nunan, D. and L. Miller (eds) (1995) *New Ways in Teaching Listening*. Alexandria, VA: TESOL.

Nuttall, C. (1996) *Teaching Reading Skills in a Foreign Language*. New edn. London: Heinemann.

Nyikos, M. (1999) The effect of key background variables on high school learning strategies. In R. Oxford (ed.) *Language Learning Strategies in the Context of Autonomy: Strategy Research Compendium: Proceedings of the First Annual Strategy Research Symposium, Teachers College*. New York: Columbia University, pp. 51–53.

Oakhill, J. and P. Bryant (1998) Factors that contribute to individual differences in children's comprehension skill: The role of inference making. Presentation at symposium: *Literacy: Integrating Research and Practice*.

OALD (1995) *Oxford Advanced Learners' Dictionary*. 5th edn. Oxford: Oxford University Press.

Obler, L. and K. Gjerlow (1999) *Language and the Brain*. Cambridge: Cambridge University Press.

O'Brien, T. (1995) Rhetorical structure analysis and the case of the inaccurate, incoherent source-hopper. *Applied Linguistics* 16(4), 442–482.

Ochs, E., E.A. Schegloff and S. Thompson (eds) (1996) *Interaction and Grammar*. Cambridge: Cambridge University Press.

O'Connor, J.D. and G.F. Arnold (1973) *Intonation of Colloquial English*. 2nd edn. London: Longman.

Odlin, T. (ed.) (1994) *Perspectives on Pedagogical Grammar*. Cambridge: Cambridge University Press.

Oller, J.W. (1976) Evidence of a general language proficiency factor: an expectancy grammar. *Die Neuen Sprachen* 76, 165–174.

Oller, J.W. (1983) A consensus for the eighties. In J.W. Oller (ed.) *Issues in Language Testing Research*. Rowley, MA: Newbury House, pp. 351–356.

Oller, J.W. and F. Hinofotis (1980) Two mutually exclusive hypotheses about second language ability: indivisible or partially divisible competence. In J.W. Oller and K. Perkins (eds) *Research in Language Testing*. Rowley, MA: Newbury House, pp. 13–23.

O'Loughlin, K. (1997) Test-taker performance on direct and semi-direct versions of the oral interaction module. In G. Brindley and G. Wigglesworth (eds) *Access: Issues in Language Test Design and Delivery*. Sydney: National Centre for English Language Teaching and Research, Macquarie University, pp. 117–146.

Olson, D. (1990) When a learner attempts to become literate in a second language, what is he or she attempting? *TESL Talk* 20(1), 18–22.

Olstain, E. and A.D. Cohen (1991) Teaching speech act behavior to nonnative speakers. In M. Celce-Murcia (ed.) *Teaching English as a Second or Foreign Language*. New York: Newbury House/HarperCollins, pp. 154–169.

O'Malley, J.M. and A.U. Chamot (1990) *Learning Strategies in Second Language Acquisition*. Cambridge: Cambridge University Press.

O'Malley, J.M. and L. Valdez-Pierce (1996) *Authentic Assessment for English Language Learners: Practical Approaches for Teachers*. Reading, MA: Addison-Wesley.

On Balance: Guidelines for the Representation of Women and Men in English Language Teaching Materials (1991) Chilton: Women in EFL Materials.

O'Neil, R.O. (1982) Why use textbooks? *ELT Journal* 36(2).

O'Neill, R., R. Kingsbury and T. Yeardon (1971) *Kernel Lessons Intermediate*. London: Longman.

On Target (1996) Windhoek: Gamsberg Macmillan.

Ortega, L. (1997) Process and outcomes in networked classroom interaction: Defining the research agenda for L2 computer-assisted classroom discussion. *Language Learning and Technology* 1(1), 82–93. Available: http://llt.msu.edu/vol1num1 [2000, Nov 3].

Oscarson, M. (1997) Self-assessment of foreign and second language proficiency. In C. Clapham and D. Corson (eds) *Encyclopedia of Language and Education, Vol. 7: Language Testing and Assessment*. Dordrecht: Kluwer Academic, pp. 175–187.

Owen, C. (1996) Do concordances require to be consulted? *ELT Journal* 50, 3, pp. 219–224.

Oxford, R.L. (1990) *Language Learning Strategies: What Every Teacher Should Know*. Boston, MA: Heinle and Heinle.

Oxford, R.L. (ed.) (1996) *Language Learning Strategies Around the World: Cross-Cultural Perspectives*. Manoa, HI: University of Hawai'i Press.

Oxford, R.L. and M. Ehrman (1995) Adults' language learning strategies in an intensive foreign language program in the United States. *System* 23, 359–386.

Oxford, R.L. and B.L. Leaver (1996) A synthesis of strategy instruction for language learners. In R. Oxford (ed.) *Language Learning Strategies Around the World: Cross-Cultural Perspectives*. Manoa, HI: University of Hawai'i Press, pp. 227–246.

Oxford, R.L. and M. Nyikos (1989) Variables affecting choice of language learning strategies by university students. *Modern Language Journal* 73, 291–300.

Oxford, R.L., M. Ehrman and M. Nyikos (1988) *Vive la différence?* Reflections on sex differences in use of language learning strategies. *Foreign Language Annals* 21(4), 321–329.

Oxford, R.L., Y.Y. Park-Oh, S. Ito and M. Sumrall (1993) Learning a language by satellite television: What influences student achievement? *System* 21, 31–48.

Pajares, M.F. (1992) Teachers' beliefs and educational research: Cleaning up a messy construct. *Review of Educational Research* 62(3), 307–332.

Papaefthymiou-Lytra, S. (1987) *Language, Language Awareness and Foreign Language Learning*. Athens, OH: University of Athens Press.

Papert, S. (1993) The children's machine: Rethinking school in the age of the computer. New York: Basic Books.

Paradis, M. (ed.) (1995) *Aspects of Bilingual Aphasia*. Oxford: Pergamon.

Paran, A. (1996) Reading in EFL: facts and fictions. *ELT Journal* 50(1), 25–34.

Parish, J. (1995) Multi-media and language learning. *FOLIO* 2(1), 4–6.

Park-Oh, Y. (1994) Self-regulated strategy training in second language reading. Unpublished PhD dissertation, University of Alabama, Tuscaloosa, AL.

Patthey-Chavez, G.E. and D. Ferris (1997) Writing conferences and the weaving of multi-voiced texts in college composition. *Research in the Teaching of English* 31, 51–90.

Paulston, C.B. (1982) *Swedish Research and Debate about Bilingualism: A Critical Review of the Swedish Research and Debate about Bilingualism and Bilingual Education in Sweden from an International Perspective: A Report to the National Swedish Board of Education*. Skoloverstyrelsen: National Swedish Board of Education.

Paulston, C.B. (ed.) (1988) *International Handbook of Bilingualism and Bilingual Education*. New York: Greenwood Press.

Paulston, C.B. (1994) *Linguistic Minorities in Multilingual Settings: Implications for Language Policies*. Amsterdam: John Benjamins.

Pawley, A. and F. Syder (1983) Two puzzles for linguistic theory: nativelike selection and nativelike fluency. In J.C. Richards and R. Schmidt (eds) *Language and Communication*. London: Longman, pp. 191–226.

Pelletieri, J. (2000) Negotiation in cyberspace: The role of 'Chatting' in the development of grammatical competence. In M. Warschauer and R. Kern (eds) *Network-based language teaching: Concepts and practice*. New York: Cambridge University Press.

Penfield, W. and L. Roberts (1959) *Speech and Brain-Mechanisms*. Princeton, NJ: Princeton University Press.

Pennington, M. (1996) *Phonology in English Language Teaching: An International Approach*. London: Longman.

Pennington, M. and M.N. Brock (1992) Process and product approaches to computer-assisted composition. In M. Pennington and V. Stevens (eds) *Computers in Applied Linguistics: An International Perspective*. Clevedon: Multilingual Matters, pp. 79–109.

Pennycook, A. (1994) *The Cultural Politics of English as an International Language*. London: Longman.

Pennycook, A. (1997) Vulgar pragmatism, critical pragmatics and EAP. *English for Specific Purposes* 16(4), 253–269.

Pepitone, J.S. (1995) *Future Training: A Roadmap for Restructuring the Training Function*. Dallas, TX: AddVantage Learning Press.

Perkins, K. (1998) Assessing reading. *Annual Review of Applied Linguistics* 18, 208–218.

Peyton, J. (2000) Immersed in writing: Networked composition at Kendall Demonstration Elementary School. In E. Hanson-Smith (ed.) *Technology-Enhanced Learning Environments*. Alexandria, VA: TESOL.

Pfaff-Harris, K. (2000) *The Linguistic Funland!* [Online]. Available: http://www.linguistic-funland.com/ [2000, Nov 3].

Phillipson, R. (1992) *Linguistic Imperialism*. Oxford: Oxford University Press.

Phinney, M. (1991) Computer-assisted writing and writing apprehension in ESL students. In P. Dunkel (ed.) *Computer-Assisted Language Learning and Testing: Research Issues and Practice*. New York: Newbury House/HarperCollins, pp. 189–204.

Piaget, J. (1950) *The Psychology of Intelligence*. Translated from *La psychologie de l'intelligence* 1947. Translated by M. Piercy and D.E. Berlyne. London: Routledge and Kegan Paul.

Pica, T. (1985) The selective impact of classroom instruction on second language acquisition. *Applied Linguistics* 6(3), 214–222.

Pica, T. (1994) Research on negotiation: What does it reveal about second language learning conditions, processes, and outcomes? *Language Learning* 44, 493–527.

Pica, T. and C. Doughty (1985) Input and interaction in the communicative language classroom: A comparison of teacher-fronted and group activities. In S.M. Gass and C.G. Madden (eds) *Input and Second Language Acquisition*. Rowley, MA: Newbury House, pp. 115–132.

Pica, T. and C. Doughty (1988) Variations in classroom interaction as a function of participation pattern and task. In J. Fine (ed.) *Second Language Discourse: A Textbook of Current Research*. Norwood, NJ: Ablex.

Pica, T., R. Young and C. Doughty (1987) The impact of interaction on comprehension. *TESOL Quarterly* 21, 737–758.

Pica, T., L. Holliday, N. Lewis and L. Morgenthaler (1989) Comprehensible output as an outcome of linguistics demands on the learner. *Studies in Second Language Acquisition* 11(1), 63–90.

Pica, T., R. Kanagy and J. Falodun (1993) Choosing and using communication tasks for second language instruction. In G. Crookes and S.M. Gass (eds) *Tasks and Language Learning: Integrating Theory and Practice*. Clevedon: Multilingual Matters.

Pica, T., F. Lincoln-Porter, D. Paninos and J. Linnell (1996) Language learners' interaction: How does it address the input, output and feedback needs of language learners? *TESOL Quarterly* 31, 95–120.

Pienemann, M. (1984) Psychological constraints on the teachability of languages. *Studies in Second Language Acquisition* 6(2), 186–214.

Pienemann, M. (1989) Is language teachable? *Applied Linguistics* 10(1), 52–9.

Pienemann, M. (1998) *Language processing and Second Language Development: Processability Theory*. Amsterdam/Philadelphia, PA: John Benjamins.

Pienemann, M. and M. Johnston (1987) Factors influencing the development of language proficiency. In D. Nunan (ed.) *Applying Second Language Acquisition Research*. Adelaide: National Curriculum Resource Centre.

Pinker, S. (1994) *The Language Instinct: How the Mind Creates Language*. New York: William Morrow Press.

Pinker, S. and A. Prince (1988) On language and connectionism: Analysis of a parallel distributed processing model of language acquisition. *Cognition* 28, 73–193.

Pinto, D. (1996) What does 'schMOOze' mean?: Non-native speaker interactions on the internet. In M. Warschauer (ed.) *Telecollaboration in Foreign Language Learning: Proceedings of the Hawai'i Symposium*. Honolulu, HI: University of Hawai'i, Second Language Teaching and Curriculum Center, pp. 165–184.

Plough, I. and S. Gass (1993) Interlocutor and task familiarity: Effects on interactional structure. In G. Crookes and S. Gass (eds) *Tasks and Language Learning: Integrating Theory and Practice*. Clevedon: Multilingual Matters, pp. 35–56.

Polanyi, L. (1981) Telling the same story twice. *Text* 1(4), 315–336.

Politzer, R. (1980) Requesting in elementary school classrooms. *TESOL Quarterly* 14(2), 165–174.

Pomerantz, A. (1984) Agreeing and disagreeing with assessments: Some features of preferred/dispreferred turn shapes. In J. Atkinson and J. Heritage (eds) *Structure of Social Action*. Cambridge: Cambridge University Press.

Pomerantz, A. and B.J. Fehr (1997) Conversation analysis: An approach to the study of social action as sense making practices. In T.A. van Dijk (ed.) *Discourse as Social Interaction*. London: Sage.

Ponsonby, M. (1987) *How Now Brown Cow?* Englewood Cliffs, NJ: Prentice Hall.

Porte, G. (1997) The etiology of poor second language writing: The influence of perceived teacher preferences on second language revision strategies. *Journal of Second Language Writing* 6, 61–78.

Porter Ladousse, G. (1983) *Speaking Personally*. Cambridge: Cambridge University Press.

Postman, N. and C. Weingartner (1969) *Teaching as a Subversive Activity*. London: Penguin.

Potter, J. and M. Wetherell (1987) *Discourse and Social Psychology: Beyond Attitudes and Behavior*. London: Sage.

Poulisse, N. and T. Bongaerts (1994) First language use in second language production. *Applied Linguistics* 15, 36–57.

Poynton, C. (1997) Language and difference and identity: Three perspectives. *Literacy and Numeracy Studies* 7, 7–24.

Prabhu, N.S. (1984) Procedural syllabuses. In T.E. Read (ed.) *Trends in Language Syllabus Design*. Singapore: Singapore University Press/RELC.

Prabhu, N.S. (1987) *Second Language Pedagogy*. Oxford: Oxford University Press.

Pratt, M.L. (1991) Arts of the contact zone. In P. Franklin (ed.) *Profession 91*. New York: Modern Language Association, pp. 33–40.

Preston, D.R. (1989) *Sociolinguistics and Second Language Acquisition*. Oxford: Blackwell.

Prior, P. (1991) Contextualising writing and response in a graduate seminar. *Written Communication* 8, 267–310.

Prowse, P. (1998) How writers write: Testimony from authors. In B. Tomlinson (ed.) *Materials Development for Language Teaching*. Cambridge: Cambridge University Press, pp. 130–145.

Prowse, P. (1999) *Double Cross*. Cambridge: Cambridge University Press.

Quinn, A. (1998) A typology for clarification of strategies in interaction. Unpublished MEd dissertation, University of Bristol.

Quirk, R., S. Greenbaum, G. Leech and J. Svartvik (1985) *A Comprehensive Grammar of the English Language*. London: Longman.

Raimes, A. (1991) Out of the woods: Emerging traditions in the teaching of writing. *TESOL Quarterly* 25(3), 407–430.

Ramanathan, V. and R.B. Kaplan (1996) Audience and voice in current L1 composition texts: Some implications for ESL student writers. *Journal of Second Language Writing* 5(1), 21–24.

Rampton, B. (1990) Displacing the 'native speaker': Expertise, affiliation and inheritance. *ELT Journal* 44, 97–101.

Rampton, B. (1995) *Crossing: Language and Ethnicity among Adolescents*. London: Longman.

Rayner, K. and A. Pollatsek (1989) *The Psychology of Reading*. Englewood Cliffs, NJ: Prentice Hall.

Rea-Dickins, P. (1994) Evaluation and English language teaching. *Language Teaching* 27, 71–91.

Rea-Dickins, P. and K. Germaine (1993) *Evaluation*. Oxford: Oxford University Press.

Ready-Morfitt, D. (1991) The role and limitations of self-assessment in testing and research. Unpublished manuscript, Second Language Institute, University of Ottawa.

Reid, J. (1995a) *Learning Styles in the ESL/EFL Classroom*. Boston, MA: Heinle and Heinle.

Reid, J. (1995b) *Teaching ESL Writing*. Upper Saddle River, NJ: Prentice Hall Regents.

Reid, J. (ed.) (1998) *Using Learning Styles in the Second Language Classroom*. Upper Saddle River, NJ: Prentice Hall.

Reid, J. (2000) Advanced EAP writing and curriculum design: what do we need to know? In P. Matsuda and T. Silva (eds) *On Second Language Writing*. Mahwah, NJ: Lawrence Erlbaum.

Reid, J. and B. Kroll (1995) Designing and assessing effective classroom writing assignments for NES and ESL students. *Journal of Second Language Writing* 4, 17–41.

Richards, J.C. (1980) Conversation. *TESOL Quarterly* 14(4), 413–432.

Richards, J.C. (1985) Listening comprehension: Approach, design, and procedure. In J.C. Richards (ed.) *The Context of Language Teaching*. Cambridge: Cambridge University Press, pp. 189–207.

Richards, J.C. (1990) *The Language Teaching Matrix*. Cambridge: Cambridge University Press.

Richards, J.C. (ed.) (1998) *Teaching in Action*. Alexandria, Virginia: TESOL.

Richards, J.C. and C. Lockhart (1991–92) Teacher development through peer observation. *TESOL Journal* 1(2), 7–10.

Richards, J.C. and C. Lockhart (1994) *Reflective Teaching in Second Language Classrooms*. New York: Cambridge University Press.

Richards, J.C. and D. Nunan (eds) (1990) *Second Language Teacher Education*. New York: Cambridge University Press.

Richards, J.C. and T. Rodgers (1986) *Approaches and Methods in Language Teaching*. Cambridge: Cambridge University Press.

Richards, J.C. *et al.* (1992) *A Dictionary of Applied Linguistics*. London: Longman.

Richards, J.C., J. Hull and S. Proctor (1998) *New Interchange*. Cambridge: Cambridge University Press.

Richardson, P.W. (1994) Language as personal resource and as social construct: Competing views of literacy pedagogy in Australia. In A. Freedman and P. Medway (eds) *Learning and Teaching Genre*. Portsmouth, NH: Boynton/Cook Heinemann, pp. 117–142.

Riggenbach, H. (1999) *Discourse Analysis in the Language Classroom, Vol. 1: The Spoken Language*. Ann Arbor, MI: University of Michigan Press.

Riggenbach, H. and V. Samuda (1997) *Grammar Dimensions: Form, Meaning and Use 2*. Boston, MA: Heinle and Heinle.

Rinvolucri, M. and J. Morgan (1990) *Once Upon a Time: Using Stories in the Language Classroom*. Cambridge: Cambridge University Press.

Rivers, W. and M. Temperley (1978) *A Practical Guide to the Teaching of English as a Second or Foreign Language*. New York: Cambridge University Press.

Roach, P. (2000) *English Phonetics and Phonology: A Practical Course*. 3rd edn. Cambridge: Cambridge University Press.

Roach, P. (forthcoming) *Phonetics: Oxford Introductions to Language Study*. Oxford: Oxford University Press.

Robb, T. (2000) *Famous Japanese Personages Project* (Kyoto Sangyo University) [Online]. Available: www.kyoto-su.ac.jp/information/famous/ [2000, Nov 3].

Robbins, J. (1997) Between 'hello' and 'see you later': Development strategies for interpersonal communication. Unpublished PhD dissertation, Georgetown University. UMI 9634593.

Robbins, S.P. (1998) *Organizational Behavior*. 8th edn. Upper Saddle River, NJ: Prentice Hall.

Robinson, P. (1980) *ESP (English for Specific Purposes): The Present Position*. Oxford: Pergamon.

Robinson, P. (ed.) (1988a) *Academic Writing: Process and Product*. ELT Documents 129. London: Modern English Publications / Macmillan / The British Council.

Robinson, P. (1988b) The management of language training. *Language Teaching* 21(3), 146–157.

Robinson, P. (1991) *ESP Today: A Practitioner's Guide*. London: Prentice Hall.

Robinson, P. (1996) Learning simple and complex second language rules under implicit, incidental, rule-search and instructed conditions. *Studies in Second Language Acquisition* 18, 27–68.

Robinson, W.P. (1979) Speech markers and social class. In K.R. Scherer and H. Giles (eds) *Social Markers in Speech*. Cambridge: Cambridge University Press, pp. 211–249.

Rogerson, P. and J.B. Gilbert (1990) *Speaking Clearly*. Cambridge: Cambridge University Press.

Romaine, S. (1994) *Language in Society: An Introduction to Sociolinguistics*. Oxford: Oxford University Press.

Romaine, S. (1995) *Bilingualism*. 2nd edn. Cambridge, MA: Blackwell.

Romaine, S. (1996) Bilingualism. In W.C. Ritchie and T.K. Bhatia (eds) *Handbook of Second Language Acquisition*. San Diego, CA: Academic Press, pp. 571–604.

Rorschach, E. and R. Whitney (1986) Relearning to teach: Peer observation as a means of professional development. *American Educator* 38(1), 40–44.

Rosenholtz, S. (1989) *Teachers' Workplace: The Social Organization of Schools*. New York: Longman.

Ross, S. (1992) Accommodative questions in oral proficiency interviews. *Language Testing* 9(2), 173–186.

Ross, S. (1997) An introspective analysis of listener inferencing on a second language listening task. In G. Kasper and E. Kellerman (eds) *Communication Strategies: Psycholinguistic and Sociolinguistic Perspectives*. London: Longman.

Ross, S. (1998) Self-assessment in language testing: A meta-analysis and analysis of experiential factors. *Language Testing* 15(1), 1–20.

Rossner, R. (1988) *The Whole Story*. London: Longman.

Rost, M. (1990) *Listening in Language Learning*. London: Longman.

Rost, M. (1991) *Listening in Action*. New York: Prentice Hall.

Rost, M. (1994) *Introducing Listening*. London: Penguin.

Rost, M. and S. Ross (1991) Learner use of strategies in interaction: Typology and teachability. *Language Learning* 41, 235–273.

Rowe, M.B. (1969) Science, silence and sanctions. *Science and Children* 6(6), 12–13.

Rubin, J. (1975) What the 'good language learner' can teach us. *TESOL Quarterly* 9, 41–51.

Rubin, J. (1994) A review of second language listening comprehension research. *Modern Language Journal* 78, 199–221.

Ruiz, R. (1988) Bilingualism and bilingual education in the United States. In C.B. Paulston (ed.) *International Handbook of Bilingualism and Bilingual Education*. New York: Greenwood Press, pp. 539–560.

Rumelhart, D. (1977) Toward an interactive model of reading. In S. Dornic (ed.) *Attention and Performance, Vol. 6*. Hillsdale, NJ: Lawrence Erlbaum, pp. 33–58.

Rumelhart, D. and J. McClelland (1986) On learning the past tenses of English verbs. In J. McClelland and D. Rumelhart and the PDP Research Group (eds) *Parallel Distributed Processing. Explorations in the Microstructures of Cognition, Vol. 2: Psychological and Biological Models*. Cambridge, MA: MIT Press, pp. 216–271.

Rutherford, W. (1977) *Modern English*. 2nd edn. New York: Harcourt Brace Jovanovich.

Rutherford, W. (1987) *Second Language Grammar: Learning and Teaching*. London: Longman.

Rutherford, W. and M. Sharwood Smith (eds) (1988) *Grammar and Second Language Teaching*. New York: Newbury House/HarperCollins.

Sacks, H., E.A. Schegloff and G. Jefferson (1974) A simplest systematics for the organisation of turn-taking for conversation. *Language* 50(4), 696–735.

Salaberry, R. (1999) Call in the year 2000: Still developing the research agenda. *Language Learning and Technology* 3(1), 104–107. A commentary on Carol Chapelle's CALL in the Year 2000: Still in search of research paradigms. *Language Learning and Technology* 1(1). Available: http://llt.msu.edu/vol3/num1 [2000, Nov 3].

Salager-Meyer, F. (1994) Hedges and textual communicative function in medical English written discourse. *English for Specific Purposes* 13(2), 149–170.

Salimbene, S. (1985) *Strengthening your Study Skills: A Guide for Overseas Students*. Rowley MA: Newbury House.

Samuda, V. (2001) Guiding relationships between form and meaning during task performance: The role of the teacher. In M. Bygate, P. Skehan and M. Swain (eds) *Researching Pedagogic Tasks: Second Language Learning, Teaching and Testing*. London: Longman, pp. 119–140.

Samuda, V. and P. Rounds (1992) Critical episodes: Reference points for analyzing a task in action. In G. Crookes and S.M. Gass (eds) *Tasks in a Pedagogical Context: Integrating Theory and Practice*. Clevedon: Multilingual Matters.

Sano, F. (1999) Strategy instruction for writing in EFL. In R. Oxford (ed.) *Language Learning Strategies in the Context of Autonomy: Strategy Research Compendium: Proceedings of the First Annual Strategy Research Symposium, Teachers College*. New York: Columbia University, pp. 70–72.

Santos, T. (1988) Professors' reactions to the academic writing of nonnative speaking students. *TESOL Quarterly* 22, 69–90.

Sato, C. (1982) Ethnic styles in classroom discourse. In M. Hines and W. Rutherford (eds) *On TESOL 1981*. Washington, DC: TESOL.

Scarcella, R.C. and R.L. Oxford (1992) *The Tapestry of Language Learning: The Individual in the Communicative Classroom*. Boston, MA: Heinle and Heinle.

Scarino, A., D. Vale, P. McKay and J. Clark (1988) *Australian Language Levels Guidelines. Book 2: Syllabus Development and Programming*. Canberra: Curriculum Development Office.

Schegloff, E.A. and H. Sacks (1973) Opening up closings. *Semiotica* 8(4), 289–327.

Schieffelin, B.B. and E. Ochs (eds) (1986) *Language Socialization Across Cultures*. Cambridge: Cambridge University Press.

Schiffman, H.F. (1997) Diglossia as a sociolinguistic situation. In F. Coulmas (ed.) *Handbook of Socio-linguistics*. Oxford: Blackwell.

Schiffrin, D. (1987) *Discourse Markers*. Cambridge: Cambridge University Press.

Schmeck, R.R. (1988) *Learning Strategies and Learning Styles*. New York: Plenum.

Schmidt, R. (1990) The role of consciousness in second language learning. *Applied Linguistics* 11(2), 129–158.

Schmidt, R. (1994a) Deconstructing consciousness in search of useful definitions for applied linguistics. In J. Hulstijn and R. Schmidt (eds) *Consciousness and Second Language Acquisition: Perspectives on Form-Focused Instruction. 1994 AILA Review*. Amsterdam: AILA.

Schmidt, R. (1994b) Implicit learning and the cognitive unconscious: Of artificial grammars and SLA. In N. Ellis (ed.) (1994) *Implicit and Explicit Learning of Languages*. London: Academic Press, pp. 165–209.

Schmidt, R. (ed.) (1995) *Attention and Awareness in Foreign Language Learning*. Honolulu, HI: University of Hawai'i, Second Language Teaching and Curriculum Center.

Schmidt, R. and S. Frota (1986) Developing basic conversational ability in a second language: A case study of an adult learner of Portuguese. In R. Day (ed.) *Talking to Learn: Conversation in Second Language Acquisition*. Rowley, MA: Newbury House, pp. 237–326.

Schmitt, N. and M.J. McCarthy (eds) (1997) *Vocabulary: Description, Acquisition and Pedagogy*. Cambridge: Cambridge University Press.

Scholfield, P. (1997) Vocabulary reference works in foreign language learning. In N. Schmitt and M.J. McCarthy (eds) *Vocabulary: Description, Acquisition and Pedagogy*. Cambridge: Cambridge University Press, pp. 279–302.

Schon, D. (1987) *Educating the Reflective Practitioner*. San Francisco, CA: Jossey-Bass.

Schumann, F.E. and J.H. Schumann (1977) Diary of a language learner: an introspective study of second language learning. In H.D. Brown, C.A. Yorio and R.H. Crymes (eds) *On TESOL 1977, Teaching and Learning English as a Second Language: Trends in Research and Practice*. Washington, DC: TESOL.

Schumann, J. (1975) Affective factors and the problem of age in second language acquisition. *Language Learning* 25, 209–235.

Schumann, J. (1978) *The Pidginization Process: A Model for Second Language Acquisition*. Rowley, MA: Newbury House.

Schwartz, B. and R. Sprouse (1994) Word order and nominative case in non-native language acquisition. In T. Hoekstra and B. Schwartz (eds) *Language Acquisition Studies in Generative Grammar*. Amsterdam/Philadelphia, PA: John Benjamins, pp. 317–368.

Scollon, R. and S.W. Scollon (1981) *Narrative and Face in Interethnic Communication*. Norwood, NJ: Ablex.

Scollon, R. and S.W. Scollon (1983) Face in interethnic communication. In J.C. Richards and R.W. Schmidt (eds) *Language and Communication*. London: Longman, pp. 156–190.

Scollon, R. and S.W. Scollon (1995) *Intercultural Communication*. Oxford: Blackwell.

Scovel, T. (1988) *A Time to Speak: A Psycholinguistic Inquiry into the Critical Period for Human Speech.* Boston, MA: Heinle and Heinle/Newbury House.

Scovel, T. (1998) *Psycholinguistics.* Oxford: Oxford University Press.

Segall, M.H. (1979) *Cross-Cultural Psychology: Human Behavior in Global Perspective.* Monterey, CA: Brooks/Cole.

Seidenberg, M. and J. McClelland (1989) A distributed developmental model of word recognition. *Psychological Review* 96, 523–568.

Seidlhofer, B. and C. Dalton-Puffer (1995) Appropriate units in pronunciation teaching: some programmatic pointers. *International Journal of Applied Linguistics* 5(1), 135–146.

Seliger, H.W. (1977) Does practice make perfect? A study of interaction patterns and L2 competence. *Language Learning* 27, 263–278.

Seliger, H.W. (1983) Learner interaction in the classroom and its effect on language acquisition. In H.W. Seliger and M.H. Long (eds) *Classroom Oriented Research in Second Language Acquisition.* Rowley, MA: Newbury House, pp. 246–267.

Selinker, L. (1972) Interlanguage. *International Review of Applied Linguistics* 10(3), 209–231.

Selinker, L. (1992) *Rediscovering Interlanguage.* London: Longman.

Selinker, L. and D. Douglas (1985) Wrestling with 'context' in interlanguage theory. *Applied Linguistics* 6(2), 190–204.

Sengupta, S., G. Forey and E. Hamp-Lyons (1999) Supporting effective English communication within the context of teaching and research in a tertiary institute: Developing a genre model for consciousness-raising. *English for Specific Purposes* 18, (supplementary issue) S7–S22.

Shapson, S. (1984) Bilingual and multicultural education in Canada. In S. Shapson and V. D'oyley (eds) *Bilingual and Multilingual Education: Canadian Perspectives.* Clevedon: Multilingual Matters, pp. 1–13.

Shapson, S. and V. D'oyley (eds) (1984) *Bilingual and Multilingual Education: Canadian Perspectives.* Clevedon: Multilingual Matters.

Sharwood Smith, M. (1981) Consciousness-raising and the second language learner. *Applied Linguistics* 2, 159–168.

Sharwood Smith, M. (1993) Input enhancement in instructed SLA: Theoretical bases. *Studies in Second Language Acquisition* 15, 165–179.

Sharwood Smith, M. (1994) *Second Language Learning: Theoretical Foundations.* London: Longman.

Shavelson, R.J. and P. Stern (1981) Research on teachers' pedagogical thoughts, judgements, decisions, and behavior. *Review of Educational Research* 51, 455–498.

Sheldon, L.E. (ed.) (1987) *ELT Textbooks and Materials: Problems in Evaluation and Development.* ELT Documents 126. London: Modern English Publications / The British Council.

Sheldon, L.E. (1988) Evaluating ELT textbooks and materials. *ELT Journal* 42(4), 237–246.

Shetzer, H. and M. Warschauer (2000) An electronic literacy approach to network-based language teaching. In M. Warschauer and R. Kern (eds) *Network-based Language Teaching: Concepts and Practice.* New York: Cambridge University Press.

Shohamy, E. (1995) Performance assessment in language testing. *Annual Review of Applied Linguistics* 15, 188–211.

Shohamy, E. (1998) Applying a multiplism approach. In E.S.L. Li and G. James (eds) *Testing and Evaluation in Second Language Education.* Hong Kong: Language Centre, The Hong Kong University of Science and Technology, pp. 99–114.

Shor, I. (ed.) (1987) *Freire for the Classroom: A Sourcebook for Liberatory Teaching.* Portsmouth, NH: Boynton/Cook.

Shore, B. (1996) *Culture in Mind: Cognition, Culture, and the Problem of Meaning.* New York: Oxford University Press.

Short, M. (ed.) (1989) *Reading, Analyzing and Teaching Literature.* London: Longman.

Showers, B. (1985) Teachers coaching teachers: Schools restructured to support the development of peer coaching teams create norms of collegiality and experimentation. *Educational Leadership* 47, 43–48.

Showers, B. and B. Joyce (1996) The evolution of peer coaching. *Educational Leadership* 53(6), 12–16.

Shulman, L. (1986) Paradigms and research programs in the study of teaching. In M. Wittrock (ed.) *Handbook of Research on Teaching.* 3rd edn. New York: Macmillan, pp. 3–36.

Silberstein, S. (1984) Language is culture: Textbuilding conventions in oral narrative. In J. Handscombe, R.A. Oren and B.P. Taylor (eds) *On TESOL 1983: The Question of Control.* Washington, DC: TESOL, pp. 67–80.

Silberstein, S. (1988) Ideology as process: Gender ideology in courtship narratives. In A.D. Todd and S. Fisher (eds) *Gender and Discourse: The Power of Talk.* Norwood, NJ: Ablex, pp. 125–149.

Silva, T. (1993) Toward an understanding of the distinct nature of L2 writing: The ESL research and its implications. *TESOL Quarterly* 27, 657–677.

Silva, T., I. Leki and J. Carson (1997) Broadening the perspective of mainstream composition studies. *Written Communication* 14(3), 398–428.

Simon, R.I. (1987) Empowerment as a pedagogy of possibility. *Language Arts* 64, 370–383.

Simon, R.I. (1992) *Teaching Against the Grain: Texts for a Pedagogy of Possibility*. Boston, MA: Bergin and Garvey.

Sinclair, J. (ed.) (1990) *Collins COBUILD English Grammar*. London: Collins.

Sinclair, J. (1991) *Corpus, Concordance, Collocation*. Oxford: Oxford University Press.

Sinclair, J. (1996) Units of meaning. *Textus* 9, 75–106.

Sinclair, J. and M. Coulthard (1975) *Towards an Analysis of Discourse*. Oxford: Oxford University Press.

Sinclair, J. and A. Renouf (1988) A lexical syllabus for language learning. In R.A. Carter and M.J. McCarthy (eds) *Vocabulary and Language Teaching*. London: Longman, pp. 140–160.

Singleton, D. (1999) *Exploring the Second Language Mental Lexicon*. Cambridge: Cambridge University Press.

Sionis, C. (1995) Communication strategies in the writing of scientific research articles by non-native users of English. *English for Specific Purposes* 14(2), 99–114.

Skehan, P. (1989a) *Individual Differences in Second Language Learning*. London: Edward Arnold.

Skehan, P. (1989b) Progress in language testing: The 1990s. In J.C. Alderson and B. North (eds) *Language Testing in the 1990s*. London: Macmillan, pp. 3–21.

Skehan, P. (1992) Strategies in second language acquisition. *Thames Valley Working Papers in English Language Teaching* 1, 178–208.

Skehan, P. (1996) Second language acquisition research and task-based instruction. In J. Willis and D. Willis (eds) *Challenge and Change in Language Teaching*. London: Heinemann.

Skehan, P. (1998) *A Cognitive Approach to Language Learning*. Oxford: Oxford University Press.

Skehan, P. and P. Foster (1997) Task type and task processing conditions as influences on foreign language performance. *Language Teaching Research* 1(3), 185–211.

Skelton, J. (1994) Analysis of the structure of original research papers: aid to writing original papers for publication. *British Journal of Medical Practice* Oct, 455–459.

Skinner, B.F. (1957) *Verbal Behavior*. New York: Appleton-Century-Crofts.

Skutnabb-Kangas, T. and R. Phillipson (eds) (1994) *Linguistic Human Rights*. Berlin: Mouton de Gruyter.

Slater, F. (1985) Teacher Quality or Quality Control? In F. Slater *The Quality Controllers: A Critique of the White Paper 'Teaching Quality'*. London: Institute of Education, University of London, pp. 10–21.

Slimani, A. (1987) The teaching–learning relationship: Learning opportunities and the problems of uptake: an Algerian case study. Unpublished PhD thesis, University of Lancaster.

Slimani, A. (1989) The role of topicalisation in classroom language learning. *System* 17, 223–234.

Slobin, D. (1971) *Psycholinguistics*. Glenview, IL: Scott, Foresman.

Smith, F. (1971) *Understanding Reading: A Psycholinguistic Analysis of Reading and Learning to Read*. Orlando, FL: Holt, Reinhart and Winston.

Smith, H.H.J. (1998) Perceptions of success in the management of aid-funded English language teaching projects. Unpublished PhD, University of Reading.

Smitherman, G.N. (1981) 'What go round come round': *king* in perspective. *Harvard Educational Review* 62, 40–56.

Smitherman, G.N. (1998) Ebonics and TESOL: 'Dat teacher be hollin at us'– What is Ebonics? *TESOL Quarterly* 32, 139–143.

Smith-Hefner, N.J. (1988) Women and politeness: The Javanese example. *Language in Society* 17, 535–554.

Soares, C. and F. Grosjean (1984) Bilingual in a monolingual and bilingual speech mode: The effect on lexical access. *Memory and Cognition* 12, 380–386.

Soars, L. and J. Soars (1993) *Headway*. Oxford: Oxford University Press.

Soars, L. and J. Soars (1996) *New Headway Intermediate*. Oxford: Oxford University Press.

Soh, B.-L. and Y.P. Soon (1991) English by e-mail: creating a global classroom via the medium of computer technology. *ELT Journal* 45(4), 287–292.

Soo, K.-S. (1999) Theory and research: Learning styles, motivation, and the CALL classroom. In E. Hanson-Smith (ed.) *Call Environments: Research, Practice, and Critical Issues*. Alexandria, VA: TESOL, pp. 289–301.

Sorace, A. (1985) Metalinguistic knowledge and language use in acquisition-poor environments. *Applied Linguistics* 6, 239–254.

Spack, R. (1988) Initiating ESL students into the academic discourse community: How far should we go? *TESOL Quarterly* 22(1), 29–51.

Spack, R. (1997) The acquisition of academic literacy in a second language: A longitudinal case study. *Written Communication* 14, 3–62.

Spada, N. (1997) Form-focused instruction in second language acquisition: A review of classroom and laboratory research. *Language Teaching* 30(2), 73–87.

Spada, N. and P. Lightbown (1993) Instruction and the development of questions in L2 classrooms. *Studies in Second Language Acquisition* 15, 205–224.

Spiro, J. (1992) Measuring Literary Skills. In C.J. Brumfit (ed.) *Assessment in Literature Teaching*. London: Macmillan, pp. 46–67.

Spolsky, B. (1985) What does it mean to know how to use a language? An essay on the theoretical basis of language testing. *Language Testing* 2(2), 180–191.

Spolsky, B. (1998) *Sociolinguistics*. Oxford: Oxford University Press.

Spradley, J.P. (1980) *Participant Observation*. New York: Holt, Rinehart and Winston.

Sproull, L. and S. Kiesler (1991) *Connections: New Ways of Working in the Networked Organization*. Cambridge, MA: MIT Press.

Srivastava, R.N. (1988) Societal bilingualism and bilingual education: A study of the Indian situation. In C.B. Paulston (ed.) *International Handbook of Bilingualism and Bilingual Education*. New York: Greenwood Press, pp. 247–274.

St John, E. and D. Cash (1995) Language learning via e-mail: Demonstrable success with German. In M. Warschauer (ed.) *Virtual Connections: Online Activities and Projects for Networking Language Learners*. Honolulu, HI: University of Hawai'i, Second Language Teaching and Curriculum Center, pp. 191–197.

St John, M.J. (1996) Business is booming: Business English in the nineties. *English for Specific Purposes* 15, 3–18.

Stanovich, K.E. and A.E. Cunningham (1992) Studying the consequences of literacy within a literate society: The cognitive correlates of print exposure. *Memory and Cognition* 20, 51–68.

Steinberg, D. (1993) *An Introduction to Psycholinguistics*. London: Longman.

Stenhouse, L. (1975) *An Introduction to Curriculum Research and Development*. London: Heinemann.

Stern, H.H. (1983) *Fundamental Concepts of Language Teaching*. Oxford: Oxford University Press.

Stern, H.H. (1992) *Issues and Options in Language Teaching*. Oxford: Oxford University Press.

Sternberg, R.J. (1987) Most vocabulary is learned from context. In M.G. McKeown and M.E. Curtis (eds) *The Nature of Vocabulary Acquisition*. Hillsdale, NJ: Lawrence Erlbaum, pp. 89–105.

Stevick, E. (1976) *Memory, Meaning and Method*. Rowley, MA: Newbury House.

Stevick, E. (1980) *Teaching Languages: A Way and Ways*. Rowley, MA: Newbury House.

Stevick, E. (1986) *Images and Options in the Language Classroom*. Cambridge: Cambridge University Press.

Stevick, E. (1989) *Success with Foreign Languages*. London: Prentice Hall.

Stoller, F.L. (1994) The diffusion of innovations in intensive ESL programs. *Applied Linguistics* 15(3), 300–327.

Stoner, J.A.F., R.E. Freeman and D.R. Gilbert, Jr (1995) *Management*. 6th edn. Englewood Cliffs, NJ: Prentice Hall.

Storey, P. (1998) Developing and validating a taxonomy of test-taking strategies. In E.S.L. Li and G. James (eds) *Testing and Evaluation in Second Language Education*. Hong Kong: Language Centre, The Hong Kong University of Science and Technology, pp. 50–65.

Stott, K. and H. Parr (1991) *Marketing Your School*. London: Hodder and Stoughton.

Street, B. (1984) *Literacy in Theory and Practice*. Cambridge: Cambridge University Press.

Strevens, P. (1977a) *New Orientations in the Teaching of English*. Oxford: Oxford University Press.

Strevens, P. (1977b) Special-purpose language teaching: A perspective. *Language Teaching and Linguistics Abstracts* 10, 3.

Stubbs, M. (1980) *Language and Literacy: The Sociolinguistics of Reading and Writing*. London: Routledge and Kegan Paul.

Stubbs, M. (1997) Whorf's children: Critical comments on critical discourse analysis (CDA) In A. Ryan and A. Wray (eds) *Evolving Models of Language*. Clevedon: British Association for Applied Linguistics in association with Multilingual Matters, 100–116.

Suid, M. and W. Lincoln (1988) *Recipes for writing: Motivation, Skills, and Activities*. New York: Addison Wesley Longman.

Sullivan, N. (1998) Developing critical reading writing skills: Empowering minority students in a networked computer classroom. In J. Swaffar, S. Romano, P. Markley and K. Arens (eds) *Language Learning Online: Theory and Practice in the ESL and L2 Computer Classroom*. Austin, TX: Labyrinth Publications/Daedalus Group, pp. 41–55. Available: labyrinth.daedalus.com [2000, February 28].

Sullivan, N. and E. Pratt (1996) A comparative study of two ESL writing environments: A computer-assisted classroom and a traditional oral classroom. *System* 29, 491–501.

Swain, M. (1985) Communicative competence: Some rules of comprehensible input and comprehensible output in its development. In S. Gass and C. Madden (eds) *Input in Second Language Acquisition*. Rowley, MA: Newbury House, pp. 235–253.

Swain, M. (1995) Three functions of output in second language acquisition. In G. Cook and B. Seidlhofer (eds) *Principles and Practice in Applied Linguistics: Studies in Honour of H.G. Widdowson*. Oxford: Oxford University Press.

Swain, M. and S. Lapkin (1998) Interaction and second language learning: Two adolescent French immersion students working together. *Modern Language Journal* 82, 320–337.

Swales, J.M. (1981) *ESP Monograph Vol. 1: Aspects of Paper Introductions*. Birmingham: Language Studies Unit, Aston University.

Swales, J.M. (1986) Utilizing the literatures in teaching the research paper. Unpublished manuscript.

Swales, J.M. (1990a) *Genre Analysis: English in Academic and Research Settings*. Cambridge: Cambridge University Press.

Swales, J.M. (1990b) Nonnative speaker graduate engineering students and their introductions: global coherence and local management. In U. Connor and A. Johns (eds) *Coherence in Writing: Research and Pedagogical Perspectives*. Washington, DC: TESOL.

Swales, J.M. (1998a) English as Tyrannosaurus rex. *World Englishes* 16, 373–382.

Swales, J.M. (1998b) *Other Floors, Other Voices: A Textography of a Small University Building*. Mahwah, NJ: Lawrence Erlbaum.

Swales, J.M. and C. Feak (1994) *Academic Writing for Graduate Students*. Ann Arbor, MI: University of Michigan Press.

Swan, M. and B. Smith (1987) *Learner English: A Teacher's Guide to Interference and Other Problems*. Cambridge: Cambridge University Press.

Swan, M. and C. Walter (1992) *The New Cambridge English Course 3*. Cambridge: Cambridge University Press.

Swanick, K. (1990) The necessity of teacher education. In N.J. Graves *Initial Teacher Education*. London: Kogan, 92–108.

Tai, J.H.-Y. (1988) Bilingualism and bilingual education in the People's Republic of China. In C.B. Paulston (ed.) *International Handbook of Bilingualism and Bilingual Education*. New York: Greenwood Press, pp. 185–201.

Tang, R. and S. John (1999) The 'I' in identity: Exploring writer identity in student academic writing through the first person pronoun. *English for Specific Purposes* 18, S23–S40 (supplementary issue).

Tannen, D. (1984a) *Conversational Style: Analyzing Talk Among Friends*. Norwood, NJ: Ablex.

Tannen, D. (1984b) The pragmatics of cross-cultural communication. *Applied Linguistics* 5(3), 47–54.

Tannen, D. (ed.) (1993) *Gender and Conversational Interaction*. New York: Oxford University Press.

Tannen, D. and M. Saville-Troike (eds) (1985) *Perspectives on Silence*. Norwood, NJ: Ablex.

Tarone, E. (1987) The phonology of interlanguage. In G. Ioup and S. Weinberger (eds) *Interlanguage Phonology: The Acquisition of a Second Language Sound System*. Cambridge, MA: Newbury House. Originally published 1978.

Tartter, V. (1986) *Language Processes*. New York: Holt, Rinehart and Winston.

Taylor, L. (1993) *Pronunciation in Action*. Englewood Cliffs, NJ: Prentice Hall.

Tella, S. (1992a) *Boys, Girls and E-mail: A Case Study in Finnish Senior Secondary Schools*. Research Report 110. Helsinki: Department of Teacher Education, University of Helsinki.

Tella, S. (1992b) *Talking Shop via E-mail: A Thematic and Linguistic Analysis of Electronic Mail Communication*. Research report 99. Department of Teacher Education, University of Helsinki. Also available as ERIC Document ED 352015.

Tench, P. (1992) Phonetic symbols in the dictionary and in the classroom. In A. Brown (ed.) *Approaches to Pronunciation Teaching*. London: Modern English Publications / Macmillan / The British Council.

TESOL (1997) *ESL Standards For Pre-K-12 Students*. Alexandria, VA: Teachers of English to Speakers of Other Languages.

Tharp, R. and R. Gallimore (1988) *Rousing Young Minds to Life: Teaching, Learning, and Schooling in Social Context*. New York: Cambridge University Press.

Thiagarajan, S. and B. Steinwachs (1990) *Barnga: A Simulation Game on Cultural Clashes*. Yarmouth, ME: Intercultural Press.

Thomas, J. (1983) Cross-cultural pragmatic failure. *Applied Linguistics* 4, 91–105.

Thomason, S.G. (ed.) (1997) *Contact Languages: A Wider Perspective*. Amsterdam: John Benjamins.

Thornton, P. and T. Dudley (1997) The CALL environment: An alternative to the language lab. *CAELL Journal* 7(4), 29–34.

Thorp, D. (1991) Confused encounters: differing expectations in the EAP classroom. *ELT Journal* 45(2), 108–118.

Tinkel, A.J. (1988) *Explorations in Language*. Cambridge: Cambridge University Press.

Tollefson, J.W. (ed.) (1995) *Power and Inequality in Language Education*. Cambridge: Cambridge University Press.

Tomasello, M. and C. Herron (1998) Down the garden path: Inducing and correcting overgeneralization errors in the foreign language classroom. *Applied Psycholinguistics* 9, 237–246.

Tomlin, R. (1994) Functional grammars, pedagogical grammars, and communicative language teaching. In T. Odlin (ed.) *Perspectives on Pedagogical Grammar*. Cambridge: Cambridge University Press, pp. 140–178.

Tomlinson, B. (1987) *Openings*. London: Penguin.

Tomlinson, B. (1994) Pragmatic awareness activities. *Language Awareness* 3(4), 119–129.

Tomlinson, B. (ed.) (1998a) *Materials Development for Language Teaching*. Cambridge: Cambridge University Press.

Tomlinson, B. (1998b) Introduction. In B. Tomlinson (ed.) *Materials Development for Language Teaching*. Cambridge: Cambridge University Press, pp. 1–24.

Tomlinson, B. (1998c) Seeing what they mean: helping L2 learners to visualise. In B. Tomlinson (ed.) *Materials Development for Language Teaching*. Cambridge: Cambridge University Press, pp. 265–278.

Tomlinson, B. (1999a) Materials development for language teachers. *Modern English Teacher* 8(1), 62–64.

Tomlinson, B. (1999b) Developing criteria for materials evaluation. *IATEFL Issues* 147, 10–13.

Tomlinson, B.J., S.B. Choo, D.A. Hill and H. Masuhara (2000) *English for Life*. Singapore: Federal Publications.

Tomlinson, B., B. Dat, H. Masuhara and R. Rubdy (2001) Review of EFL coursebooks. *ELT Journal* 55(1).

Tomlinson, B. and H. Masuhara (2000) Using simulations on materials development courses. *Simulation and Gaming: An Interdisciplinary Journal of Theory, Practice and Research* 31(2), 152–168.

Triandis, H.C. (1995) *Individualism and Collectivism*. Boulder, CO: Westview Press.

Tribble, C. (1996) *Writing*. Oxford: Oxford University Press.

Trimble, L. (1985) *English for Science and Technology: A Discourse Approach*. Cambridge: Cambridge University Press.

Trimble, M., L. Trimble and K. Drobnic, (eds) (1978) *English for Special Purposes: Science and Technology*. English Language Institute, Oregon State University.

Trudgill, P. (1974) *The Social Differentiation of English in Norwich*. Cambridge: Cambridge University Press.

Trudgill, P. (1990) *The Dialects of England*. Oxford: Blackwell.

Trudgill, P. (1995) *Sociolinguistics: An Introduction to Language and Society*. 3rd edn. London: Penguin.

Trudgill, P. and J. Cheshire (eds) (1998) *The Sociolinguistics Reader, Vol. 1: Multilingualism and Variation; Vol. 2: Gender and Discourse*. London: Arnold; New York: St Martin's Press.

Trudgill, P. and J. Hannah (1995) *International English*. 3rd edn. London: Edward Arnold.

Truscott, J. (1998) Noticing in second language acquisition: A critical review. *Second Language Research* 14, 103–135.

Tsui, A.B.M. (1993) Helping Teachers to Conduct Action Research in ESL Classrooms. In D. Freeman and S. Cornwell (eds) *New Ways in Teacher Education*. Virginia, TESOL: pp. 171–175.

Tsui, A.B.M. (1995) *Introducing Classroom Interaction*. London: Penguin.

Tsui, A.B.M. (1996a) Learning how to teach ESL writing. In D. Freeman and J.C. Richards (eds) *Teacher Learning in Language Teaching*. New York: Cambridge University Press, pp. 97–119.

Tsui, A.B.M. (1996b) Reticence and anxiety in second language learning. In K. Bailey and D. Nunan (eds) *Voices from the Language Classroom*. New York: Cambridge University Press, pp. 145–167.

Tsui, A.B.M. (1997) Awareness raising about classroom interaction. In L. van Lier and D. Corson, (eds) *Encyclopedia of Language and Education, Vol. 6: Knowledge About Language*. Dordrecht, Kluwer, pp. 183–194.

Tsui, A.B.M. (in press) *Understanding Expertise in Language Teaching*. Cambridge: Cambridge University Press.

Tsunoda, T. (1985) *The Japanese Brain: Uniqueness and Universality*. Tokyo: Taishukan.

Tuffs, R. (1995) Language teaching in the post-Fordish era. *System* 23(4), 491–502.

Turner, J. (1998) Assessing speaking. *Annual Review of Applied Linguistics* 18, 192–207.

Ulichny, P. (1996) What's in a methodology? In D. Freeman and J.C. Richards (eds) *Teacher Learning in Language Teaching*. New York: Cambridge University Press, pp. 178–196.

Underwood, M. (1989) *Teaching Listening*. London: Longman.

Ur, P. (1981) *Discussions That Work*. Cambridge: Cambridge University Press.

Ur, P. (1984) *Teaching Listening Comprehension*. Cambridge: Cambridge University Press.

Ur, P. (1988) *Grammar Practice Activities*. Cambridge: Cambridge University Press.

Ur, P. (1996) *A Course in Language Teaching: Practice and Theory*. Cambridge: Cambridge University Press.

Valdes, J.M. (ed.) (1986) *Culture Bound. Bridging the Cultural Gap in Language Teaching*. Cambridge: Cambridge University Press.

van Dijk, T. (1972) *Some Aspects of Text Grammars*. The Hague: Mouton.

van Ek, J. (1973) *The 'Threshold Level' in a European Unit/Credit System for Modern Teaching by Adults*. System Development in Adult Language Learning. Strasbourg: Council of Europe.

van Essen, A. (1997) Language awareness and knowledge about language: An overview. In L. van Lier and

D. Corson (eds) *Encyclopedia of Language and Education, Vol. 6: Knowledge About Language*. Dordrecht: Kluwer Academic, pp. 1–9.

van Lier, L. (1988) *The Classroom and the Language Learner: Ethnography and Second Language Classroom Research*. London: Longman.

van Lier, L. (1989) Reeling, writhing, drawling, stretching, and painting in coils: Oral proficiency interviews as conversation. *TESOL Quarterly* 23(3), 489–508.

van Lier, L. (1995) *Introducing Language Awareness*. London: Penguin.

van Lier, L. (1996) *Interaction in the Language Curriculum: Awareness, Autonomy and Authenticity*. London: Longman.

van Lier, L. (1998a) All hooked up: An ecological look at computers in the classroom. In J. Fisiak (ed.) *Festschrift for Kari Sajavaara on his Sixtieth Birthday*. Poznan: Studia Anglica Posananiensia 33, pp. 281–301.

van Lier, L. (1998b) The relationship between consciousness, interaction and language learning. *Language Awareness* 7(2 and 3), 128–145.

van Lier, L. and D. Corson (eds) (1997) *Encyclopedia of Language and Education, Vol. 6: Knowledge About Language*. Dordrecht: Kluwer Academic.

van Lier, L. and N. Matsuo (1999) Varieties of conversational experience: Looking for learning opportunities. *Applied Language Learning*, 10(2).

Vandergrift, L. (1996) The listening comprehension strategies of core French high school students. *The Canadian Modern Language Review* 52, 200–223.

Vann, R., F.D. Lorenz and D.E. Meyer (1991) Error gravity: Faculty response to errors in the written discourse of nonnative speakers of English. In E. Hamp-Lyons (ed.) *Assessing Second Language Writing in Academic Contexts*. Norwood, NJ: Ablex, pp. 181–195.

Varela, E. (1999) Using learning strategy instruction to improve English learners' oral presentation skills in content-based ESL instruction. In R. Oxford (ed.) *Language Learning Strategies in the Context of Autonomy: Strategy Research Compendium: Proceedings of the First Annual Strategy Research Symposium, Teachers College*. New York: Columbia University, pp. 76–77.

Varonis, E. and S. Gass (1985) Native/nonnative conversations: A model for negotiation of meaning. *Applied Linguistics* 8, 71–90.

Vaughan-Rees, M. (1995) *Rhymes and Rhythm*. London: Macmillan.

Vilmi, R. (1995) International environment activity. In M. Warschauer (ed.) *Virtual Connections: Online Activities and Projects for Networking Language Learners*. Honolulu, HI: University of Hawai'i, Second Language Teaching and Curriculum Center, pp. 205–207.

von Elek, T. (1985) A test of Swedish as a second language. In Y.P. Lee, R. Lord, C.Y.Y. Fok, and G. Low (eds) *New Directions in Language Testing*. Oxford: Pergamon, pp. 47–57.

Vygotsky, L.S. (1978) *Mind in Society: The Development of Higher Psychological Processes*. Cambridge, MA: MIT Press.

Vygotsky, L.S. (1986) *Thought and Language*. Cambridge, MA: MIT Press.

Wagner, S.T. (1981) The historical background of bilingualism and biculturalism in the United States. In M. Ridge (ed.) *The New Bilingualism: An American Dilemma: Proceedings of a conference sponsored by the Center for Study of the American Experience, The Annenberg School of Communications, University of Southern California, May 1980*. Los Angeles, CA: University of Southern California Press, pp. 29–52.

Wajnryb, R. (1993) *Classroom Observation Tasks: A Resource Book for Language Teachers and Trainers*. Cambridge: Cambridge University Press.

Wajnryb, R. (1996) Death, taxes and jeopardy: Systematic omissions in EFL texts, or life was never meant to be an adjacency pair. Paper presented at the 9th Educational Conference, Sydney.

Walker, E. (1997) *The Relationship Between Learner Age and Anxiety in Foreign Language Learning*. Department of Curriculum Studies, University of Hong Kong.

Wall, D. (1996) Introducing new tests into traditional systems: Insights from general education and from innovation theory. *Language Testing* 13(3), 334–354.

Wallace, C. (1992a) Critical literacy awareness in the EFL classroom. In N. Fairclough (ed.) *Critical Language Awareness*. London: Longman, pp. 59–92.

Wallace, C. (1992b) *Reading*. Oxford: Oxford University Press.

Wallace, M. (1980) *Study Skills in English*. Cambridge: Cambridge University Press.

Wang, Y.M. (1993) E-mail dialogue journaling in an ESL reading and writing classroom. Unpublished PhD dissertation, University of Oregon at Eugene.

Wardough, R. (1998) *An Introduction to Sociolinguistics*. 3rd edn. Malden, MA: Blackwell.

Warschauer, M. (1995a) *E-mail for English Teaching*. Alexandria, VA: TESOL Publications.

Warschauer, M. (ed.) (1995b) *Virtual Connections: Online Activities and Projects for Networking Language Learners*. Honolulu, HI: University of Hawai'i, Second Language Teaching and Curriculum Center.

Warschauer, M. (1996a) Comparing face-to-face and electronic communication in the second language classroom. *CALICO Journal* 13(2), 7–26.

Warschauer, M. (1996b) Motivational aspects of using computers for writing and communication. In M. Warschauer (ed.) *Telecollaboration in Foreign Language Learning: Proceedings of the Hawai'i Symposium*. Honolulu, HI: University of Hawai'i, Second Language Teaching and Curriculum Center.

Warschauer, M. (1997) Computer-mediated collaborative learning: Theory and practice. *Modern Language Journal* 81(3), 470–481.

Warschauer, M. (1998) Online learning in sociocultural context. *Anthropology and Education Quarterly* 29(1), 68–88.

Warschauer, M. (1999) *Electronic Literacies: Language, Culture, and Power in Online Education*. Mahwah, NJ: Lawrence Erlbaum.

Warschauer, M. and R. Kern (eds) (2000) *Network-Based Language Teaching: Concepts and Practice*. New York: Cambridge University Press.

Warschauer, M., H. Shetzer and C. Meloni (2000) *Internet for English Teaching*. Alexandria, VA: TESOL Publications.

Weigle, S. (1994) Effects of training on raters of ESL compositions. *Language Testing* 11(2), 197–223.

Weinreich, U. (1953) *Languages in Contact: Findings and Problems*. New York: The Linguistic Circle of New York.

Weinreich, U. (1968) *Languages in Contact: Findings and Problems*. The Hague: Mouton.

Weir, C.J. (1988) The specification, realization and validation of an English language proficiency test. In A. Hughes (ed.) *Testing English for University Study*. ELT Documents 127. London: Modern English Publications / The British Council.

Weir, C.J. (1990) *Communicative Language Testing*. London: Prentice Hall.

Weir, C.J. (1993) *Understanding and Developing Language Tests*. London: Prentice Hall.

Weir, C.J. and J. Roberts (1994) *Evaluation in ELT*. Oxford: Blackwell.

Weir, C.J. and A.H. Urquhart (1998) *Reading in a Second Language: Process, Product and Practice*. London: Longman.

Weissberg, R. and S. Buker (1990) *Writing Up Research: Experimental Report Writing for Students of English*. Englewood Cliffs, NJ: Prentice Hall.

Weitzman, E.A. and M.B. Miles (1995) *A Software Sourcebook: Computer Programs for Qualitative Data Analysis*. Thousand Oaks, CA: Sage.

Wells, G. (1986) *The Meaning Makers: Children Learning Language and Using Language to Learn*. London: Hodder and Stoughton.

Wells, G. (1991) Apprenticeship in literacy. In C. Walsh (ed.) *Literacy as Praxis: Culture, Language and Pedagogy*. Norwood, NJ: Ablex.

Wells, J.C. (1982) *Accents of English*. Cambridge: Cambridge University Press.

Wells, J.C. (1990) *Longman Pronunciation Dictionary*. London: Longman.

Wenden, A. (1991) *Learning Strategies for Learner Autonomy: Planning and Implementing Learner Training for Language Learners*. Englewood Cliffs, NJ: Prentice Hall.

Werlich, E. (1976) *A Text Grammar of English*. Heidelberg: Quelle and Meyer.

West, M. (1953) *A General Service List of English Words*. London: Longman.

West, R. (1994) Needs analysis in language teaching. *Language Teaching* 27, 1.

White, G. (1998) *Listening*. Oxford: Oxford University Press.

White, L. (1987) Against comprehensible input: The input hypothesis and the development of second-language competence. *Applied Linguistics* 8, 95–110.

White, L. (1989) *Universal Grammar and Second Language Acquisition*. Amsterdam/Philadelphia, PA: John Benjamins.

White, L. and P. Lightbown (1984) Asking and answering in ESL classes. *The Canadian Modern Language Review* 40(2), 228–244.

White, R. (1988) *The ELT Curriculum: Design, Innovation and Management*. Oxford: Blackwell.

White, R. (1998) *New Ways in Teaching Writing*. Alexandria, VA: TESOL.

White, R. and V. Arndt (1991) *Process Writing*. London: Longman.

White, R., M. Martin, M. Stimson and R. Hodge (1991) *Management in English Language Teaching*. Cambridge: Cambridge University Press.

Widdowson, H.G. (ed.) 1974–(1980) *English in Focus*. Series of books. Oxford: Oxford University Press.

Widdowson, H.G. (1975) *Stylistics and the Teaching of Literature*. London: Longman.

Widdowson, H.G. (1978) *Teaching Language as Communication*. Oxford: Oxford University Press.

Widdowson, H.G. (1983) *Learning Purpose and Language Use*. Oxford: Oxford University Press.

Widdowson, H.G. (1984a) *Explorations in Applied Linguistics 2*. Oxford: Oxford University Press.

Widdowson, H.G. (1984) Reading and communication. In J.C. Alderson and A.H. Urquhart (eds) *Reading in a Foreign Language*. London: Longman.

Widdowson, H.G. (1989) Knowledge of language and ability for use. *Applied Linguistics* 10(2), 128–137.

Widdowson, H.G. (1990) *Aspects of Language Teaching*. Oxford: Oxford University Press.

Widdowson, H.G. (1992) *Practical Stylistics*. Oxford: Oxford University Press.

Widdowson, H.G. (1995a) Discourse analysis: A critical view. *Language and Literature* 4(3), 157–172.

Widdowson, H.G. (1995b) Review of Fairclough (1992), *Discourse and Social Change*. *Applied Linguistics* 16(4), 510–516.

Widdowson, H.G. (1998) Context, community and authentic language. *TESOL Quarterly* 32(4), 705–716.

Widdowson, H.G. (2000) On the limitations of linguistics applied. *Applied Linguistics* 21(1), 3–25.

Wigzell, R. (1992) Efficiency, cost-effectiveness and the privatisation of foreign language learning. *System*, 220(1), 15–31.

Wilkins, D. (1976) *Notional Syllabuses*. London: Oxford University Press.

Wilkins, D., C.J. Brumfit, C. Bratt-Paulston (1981) Notional syllabuses revisited: A response, some comments and a further reply. *Applied Linguistics* 2(1), 90–100.

Williams, D. (1983) Developing criteria for textbooks evaluation. *ELTJournal* 37(3), 251–255.

Williams, M. and R.L. Burden (1997) *Psychology for Language Teachers*. Cambridge: Cambridge University Press.

Williams, R. (1982) *Panorama*. London: Longman.

Willis, D. (1990) *The Lexical Syllabus: A New Approach to Language Teaching*. London: HarperCollins.

Willis, D. and J. Willis (1987) Varied activities for variable language learning. *ELT Journal* 41(1), 12–18.

Willis, J. (1981) *Teaching English Through English*. London: Longman.

Willis, J. (1996) *A Framework for Task-Based Learning*. London: Longman.

Willis, J. and D. Willis (1988) *Collins COBUILD English Course*. London: Collins.

Willis, J. and D. Willis (eds) (1996) *Challenge and Change in Language Teaching*. London: Heinemann.

Winter, E.O. (1977) A clause-relational approach to English texts: A study of some predictive lexical items in written discourse. *Instructional Science* 6(1), 1–92.

Winter, E.O. (1982) *Towards a Contextual Grammar of English*. London: Allen and Unwin.

Wolff, H. (1964) Intelligibility and inter-ethnic attitudes. In D. Hymes (ed.) *Language and Culture in Society*. New York: Harper Row.

Wolfram, W. (1993) Ethical considerations in language awareness programs. *Issues in Applied Linguistics* 4, 225–255.

Wolfram, W. (1997) Dialect in society. In F. Coulmas (ed.) *Handbook of Sociolinguistics*. Oxford: Blackwell.

Wolfson, N. (ed.) (1989) *Perspectives: Sociolinguistics and TESOL*. New York: Newbury House.

Wolfson, N. and E. Judd (eds) (1983) *Sociolinguistics and Language Acquisition*. Rowley, MA: Newbury House.

Wong, R.F. (1987) Learner variables and prepronunciation considerations in teaching pronunciation. In J. Morley (ed.) *Current Perspectives on Pronunciation: Practices Anchored in Theory*. Washington, DC: TESOL.

Woods, P. (1988) Pulling out of a project: twelve tips for project planners. *ELT Journal* 42(3), 196–201.

Woodward, T. (1992) *Ways of Training*. London: Longman.

Wright, A. (1996) *Story-Telling with Children*. Oxford: Oxford University Press.

Wright, A. (1997) *Creating Stories with Children*. Oxford: Oxford University Press.

Wright, S. (1998) The effect of simulations on second language development. *CAELL Journal* 8(2), 3–10.

Wright, T. (1994) *Investigating English*. London: Edward Arnold.

Wright, T. and R. Bolitho (1993) Language awareness: A missing link in teacher education? *ELT Journal* 47, 4.

Wright, T. and R. Bolitho (1997) Language awareness in in-service programs. In L. van Lier and D. Corson (eds) *Encyclopedia of Language and Education, Vol. 6: Knowledge About Language*. Dordrecht: Kluwer Academic, pp. 173–181.

Young, D. (1988) Bilingualism and bilingual education in a divided South African society. In C.B. Paulston (ed.) *International Handbook of Bilingualism and Bilingual Education*. New York: Greenwood Press, pp. 403–428.

Young, R. and M. Milanovic (1992) Discourse variation in oral proficiency interviews. *Studies in Second Language Acquisition* 14(2), 403–424.

Yule, G. (1996) *Pragmatics*. Oxford: Oxford University Press.

Yule, G. (1997) *Referential Communication Tasks*. Mahwah, NJ: Lawrence Erlbaum.

Yule, G. and W. Gregory (1989) Survey interviews for interactive teaching. *ELT Journal* 43(2), 142–149.

Yule, G. and D. Macdonald (1994) The effects of pronunciation teaching. In J. Morley (ed.) *Pronunciation Pedagogy and Theory: New Views, New Directions*. Alexandria, VA: TESOL.

Yule, G. and E. Tarone (1991) The other side of the page: Integrating the communication strategies and negotiated input in SLA. In R. Phillipson, E. Kellerman, L. Selinker, M. Sharwood Smith and M. Swain (eds) *Foreign/Second Language Pedagogy Research*. Clevedon: Multilingual Matters.

Yule, G., T. Mathis and M. Hopkins (1992) On reporting what was said. *ELT Journal* 46, 245–251.

Zamel, V. (1982) Writing: The process of discovering meaning. *TESOL Quarterly* 16, 195–209.

Zeichner, K. (1998) The new scholarship in teacher education. Vice presidential address presented at the annual meeting of the American Educational Research Association, San Diego, CA.

Zhang, S. (1995) Reexamining the affective advantage of peer feedback in the ESL writing class. *Journal of Second Language Writing* 4, 209–222.

Zhao, Y. (1996) Language Learning on the world wide web: Toward a Framework of Network Based CALL. *CALICO Journal* 14(1), 37–51.

Zoubir-Shaw, S. and R. Oxford (1995) Gender differences in language learning strategy use in university-level introductory French classes: A pilot study employing a strategy questionnaire. In C.A. Klee (ed.) *Faces in the Crowd: Individual Learners in Multisection Programs*. Boston, MA: Heinle and Heinle.

Zuengler, J. and B. Bent (1991) Relative knowledge of content domain: An influence on native- non-native conversations. *Applied Linguistics* 12(4), 397–415.

Index

business letters 134, 189
business management 199, 204

CA *see* contrastive analysis
CALL *see* computer assisted
   language learning (CALL)
CALLA *see* Cognitive
   Academic Language
   Learning Approach
   (CALLA)
Cambridge International
   Corpus 44
*Cambridge International
   Dictionary of English*
   (CIDE) 43–4
Cambridge Language Survey
   see Cambridge
   International Corpus
Canada
   immersion programmes 90
   immigrant women 106
   Official Languages Act (1969)
   95
Canadian English 3
care-taker speech 84, 121, **219**
career orientation, and strategy
   use 171
carrying out instructions 173
CARS (creating a research
   space) model, of article
   introductions 134, 188 Fig.
   27.1
case studies 30, 132, 162, 164
   of minority language children
   in the classroom 23
casual talk 50–1
categorical perception 81, **219**
CD-ROMs 110, 112
censorship, of materials 68
certification, assessment for
   138
chat rooms 208
child-directed speech (CDS) 84,
   219
child language acquisition
   longitudinal studies 88
   stages of development 84
children
   and care-takers interaction 84
   help towards bilinguality 96
chronemics 203
CIDE (*Cambridge International
   Dictionary of English*) 43–4
circumlocution 168
Civil Rights Movement 202
clarification 40
classical humanist paradigm
   180, 181
classroom
   comparison of traditional and
   computer-enhanced 108

computer-networked 32
institutionalised and ritual
   setting 50
social dynamics of 40
task-based learning in 176
virtual 32
'classroom dialect' 174
classroom discourse 115–16,
   214
and students' writing 189
classroom distance learning 112
classroom interaction 49–50,
   120–5, 214
language used by the teacher
   120
observable aspects 121
unobservables in 121, 123
classroom observation 114–19,
   164
functions of 114
interaction analysis 120
second language 115
classroom pedagogy 74
classroom-based evaluation 149,
   150, **219**
factors in 146–7 Fig. 21.2
clause-relational analysis 52
cloze passages 111, 139
CLT *see* communicative
   language teaching
CMC *see* computer-mediated
   communication
coaching 76
co-articulation 83
COBUILD (Collins
   Birmingham University
   International Language
   Database) project 38, 43,
   46
code-switching 82, 103–4, **219**
   and identity 105–6
cognition, and language 97
Cognitive Academic Language
   Learning Approach
   (CALLA) 108, **219**
cognitive apprenticeship 77–8
cognitive approaches 52, 108
cognitive deficit theory, and
   restricted code 102
cognitive depth 44
cognitive domain, and language
   awareness 162
cognitive processing
   approach 80, 169
   of extended written texts 52
   universals in human 203
cognitive psychology 23
cognitive science 80, 85, 97
cognitive strategies
   in language learning 167
   listening 11

cohesion, text 23, 25, 52
collaborative decision-making
   154
collaborative evaluation 146,
   147, 149, 150, **219**
collaborative writing 29, 32, 191
collectivism, vs. individualism
   203
collocations 52
colonialism 3, 4, 105, 204
COLT (Communicative
   Orientation of Language
   Teaching) 116
communication
   high-context and low-context
   203
   'out-of-awareness' aspects of
   203
   see also intercultural
   communication; on-line
   communication
communication strategies 120,
   168
   in oral language 17, 18
communicative approach 15,
   18, 36–7, 39, 107, 131, 183
communicative competence 8,
   36, 57, 67, 152, 174–5, **219**
   of the bilingual 93
   and curriculum design 157
   sociolinguistic 103
communicative language
   teaching (CLT) 2, 8, 36–7,
   116, 152, 201, **219**
   and assessment 139
   focus on form within 40
   and pronunciation 57
   and sociolinguistic aspects
   103
   and task-based learning
   174–5, 214
communicative needs 140,
   174–5
   and EAP 127
Communicative Orientation of
   Language Teaching
   (COLT) 116
communicative purpose, and
   identification of genre 189
communicative stress 46
communicative syllabus 157,
   158, 174
communicative tasks 153, 173
Community Language Learning
   14, 57
comparative methodology 55
compensatory strategies, in
   language learning 168
competence
   Chomsky's 8, 35
   conversational 53